IT'S A LIVING
Work in Modern Society

IT'S A LIVING
Work in Modern Society

GALE MILLER
Marquette University

ST. MARTIN'S PRESS NEW YORK

Library of Congress Catalog Card Number: 80–52391

Manufactured in the United States of America
54321
fedcba
For information, write St. Martin's Press, Inc.,
175 Fifth Avenue, New York, N.Y. 10010

cover design: Tom McKeveny
typography: Charles Thurlow

cloth ISBN: 0–312–43907–5
paper ISBN: 0–312–43908–3

Acknowledgments

Material on pp. 111, 114–115 reprinted with permission from Jaber F. Gubrium and David R. Buckholdt, "The Production of Hard Data in Human Service Institutions," *Pacific Sociological Review* 22 (January, 1979): 115–136.

Table 8.1, p. 255, reprinted with permission of the author from Ichak Adizes, *Industrial Democracy: Yugoslav Style* (Los Angeles: MDOR Institute, 1977), p. 34.

Contents

Preface

This book is intended to help students understand the sociology of work by encouraging them to look beyond the traditional limits of the field. Conventional definitions of work have been so restricted that many of the ways human beings make their livings have been ignored. Until recently, sociologists have confined their attention to those forms of work for which people are directly paid. Yet work includes not only the occupations of the assembly-line worker and the secretary, but also the activities of the housewife, the peasant farmer, and the streetcorner hustler—among many others.

This enlargement of our field of vision to include wageless peasants as well as salaried office workers is closely tied to the perspective of this book, that of the sociology of knowledge. This point of view encourages us to take seriously the many ways people make sense of their lives and find meaning in their work. It allows us to see that the meanings workers ascribe to the ways in which they make a living are no less worthy of study than the findings and theories of academic researchers.

The approach I have taken in *It's a Living* builds on Edwin Sutherland's fertile research in the 1930s and on more recent work from interactionist and phenomenological perspectives. The writings of Eliot Freidson, Joyce Stephens, Peter Manning, John Hall, Lee Braude, and Bettylou Valentine have, in particular, enriched this book. The ideas of scholars in other disciplines, especially in anthropology and history, also have much to offer sociologists of work. The specific contributions of many of these people are discussed in the chapters that follow, but the work of Edmund Leach and of Yolanda and Richard Murphy deserves special mention here.

I am indebted to many people for their help in more personal ways. I am grateful to the scholars who read parts or all of the manuscript: Eliot Freidson, Richard Hall, Roland J. Pellegrin, and several anonymous reviewers. George Ritzer deserves special thanks not only for his helpful criticism but also for encouraging my original interest in the field. I wish to thank David Buckholdt, who has used his position as department chairperson at Marquette University to foster efforts such as this. Mary Magestro, Laurie Mallon, Laurie Gunderson, and Irene Cunningham of Marquette typed several drafts, and I appreciate their help. I am deeply indebted to Bob Woodbury, Emily Berleth, and Elaine Romano of St. Martin's Press. Finally, and above all, I wish to acknowledge the contributions of Diane Miller, contributions—and sacrifices—which go well beyond her assistance with this book. The book is dedicated to her.

For Diane Miller

IT'S A LIVING
Work in Modern Society

Chapter One

WORK AS A HUMAN REALITY

Among the various theoretical perspectives that make up contemporary sociology is the *sociology of knowledge* (Berger and Luckmann, 1966; Schutz, 1967; Schutz and Luckmann, 1973). This perspective assumes that objects and events have no intrinsic meaning separate from the meanings human beings create as they act and interact. The reality of an object or event depends instead on the ways in which human beings interpret it, and, for this reason, it is possible for the same object or event to have many realities. Thus, according to the sociology of knowledge, we live in a world of many realities that are socially constructed (i.e., created through social interaction). One consequence of this viewpoint is the recognition that although socially constructed realities provide people with a way of organizing and understanding their experiences, those realities can be changed; when change occurs, new ways of organizing and understanding experience develop. Another consequence is the recognition that not all individuals or groups share the same reality; rather, much of the conflict that characterizes human life arises from the differing realities that individuals and groups construct.

The perspective offered by the sociology of knowledge is quite different from that of common sense or everyday life. Common sense tells us that reality is a single, unitary entity that exists outside the human mind and limits our choices in everyday life. It is certainly not a product of our actions, interactions, and interpretations. An important reason why we experience reality as an external and independent force is that our knowledge about the world is shared with others. This knowledge may be highly sophisticated and systematically organized, as with many philosophical, theological, and scientific theories, or it may be based on less sophisticated and formalized ideas and experiences that people share in the normal course of everyday life. In either case, such knowledge is our basis for knowing what reality is, and it typically locates the source of reality outside the individual—such as in a divine plan or as a part of the natural order of things. Thus, the view of reality characteristic of everyday life assumes that there are "facts of life" all people must recognize and take into account. The sociology of knowledge perspective, on the other hand, argues that the "facts of life" are quite variable among individuals and groups because they are creations of the human mind.

One way to grasp the link between reality and knowledge is to look at areas of life that are changing, because these changes involve the destruction of old realities and the construction of new ones. An especially important example today is the changing reality of sex roles. One old reality declares that women and men are "naturally" different in their dispositions and abilities. Such activities as cooking, cleaning house, and tending children, for example, are better suited to the dispositions and abilities of women, whereas men are better suited for other activities. Various philosophical, theological, and scientific theories, which state that women are naturally more emotional, passive, and nurturant than men, support this reality. The shared experiences of everyday life, which indicate that men and women are ineffective and unhappy when they try to do things that are not natural to their sex, are also thought to support this reality. Both men and women can see how unhappy and ineffective men are when they must take care of the house and children during the absence of their wives. Similarly, the experiences of everyday life provide many examples of women who, in trying to compete with men, are unhappy and ineffective.

More and more people today are challenging this reality. They note that the absence of training and skills accounts for much of the past unhappiness and ineffectiveness of men and women. Men who know how to take care of a house and children, for example, are neither unhappy nor ineffective. It is also true that men and women have not always received support when they have attempted to do things that are associated with the other sex. Part of the past ineffectiveness and unhappiness of career women can be traced to the efforts of men to embarrass, if not get rid of, them. Finally, critics point out that much of the evidence for the old reality is selective. Only those aspects of everyday experience that confirm the reality are called upon, while the contradictory aspects of everyday life are ignored. For example, those who hold that men cannot cook ignore the evidence of those men who are quite capable at a barbecue grill. And those who maintain that women cannot do heavy factory labor ignore the fact that women often move heavy furniture in order to clean a room.

Fundamental to the current changes in sex roles, then, is a challenge to old realities about men and women and the development of new ones. Like the old realities, the new ones will be experienced as "facts of life" that are beyond the control of human beings. Similarly, they will be based on knowledge that is gathered from sophisticated research and theory and from the experiences of everyday life. And the new realities, too, will be subject to challenge as inaccurate because, like all the realities created by human beings, they are based on selective and oversimplified views of the diverse and contradictory experiences that make up human life.

THE SOCIAL CONSTRUCTION OF WORK

Like sex roles, work is experienced as a simple and unavoidable fact of life by most people. This statement is as true for those so-called primitive people who rise early in the morning to hunt animals or to gather fruits and vegetables as it is for modern workers who rise early in order to get to their jobs on time. How work is interpreted, however, is another matter and it is a central concern of this book. In order to understand the variety of realities associated with work, it is necessary to use the sociology of knowledge perspective, and this requires a step back from the normal assumptions of everyday life in order to look at work as a socially constructed reality. This approach to work also includes several other features.

First, the approach requires that human beings be treated as the major sources for creating and changing the realities associated with work. Many other sociological perspectives look for the causes of human action in such variables as wealth, age, sex, and race. While these factors are treated as potentially important human limitations within the sociology of knowledge perspective, the ultimate "causes" of social reality are thought to be human actions and interactions (MacIver, 1964). More concretely, the sociology of knowledge perspective requires that we treat work as having no intrinsic meaning; rather, human beings create the meaning associated with work as they construct reality.

A second feature of the approach to work recommended here is the setting aside of popular conceptions of what is and what is not "real work." Any activity that is used to make a living may be treated as a type of work (Polanyi, 1957). Conventional occupations found in the factory or the modern office, for example, are types of work. But work includes more than these. The activities of homemakers who make important contributions to the livelihood of families also constitute work. Even criminal activities, if they are undertaken as a livelihood, may be thought of as work. Theft, the sale of drugs, and prostitution are examples. Finally, the above definition of work can include the activities of "Moonies," Hare Krishna devotees, and others who solicit donations in public places—providing they are undertaken to earn a living.

A third feature of the approach we will follow is a concern for the ways in which the requirements associated with work are justified (Berger and Luckman, 1966). The body of knowledge associated with a type of work is crucial in understanding how it is justified, because knowledge includes both information about how to do the work and a set of values for evaluating it. These values are images of what work should be. Just as the knowledge we have about sex roles tells us which activities and relationships of men and women are legitimate, so the knowledge we have about work tells us which work experiences are legitimate or illegitimate. In both cases, that knowledge may be based on either sophisticated theories and research or on everyday experience. The example of sex roles is instructive for one more reason: it shows that the knowledge that guides our judgment about what is legitimate may be used to justify unequal relationships. An important feature of the sociology of knowledge approach, then, is a concern for the ways in which our interpretations of the "facts of life" can be used to justify the power of some people and the subordination of others.

Finally, in developing the sociology of knowledge approach to work not all types of research projects are equally useful. The most important problems for this approach are the ways in which reality is socially constructed and changed, and, for this reason, the most appropriate research materials are found in descriptive accounts of the development of social realities (Douglas, 1970). The descriptive accounts may be of two general types. First, historical descriptions are useful, because they provide us with a basis for understanding the general process through which current realities have emerged. Studies of the early factory, for example, provide a basis for comparatively understanding how the early and late stages of industrialization are alike and different. Second, descriptive accounts of existing groups are useful, because they provide insight into the ways in which everyday circumstances affect social reality. The social reality that characterizes a particular factory, for example, is not a simple consequence of history; rather, the historically based reality is interpreted in light of the immediate problems and relationships of the work place. In this way, the historically based reality is continually changed through human actions and interactions. In sum, those research projects that are based on the assumption that social reality is "caused" by human beings and not by "variables" are most useful to developing this approach to the sociology of work.

The rest of this chapter deals more fully with some general issues associated with the sociology of knowledge and, particularly, with their implications for studying work. Because such a discussion can easily become overly abstract and difficult to apply to human experience, it is important to begin with a concrete example of how work can be organized and pursued. The example provided in the next section is adapted from studies by Richard Murphy (1960) and by Yolanda and Richard Murphy (1974) of the Mundurucú Indians who live in the Amazon valley of Brazil. The Mundurucú illustrate well the abstract issues and concepts central to this book. The interpretation of work in Mundurucú life can also be usefully compared to the realities of modern work discussed in later chapters of this book. It must be recognized from the outset, however, that the Mundurucú provide only one example of how work is socially constructed in so-called primitive societies. Those societies are as diverse as the ones that are typically classified as modern.

THE REALITIES OF MUNDURUCÚ LIFE

Although many Mundurucú continue to live in scattered villages in the Amazon valley of Brazil, there is little joint activity among them today. This style of life is very different from the one that existed in the past, when the villages were linked in a variety of cooperative activities. The most important of these activities was warfare; indeed, the Mundurucú continue to be recognized as one of the fiercest of the many warring tribes that occupied the Amazon valley prior to the twentieth century. Their emphasis on war and violence is reflected in the practice of headhunting, that is, of cutting off the heads of their fallen enemies. The heads were returned to the village and displayed publicly as symbols of the greatness of Mundurucú warriors. In addition, the warriors who were most successful at headhunting were accorded great respect within the village, as were their families.

Much of the traditional way of life is gone today. The Mundurucú do not engage in war or headhunting anymore, although both continue to be important symbols in the lives of Mundurucú men. The tribe is also less important because there is little demand for intervillage cooperation. In large part, the traditional way of life has been undermined by contact with outsiders (particularly government officials, missionaries, and traders), who have used and continue to use the Mundurucú to achieve their aims. Sometimes the outsiders have imposed their ways without the consent or cooperation of the Mundurucú, but the Mundurucú learned early that cooperation with the outsiders promised them many of the material goods they desired. Even before the start of the twentieth century, for example, the Mundurucú were sometimes working as mercenaries for traders who wished to subdue other tribes in the area that interfered with peaceful trade. Today the cooperation between the Mundurucú and outsiders is different, but its impact on the lives of the people continues. Indeed, it is impossible to understand their contemporary way of life without reference to their association with outsiders.

The traditional Mundurucú way of life is threatened today. The Mundurucú population itself has declined from about 5,000 in the nineteenth century to less than 1,300 in the mid-twentieth century. The dwelling places of the remaining people have changed significantly as well. While some still live in traditional village settings, others live in a Catholic mission, a government-sponsored Mundurucú post, or a variety of private households scattered among the non-Mundurucú Brazilians who live in the Amazon valley. Even within the village settings, the traditional way of life is only partially preserved. This is reflected not only in the decline of warfare but also in the changing work of the people. Traditionally, the Mundurucú have made their livings by hunting, fishing, gardening, and gathering wild vegetables and fruits. Today the collection and sale of rubber to traders occupy a large part of their time. There are, however, some villages in which tradition is better preserved than in others. One such village, Cabruá, is a good example of the survival of tradition in the face of modernization.

Life in Cabruá

Cabruá is a small village containing only sixty-seven people and five houses. The village itself takes up a small space, but the economic activities of village members (hunting, fishing, gardening, and gathering wild fruits and vegetables) take them into the surrounding forest. Thus, the way of life in Cabruá allows the inhabitants to occupy a larger region than just the village proper. Because the Cabruá people live in direct relation to nature, they are significantly influenced by it. For example, their gardens, which are created by slashing and burning an area in the forest, last only two or three years because the forest begins to retake them after this amount of time. The availability of animals to hunt and wild fruits and vegetables to gather is also affected by conditions in the forest. In addition, Cabruá life is influenced by the climatic patterns of the region. Heavy rains fall about six and a half months of the year, and the rest of the year is very dry. Fishing does not occur during the wet season because small rivers near the forest overflow their banks and it is too difficult and dangerous for the Mundurucú, equipped only with bows and arrows, to walk through the water in pursuit of fish. During the dry season the villagers move to the banks of larger rivers, where they fish from canoes and collect rubber for trade.

Just as the natural environment of the region influences Cabruá life so too do the roles and social relations which have emerged with the social construction of Cabruá life. Indeed, to speak of Cabruá as having a single reality is to oversimplify that social world, because the village offers two primary definitions of reality that are linked to the activities and relationships of men and women.

Officially, at least, Cabruá life is dominated by men. They are the only persons allowed to hunt, the most prized economic activity in the village. Trade with outsiders cannot occur without a man (preferably the chief) acting as the official representative of the village. The dominance of men is also evident in the role of the chief, always a man. The chief's household violates the usual pattern of matrilocality in the village. *Matrilocality* refers to the practice of locating the family within the village of the woman. The Mundurucú man typically marries a woman from another village and moves there. In any single village women are thus the most stable component of the adult population. The chief and his family, however, are the exception because the woman he marries either already lives in or moves to his village (i.e., the family is *patrilocal*). This practice, together with that of passing the role of chief from father to son, assures male continuity in leadership positions.

The most important center of the men's world is the "men's house." This is a separate building in the village and the permanent residence of all adult males, whether married or not. Within the men's house a unique set of social relationships, which is denied to women, exists. The relationships that are established are important in separating the reality of Cabruá men from that of the women, as we shall see shortly. The men's house is also the location of the *karökö*, which are sacred musical instruments. They are related to spirits (*karökö ejewot*) that protect the village and that must be placated from time to time. Because the spirits like to hear the *karökö* played, the men play them on occasion. The *karökö* are also symbolically fed everyday. The importance of the *karökö* goes beyond the spiritual realm, however. They are symbols of male dominance and, for this reason, women are never allowed to see them.

The symbolic importance of the *karökö* can be traced to a myth that is shared by Cabruá men. According to the myth three women were given the *karökö* by the spirits, and they were able to use these instruments to take control of the village from men. For example, they forced the men to cook and do other "womanly" activities. Most important, the women were able to force the men into sexual intercourse. The men could not refuse because of the spiritual power which goes with possession of the *karökö*. The women lost their power, however, because they were unable to hunt, and the spirits associated with the *karökö* prefer meat to other foods. The men thus retook control of the village by offering the *karökö* meat, and the women were forced into a subordinate role, which requires that they not look at the *karökö* and that they be sexually available to their husbands at all times. Sexual intercourse, then, has symbolic importance in the reality of the men's world, further reflected by the use of gang rape to punish women who stray too far from community rules. Women who look at the *karökö* and those who are too promiscuous may be subject to this punishment, as may any women who do not follow the demands of male authorities outside the village. For example, one girl was gang raped for running away from a mission school.

In sum, the most important social realities for the men are their ties to the spiritual realm and their control over hunting. Male power is precarious, however, because it rests on the control of the *karökö*, which, potentially at least, could be retaken by women. Control over sexual intercourse is vital because it is one way in which the male reality is affirmed in everyday life. It is, in other words, a symbol of power and not just a means of reproduction or a source of physical pleasure.

The Cabruá men's world is quite different from that of the women. Much of this difference is related to the physical separation of men and women in the village. Men spend much of their time hunting in the forest, whereas women spend most of their time in the village or in the gardens which are nearby. Even when men and women work together, they usually divide the project into men's and women's work. When gardens are cleared and planted, for example, the men and women work at separate activities that involve little contact with the opposite sex. The separation of men and women is also apparent in their residences. A man spends most of his time in the men's house, whereas a woman lives with her children and adult female relatives in a separate house.

An important difference between men and women, then, is the center of their activity. The men's reality is created through interactions in collective settings—the hunting group, the men's house, and so forth. The women's reality is primarily created through interactions in their houses, the gardens, and the farina shed. The farina shed is a building where manioc (a plant cultivated in Cabruá gardens) is turned into farina, a meal-like substance basic to the Cabruá diet. It is also sold to outsiders. Because gardening, making farina, and other female work activities are burdensome, women typically work in groups. Women's groups are also encouraged by the men's practice of demanding sexual intercourse with any woman found alone outside the village. Thus, most aspects of the women's lives involve other women, and from these settings and interactions, a women's reality has developed in the village of Cabruá.

In some ways the women's reality is the opposite of the men's. The women, for example, share no myths about the sources of their current situation and they are quite cynical about the men's myths. But the difference goes deeper—the very bases of male and female knowledge are distinct. Male knowledge is based on everyday life experiences in the men's house, in hunting parties, and other sexually segregated settings. This knowledge is supplemented by a set of general symbols and explanations (e.g., myths) that the men share. The women have no general symbols and explanations that they share; rather, their reality is based exclusively on their everyday experiences. For this reason they live in a world that is qualitatively different from that of the men, one that is highly secular and pragmatic. For the women, a more important question than how they originated is how they are going to deal with the immediate problems of everyday life.

The Cabruá women deal with their problems in two general ways. Manipulation—allowing the men to be officially in charge, but directing the flow of activities and decisions from the background—is one way. The practice of trading with outsiders provides an example. Although the men are always the official representatives of the village, if the materials being traded involve the women's world, then the deal is not consummated without the approval of the woman in charge of the household within which the goods were produced. Similarly, women have some control over their sex lives, although it is indirect. Wives sometimes subtly indicate their desires to their husbands through glances and other nonverbal communications. Women also sometimes purposely wander into the forest alone in order to just happen upon their husbands or other men with whom they wish to have sex. This manipulative strategy almost always succeeds because the men place high value on sexual intercourse, particularly adultery, and they are unlikely to turn down the opportunities women provide. Looked at one way, the men are captives of their own symbols and, for this reason, women can manipulate them. A final way in which women manipulate men is through indirect ridicule and gossip. Many Cabruá women enjoy listening to the men play the *karökö* because they can make fun of those who are incompetent. Similarly, the women often gossip about the men loudly enough so that their comments can be overheard in the men's house. A favorite topic is the shortness of the men's penises or their inadequacies at sexual intercourse. This is an effective strategy because the men find such gossip personally insulting and threatening, but they seldom are willing to challenge it; rather, they deal with it by retreating into the forest or ignoring it. It is also effective because it challenges the high symbolic value the men place on sex. The women counter the male world by indirectly noting that the men do not measure up to their shared images of themselves.

Besides manipulating the men in subtle and sometimes hidden ways, a second way they deal with common problems is through direct efforts. These efforts are made possible by the extreme separation of men and women in Cabruá. When the men return from hunting, for example, they deposit their kill with "their women"—their wives or, if single or divorced, their mothers. The women dress the animals and divide the meat among themselves so that everyone shares in the bounty of the hunt even if representatives of each household did not kill the same number of animals. Women have exclusive control of the process of dressing and dividing the meat. Similarly, they control decisions about the preparation of farina. The separation of men and women also means that women largely determine the ways in which children are raised. Women also act directly to control each other in order to minimize the chances of gang rape. Gossip is one means of such control, and it is effective because the women spend most of their lives together. The respect and cooperation of other women is important under such circumstances. Any woman who becomes too promiscuous or otherwise strays too close to a gang rape is typically brought back into line by other women before she must face the more brutal wrath of the men.

The women of Cabruá are not, then, the passive followers of omnipotent men, as the men's reality indicates. They are active in shaping their world and reality. Indeed, because they have greater control than the men over such basic activities as child rearing and food preparation, the women can be seen as the cornerstone of the Cabruá life. The men's activities of hunting, fishing, clearing the forest for gardens, and playing the *karökö* are, then, supplementary to "women's work." Certainly this is the way that the women of Cabruá see their world. The fact that this interpretation flies in the face of the men's reality indicates that the bodies of knowledge used by men and women are different. The men base their reality, in part, on myth and the symbolic importance of hunting and controlling sexual intercourse. The women, on the other hand, base their reality on the knowledge they glean from everyday life and the many contradictions it entails.

The two realities that make up Cabruá life are important in understanding the heritage of the Mundurucú, but they arise within a village setting which is somewhat isolated from outsiders. These realities break down when the Mundurucú move to new settings which involve different activities and relationships. Human realities are thus precarious. Because they are socially constructed, realities can be socially changed to meet the changing circumstances of everyday life. The Mundurucú who live along the Cururú River provide a good example of how modernization has affected their realities.

Life along the Cururú

The Mundurucú along the Cururú River are not completely separate from those who live in Cabruá and similar villages. Many Cabruá residents, for example, move to the Cururú region during the dry season in order to fish and collect rubber for trading with outsiders. Rubber is created by cutting into, or tapping, a rubber tree and collecting the tree's sap. The sap is then poured onto a pole which is rotated above a fire.

The heat causes the sap to become a ball of raw rubber, which is added to each day until it becomes large enough to trade. Each year more and more residents of Cabruá and other traditional villages decide to remain in the Cururú region during the rainy season when rubber cannot be collected. Those who remain may settle in the Catholic mission, in the government post, or in the various villages and private households along the river. The total Mundurucú population in the Cururú region in 1952, when the study was undertaken, was 700, which included 200 persons in the mission, 70 to 80 in the government post, and the rest in scattered villages and households.

Several appealing features about life in the Cururú region encourage people to settle there. First, it is possible to fish all year round in the river, and fishing is a more dependable source of food than hunting. Second, permanent settlement along the Cururú eliminates the long annual treks from the village to the river and back again. Third, and perhaps most important, goods from local traders are readily available. Persons living in traditional villages are dependent on itinerant traders, who often cheat them. In the Cururú region the traders are more numerous than in the outlying villages (the most important at the government post and Catholic mission), and the Mundurucú perceive them as more willing to offer a fair deal. The fairness of the exchange is important because, rather than sell their goods for money, the Mundurucú trade them for other goods. This means that the Mundurucú cannot seek out larger national markets where their goods can be exchanged for money. Barter is thus based on a local market, and some local traders are fairer than others. The two most important goods traded by the Mundurucú are rubber during the dry season and farina during the rainy season. Even with those objects of trade, however, the Mundurucú are often in debt to traders, who advance them goods in anticipation of future rubber or farina production. The continuing problem of being in debt increases the importance of dealing with a fair trader.

One change which accompanies permanent residence along the Cururú, then, is financial debt to outsiders, but there are other important changes. Changes in village life and in the household are particularly notable.

Whole villages do not move to the Cururú at once; rather, individuals and households move at different times. Sometimes those who move are able to settle near relatives or old village members, but often this is impossible. An important limiting factor is the availability of rubber trees to be tapped. Unlike the traditional village economy, which is based on the shared use of the forest and gardens, rubber collecting is based on private property. Specifically, each rubber collector controls a set of trees which make up his "rubber avenue"; others may not tap those trees. The availability of uncontrolled trees thus limits the migrant's choice. The problem is worsening because, as more people become dependent on the rubber trade for their livelihoods, they must take control of two and three rubber avenues, instead of just one for part-time rubber collection.

Because different people settle along the Cururú at different times, villages along the Cururú are often made up of very diverse populations, and the old pattern of segregating men and women is breaking down. There are, for example, no men's houses, nor do the households within the villages include large numbers of related women. Rather, village and household life are centered in the *nuclear family* (husband, wife, and their children), although two or three nuclear families occasionally share the same house. Even when several nuclear families live together, however, the old pattern of matrilocality is often ignored. But the importance of the new way of life goes beyond living arrangements. The most basic sources of the separate realities of men and women found in the traditional village are different, but these differences can no longer be maintained outside the village. It is difficult, for example, to maintain separate realities when the most important person in your life is your husband or wife and not members of your own sex.

The destruction of the old realities is also encouraged by new work arrangements. The process of collecting rubber does not require a group, as with hunting, and so modernization has undermined much of the traditional basis for men's knowledge and reality. Indeed, when rubber collectors need help, they typically enlist the aid of their wives or children. Similarly, when the men of the Cururú hunt, they typically go alone because they have guns and do not need a group to chase and kill the animals. Fishing has also become a private activity which does not involve persons outside the nuclear family. The conditions of life along the Cururú have also undermined the women's reality found in the traditional village. Cooperative gardening does not occur in this world; rather, men and women of each household clear the forest and plant and harvest their own gardens. Even farina making has changed. Although many villages have a public farina shed, each household uses it privately on a rotating schedule. Thus, the husband, wife, and children of each household are the producers of farina. One consequence is that the farina shed is no longer a source for creating a unique women's reality.

In sum, the world of the Cururú region is different from that of the traditional village. The old sources of knowledge and reality have been destroyed and new ones have evolved. The most important source of reality in Cururú village life is the private household. Through their various work and other social activities, the members of each household create realities distinct from those of other households. For this reason the modernization of the Mundurucú is a "mixed blessing." Certainly, much of the cruelty that characterizes male-female relations in the traditional village is absent here, because husbands and wives live and work together. Much of the male concern for sexual superiority is also absent in the Cururú world. The new realities of private households, then, offer many advantages to the women, who are the strongest advocates of modernization. But these new realities also entail costs.

Much of the male and female camaraderie of the traditional village is lost in the Cururú villages. For example, it is difficult to obtain help when a household cannot handle a job by itself. The pursuit of the material goods offered by the traders also constrains the modernized Mundurucú, because they must work continuously to accumulate enough rubber and farina to trade. In the traditional village the major aim of work is to sustain the community and, if a hunt is especially successful, the hunters can take a day or two off. The Cururú workers have no such luxury because earning a livelihood from rubber collecting is demanding work. Unlike the part-time migrant worker from the traditional village who spends about three months along the Cururú and devotes about four days a week collecting rubber from his single rubber avenue, the full-time Cururú resident devotes five days a week and five months a year to collecting from his two or three rubber avenues. Another indicator of the demanding nature of the work is expressed in the concerns of the women. In the Cururú villages the wives assess their husbands as workers, and a "good worker" is one who collects a great deal of rubber. Those husbands who lag behind others often face angry wives who want them to increase their productivity. In the traditional village, on the contrary, women do not worry about whether their husbands are "good workers" or not. Within a cooperative economy that is irrelevant so long as a person is an adequate worker. Certainly wives do not nag their husbands to become better hunters.

Finally, the changing circumstances and realities of Mundurucú life bind women to men in new ways. In the traditional village women are bound to men in highly ritualized ways, but the women are not economically dependent on the men, except for help in such activities as clearing the forest and hunting for meat. None of these activities is absolutely vital to the survival of the women, however, because they can clear the forest themselves if necessary, and the meat obtained from hunting is not the most important source of food for the village. Its primary value is symbolic. Indeed, the relative unimportance of the men in the traditional village is reflected in the high divorce rate there. A divorce is easily obtained since a man is considered divorced from his wife any time he refuses to give her the meat he has killed while hunting. Divorced women in the traditional village do not have to worry about starving, however, because they live in a household of female relatives who control meat distribution and will share with them. In contrast, although the Cururú women appear to be more equal, underlying this equality is dependence on the husband as a rubber collector. The rubber avenue of a household belongs to the man alone. Divorce cuts a woman off from this source of livelihood, and the absence of relatives who will share with her worsens the problem. Similarly, cultivating a garden and making farina are difficult for a divorced woman who does not have relatives to help with these onerous tasks. As time passes, new networks of sharing and aid may develop which parallel those of the traditional village, but at the time of the Murphys' studies, the center of Cururú life was the nuclear family, and when it broke down the family members were often alone.

This description of the Mundurucú demonstrates how social realities are created through social interaction and vary with changing circumstances. The Cabruá realities of men and women reflect the differing types of knowledge available to them in their differing social circumstances. These realities, however, break down when the Mundurucú move to the Cururú region, because the nature and source of knowledge are changed.

Based on the changing circumstances of their lives and sources of knowledge, people create new realities for understanding and dealing with their worlds. These realities are good indications of the ways in which human beings actively interpret and organize their lives. The new realities are not "caused" by modernization or some other change; rather, they are human interpretations of change (Gusfield, 1967, 1975). Nor can the new realities be easily classified as "good" or "bad." A better approach is to see them as having different consequences for different people, who experience them as independent "facts of life," offering both new opportunities and new constraints. In sum, social realities are human interpretations of the world that are created in response to the practical circumstances and problems of life and that offer "mixed blessings" for individuals.

MUNDURUCÚ LIFE AND THE SOCIOLOGY OF KNOWLEDGE APPROACH TO WORK

Based on the various realities of Mundurucú life, it is now possible to develop further the sociology of knowledge approach to work. Three of the most important issues considered by this approach are: (1) how official statements about the world are related to the social realities of everyday life; (2) how myths are created and used in everyday life; and (3) how social change affects the social realities of everyday life. The several social realities making up Mundurucú life may be used as a beginning point for dealing with these issues.

Official Statements and Everyday Life

The Mundurucú are a useful example for developing the sociology of knowledge approach because they have been studied by anthropologists who are sensitive to the changes and contradictions in everyday human life (Murphy, 1971). In studying human beings it is never sufficient to look only at the official statements they make about themselves. To do so is to miss the way that official statements fail to capture the ongoing, everyday life of the group. To consider only official statements is to overlook the ways in which human beings act to create realities and to influence the circumstances of their lives.

The active nature of human beings is quite evident in the village life of Cabruá. Women there are officially powerless, but unofficially they are the major sources of power, because they control the preparation and distribution of food in the village. Their production of farina, which is the most important food of the village, is one indication of that control. The preparation and distribution of meat, which the hunters turn over to them, is another. The women carry out these tasks without advice from the men who, as powerful village officials, cannot be bothered with such mundane matters. One consequence of this pattern of life, as we have seen, is that women can negate the economic impact of divorce. Similarly, male control over sexual intercourse is not so exclusive as the official statements indicate. Wives can encourage or discourage their husbands' sexual interests in a variety of ways. Indeed, wives often control their husbands by having extramarital affairs when their husbands have angered them. Public knowledge of such affairs is humiliating to the husband and an effective means of unofficial control by the wives. Finally, Cabruá women collectively act to restrain women who are in danger of being gang raped by the men.

The everyday life of Cabruá, then, is not what it seems to be when only the official interpretations of the village are considered. The men and women who live there are involved in a constant process of negotiation; sometimes the outcome of their interaction is consistent with the official male view and sometimes with the unofficial female view. In either case, the residents of Cabruá are not passive players of traditional social roles. The active, negotiating nature of Cabruá villagers is important because it is characteristic of all human beings in all situations, regardless of what the official statements may be.

Official statements about the "way things are" are important, however, because they reflect the realities of some people within a group or society. They do this in two general ways. First, official statements offer an explanation for how the group has arrived at its present situation. The myth about the *karökö* shared by Cabruá men is an example. A second way in which official statements reflect reality is by indicating the way that life should be. Put differently, official statements are also moral statements, because they are one basis for distinguishing good from bad, natural from unnatural, desirable from undesirable. Again, the myth of the *karökö* is based on the assumption that men should dominate women and, consequently, that men should consciously act to protect their power from women. Gang rape, the men's house, control over hunting, and the hiding of the *karökö* from the women's view are concrete examples of how the men seek to protect themselves symbolically.

When the historical and moral aspects of official statements are combined, their full importance becomes evident. They are justifications for a way of life and the reality that gives it meaning. They are also interpretations of the past, present, and sometimes the future, and, as such, they do not fully reflect the ongoing activities and interactions of people in everyday life. Instead, they provide a way of making sense out of everyday life by pointing to some events, actions, and objects as important and others as unimportant. For Cabruá men the hunt is more important than the preparation and distribution of the meat. Thus, sharing meat with one's estranged wife is less important and less threatening than having women take part in the hunt. Similarly, the women's lack of desire to see the *karökö* is less important than the male awareness that they cannot look upon these sacred instruments. Official statements and explanations, then, are quite important because they may be used as symbols of dominance and group solidarity (Duncan, 1962, 1968). For this reason, they can be treated as a type of myth, used to legitimate a social reality (Barthes, 1972; Leach, 1954). To understand this statement we must investigate the role of myths in social life.

Myth and Everyday Life

For many people the word "myth" means a false statement about the world. For instance, they might see the myth of the *karökö* as an example of superstition which keeps the Mundurucú from seeing "reality." There are two major problems with this view of myths. First, it assumes that there is an ultimate reality, independent of the interpretations of human beings. The problem with this assumption becomes obvious when the bases for ultimate reality are explored. If those who see myths as worthless are asked to describe what they mean by ultimate reality, they will usually respond by giving some interpretation of the world they accept. The myth of the *karökö* is seen as unreal or superstition because it does not fit in with their interpretation. A second problem with the conventional use of the word "myth" is that it is often linked to an implicit assumption that only "primitive people" have myths. This argument is difficult to sustain when our "scientific and rational" lives are critically examined. For example, many people who would laugh at the myth of the *karökö* and call it superstitious accept without question the claim that Jesus was conceived by a virgin. The fact that this claim does not fit with our experiences in everyday life is irrelevant for those who believe in it. It is a reality to them, just as the myth of the *karökö* is a reality to Cabruá men.

Some people use the words "myth" and "ideology" interchangeably, because they see both as sets of ideas which reflect and justify the power of a group or segment of society. Karl Marx and Friedrich Engels (1845–1846/1969) claim, for example, that each new ruling class attempts to show that its social interests represent the interests of the whole society by constructing explanations and justifications which demonstrate the rationality and universal truth of its ideas and interests. From this point of view, the myth of the *karökö* represents the need of the Cabruá men (the rulers) to provide an explanation for their power in order to control the women (the ruled). A major problem with this claim is that it can easily be taken too far. Implicit in it is the assumption that the ruled accept the myth as valid, which is not necessarily true (Murphy, 1971). Indeed, the Cabruá women are a useful example, because they openly scorn the men's explanations for the division of the sexes.

A better approach is simply to define myths as images of the world (Gusfield, 1973b). As images, myths may take a variety of forms. They may be found, for example, in presentations of the mass media, in various forms of art, in political and religious dogma, and in many scientific theories. Some myths may also be used to justify the dominance of some persons over others or to justify social change, and these are the most important myths considered in the analysis of work in this book.

Myths, then, are real because we believe them to be real, and they are important because they help us to make sense out of the world—that is, they help us create reality (Thomas, 1923). The reality of myths is, however, variable. Not everyone in Cabruá believes in the myth of the *karökö*, and not everyone in the Western world believes in the myth of virgin conception. Even those who believe in these myths do not use them all the time. An American couple who return from Christmas services at their church and confront their pregnant teen-age daughter, for example, are unlikely to be convinced that virgin conception has occurred again. In a similar way, the Cabruá men use the myth of the *karökö* situationally, but when they do use it, the myth is a statement of reality.

The reality the myth conveys may be conservative and justify the existing situation, but this is not always the case. An important aspect of social movements which are primarily concerned with change is the creation of myths which help members to make sense out of the present, justify their efforts at change, and point to a new future (Gusfield, 1973b). Myth making, then, is an important feature of human life, because it is a way of giving life continuity. For this reason, an important part of mythmaking is the creation of tradition.

Tradition, like the "facts of life," is typically experienced as a given, something that must be accepted. One reason for this belief is that we assume tradition to be an accurate portrayal of the past, which, after all, cannot be changed. But this perception of tradition ignores the ways in which we continuously create history and tradition by generalizing from current situations (Gusfield, 1973a, 1975). The way of life which characterizes Cabruá villagers is today thought of as traditional by the Mundurucú, but it is very different from the Mundurucú way of life during headhunting days. Today the Cabruá people are peaceable, cooperate little with other villagers, and consider tribal affiliations unimportant. The reason for the disparity between historical fact and what is considered traditional is that tradition and history are created in the present; they are primarily concerned with explaining the present by linking it to a continuous historical process. This mythmaking tendency is found in Cabruá, but it is also evident in our use of bits and pieces of history to indicate the universal features of "human nature." Thus, we are sometimes told that it is human nature to place self-interest above all other considerations, and people who use this argument support it with numerous concrete examples in the recent and distant past. Those same people often become angry, however, when a similar argument is made about the motives of those who have died in war or those who framed the Constitution. These pieces of history are interpreted within a different tradition based on a different vision of human nature.

For the purposes of this analysis, the most important work-related myths are those dealing with (1) the need for work, (2) the present organization of work, and (3) the rewards of work. Myths may either justify or undermine current interpretations of each of these aspects of work; thus, work-related myths may encourage conservative or radical actions, but in either case they provide a framework for understanding work. In Cabruá, the major source of mythmaking is the men and, consequently, Table 1-1, which summarizes Cabruá work myths, deals only with the men's reality.

The Cabruá myth about the need for work defines men's work primarily as hunting because it is necessary for food and because it is a traditional and spiritually important activity. The importance of hunting is reflected in the desire of the spirits associated with the *karökö* to be fed meat. The official interpretation of why women's work is needed derives from the men's preoccupation with controlling women. Women's

Table 1-1 • Work-Related Myths of Cabruá Men

Need for Work	*Organization of Work*	*Rewards of Work*
Men: Hunting is a sacred activity that is prized by the spirits of the *karökö* and, therefore, necessary	Work is rigidly divided according to sex Group work is thought of as desirable for both men and women	Men: Hunting is spiritually important for the village, and outstanding hunters have a right to enjoy high prestige
Women: Women are a perpetual threat to the dominance of men and they must be controlled. One form of submission is doing women's work		Women: No rewards are given

work is recognized as an important source of food, but it is also a symbol of submission to male dominance: women must do less valued work to keep them in their place.

The Cabruá myth about the proper organization of work is also made up of two parts. First, it argues that work is best organized along sexual lines and in segregated groups. There is, then, men's and women's work. The second part of the myth stresses the need for cooperative work. Both men and women should work in groups. Indeed, working individually is sometimes taken as a sign of sorcery or witchcraft, and the penalty for sorcery is death.

Finally, there is the Cabruá myth about the rewards of work. It states simply that male hunters enjoy the satisfaction of placating the spirits who are important to the village, and those who are the best hunters have a right to greater prestige than other men. This myth says nothing about the rewards of women's work, and that omission distinguishes it from many of the paternalistic myths found in other societies. Whereas Cabruá men do not see women as happy or satisfied with their work, other, more paternalistic interpretations argue that women find their work rewarding because it is natural for their sex or because they are childlike and find simple activities satisfying.

There are three important features of the Cabruá men's myths that are also characteristic of other myths about work. First, the myths do not deny the importance of work as a way of making a living, but they give it more general meaning. Put differently, work activities, organizations, and rewards are made symbolic within myth. Second, the Cabruá myths concentrate on only one aspect of the men's work. The most important work activity is hunting, whereas fishing, clearing gardens, collecting rubber, and building houses are not mentioned. Cabruá work myths, like others, are oversimplifications of everyday life because they concentrate on what is symbolically most important to the mythmakers (Manning, 1977). Finally, work myths are not used all of the time by Cabruá men; rather, they are shared images that are used within concrete situations to explain and justify the Cabruá men's reality. Each of these features of Cabruá work myths will be evident in the work myths that are discussed in later chapters of this book.

The Impact of Social Change on Social Realities

Central to a sociology of knowledge approach to work is a recognition of the disparity between everyday life and our explanations of the world. The disparity exists because life is too complex to be captured in explanatory statements. Fundamental to our explanations is the creation of myths, and an important part of mythmaking is the creation of history or tradition. But our myths and traditions are tenuous, and they can be changed through new interpretations. New interpretations arise from the changing circumstances of everyday life. Thus, the study of social change is basic to a sociology of knowledge approach to work. These new interpretations will also differ from everyday life, and they will become associated with new myths and traditions. Again, the Mundurucú provide an example.

Life along the Cururú River is quite different from life in Cabruá. Gone are many of the symbols of male superiority and female inferiority. Also gone are many of the sources of male and female solidarity. What is emerging is a way of life that is based on the private household, typically made up of only one nuclear family. Equally important, this way of life is based on trade, which means that outsiders now control many of the most important items needed to live. Even farina, which in Cabruá is primarily produced for village consumption, is produced as an item of trade in the villages along the Cururú. These changes in family, village, and economic life also have had an impact on patterns of dependence among the Mundurucú who have become modernized. For example, the husband-wife relationship has changed, so that many of the old male-female antagonisms are absent, although men and women are now dependent on one another in new ways. Equally important is the increasing dependence of Cururú residents on traders, who can substantially affect the lives of the Mundurucú by changing the terms of their deals. This dependence is most obvious in the more or less permanent indebtedness of most Cururú residents. Indebtedness to traders is important for understanding the practical problems of everyday life for the Mundurucú, but it is also culturally important.

The most important source of official statements that justify the new Mundurucú-trader relationship is the group of priests who run the mission and are heavily involved in trade themselves. As with the official statements of the men in Cabruá, there is often a disparity between action and explanation. Much of the priests' rationale for running the mission is to bring Christianity to the area, but the Mundurucú typically treat these efforts as the women in Cabruá treat male pronouncements: they resist in subtle and indirect ways. On days of special Christian significance, for example, the priests exert pressure to come to gatherings, attend Mass, and receive the Sacraments, but the Mundurucú use these times to deliver rubber, enjoy the coffee and sweets provided by the nuns, dance, and visit with relatives and friends (Murphy, 1960). Similarly, the priests often try to influence the selection of the chief by refusing to recognize anyone who does not accept the mission and Christianity and who will not carry the priests' message to the Mundurucú. Though they usually have their way, the typical Mundurucú response is simply to ignore the new chief and to do as they please.

In sum, the new activities and social relationships that characterize life along the Cururú have given rise to new relationships of dominance and dependence. For this reason, the most important mythmakers are no longer the men but the traders and, particularly, the priests at the mission. As life becomes more settled in this area, it is likely that new historical explanations for the current Mundurucú way of life will also emerge. In developing these explanations, the Mundurucú will give Cururú life a traditional base much as they have previously done in Cabruá.

MUNDURUCÚ LIFE AND THE STRUCTURAL BASES OF SOCIAL REALITIES

To this point we have identified three important problems for building a sociology of knowledge approach to work: (1) how official statements about work and the observable actions of persons in everyday life are related; (2) how myth and the creation of tradition help to explain current work patterns and point to desired future states; and (3) what the impact of social change is on social realities. Each of these will be central to the discussions of the major types of work that make up the rest of this book. Before turning to these discussions, however, it is important to consider the structural bases for the creation of social realities. The Mundurucú are also helpful in this endeavor. The two most important structural bases for building social realities are time and space.

Time

Although time is a universal feature of human existence, it can be experienced in very different ways. One way is to use a clock, which organizes time as an orderly process of moving from one temporal unit to another. Nature also organizes time, but natural time is much less predictable than clock time. Although it too involves a movement through temporal units (such as seasons), the length of the time units is quite variable. For example, sometimes winters are long and sometimes they are short; indeed, sometimes winter is interrupted by a warm period before it resumes again. There are, then, a variety of ways individuals and groups can experience time, and the way time is experienced has important implications for how work is organized and experienced (i.e., how it is given reality).

There are three major ways in which time can be organized and experienced: diachronically, synchronically, and apocalyptically (John Hall, 1978). *Diachronic time* assumes a connection between the past and future. Thus, events and decisions occurring in the past are seen as vital for understanding the present, and present events and decisions are seen as important determinants of the future. *Synchronic time* assumes that the only reality is the present. What has occurred in the past is irrelevant to the present, and the present has no meaning for the future. In other words, we can only influence the world in the present. *Apocalyptic time* assumes that this world is irrelevant and the only important concern of an individual should be with transcending this world and entering another better one. Persons who experience time apocalyptically often must deal with the world of diachronic and synchronic time, but only as a way of achieving another world. The orientation toward the future of those who experience time apocalyptically means that much of their lives is directed toward a timeless state, because in the future the divisions of life into past, present, and future will be irrelevant.

To the extent that people live in a world of multiple realities, it is possible for them to experience time differently, depending on the realities of the situations in which they find themselves. Although most of us assume that we live in a world of diachronic time, this is not always true. Many events that are called play, for example, are based on a synchronic interpretation of time. Players tend to get totally caught up in the game and to lose awareness of how their activity is linked to the past and future. They also tend to treat the present as inconsequential for the past and future. An example of this tendency is offered by Julian Roebuck and Wolfgang Frese (1976) in their study of the Rendezvous—an after-hours club in an eastern city. Among the regular patrons of the club are a group of small-time racketeers who are friends of the club manager and a group of young women who are employed at a variety of conventional occupations. Periodically, the manager holds a private party in his office in the back of the club. These parties are based on a synchronic interpretation of time, because whatever occurs during them is treated as unconnected to other aspects of the participants' lives. Typically, the participants have sexual relations with one or more of the persons at the party, but when the party is over the racketeers return to their dates for the evening (many of whom wait in the public area of the club) and the women return to their normal activities within the club. Synchronic time best describes the experience because none of the participants would want their actions at the party to be the basis for making moral judgments about them later in other situations. The party is a self-contained event that has no connection to the past or present.

Just as synchronic time is associated with some situations, so apocalyptic time is characteristic of others. When people begin to talk of life in heaven, for example, they typically speak of it in an apocalyptic way, because heaven is seen as qualitatively different from this world. The aging process is irrelevant to such discussions because past, present, and future are not assumed to be a part of this spiritual world. Indeed, the conclusion to such discussions is often a statement that life in heaven just "is." People who believe in a hereafter base their everyday lives on diachronic time, but they experience it in the same way as members of many so-called mystical cults (such as the Hare Krishna), who are also concerned with transcending this world. The tendency to use apocalyptic time in discussing the future is not just limited to religious issues, however; many secular and political movements that are concerned with transforming present realities also treat time apocalyptically. Many socialists, for example, conceive of a truly socialist future in an apocalyptic way, because they assume that the major forces shaping the past and present will be absent from this new world.

Time, then, is experienced differently from situation to situation, but because work tends to occur in similar and routine situations, it is possible to categorize different types of work realities based on the ways in which time is organized and experienced within them. Following the lead of Julius Roth (1963), we will refer to these general arrangements of time as *work-related timetables* and discuss examples of diachronic, synchronic, and apocalyptic timetables in later chapters. For the present, it is important to recognize that there are differences even among timetables of the same general type. For example, the three Mundurucú groups we have identified—Cabruá women, Cabruá men, and Cururú workers—all experience time as diachronic, but their timetables are essentially different. The kinds of work performed and the degree to which the work is continuous or discontinuous help explain the differences in the work-related timetables of these workers. Table 1-2 summarizes how the three Mundurucú workers experience diachronic time.

Table 1-2 • Work-Related Timetables of the Mundurucú

Subgroup	*Experience of Time*	*Timetable*
Cabruá Women	Diachronic	Based on the continuous requirements of village and household life
Cabruá Men	Diachronic	Based on the discontinuous processes of nature and requirements of village life
Cururú Workers	Diachronic	Based on the continuous demands of the local market and the material desires of the workers

The social reality of Cabruá women's work is based on a timetable that is continuous because the demands of the village and household are continuous. Although Cabruá women do not tend their gardens or make farina every day, they are engaged in some type of work every day. They certainly cannot make large amounts of farina one day and take the next day off from work. Cooking, child care, and other forms of Cabruá women's work preclude such an organization of work. Cabruá men, on the other hand, have a work-related timetable which is discontinuous and allows for taking time off from work. This is possible because Cabruá men's work is based on the discontinuous processes of nature and requirements of the village. Cabruá men, for example, do not need to clear the forest for gardens every day because it takes two to three years for the forest to take over the existing gardens. Similarly, Cabruá men cannot fish or hunt every day because the natural conditions necessary for hunting and fishing are sometimes absent. Even when natural conditions are right, Cabruá men work discontinuously, because the village has no way of preserving and storing many of the products of their work. Men who have had an especially successful hunt, for example, can plan on taking a day or two off from work, because it will take that long for the village to consume the available meat supply.

All of this changes with a permanent move to the Cururú region, because work there is primarily based on the continuous demands of the local market. In the Cururú region, both men and women work continuously because there is a constant demand for rubber during the dry season and for farina during the rainy season. The continuous demand of the market is reinforced by the continuing desires of the Mundurucú for the material goods controlled by the local traders. Thus, the demand for work cannot be separated from the desires and needs of the populace. In Cabruá the desires and needs are primarily oriented toward subsistence (simply making a living), whereas the desires and needs of the Mundurucú living in the Cururú region are larger in scope and, consequently, work is continuous. One general conclusion that can be drawn from the Mundurucú example is that the felt need to work will persist and may even intensify to the extent that the desires and needs of people for material goods persist and expand. An important consequence of modernization, then, is that it may provide opportunities for developing new desires and needs, and, if this occurs, the work-related timetables of the group will be affected (Sahlins, 1972).

Space

The second structural base for building social realities is space. In a general sense, space refers to the territorial area within which people act and interact. Looked at this way, the space of the Cabruá men's reality is larger than that of the women, because they roam great distances into the forest in the course of hunting. The women, on the other hand, are primarily confined to the general vicinity of the village.

A more sociological use of the term "space" is to define it as locations for human action and interaction (Freilich, 1963). Such a definition deemphasizes the size of the space and stresses the nature of the action and interaction that occur within it. It is the actions and interactions of persons that are most important in building social realities. Social realities, then, are located in space and some are associated with large territories and some with small territories.

To the extent that a social reality includes work, it can be treated as a *work-related community* (Holzner, 1972). An important feature of work-related communities is the sense members have of belonging to a group made up of similar people who are facing similar problems. Put more formally, work-related communities are based on a *consciousness of kind* (Gusfield, 1975). But work-related communities are not permanent features of social life. They develop when people get together and create them, and they disappear when the members leave. An important factor distinguishing different types of work-related communities, then, is time. Some work-related communities are very enduring, whereas others shift gradually over time and still others are quite fleeting. This is evident in the types of work-related communities found among the Mundurucú and summarized in Table 1-3.

The work-related community of the Cabruá women is highly enduring because it is based on a stable population. The practice of matrilocality assures that the female household members will be stable. In addition, the community of Cabruá women is based on the settings within which women work. The garden and the farina shed are especially important, because they are settings within which women spend much of their time. The social relationships that develop in these settings give rise to a consciousness of kind among the women. Thus, the

Table 1-3 • Work-Related Communities of the Mundurucú

Subgroup	*Degree of Permanence*	*Basis of the Community*
Cabruá Women	Enduring	Based on the enduring population of the household and the other regular collective settings of women's work
Cabruá Men	Shifting	Based on the shifting membership of the men's house and the men's work groups
Cururú Workers	Mixed	Based on the enduring membership of the household, the shifting membership found in work settings, and the fleeting nature of local events

women live in the same village as the men, but they belong to a different community.

Indeed, the work-related community of the Cabruá men is less enduring that that of the women, partly because of the practice of matrilocality. The composition of the men's house is changed whenever a man marries a woman in another village or whenever a divorce occurs, because the divorced man often returns to his home village. Another reason for the shifting nature of the men's community is their work, which is often intermittent and seldom involves all of the men at one time. A hunting party, for example, usually includes only some of the residents of the men's house. Thus, the consciousness of kind found in the Cabruá men's community is less enduring than in the women's community. It is still present, however, and its importance is reflected in the significance attached to the *karökö* by the men. Indeed, these musical instruments are the most important symbol of the Cabruá men's consciousness of kind (their community).

The work-related communities of the Cururú region are more varied than in Cabruá and, for this reason, they are classified as mixed in Table 1-3. The most enduring work-related community is the household, which is the center of social life for most of the Mundurucú who live here. A more shifting community is the village, which is made up of persons who occasionally help each other with work projects. Finally, there is a fleeting work-related community that emerges with local ceremonies and events. Christian holidays provide one setting for the rise of these communities, because a large number of Mundurucú travel to the mission to trade their goods, dance, eat, drink, and see friends and kin. These communities are fleeting because they disappear when the participants go home. Within the time and social limits of the settings, however, a consciousness of kind may develop and provide the participants with a sense of community affiliation.

One general conclusion that emerges from the Mundurucú example is that work-related communities develop, in part, as a consequence of the segregation of individuals and groups. An important basis for the male and female communities in Cabruá is the physical separation of men and women. But segregation is not always physical; it can also be social. In this case, people may be in close physical proximity but be socially distant because they fail to interact with one another. Many contemporary urban communities are based on social segregation. But social and physical segregation can break down, and when this occurs an important basis for community is destroyed, although a new community may emerge to take its place. The segregation of men and women in Cabruá, for example, is broken down in the Cururú villages, but in place of the male and female communities, a new community has arisen—the private household. Segregation is also an important source for the development of myths. Myths provide an explanation for how and why segregation has developed, and they are often used as justifications for maintaining segregated communities.

To this point, the discussion has centered on the Mundurucú and the various realities that characterize them. The rest of this book is concerned with the work-related realities of modern society, but it should be noted that the general characteristics associated with Mundurucú realities are also found in modern societies. Thus, the Mundurucú provide a point of comparison for understanding the work-related realities of modern society. These realities will be discussed in detail in later chapters, but first it is important to gain a more general overview of the analysis we will present in this text.

OVERVIEW OF THE BOOK

Contrary to the picture that is sometimes painted of nonindustrial ways of life, the Murphys' analyses of the Mundurucú show the diversity and complexity of this world and the contradictions found in it. At the same time, Mundurucú life is less diverse than modern life, in which vast numbers of people encounter each other in a variety of specialized roles and settings. Unlike the Cabruá residents, who share much of their work and thereby build social realities that are shared by large portions of the village, modern workers perform jobs that are so specialized that the realities created in work settings are shared by only small segments of the whole society. For this reason, some sociologists of work are primarily concerned with identifying and describing the unique social realities of those in particular lines of work or work settings (Bensman and Lilienfeld, 1973). Indeed, some of the most insightful and important studies in the field use this approach (Hughes, 1970).

But there is another approach to studying the diverse work-related realities of modern society. Sociologists who use this approach classify general work roles and situations into types. These types are then used to divide up the world in order to make sense of it. An important advantage of such an approach is that it encourages the analyst to look for similarities among the various lines of work that make up a type. A major disadvantage is that many of the unique aspects of specific work roles and settings may be ignored.

While recognizing its disadvantages, this book is based on the second approach to work-related realities. Specifically, the remaining chapters deal with six general types of work: peasant work, industrial work, professional work, hustling work, household work, and countercultural work. Although this typology leaves out some lines of work found in modern societies (such as entertainment and sales), it does take into account the major types of modern work situations.

Peasant work is based on a rural and traditional way of life, within which a balance is sought between producing for subsistence (for immediate household use) and for sale to others. In some ways, peasant work is similar to work among the Mundurucú, who also produce for subsistence and sale. There are some differences between them, however, and they will become apparent as the work of the French peasantry is discussed in the next chapter.

Unlike peasant work, industrial work is exclusively directed toward production for sale, it is centralized in a work place that is separate from the home (such as a factory), and it is organized as a set of highly specialized, routine actions and decisions which culminates in products (i.e., goods or services). The routine actions often require machines, which may influence, if not dominate, the worker. Industrial work is most obvious in the factory, where mechanization and specialization are highly developed, but it is also characteristic of other work settings. Office settings are an important example. Indeed, many recent developments in office machinery and organization are encouraging the industrialization of some parts of the office. This issue and others will be discussed in chapter three.

Because industrial work is organized around the interests and authority of organizational officials, such as factory and office managers, it can be described as work based on the "organizational principle" (Freidson, 1973). Professional work, on the other hand, is organized around the shared goals and interests of members of the same occupation and can therefore be described as based on the "occupational principle." The unique organization of professional work is partly related to the ability of professionals to "monopolize" the knowledge and skills associated with their work by limiting its public availability. Indeed, professional knowledge and skills are made available to the public primarily through the services of the professional worker and through training programs which restrict the number of students. Further encouraging the professional control of limited areas of human knowledge are licensing laws and other forms of legislation restricting the professional practice and government regulatory and funding agencies, which are used to justify and expand professional knowledge. In addition, professional work is usually less specialized and mechanized than industrial work. Many of these features of professional work are changing today, and new models of professionalism are developing. These issues form the nucleus of chapter four.

Typically, when the modern worker is discussed, the image that comes to mind is that of an industrial or professional worker who is regularly employed. One problem with this image is that it excludes a large number of persons who work irregularly at a variety of jobs. Included in this category of workers are the retired, who often supplement their social security by doing odd jobs; migrant workers, who harvest crops in summer and try to find other incomes in winter; persons holding low-paying and insecure jobs (such as dishwashers); and, finally, some people involved in crime. These and similar ways of making a living are classified here as types of hustling work, and they are discussed in chapter five. An important aspect of such work is how public welfare, unemployment, and "rehabilitation" programs influence the lives of those employed at it.

Another type of work that is often left out of official assessments of the modern economy is household work, much of which is associated with the unpaid role of the housewife. Chapter six is largely concerned with the activities and problems of these workers. It is also concerned with the ways in which problems found in work places outside the home intrude upon family life, especially in homes where the husband and wife are both pursuing outside careers. Household work, then, is a more general topic than just how to cook or clean, since it also involves such basic issues as child rearing and husband-wife relationships.

Each of the five types of work described above are linked to social realities that give them meaning. Indeed, many are associated with several competing realities that point to different aspects of the everyday lives of workers. An important part of the chapters that follow, then, is the identification of these realities and the myths that are associated with them. Each of the types of work is also based on differing ways of organizing time and space, another important topic in the following chapters.

If we were to limit the discussion of modern work to only five types, however, much of the variety and richness of modern life, which partly stems from the presence of alternative communities and social movements, would be ignored. These communities and movements are intentionally organized as alternatives to conventional life. They include several of the communes created by disaffected youth during the 1960s and 1970s, but they also include many enduring communities, such as the Hutterites and the Amish, who trace their beginnings to the nineteenth century or before. Chapter seven is concerned with these alternatives to conventional work, and it provides a brief summary of some of their most important features.

Chapter eight is concerned with the changing social realities associated with modern work. The most important trend is the renewed interest in giving power to workers and clients who have been denied it in the past. The diverse persons and settings affected by this trend are described here as parts of the *empowerment movement*, which many observers feel offers hope for building more equitable and democratic work places in modern society. Three examples of empowerment—of factory workers, low-level office workers, and the clients of professional workers—are discussed in this chapter as well as some more general issues involving the potential of the movement to fulfill the predictions and dreams of its advocates.

The final chapter attempts to bring together the diverse issues discussed in the earlier chapters. That is done by looking at two important theoretical and empirical problems facing both sociologists and workers themselves as they go about their everyday lives. The first problem involves the organization of work opportunities in modern society. Since much of the academic and popular analysis of this problem concentrates on the ways in which the value of workers and their opportunities to work are affected by supply and demand factors, this chapter includes a discussion of how modern work is organized within labor markets where workers are assigned differing monetary values. The second problem this chapter looks at concerns the need to work. It is argued that the need to work is related to the general ways in which we define our basic human needs and wants. In modern societies, advertisers attempt to convince us that we "need" to buy their products in order to be truly happy, fulfilled, or respectable, and most people willingly increase the goods and services they want and deem necessary for a proper way of life as their wealth increases. One outcome is that modern people experience the need to work just as intensely as those in the past who were on the brink of extinction; we convince ourselves that we must continue to work in order to assure ourselves of the "good life." Making a living, in other words, is a matter of human definition and interpretation.

CONCLUSION

A sociology of knowledge approach to work tries to identify the social realities that give work meaning. These realities are created out of the social actions and interactions of people in their everyday living and the formal theories and explanations of a group. An important part of the task of creating reality is mythmaking, since myths are explanations of the present situation which may be used to justify the status quo or change. Because they explain and justify, myths are often historical, and they point to continuities between the past and present. Social reality is also based on time and space. It is a sense of time that makes human experience orderly, because it provides the individual with a framework for interpreting an experience in relation to other experiences. For this reason, diachronic, synchronic, and apocalyptic views of time are important, because they provide people with different frameworks for interpreting their experiences. Space is important, because it is within specific locales that people create and sustain social realities. If these realities give rise to a consciousness of kind among the participants, then a community exists. Because social realities are humanly created and maintained, however, they can also be changed. An important source of change is everyday life, but changes in theory or myth can also encourage people to reinterpret their worlds, and this reinterpretation can then become the basis for a new social reality.

This book attempts to identify and discuss the most important types of one human reality—work. Admittedly, it offers an oversimplification of the many different kinds of work. In a sense, the book is actually a mythmaking enterprise because it offers an explanation for the rise and persistence of the types of work found in modern society. Unlike some of the other myths discussed here, however, this analysis is not intended to justify existing relations of inequality, nor is it concerned with presenting and justifying an alternative way of life that promises full equality, prosperity, and self-actualization to all. If we were to name the myth offered here, we might call it the myth of humanism, which assumes that human beings create reality through social action and interaction.

Because reality is based on personal negotiation (social interaction), it reflects the many different interests that arise when people deal with the practical problems of everyday life. It is not possible, then, to conclude this analysis by describing an ideal world in which work is devoid of conflict, frustration, and change; rather, we must content ourselves with a less inspiring question: What will be the most important problems of everyday life in the future, and how are we likely to interpret them? The myth of humanism rejects the notion that we have necessarily arrived at the present because of divine intervention, social evolution, or economic imperatives. We have arrived at the present through a variety of avenues that reflect differing, even contradictory, goals, and because it too will be a human creation, the future will also be contradictory and uncertain.

Chapter Two

PEASANT WORK

Because the word "peasant" is used in a variety of ways, it is important to begin by defining it. A highly regarded anthropological definition states that *peasantry* are a unique, rural, economic type, who have some of the characteristics of both primitive and modern ways of life (Wolf, 1966). The word "primitive" is used in this definition to indicate a way of life based on tribal membership in which the primary object of work is to obtain the resources needed for subsistence or short-run survival. In primitive society the most important unit of work is the *household*, which includes everyone who lives in the same building or space whether they are related through family ties or not. The major centers of work for the Mundurucú of Cabruá, for example, are the men's work groups, which are centered in the men's house, and the women's work groups, which are centered in the several households headed by women. Within the households, everyone is usually expected to work in some way.

The term "modern," on the other hand, is used in this definition to indicate a way of life based on an affiliation with a state or government. The object of work is to obtain money, which can be exchanged for goods or saved. Thus, modern work is not just directed toward immediate survival but may be used to increase wealth. Finally, the word "modern" assumes that the household is primarily a unit of consumption and that production occurs elsewhere.

The peasantry clearly have characteristics of both primitive and modern ways of life. A major goal of peasants, for example, is to acquire the resources needed to survive in the short run, and the peasant work force is largely composed of members of the household. The peasantry have some modern characteristics as well. Peasants produce some goods for sale to outsiders, and they use the money to buy material goods or to pay their rent and taxes. The fact that peasants must pay taxes indicates one way in which they are connected with the state. There are, then, several reasons for classifying the peasantry as an intermediate economic type with both primitive and modern economic characteristics.

An important problem with the definition stated above, however, is that it is static: it does not fully reflect the diverse and changing nature of the peasantry as they have developed in various parts of the world. There are very important differences among peasants found in Europe, Southeast Asia, and Latin America, for example. Important differences are also evident in the stages of history of a single peasant village. Because of these problems, some anthropologists are attempting to create new classifications which take account of the many subtle variations found in contemporary rural life (Halperin and Dow, 1977).

For the purposes of this chapter, a different, less elaborate and sophisticated approach is taken. The peasantry are treated as having some of the characteristics of primitive and modern ways of life, but it is assumed that the specific mixture of these characteristics differs from one peasant community to another and changes over time. Generally, the peasantry are becoming increasingly modern, but modernization is being resisted in a variety of ways and by a variety of people. It is not possible, then, to describe a universal and smooth evolutionary process through which peasants become modern; rather, for the peasant modernization is made up of many roads which lead in many directions, some of them smooth, others rough. This is so, because peasants (like other human beings) are active in responding to the problems and opportunities of life.

Because no single evolutionary process can be described, this chapter is not concerned with all of the forms of peasant life found in the contemporary world. It concentrates instead on French peasants, who, unlike the peasants of Asia and Latin America, have no direct experience with colonialism. The French peasant experience is, then, only one of a number of peasant experiences extant in the contemporary world. It is important, however, because it is based on a long historical process which provides insight into the ways in which modernization is both embraced and resisted by peasants.

Although the peasant experience in France will reveal a great deal about the more general environment of rural life, it should not be inferred that peasants are the only inhabitants of that environment. A variety of nonfarmers coexist with the peasants. The relationships of peasant farmers with others who also live in rural areas is an important topic, which this chapter will also explore.

A brief overview of the historical problems of the French peasantry is provided in the next section. With this overview as a basis, the realities of peasant life, myths about peasant work, and the changing circumstances of contemporary peasant life can then be discussed.

THE SOURCES AND COMPONENTS OF THE FRENCH PEASANTS' DILEMMA

For many historians a major watershed in the history of the French peasantry is the French Revolution (1789–1799). One consequence of this revolution was the emergence of Napoleon as the leader of France, but equally important were the changes in the French people's outlook that occurred at this time. The French Revolution was an attack on the traditional monarchy and aristocracy which controlled the major institutions of the country. Central to the new outlook was nationalism, through which the new French leaders hoped to both destroy the old monarchical and aristocratic loyalties of the people and to build new loyalties to a unified French government and culture. The new outlook continued to have an influence after the French Revolution; indeed, it is basic to understanding the agricultural policies of the French government for the past 200 years. The various governmental efforts at land reform, which have sought to break up the large landholdings of aristocrats, the Catholic Church, and some peasants, provide evidence of the continued vitality of the outlook. So too do the efforts to get peasant farmers to use modern farm equipment and farming techniques.

This view of the origins of the French peasants' situation today should not be used to oversimplify the relationship between the peasantry and the government, however. To obtain a balanced view, the relationship between government policies and everyday life must be considered. This requirement is especially important in considering rural France, because historically the countryside has been a separate world from Paris and the other political and economic centers of this country. Indeed, throughout French history the countryside has been made up of many localized worlds that have little in common with each other, much less the cities. Karl Marx (1852/1964), for example, described rural France as a sack of potatoes of differing sizes and shapes with little in common other than the fact that they are all potatoes.

Localism and Resistance to Modernization

Because of the isolated and localized nature of rural France, the government's efforts at land redistribution have prompted a variety of reactions. Although many rural areas experienced land reform during the nineteenth century, it is a mistake to assume that these policies were implemented everywhere. In particular, government efforts to stop the practice of primogeniture—that is, of passing the farm on to the eldest son—were resisted by peasants, who did not want to see the farm divided into small, uneconomic parts. One way in which this was done was to prevent daughters from marrying (Zeldin, 1973). So long as they did not marry, it was not necessary to give up part of the family's land as a dowry. Another strategy was to encourage marriage among cousins so that the land remained in the family, if not in the household (Jolas and Zonabend, 1977). Indeed, the best of all possible alternatives was a double marriage in which two members of each household married, because an equal land exchange could then be negotiated.

The French peasantry, then, were active in shaping the ways in which government policies were implemented in their regions. Sometimes they presented a united front because they shared a common interest. The government unwittingly promoted such a united front because its officials—tax collectors, bailiffs, forest guards, and the like—insisted on compliance with national laws and often ignored local customs (Weber, 1976). The peasants' resentment of these officials is perhaps best reflected in the prayers of the farmers in the Limousin region, which included the line: "Deliver us from all evil and from justice" (Weber, 1976: 50). But justice was not always perceived in the same ways by peasants. For example, sometimes family members who were being denied their legal share of the family farm would seek redress in the government's courts. Thus, government policies were not always resisted; rather, they were perceived in light of the ongoing practical problems of the various kinds of people who made up rural France during the nineteenth and early twentieth centuries.

The local institutions of the rural areas were an important arena of confrontation between the old and new. A major local institution was language. Although the peasantry were citizens of France, many of them did not speak the language; rather, they spoke local and regional languages. As late as 1863, for example, 25 percent of the French population did not speak any French, and most of these people were in rural areas (Weber, 1976). But this figure does not fully reflect the importance of local languages, because many of the people who could speak French did not do so except when dealing with government officials and other outsiders. Within the village and the household, the local language was often used exclusively. The persistence of local languages is important because it was one basis for separating the peasantry from government officials and others wishing to modernize them. It was also an important basis for building unique social relationships and customs in each rural area.

Among the local customs that were of special importance were the festivals, which occurred periodically to celebrate religious events and personages (e.g., celebrations for saints) as well as such mundane events as the changing of seasons. Government officials often treated these local festivals, like the language, as undesirable and tried to control them (Weber, 1976). A major concern of the officials was the tendency of peasants and other local residents to get drunk and otherwise engage in traditional, but "disorderly," behavior that often violated government laws. Teachers, priests, and other village notables often shared the government officials' concerns.

Divisions in Rural France

To this point the discussion has centered on two competing realities: the local-traditional reality and the national-modern reality. This imagery is an oversimplification because it implies that people were totally committed to either tradition or modernization. This was not the case; rather, each local area was made up of a number of people and realities that typically mixed traditional and modern themes. One set of local realities was based on sex. During the nineteenth century, for example, the French province of Provence was made up of a number of villages in which men's reality was created in a variety of sexually segregated places within the village and in the surrounding fields (Roubin, 1977). The most important of these places was the wine cellar, where men met on a daily basis to drink and talk, but also to seek protection from the weather, since cellars are usually cooler in summer and warmer in winter than other places. Women's reality was primarily constructed in the home, garden, and farm buildings, particularly the stables. There women sometimes ran into each other as they worked, but more important were the regular nightly meetings in the stables. Thus, two major work-related communities, based on the differing activities and spaces of men and women, coexisted in the villages of Provence.

But the divisions prevalent in traditional French rural life went beyond male and female realities; people were divided as well by their levels of wealth, prestige, and lines of work. Some of the different kinds of people have already been noted: government officials, teachers, and priests. In addition, most traditional peasant villages included one or more families of great wealth and prestige. Sometimes they lived in the village permanently, and in other cases they lived there only part of the year. In either case they were important political and economic forces in the village. They were also major employers of local men and women who had little or no land of their own and were dependent on outside employment in order to make a living (Morel, 1977). The traditional peasant village also included a number of craftspeople and retailers who served the local public. Even the category of peasant farmer included a variety of types of workers, based on the size of their farms and whether they owned or rented the land. Finally, the traditional peasant village included a sizable group of people who begged and scavenged for their livings. In the village of Minot, for example, these individuals were called woodspeople, because they lived in the woods where they built shacks for homes, planted small gardens, hunted (often illegally), and gathered wood (Jolas and Zonabend, 1977). They often supplemented their work activities by doing odd jobs in the village and gathering fruits and vegetables in the collectively owned areas around privately owned farm land.

The traditional French peasant village, then, included different kinds of people who were divided in their activities, spaces, and realities. Each of these groups was affected in different ways by the continuing drive for unification and modernization. It is thus too simplistic to view unification and modernization as the result of the self-interested actions of government officials who sought to improve their political and economic positions. Although self-interest is an important feature of the historical process affecting the peasantry, there were many different people pursuing their own interests who were active in the process.

The Complexity of the Peasants' Dilemma

Finding a mixture between modern and traditional ways of life can be seen as the "peasants' dilemma," and that dilemma is not simply reducible to good and evil forces (Wolf, 1966). The complexity of the peasants' dilemma can be seen by weighing the competing advantages and disadvantages of modernization versus traditionalism. Those who wish to preserve the traditional rural way of life point to the ways in which peasants have historically shared with one another in order to get through hard times. A peasant household that had been devastated by disease, crop failure, or death of their livestock, for example, could be certain that others in the village would help. The proponents of tradition also call attention to the many festivals and other local events, which have traditionally given peasant life a charm and vibrance not found in other parts of France. Finally, they point to the close-knit peasant family, which often includes several generations of relatives who all contribute to the livelihood of the household. From the traditionalists' point of view, these features of peasant life are incompatible with modernization, which stresses individualism, materialism, and nationalism.

The modernizers, on the other hand, emphasize the abject poverty that is the cornerstone of traditional peasant life. Looked at this way, sharing is not so much an expression of peasant compassion as a necessary part of surviving in an uncertain world. Each household feels responsible to those who have been devastated, because they know that they could also easily be reduced to begging and scavenging. In addition, not all of the beggars and scavengers were equally likely to receive help from the various segments of the village. In Minot, for example, the woodspeople were in constant conflict with the wealthier farmers, who naturally did not want the woodspeople stealing their crops or hunting in unauthorized areas (Jolas and Zonabend, 1977). The modernizers also stress the ways in which local customs encourage suspicion and hostility toward outsiders. Put differently, the charm and vibrancy of local life obscure the underlying provincialism and lack of alternatives available to local residents. The inability of many to speak French is one example of rural provincialism and lack of opportunity. Similarly, the traditionalists do not always recognize that local festivals, daily meetings in wine cellars, and similar events were often important sources for the alcoholism prevalent in some traditional villages. Finally, the modernizers note that the large peasant family was often filled with conflict, and it was seldom based on equality. The separation of the men's and women's worlds in the villages of Provence is one reflection of the divisions sometimes characteristic of traditional peasant households (Roubin, 1977). An important source of conflict was the relationship between the father and eldest son, because the son could not take full control of the farm until the father stepped aside. This often did not occur until the son was middle-aged. Similar types of family disputes occurred over the delay of daughters' marriages to protect the family's land.

The peasant's dilemma is, then, a complex and sometimes subtle problem which affects rural residents in different ways. The many sources of modernization and unification can have a variety of effects (Weber, 1976). The building of roads, which link rural France with the cities, for example, has been important in improving the standard of living of the peasantry, but it has also provided new opportunities for contact with urbanites (particularly tourists), who often bring new concerns and ways of life into the village. Similarly, military service has been an important source of modernization, because the young men who return home often bring with them new commitments and ideas. It has also heightened the self-consciousness of many young men, because they have found themselves being treated as a distinct social segment while in the military (Hélias, 1978; Morin, 1970). Thus, young men who otherwise feel no affiliation or attachment to one another find that while they are in the military, they are all considered the same because they come from the same general region of the country and they are all peasants. Upon returning from military service, these attachments and the collective identity associated with them may become the basis for a new commitment to tradition. But young men are not the only sources of modernization. Young women too have often migrated to the city to work for a time, and when they return they have also brought back a new commitment to both modernization and tradition.

Other mixtures of modernity and tradition are found in the church, local and national political parties, schools, government agricultural agencies, and markets where peasants and urbanites mingle. But the impact of these institutions varies from village to village, because their influence is mediated by the ongoing relationships and activities that make up peasant everyday life. It is to the social realities of peasant everyday life that we turn next.

THE SOCIAL REALITIES OF PEASANT LIFE

Because of the diversity of French peasant life, it is impossible to describe it fully in a short treatment such as this chapter. We can only create a composite image of this world that reflects its general characteristics but obscures some of the unique features of each village and region. We will do that here by focusing on the household of the peasant farm and, particularly, on the work of adult men and women. The term "peasant farmer" is used throughout to indicate all those persons who gain their primary livelihoods from agriculture, including both those who own and those who rent their farms. It also includes both farmers who live on the land and those who live in nearby villages, although most of the discussion will deal with the village dwellers.

There are five overriding themes that characterize the traditional social realities of the French peasantry. First is a concern for the land. Although those who own and those who rent land place differing degrees of emphasis on this value, the land is generally considered to be an important means of making a living and a major symbol of a family's success and standing in the village. Some indicators of the importance of the land have already been noted: the preservation of primogeniture and the delaying of daughters' marriages in order to keep the family farm together. The importance of the land and farming is reflected in other areas as well. Peasants do not speak of becoming a farmer, for example. One can become a teacher, priest, factory worker, or sailor, because each of these occupations requires the acquisition of skills and knowledge outside the household and the farm, but peasant farmers simply continue to do and be what they have been since childhood—peasants (Hélias, 1978). The counterpart to the knowledge and skills of other occupations is the land, because that is something that peasants can possess. When asked to describe their work, for example, peasant farmers typically talk about the size and quality of their farmland and not the skills and knowledge that are involved in cultivating it (Mendras, 1970). The land is important, then, because it is a necessary condition for being a peasant, and the social realities of peasant life are based on the knowledge and everyday experiences associated with cultivating the land.

A second and related theme is the high value placed on food in the traditional peasant way of life. This concern is clearly linked to the uncertainties and poverty of the peasantry and shows up in a variety of ways. Many large landholders who hire workers, for example, apportion noon meals by the amount of work done. The largest portions go the the best workers, regardless of whether they are the landowner or someone else (Hélias, 1978). The importance attached to bread in some areas is another indication, because bread is a staple in the diets of many peasants. Perhaps the best reflection of the high value placed on food is found in the language and stories of the peasants. In the village of Pouldreuzic in Brittany—a French region where change has traditionally been resisted—there are many stories about peasant children who eat until they are full, but they continue to have feelings of hunger, because hunger is endemic to peasant life. More directly to the point are the keys to health of the peasants in Pouldreuzic: "*debri mad, kaohad mad, koused mad* ("eating well, shitting well, sleeping well")—the last . . . dependent on the first two" (Hélias, 1978: 266). In a world of uncertainty and poverty, it is not surprising that both the land and the food produced from it have important practical and symbolic value.

A third theme in the social realities of traditional peasant life is the division of the world into "Them" and "Us." This division is evident in the village, where peasants distinguish themselves from persons of higher and lower rank. But the division also seems to be made in the politics of the village. In Pouldreuzic the population is divided between the Whites and the Reds (Hélias, 1978; Morin, 1970). Historically, this division has been important because the Whites have been conservative supporters of the church and aristocracy, and the Reds have supported the general aims of the French Revolution. Though less important today, the division still becomes symbolically important from time to time, particularly during elections when each side prepares to do battle at the polls. The White-Red distinction may emerge on other occasions as well. In describing his childhood in Pouldreuzic, for example, Pierre-Jakez Hélias (1978) notes that his selection as an altar boy had important political implications, because his family was committed to the Reds and therefore opposed the political commitments of the local priests. But if he declined the opportunity, then all of the altar boys would be from families committed to the Whites, and such an honor should not be monopolized by the Whites.

An important feature of the divisions found in the village is that they are localized and concern problems of everyday life. Thus, the priest may belong to a different political faction, and he may cater to village elites, but he is still encountered as a human being because he is a resident of the village.

There is another division between Them and Us, however, that is more bothersome for peasants. This is the division between the localized world of the village and farm and the outside world of the French government, large corporations, and international powers (such as the United States and the Soviet Union). These outsiders are experienced as distant, impersonal, mysterious, and dangerous sources of power which peasants cannot understand or control. This feature of peasant reality is apparent in the everyday talk of village residents, who speak of these external influences on their lives in ways that reflect both their resentment and their resigned acceptance of this fact of life.

The importance of outside forces is also evident in those everyday activities which are designed to reduce the power and uncertainty of such forces. One of the reasons why many peasant homes have few windows, for example, is that the French government once instituted a property tax based in part on the number of windows in a house. In order to combat this policy, the peasants simply built homes with fewer windows (Wylie, 1964). Similarly, many peasants intentionally maintain a shabby appearance on the outside of their homes, because they fear that their taxes will be increased if the exteriors are improved. A more important reflection of the power of outsiders and uncertainty about them is the tendency of traditional peasants to avoid investing in long-term agricultural pursuits. In Peyrane, for example, tradition-oriented peasant farmers used to resist planting orchards—particularly olive trees, which take twenty years to mature—because they thought the orchards would be destroyed in the event of a war (Wylie, 1964). That was the pattern in the last two wars involving Europe, and for a long time, with the international powers continuing to act in antagonistic ways, the possibility of war was thought of as real and an important consideration in making decisions about agricultural investments.

A fourth theme in the social realities of the traditional peasant is a fatalistic interpretation of the world. The peasants attribute the causes of events to sources beyond their control and understanding. The uncertainties of the outside world are an important source of peasant fatalism, but it also stems from the uncertainties and poverty often associated with making a living from the land. In Pouldreuzic, the fatalistic view has been expressed historically as a belief in the "World Bitch" who could attack people at any moment (Hélias, 1978). The World Bitch's presence could be seen in the sudden destruction of a crop, which could mean that a family, unable to pay its rent, must leave the land. Several outcomes might accompany such a tragedy, but typically the husband, wife, and small children would turn to begging and the older children would be forced to leave the family and support themselves as apprentices, domestics, or similar types of workers. At other times, the World Bitch could appear as a nagging doubt or anger about one's fate in life. The prescribed solution to this problem would be to work as hard as possible in order to get rid of these thoughts. In any case, the reality of the World Bitch is not separable from the problem of poverty and the uncertainties of peasant life. Indeed, as Hélias notes, "It was mute and sly so that nothing ever warned you of its arrival: that was the tragedy" (Hélias, 1978: 18).

Although the fatalism of traditional peasants often encourages a resigned attitude of acceptance of the problems and limitations of life, it is also associated with an emphasis on persevering in the face of uncertainty and poverty (Mendras, 1970). Respectable peasants do not give in to the forces that make life difficult; rather, they continue to work and do the best that they can under the circumstances. As noted above, nagging doubt and anger are solved by working as hard as possible until the doubts go away. An emphasis on the desirability of work is, then, a fifth theme making up the social realities of traditional peasant life. Work is not desirable, however, because it is inherently enjoyable or satisfying. Work is a kind of self-discipline that is a basic and required feature of peasant life: it is not something to debate or worry about. A more appropriate subject for worry is whether work will be available in the future.

The five interrelated themes that make up traditional peasant social realities—a high regard for the land, a high regard for food, a tendency to divide the world into Them and Us, a fatalistic outlook, and an emphasis on the desirability of work—run throughout life in rural France. They are developed differently, however, depending on the circumstances of each household and village. Even more important in their development are the differences between the worlds of peasant men and women, most notably the differences in time and space, as summarized in Table 2-1.

The World of Traditional Peasant Men

Because peasant men spend much of their time cultivating the land, a major source of timing in their lives is the land and related factors, particularly the weather. At the simplest level, the amount of land controlled by a household is important, because small landholders have less work to do than large landholders. A more important factor is the relationship between working the land and the seasons. During spring and summer the pace and intensity of work are greater because crops must be planted and harvested. During other times of the year, however, peasant men may spend the whole day trimming the hedge around their fields because they have nothing else to do. The relationship between the land and time can also be noted in the talk of peasant men, because they evaluate each season and year based on its level of productivity: a "good" season or year is one which has resulted in a big crop (Mendras, 1970).

Table 2-1 • Sources of Traditional Peasant Realities

Group	*Work-Related Timetables*	*Work-Related Communities*
Peasant Men	Diachronic: based on the discontinuous processes of nature, the household, the village, and national government	Enduring: based on the enduring memberships of the household, extended family, and village
Peasant Women	Diachronic: based on the continuous processes of the household and the discontinuous processes of nature and the village	Enduring: based on the enduring memberships of the household, extended family, and village

Although men experience time diachronically, the flow of time is not based on the clock but on more or less self-contained time units which occur as cycles (Mendras, 1970). The seasons, for example, are related to one another, but they can also be experienced as separate time units within which certain activities occur. With this perspective on time it is possible to talk about having finished one's work for that season, while a more continuous organization of time is often associated with the feeling that one's work is never finished. Whereas, traditionally, peasant men have experienced time from the former perspective, today, with the modernization of agriculture, they are experiencing a new conception of time. This is a problem for many, especially the old. As Henri Mendras notes: "The dying father will have the feeling that he is leaving a farm in progress, hence unfinished, while in the past he took leave having 'run the race,' having 'served his time,' leaving his son the task of carrying on" (Mendras, 1970: 73).

The processes of nature form one basis for the discontinuous cyclical conception of time held by traditional peasant men, but there are others which complement it. One of the most important is the arrangement of village events. In the nineteenth and early twentieth centuries, peasant villages often marked the phases of life by a variety of celebrations and events. Many of these events have disappeared, but most villages continue to celebrate some. In Peyrane, for example, the year is marked by four major celebrations—All Soul's Day, Midnight Mass at Christmas, the festival of the village's patron saint, and the festival of the patron of the volunteer firemen (Wylie, 1964). In addition, the work lives of peasant men are influenced by marriages and deaths, because both weddings and funerals are events of community-wide significance. Some wedding celebrations, for example, last for three days. Finally, in those villages where religion is important, the workweeks may be divided by Sunday church services and the socializing that accompanies them (Wylie, 1966). Although these events occur at regular intervals, they break up the normal course of the men's work and thus create a work-related timetable that is discontinuous.

The timing of peasant men's work is also affected by the cycles of the household. Many peasants keep livestock in a building near their houses, whether they live in the country or in the village. Although peasant women may do most of the work in tending those animals, the men have some responsibilities in this area. One example is the slaughtering of a pig (if the family is lucky enough to own a pig), from which salted pork is made (Hélias, 1978). This event usually occurs at about the same time each year and may involve rituals, particularly if a man specializing in slaughtering and butchering is hired to supervise the process. The event may also be followed by a celebration (a "pig feast") at which wine and salted pork are served to close friends and relatives.

Finally, the timing of the traditional peasant men's work is influenced by the discontinuous and sometimes unpredictable processes of national government. One example is the requirement that young men do eighteen months of military service, but the government is important in other ways too. Perhaps most important are the government's agricultural policies. Programs of land redistribution and modernization are seldom forced on the peasantry without some minimal level of local support, but the impact can still be substantial. One example is the attempts of government officials to introduce hybrid corn into many rural areas (Mendras, 1970). Some peasants have resisted these policies, because they see the cultivation of hybrid corn as having at least three major consequences that would disrupt the pace and timing of their lives. First, the proper cultivation of hybrid corn involves the use of farming techniques and implements that are new and require a considerable financial investment. Second, successful cultivation of hybrid corn means that farmers must produce and sell it in large quantities in order to pay back their investment. Third, the profitable cultivation of hybrid corn requires that most of the peasants' land be devoted to corn. Thus, the raising of other crops, such as wheat, would be curtailed, if not eliminated. Also, the raising of cattle for slaughter might need to be eliminated so that more land could be used for growing corn. The remaining cattle would be kept for their milk—a commodity for which less land is needed and which can be sold easily in the market. Thus, the introduction of hybrid corn entails a number of consequences that alter both the kinds of work activities engaged in by peasant farmers and the pace at which they work.

In sum, the social reality of traditional peasant men is constructed from the timing of their lives and work. They live in a world of diachronic time, but past, present, and future are seen as discontinuous, reflecting the uncertainties of their lives.

Another major factor in the building of peasant men's social reality is space. Consciousness of kind is created in the household, extended family, and village. Because each of these social units is made up of stable membership, the work-related communities of traditional peasant men are enduring.

In many respects, the center of peasant life is the household, because it is the unit within which most of life's activities take place. A husband, wife, children, and sometimes the children's grandparents will live and work together in order to make ends meet. At least in winter, the members of the household are also brought together by the need for heat, which is usually only available in the room with the family's fireplace (Wylie, 1964). Based on the relationships that develop in the fields and the house, a sense of community may develop within the household. It is possible, however, to overstate the closeness of the household group; indeed, several features of peasant life tend to separate members of the household. Much of the work of men and women, for example, occurs in separate places, and many of their leisure activities also involve different places and people. Thus, although the household is important for building peasant community and identity, it is not the only one.

Another important source for building consciousness of kind is the *extended family*, made up of relatives living within the same general region. An obvious but key way in which the extended family can be important is through visits in the home, church, and other areas of the peasant village. The exchange of information, gossip, and complaints that occur during these encounters is important in giving the family members a sense of identity based on their common experiences and their differences from "Them." The extended family is also important in building social reality because it is a source of aid for those in need (Wylie, 1966). If a man needs money, machinery, or workers, for example, he can depend on the extended family to provide aid. Some students spend their entire summer vacations traveling from one relative's farm to another helping with the work that must be done. Similarly, family members who are not in school and do not own their own land often turn to relatives for employment. In some cases this employment may last for several years.

Indeed, the extended family is so important that sometimes "fictional" kinship ties between families that have no relatives in the region are created. One example is the relationship between the Malinge and Faligand families in the region of Chanzeau (Wylie, 1966). The Malinges are an older, childless couple who own the land farmed by the Faligands. The Faligands are younger and have a number of children. Neither family has close relatives in Chanzeau, and, consequently, they have created a fictional family in which "the Malinges act like parents to the Faligands and, more important, like grandparents to the Faligand children, babysitting for them and bringing them treats. The two families also gather together after church, just as close relatives do" (Wylie, 1966: 192).

Finally, besides the household and extended family, some parts of and events in the villages are important for creating a consciousness of kind among peasant men. Some of these events have already been noted: marriages, funerals, and the celebration of religious and local holidays all provide settings within which peasant reality is created, sustained, and sometimes changed. For village residents there are other places where men may gather on a more regular basis to talk, drink, eat, and play. In Peyrane one center of male activity is the café, where the men sometimes play *boules* (a game similar to lawn bowling) and *belote* (a card game) (Wylie, 1964). In Chanzeau, on the other hand, the center of social activity is the church, although socializing begun there often ends up in cafés (Wylie, 1966). A final way in which the village is important as a place for building peasant reality is in the regular economic exchanges which occur there. Many peasants depend to some degree on the village to sell their farm produce, and they also pay for village services (such as welding) with fruits and vegetables from their gardens. These regular relationships provide settings for interaction and the creation of a consciousness of kind. The exchanges also make it difficult for tax collectors to estimate the total income of peasants, who refuse to acknowledge that such exchanges are forms of income (Wylie, 1964).

The five central themes of the peasant men's reality are thus created within a discontinuous experience of time and a set of relationships centered in the local area. Because both husband and wife occupy the same household, they share many experiences and problems. Their sense of social reality, time, and space are, then, somewhat similar. But there are some differences between them that must be noted.

The World of Traditional Peasant Women

As with men's work, cycles of nature also affect traditional peasant women's work. During planting and harvesting times, for example, women may work in the fields with their husbands. Peasant women are also affected by the cycles and events of the village, though these events have different implications for women and men. The village celebrations usually mean that the men can abandon their work for a while, whereas women often experience these events as disruptions in their usual work routine. Although they must continue to cook and clean, they cook different foods and clean for different reasons. One example of the impact of village events on peasant women's work is "Fat Days," which are the three days just before Ash Wednesday, after which fasting is required twice a week for the duration of Lent (Hélias, 1978). Fat Days are an opportunity to prepare for the fasts by being as gluttonous as possible. One of the consequences of this celebration is that women have to clean their houses thoroughly and prepare large amounts of food, particularly cake, because village residents spend these three days walking from house to house to visit and trade pieces of cake. Thus, although women's work is affected by some of the same forces as men's work, the consequences are often different. Holidays provide men with a break from work and women with a chance to do different, though often more, work.

The most important difference in the timing of work is evident in the ways men and women deal with the household. Men have household responsibilities, but they are largely discontinuous, whereas women deal with the continuing demands of the household, such as cooking, cleaning, and much of child care. A girl in Peyrane describes her mother's workday in the following way:

> Maman gets up at five o'clock; she lights the fire and heats a cup of coffee for papa and then she gets breakfast, comes and wakes us up and pours out our breakfast. Then she feeds the rabbits and goats, lets the chickens out and feeds them. She breaks an egg to feed the little chicks. Then comes breakfast with papa. Then she takes the goats out, sweeps the house, washes the dishes, dusts ["raises the dust"], cleans the bedrooms, wet-mops the tile floor of the kitchen, bedrooms, and hall. Then she gets dinner ready, washes my sisters' smocks. Then she sets the table and we have dinner. Then she sweeps around the table and does the dishes again. She ties the asparagus into bunches, washes them and carries them down the road. Then she goes into the vineyard to help papa with the work he has been doing all morning. Then she comes back and fixes *gouter* [a snack] for papa and continues her work. Then she goes out to get grass for the rabbits. When she comes back it is dark and she feeds them and the chickens, closes them up in their coop and gathers the eggs. She feeds the goats and chicks and closes the chicks up in their box. Then she goes to milk the goats. Before she went out for grass she prepared supper, sorted the vegetables, and lit the fire. When she gets back after dark, she sets the table and we have supper. Then we go to bed. Maman mends our clothes. Papa listens to the radio or reads the newspaper. Then they go to bed because the next day they have to go out early to cut asparagus (Wylie, 1964: 269).

This woman lives on a farm that is some distance from the village. For women living in the village, the daily pattern of work is somewhat different, although they may do the same types of work. An important distinguishing feature of village life is the opportunity village women have to arrange their work so that they can get out of the house and see other women at some point in the day. In Peyrane a common practice is to do some marketing each day (Wylie, 1964). While shopping, the women can catch up on the latest news and gossip and take a break from the isolation of much of their housework. Even with trips to the market, however, peasant women are almost always working, because they usually combine their work and leisure. In the case of the farm wife described above, for example, the rest period at the end of the day also includes mending clothes. The combining of work and leisure is also evident in the lives of village women. Indeed, leisure time of any sort is especially difficult to come by for those women who supplement the family income by working for others, such as taking in sewing or doing domestic work.

Because husbands and wives live in the same household and belong to the same extended family, much of the space they occupy is similar. They both participate in the household gatherings before the fireplace and in the visits with members of the extended family and friends. Within these places a consciousness of kind may develop that ties husband and wife together.

There are other places, however, which are dominated by women and which provide them with an opportunity to build unique work-related communities (Reiter, 1975). Among those places are the grocery store, bakery, butcher shop, and other markets in the village. In these settings women can exchange information and gossip, but they can also create a world of their own there. A more important center for building a unique women's reality is the home, because it is the center of peasant women's lives. In Peyrane women are discouraged from going to the café except on Tuesday nights, when movies are shown (Wylie, 1964). Consequently, women meet in their homes, where they often share coffee and sew or knit as they talk. Perhaps because the home is an important meeting place for women, peasant women's reality includes an emphasis not found in the men's world on a clean, orderly home. In Pouldreuic, for example, no self-respecting peasant woman would allow the beds to be unmade, because it would reflect badly on her competence as a housekeeper (Hélias, 1978).

Because the work of men and women involve somewhat different patterns of time and space, then, the sexes experience the central themes of peasant reality in different ways in rural France. These differences are important in understanding the traditional peasant way of life, but they are also important in understanding the impact of modernization on traditional social realities.

The World of Modern Peasants

The French government, the schools, the church, and other official agencies have been important sources for modernizing peasant farming, and despite traditional distrust of these agencies, members of peasant households have often embraced the opportunities they offered. The persons most likely to accept modernization are young people and women (Mendras, 1970; Morin, 1970). Both recognize the material advantages of modernization, and they place much less emphasis on traditional activities and relationships than do many older men. Women readily see the usefulness of washing machines and other appliances in reducing drudgery and in allowing them leisure time. The young people, particularly the males, are more likely to emphasize the economic advantages of the modernized farm. Whatever the reasons for embracing it, modernization has brought with it a number of important changes in life style for the peasant.

The most general change is the organization of farm work for production of goods that can be sold in a national market. Such production often requires the farmer to specialize in one or two products, which reduces the self-sufficiency of the household because most of the resources needed for living must now be purchased from others. It also requires a large investment in land and new farm equipment. These investments and the commitment to large-scale production often entail new relationships with outsiders. Modern farmers, for example, find government agricultural experts to be vital links between their day-to-day activities and the developments in government policy and agricultural research. The experts provide information both about new farming techniques and about the availability of credit from public and private sources. Credit is vital to the operation of the modern farm because investment in new land, equipment, and crops cannot wait until money has been saved. Finally, investment and modernization encourage planning and recordkeeping by the farmer. It is no longer acceptable to live from season to season; rather, long-term plans must be made and records kept in order to anticipate future market demands and opportunities and to use one's land, money, equipment, and credit effectively.

Each of these developments flies in the face of the practices of traditional peasant farmers, who stress independence, subsistence, self-sufficiency, and diversified agriculture. Thus, many traditional farmers have resisted modernization, but in the longrun they lose because their children are unwilling to take over the farm or because they must sell to the modernizers for some other reason. Even within the household, the traditional peasant farmer often loses to his wife and children, who introduce modernization despite his reservations. Indeed, the farmer may encourage his wife and children's efforts, because he recognizes that he has become an anachronism.

But all peasant men do not respond by resigned acceptance; some use the opportunities of modernization to achieve their private ends. Traditionally the use of credit has been frowned upon, both by farmers, who see it as endangering the household's ability to provide for itself, and by experts, who fear default on the debts. But because of the ready availability of government credit today, many traditional farmers have used government loans to buy tractors, which are really unnecessary for farming their small, scattered plots of land but which increase their prestige among their peers (Mendras, 1970). The fact that the tractor increases the productivity of the land and the farmer's income very little is not important, since these men know that the government will not take legal action against them for failing to repay the loan. Thus, modernization is occurring in a variety of ways, and it is not a simple evolutionary process based on the power of the French government.

Because social reality is based on the circumstances of everyday life, an emerging—modern—reality can be seen in much of rural France. It is replacing the fatalistic emphasis on the land, food, and work—even the provincial division of the world into Them and Us, in part because Them and Us are becoming the same. There are three important features of the emerging modern reality: faith in the future, concern for experiencing the outside world, and the creation of new traditions. Perhaps the best reflection of the emerging faith in the future is the willingness of some peasant families to make investments. Buying land and equipment is one example, but there are more subtle indicators. In Peyrane, for instance, farmers oriented toward modern agriculture have begun to plant orchards, including olive trees that take twenty years to mature, and this contrasts with the traditional fatalistic emphasis on investing only in crops that produce in the shortrun out of fear of another war (Wylie, 1964). The concern for seeking contact with the outside world is expressed in efforts to draw tourists to peasant villages, but also in the high value modernizers place on travel in France and abroad (Morin, 1970).

Finally, new traditions are emerging in rural France. There is, for example, a new interest in collecting antiques (traditional peasant furniture) and buying old peasant homes and restoring them (Hélias, 1978; Morin, 1970; Wylie, 1964). Much of this activity involves the sons and daughters of peasants who have gone to the city to make a new life. They return to their home villages from time to time in search of their heritage, and in seeking it they give new meaning to the objects and events of traditional peasant life—a meaning often based on romantic

Table 2-2 • Sources of Modern Peasant Realities

	Work-Related Timetables	*Work-Related Communities*
Modern Peasants	Diachronic: based on the discontinuous processes of nature and the continuous processes of the national market	Mixed: based on the enduring membership of the household and village, the shifting membership of local associations, and distant-fleeting relations with national associations

nostalgia. Thus, the traditional peasants are often remembered as much more interesting, humane, and insightful than they really were. The creation of this tradition is also encouraged by the urbanites' new interest in "natural" food and in the life style of the traditional peasantry. The city dwellers look upon the rural way of life, with its clean air and close ties to nature, as not only desirable but in many ways superior. Associated with the revived interest in the peasant way of life is a new pride in being a peasant. The modernizers see peasants as strong, independent persons who resent and resist control; often ignored is the fact that this independence may have arisen from a sense of feeling uncomfortable and inferior in the presence of more urbane people. In sum, the modernizers, in their search for the traditional, are reinterpreting history and giving it new meaning and reality.

As with traditional peasant realities, the emerging realities are also based on time and space. The most important work-related timetables and communities are summarized in Table 2-2.

Much of modern peasant work continues to be influenced by the discontinuous processes of nature, with different seasons involving different levels of work intensity. These seasonal shifts are not so dramatic for modern farmers, however, because they spend much of their winters and other slack times in a variety of work-related activities. For example, they maintain their farm equipment, learn new farming techniques, and plan for the future. Equally important are the modern farmers' efforts to increase their profits by joining local cooperatives. These organizations engage in a variety of activities, but the most important are collectively buying and sharing farm equipment, buying the goods of local farmers and storing them in order to raise the price in the national market, and sometimes engaging in militant action, such as protesting low prices by blocking roads (Wylie, 1966). In addition, some modern peasant farmers belong to national associations, which attempt to influence government policies and prices at the national level (Franklin, 1969; Wright, 1964). The modernization of the farm, then, involves a shift in the timing of peasant work. Much of the field work of the farmer (e.g., plowing, planting, and harvesting) can now be done faster, but the time that is saved is now devoted to other work-related activities.

The work-related communities of the modern peasant family are also somewhat different. The enduring memberships of the household and village continue to be important, but these stable sources for building a consciousness of kind compete with the less enduring relationships formed in local and national associations. The associations include both men and women, and they encourage the development of a common identity among all of the farmers of France. Indeed, they are frequently important means for breaking down the old division between the men's and the women's worlds, because women are major supporters of modernization and they often play an active role in the planning and budgeting activities that are central to the modern farm and farmers' associations. Although there are still times when men and women are separated, one consequence of the modernization of rural France is the undermining of old sex-based, work-related timetables and communities and the appearance of new forms of relationships which encourage the development of new social realities. Basic to understanding these emerging realities is the way in which the enduring relationships of the household, extended family, and village are altered by the shifting relationships between local farmers and national organizations.

In sum, the everyday experiences of peasants are changing. Some of these changes are problematical and lead to painful choices and conflicts. Based on these choices and conflicts, different types of knowledge and social reality are being created. The peasants' experience of history and modernization is quite different from the interpretation of it given by government officials, academic theorists, and others who seek to identify and explain the essential characteristics of the peasantry. These explanations are a major source for myths about peasants, which we will explore next.

MYTHS ABOUT PEASANTS

Perhaps because so many outsiders have been concerned about the changing circumstances of peasant life, many of the most important myths are either attacks on peasants for not changing fast enough or glorifications of them as the last vestiges of human compassion in an increasingly brutal and impersonal world. In the latter case the concern is with slowing changes affecting the peasantry. Two sources of myth-

Table 2-3 • Literary Myths about Peasant Work

Type of Myth	*Need for Work*	*Organization of Work*	*Rewards of Work*
Romantic-Traditionalist	Based on material need and tradition	Centered in the household and directed toward sharing	Material survival and spiritual and communal satisfactions
Critical-Modernist	Based on material need	Reflects the ignorance of the peasantry	Material survival

making concerning the French peasants are novelists and academics. Their myths are worth exploring here, along with an alternative to the explanations they offer.

Literary Myths

Myths that glorify the French peasantry and those that attack them are both evident in French literature. Some novelists depict peasants as shortsighted, greedy pursuers of land (Zeldin, 1973); others describe the same people as survivors of a romantic past which we must regain. These two themes in French literature can be thought of as the *romantic-traditionalist myth* and the *critical-modernist myth*. Their explanations of peasant work are summarized in Table 2-3.

The romantic-traditionalist myth argues that peasants consider work necessary both because of their material needs and because it is a traditionally sanctioned activity reflecting peasant courage (Mendras, 1970). Thus, peasants are not greedy but are instead conforming to a traditional way of life. Similarly, the organization of traditional peasant work is explained by the ways in which tradition, family, and village relationships dominate peasant life. Because the romantic-traditionalist myth considers these institutions and relationships better than those of the city, the proponents of the myth often point to the extensive sharing that occurs in peasant villages. Finally, this explanation of peasant work identifies the primary rewards of peasant work as material survival and a sense of spiritual and communal satisfaction that comes with working the land and being in close social contact with family and neighbors.

The critical-modernist myth depicts peasant work in the opposite way. Peasants work because they are poor and they cannot live without working. Indeed, the problem of survival is so important to the peasantry that their primary motive in work and other aspects of life is greed. The traditional organization of peasant work is explained in terms of the shortsighted and ignorant nature of people who cannot even recognize their own best interests. Finally, the only reward of work for peasants is material survival. Peasants cannot derive spiritual and communal satisfactions from work because they are totally consumed by their greed.

Each of these explanations contains a certain amount of truth. There is no doubt that peasants have little choice about working because they have traditionally been very poor. But they also believe in the desirability of work, which may reflect either courage or greed. A major problem with both myths is that they neglect the time devoted to leisure by peasants. Although peasants emphasize the desirability of work, they also "waste" a great deal of time at village festivals, weddings, and other events. It is important to recognize, then, that the value placed on work is often contradicted by relationships and activities in everyday life. Other general cultural themes are also sometimes contradicted in practice. For example, although traditional peasants profess to a certain fatalism (as personified in the World Bitch), they often encourage their children to stay in school in order to gain the knowledge and skills needed to leave farming. Fatalism is thus a cultural theme used to explain some events, but in other instances the peasants adopt a nonfatalistic view.

The romantic-traditionalist and critical-modernist myths are oversimplifications because they are based on the assumption that peasants act consistently from the same set of perceptions and motivations. This is clearly not the case. Peasants do sometimes share, but they do not always share with everyone in the village, and they may even hide some of their wealth to avoid sharing it. Similarly, the persistence of traditional farming practices is partly based on the isolation of the peasant village and the farmer's lack of knowledge about modern agricultural techniques, but it is also based on the fact that modern agricultural techniques work best on large farms, where the farmer has sufficient money to invest in modern equipment and seed. The average peasant works several tiny plots of land and has little or no excess money to invest in modern equipment and seed. Finally, peasants do receive gratification from their work on the land and their relationships with others in the household, extended family, and village, but it is possible to overstate these rewards of work. It must be remembered that French peasants value the availability of work, but they seldom talk about the satisfactions of doing it.

Though the myths are oversimplification, many people have inferred ways of dealing with the peasantry from them. The romantic-traditional myth is often adopted by persons seeking to protect and preserve the traditional peasantry. In taking this position, the romantic-traditionalists often discourage efforts at modernization and, consequently, help to preserve many of the inequalities and hardships of traditional peasant life. In like fashion the critical-modernists often support policies that are harsh and insensitive to the hardships accompanying modernization. Based on their assumptions, peasant complaints about programs of modernization can be ignored because the peasants are incapable of seeing their own long-term best interests. These myths are important, then, because they are more than images found in novels: they are held by various French people, who may use them to construct political policies affecting peasants.

Academic Myths

Although their theories are not so crude as the myths of French novelists, anthropologists and other social scientists are also an important source for myths about peasants. Such analysts have devoted most of their attention to peasants in Asia and Latin America, but their theories have some application to the French case. Two competing anthropological theories that are of special interest are the *myth of the conservative peasant* and the *myth of the radical peasant*. Like the myths of the novelists, each of these myths attempts to explain peasant work (see Table 2-4) and can be used to develop public policy.

The myth of the conservative peasant tries to explain why peasants are often resistant to modernization. The general conclusion is that the practical circumstances of peasant life give rise to a moral outlook that emphasizes traditional practices, the sharing of wealth so that everyone lives at about the same economic level, fatalism, desire to reduce risk and uncertainty (Banfield, 1958; Erasmus, 1968; James Scott, 1976; Wolf, 1957). In support of this conclusion, the myth emphasizes material survival in explaining both the need for work and its primary rewards, but the most important feature of this myth is its explanation of the persistence of the traditional forms of peasant work organization. The reason is that such patterns of organization reduce the uncertainties of life; traditional peasant farming techniques and patterns of sharing guarantee survival, even if the peasant cannot hope to get rich from them. George Foster (1965) offers this explanation in his concept of "the limited good." He argues that peasants perceive the world as made up of limited resources (e.g., land, money, power, and even affection), and consequently one person's gain is another's loss. Traditional patterns of work persist because peasants see modernization as offering some people new advantages, but they are afraid that they will lose as a result.

The myth of the radical peasant shares some of the assumptions of the myth of the conservative peasant. Most basically, both stress the priority peasants give to material survival, but they differ on why survival is a problem and why peasants act to preserve traditional work.

Table 2-4 • Academic Myths about Peasant Work

Type of Myth	*Need for Work*	*Organization of Work*	*Rewards of Work*
Myth of the Conservative Peasant	Based on material need	Based on peasant suspicion, competition, and the notion of the "limited good"	Material survival
Myth of the Radical Peasant	Based on material need, which is partially created by exploiting elites at the local, national, and international levels	Reflects the exploitation of peasants by elites	Material survival

The proponents of the myth of the radical peasant point to the ways in which peasants are controlled and repressed by local, national, and international elites, who profit from them (Huizer, 1970). These elites are responsible for creating a world of limited resources, and thus peasant conservatism is rooted in repression rather than in any inherent peasant characteristics. To demonstrate this point, proponents often point to the long history of peasant protest in many parts of the world. Underlying this explanation then, is an image of peasants as people who desire modernization but who are locked into a repressive situation in which traditional practices are forced on them by elites.

Again, each of these images of the peasantry is an oversimplification. Segments of the French peasantry have resisted modernization, and part of that resistance is related to the conservative characteristics identified by anthropologists, but part of it is also related to the past experiences of peasants with modernization (Niehoff and Anderson, 1966). Very often land reform and other modernization efforts have resulted in increased wealth for large landholders and a loss for most peasants. Whether intended or not, government policies have had repressive consequences for peasants. Similarly, there are examples of radical peasant groups in France, but the major sources of modernization have been such nonradical persons as schoolteachers, agricultural experts, young men seeking a better standard of living, and women seeking to reduce the drudgery of their lives. Thus, each of these myths is an oversimplification of the everyday lives of peasants, and each fails to take account of the contradictions found in rural France.

In part, the oversimplifications found in these theories result from the policy commitments of many of the theorists. Those who see peasants as inherently radical are often committed to building grass-roots organizations which encourage peasant self-help and protest against the elites who control them (Huizer, 1970). The assumption is that peasants will cooperate to improve their situation if they are in charge, and the goals of the organizations are clearly in the peasants' best interests. Those who see peasants as inherently conservative doubt the efficacy of grass-roots organizations, because they feel that peasants are incapable of cooperative action so long as they live in a world of scarcity, fatalism, and the "limited good." Indeed, these theorists sometimes go so far as to claim that radically inspired programs of self-help encourage peasant dependence and fatalism, because the program directors prefer to deal with docile peasants who will do as they are told (Erasmus, 1968). The assertive and independent peasants who are often pointed to as examples of the inherently radical character of peasants are avoided, because they have ideas that do not fit into the plans of the organizers. The proponents of the myth of the conservative peasant thus tend to point to the need for new approaches to modernization—approaches that directly attack the peasants' conservative tendencies.

The Humanistic Approach

There is at least one more approach to understanding peasants and their relationships to programs of modernization—the humanistic approach. It recognizes that peasants are really a diverse people with diverse interests. Various segments of the peasantry assess public policies and programs intended to change their world based on their interests and the problems they experience in everyday life (Popkin, 1979). Because peasants are neither inherently conservative nor radical, they typically resist some parts of modernization and embrace other parts. What ultimately emerges are compromises that reflect the efforts of peasants to deal with their environments, and government policies are only one part of these environments. The fact that conservative and radical observers are likely to perceive these compromises as signs of peasant irrationality or powerlessness is a sign that mythmakers tend to dehumanize others as they seek to identify the single universal motive that dominates the lives of peasants.

CONCLUSION

A basic tenet of the sociology of knowledge approach is that knowledge and social reality are primarily created out of the circumstances of everyday life. The situation of French peasants, who have traditionally lived in a localized world that is highly uncertain and divided into cycles of time and activity, provides evidence for the truth of this tenet. The emphasis on land, food, work, fatalism, and a Them-Us division are, then, reflections of the practical circumstances of life. How these themes are developed is, of course, variable because interpretation is an integral part of that development. Much of the traditional knowledge of French peasants is disappearing because the practical circumstances of life are changing, and alternative interpretations of the world are being introduced through schools, government agencies, the mass media, and even the church. Basic to the changing realities of rural life are changes in work-related timetables and communities, because these are the primary frameworks within which knowledge and social reality are created. An especially important factor in the situation of the French peasantry is the destruction of old sources of social and physical segregation, which sustained traditional knowledge and realities. Thus, the building of roads and the teaching of French in rural areas are important because they are two of the ways in which the segregation of the peasantry has been attacked and new circumstances of life have been created.

Although some of the material presented here is unique to France, the general points of the chapter have wider application. The "peasants' dilemma" of finding a middle position between modernization and tradition is widespread. Many of the features of the traditional peasantry's realities are also found in other parts of the world. The work-related timetables and communities described here are common to other peasants, for example. Certainly the major characteristics of the myths about peasants are found in other places where large numbers of peasants live. Finally, many of the same sources of change discussed here affect peasants in other parts of the world. Indeed, the contemporary debate about the future of the peasantry in France is carried on in many countries. The debate predicts two possible outcomes: either peasants will become fully modernized farmers or a new type of peasantry, with a new mixture of modern and traditional characteristics, will emerge.

The first prediction claims that a "rural bourgeoisie" is emerging which has the same interests and characteristics as other modernized segments in France (Mendras, 1970; Morin, 1970). Peasants are seen as having little interest in maintaining the family farm or traditional village practices. They are interested in achieving a high standard of living, political influence, and a cosmopolitan way of life which is not limited to the local area. Although the rural bourgeoisie may represent only a minority of French farmers today, it is argued, they will eventually come to dominate the countryside as they buy up land made available by the children of peasants who no longer want to carry on family traditions. Concomitant with the rise of large farms, the farming process will be industrialized, because such methods result in greater efficiency and profitability. This development will give rise to full-time farm workers who are employed by the large landholders, and these workers will have to deal with many of the same problems that plague other industrial workers, particularly factory workers. Already some French academics have begun to study farm workers, using alienation scales similar to those used in studying factory workers (Franklin, 1969).

The alternative prediction is that a new type of peasantry—a so-called postpeasantry—is developing (Gamst, 1974). The new peasants are likely to work in factories or other nonfarm settings, but they will continue to live in the village and may continue to work the family farm. An important difference between peasants and postpeasants is that the latter will not depend on the land as a major source of their livelihoods. Because the postpeasantry will maintain their ties to the village and land, it is likely that old realities and traditions will be preserved in somewhat altered form. The land, for example, will continue to have important symbolic value, because it represents the owners' links to their heritage and not because it is indispensable in making a living. Similarly, traditional village events are likely to be preserved because they symbolize a heritage, not because they have important meaning in the day-to-day lives of postpeasants. Finally, the World-Bitch and other reflections of fatalism may be preserved as stories to be shared with children and friends, but not as explanations for the problems of everyday life. The new problems of everyday life will require new explanations.

Current evidence indicates that both these predictions may come to pass (Franklin, 1969; Wright, 1964). This development should not be surprising, since peasants have always been a diverse and independent segment of French society. What would be surprising is for all peasants to respond to the developing opportunities and problems in the same way. At the same time, it must be recognized that the development of both the rural bourgeoisie and postpeasants depends on the destruction of the social and physical separations between the traditional localized area and the larger urbane world of cities and the nation. Those rural areas that continue to be isolated and segregated from the rest of France because of language differences, inadequate roads, the absence of schools, or the government's lack of concern are likely to continue the traditional peasant way of life. The processes of modernization, then, do not affect all peasants in the same ways.

Chapter Three

INDUSTRIAL WORK

Historically the process of industrialization and the building of factories have been closely linked, because industrialization is associated with the transfer of work from the household to the factory. An example of this transfer is found in the history of shoe manufacturing in Lynn, Massachusetts (Dawley, 1976). Until the middle of the nineteenth century shoe manufacturing took place in the household of master craftsmen, who worked with members of their families, apprentices, and journeymen (established shoemakers who did not have their own businesses) to produce shoes for customers in the local area, including Boston, which is nearby. Some shoemakers also sold some of their shoes to local shopkeepers, who resold them in other towns and cities. So long as shoemaking was done in the masters' households, the work process was quite diverse, because it varied from household to household. One reason for the diversity was the relationship among the workers, which was one of close personal cooperation in the work setting. In addition, most of the workers lived together, so that problems and relationships that developed outside work could easily affect the work process. Another indication of the impact of personal relations on the work of the household was the practice of some masters of putting off work when other, more interesting opportunities developed. Thus, the household members might choose to go fishing and delay shoemaking for another day. One reason why this could be done was that the household sold most of its output in the local area, and there was a limit to how many shoes could be sold.

This pattern of work changed in the middle of the nineteenth century when shopkeepers expanded their shoe market by traveling to more distant cities along the eastern seaboard to sell their shoes. Because the local shoemaking households could not or would not produce enough shoes for the shopkeepers, the latter dealt with their problem by signing shoemakers to contracts specifying the number of shoes to be made and by turning parts of their shops into shoemaking centers. These measures increased the control of the shopkeeper over the manufacturing process and, presumably, cut down on the amount of time spent at nonwork activities. But even these changes did not result in enough shoes, and so the shopkeepers continued to expand their operations. For example, they began to sign contracts with shoemakers in towns near Lynn and, ultimately, they built factories within which large numbers of workers could be brought together and supervised.

With the rise of the factory the time when workers could chose to work or not came to an end, as did many other features of the household. Most important was the transformation of the traditional work skills and activities of master craftsmen, who were divided into groups within the shoe factory. Each group supervised workers who were specialists at one aspect of shoemaking. The old master craftsman, who could make a pair of shoes from start to finish, was thus replaced by a number of people who had fewer skills but who could make more shoes in less time.

Another factor that increased worker productivity was the sewing machine. Although the sewing machine was invented before the rise of the factory, it was so expensive that few master craftsmen could afford to buy it. The machine took on new significance, however, with the rise of the factory, where the emphasis was on large-scale production for sale in a large market. Within this type of enterprise, an investment in the sewing machine was economical, and it resulted in increased productivity, because workers no longer had to stitch together shoes by hand.

The shoe factory did not arise overnight; rather, shopkeepers introduced factory processes over the course of many years. Some of them were more calculating than others, and so there were many different paths to the industrialization of shoemaking. An important part of the process was the way in which workers resisted aspects of industrialization. Some master craftsmen resisted by retreating into traditional practices, even though such practices lowered their standard of living. Others went to work in factories, but they joined worker associations and occasionally protested, even going on strike (Dawley, 1976; Warner and Low, 1947).

Basic to industrialization, then, is the rise of the factory as the central place for manufacturing, but the process was by no means uniform and was marked by conflict. Shoe manufacturing in Lynn and other New England towns is only one example: somewhat different paths to the factory are found in other industries. In textiles, for example, the craftsmen were incorporated into the factory, but they did not specialize until later phases in the development of the industry (Wallace, 1978). In the steel industry the demise of the master craftsman was accompanied by an increase in the skill of workers, who had been relegated to unskilled jobs in less industrialized settings (Stone, 1974).

It should be noted here that the factory had an impact not just on men, but on women as well. For some women the rise of the factory meant that they were left at home to become more or less full-time housewives, but other women left their homes to seek employment in factories, which provided them with new opportunities and problems. Like their male counterparts, the early women factory workers responded to their work problems in a variety of ways, and they were certainly not opposed to joining in strikes and other militant actions under the right circumstances (Dublin, 1979; Foner, 1977).

It is possible to overstate the connection between factory work and industrialization, because many of the most important features of the factory are found in other work settings (Berg, 1979; Faunce, 1968). Much contemporary office work, for example, has been transformed in the same way shoemaking was transformed in Lynn. Many occupations in the crafts which have survived into this century are also undergoing this transformation. Longshoremen (dock workers) and members of the building trades (construction workers), for example, are being reorganized so that the building process is streamlined, based on the specialized activities of the workers (Herb Mills, 1976, 1977; Pilcher, 1972; Riemer, 1979). For purposes of this chapter, then, *industrial work* includes not just factory work but any type of work which takes place in a central location, is organized around machines, and is broken down into a series of specialized tasks that are supervised and coordinated. This definition of industrial work eliminates some forms of craft and office work: private secretaries, for example, are not industrial workers because their work activities are too varied and dispersed. Typists in typing pools, on the other hand, are clearly industrial workers, because they spend most, if not all, of their day at their typewriters, where their work is coordinated and controlled by supervisors but also by the flow of letters and other items that need to be typed.

Because industrialization is so closely linked to the rise of the factory, it is possible to identify the most important features of industrial work in this setting. But it is important to recognize that contemporary factories are not like earlier types. Most contemporary factories have work organizations, management practices, and personnel policies that are distinct from those found in the early factories of Lynn and other places. We will explore the unique characteristics of contemporary industrial work next and follow that by discussions of the social realities of industrial workers and myths associated with them.

THE TRANSFORMATION OF INDUSTRIAL WORK

The period between 1880 and World War I is vital in the development of contemporary industrial work, because it was then that factory work became streamlined, managers took control of the factory, and new offices and policies were developed to deal with the work and nonwork aspects of employees' lives (Nelson, 1975; Noble, 1977). These are the core features of the "new factory" still prevalent today. A similar pattern of development is found in the rise of the "new office," which is discussed later in this section. These historical developments are basic to understanding the social realities of contemporary industrial workers, whether they work in a factory, an office, or on the docks where ships are loaded and unloaded.

The New Factory

Although the early factories, such as those of Lynn, were substantially different places to work than the households of earlier times, these factories are best seen as intermediary work settings between the household and the new factory. Work in the early factories, for example, was seldom organized to achieve maximum productivity; rather, workers often had to walk up and down stairs in order to obtain the materials they needed, and when they finished they had to deliver their goods some place else in the factory. In addition to their inefficiency, the early factories were relatively unsafe. They had no electricity, and so light and ventilation were problems for workers. Most important, the early factories were made of wood and were highly susceptible to fire.

Another less-than-ideal feature of the early factories was the power granted to foremen, who supervised and organized workers. Foremen were usually men who had worked their way up through the ranks and had direct experience of the production process. They were a separate group from the managers, who typically had much less knowledge or interest in the production process. Foremen determined the pace of work and the ways in which it was to be done. In addition, they were primarily responsible for staffing their sections of the factory. This responsibility included the power to discipline and, if necessary, fire workers. Equally important were the recruitment and hiring activities of foremen, who developed informal networks of contact with various segments of the community; when new workers were needed, they tapped these networks. Finally, foremen had great control over the pay of their workers: they determined the wages of some workers and established piece rates for others. The *piece-rate approach* is a method of payment in which workers receive a specific amount of money for each item or batch of items they produce. A basic issue for piece-rate workers, then, is the amount of money that is associated with each item or batch. In the early factory the foremen had great control over rate determination, and, as with other areas of foremen control, workers could seldom object to management because managers almost always supported foremen. When they did not support them, it was usually because they felt that piece rates were too high.

The new factories that emerged in the period from 1880 to 1920 were different. First, most of them were built of steel and concrete, thus reducing some of the threat of fire. They were also one-story structures, so that much of the earlier drudgery of carrying materials up and down stairs was eliminated. Most important, the new factories had electricity, which not only allowed for better lighting and ventilation, but also helped streamline the work process. Sometimes work was organized around the assembly line, but other electrified forms of conveyance were also used to coordinate the activities of workers.

The rise of the new factory was also accompanied by a decline in the power of foremen. In part, that power was undermined by the development of the assembly line and other mechanical means of coordinating work, but it was also undermined by the rise of scientific management (Nelson, 1975; Noble, 1977). *Scientific management* is a style of management associated with Frederick Taylor and his followers, who believed that a truly efficient and profitable enterprise is one based on scientific study and organization of the work place. Because Taylor was an engineer, he defined science in mechanical terms: just as a machine is made up of many small movements that are coordinated to achieve efficient operation, so the factory can be studied in terms of the small movements that make it up. When these movements are identified, work can be reorganized so that each worker does a few movements that are highly efficient. Although it is a popular claim that the fragmented work of the contemporary factory can be traced to the development of the assembly line, this claim is only partially true: scientific managers took advantage of the fragmentation made possible by the assembly line.

Taylor and his followers emphasized four major issues in developing their approach. First, they were concerned with developing new forms of conveyance for the orderly and efficient movement of materials through the factory. Efficient operations cannot be achieved unless materials are moved properly. Second, they conducted time and motion studies of workers to determine the most efficient ways to organize their work and to pay them. Time and motion studies involve the observation and timing of worker activities and, based on the data, the reconstruction of the work process to make it "maximally efficient." Related to the collection of time and motion data was the creation of new accounting procedures for assessing the costs and outcomes of the work process.

Evidence of this third feature of scientific management is most easily seen in the proliferation of forms that had to be completed by supervisors in different sections of the factory. Finally, Taylor rejected the notion that secure wages encourage productivity; rather, he argued that high productivity results only when worker output and pay are linked. Thus, scientific management encouraged a piece-rate method of payment, and time and motion studies were the major way of determining the pay rates offered workers.

Each of these features of scientific management encouraged a decline in the power of foremen. The development of new forms of conveyance made much of the foremen's work obsolete, because managers controlling factory machinery could now regulate the pace and organization of work. The time and motion studies of scientific managers also undermined the foremen's power, because they were used as the basis for organizing work, assessing its efficiency, and setting pay rates. Put differently, the foremen's expertise, based on years of experience, was made irrelevant because new "scientific" criteria of evaluation were being used. The primary activities of foremen in the new factory were filling out forms and making sure that the machinery and workers were operating smoothly.

Although scientific management undermined the power of foremen, it had little impact on many of the recruitment and disciplining aspects of this job. These features of foreman power were eroded by the development of company *welfare practices,* which are the basis for the contemporary personnel department. Company welfare policies have a long history in the United States, dating back to the development of company towns in rural areas, particularly in the South. Libraries, schools, churches, restaurants, and other community facilities were features of those towns, meant to attract and keep workers. The factory managers in these early towns often rigidly controlled the governments and police forces in order to fight unionization, drunkenness, and other threats to their businesses. Around 1900 a number of strikes occurred which led other factory managers to consider the applicability of welfare programs in more urban settings. New associations of social workers and others interested in improving the situation of factory workers and minimizing strikes and unions also supported the idea. These associations encouraged the development of a variety of company welfare programs: building libraries, reading rooms, and dining areas in factories, offering medical and educational services to workers, creating safety programs, placing suggestion boxes around factories, creating company-sponsored kindergartens for the workers' children, and sponsoring gardening and other clubs for workers and their families. It was assumed that such efforts would improve the workers' life styles, but more important was that the welfare programs would result in higher profits based on the increased dependability and productivity of the workers.

Those companies that were most committed to welfare programs often hired full-time welfare secretaries, who created and directed programs within the factory. The activities and problems of these people are instructive, because they indicate the extent to which the programs were used to control workers. Elizabeth F. Briscoe, highly influential welfare secretary for the Joseph Bancroft and Sons Company from 1902 until her death in 1919, is a notable example (Nelson, 1975). Although Briscoe administered a variety of programs, she identified her most important activities as creating and maintaining a proper moral atmosphere among workers in the factory and in their homes, encouraging "responsible" labor legislation, and informing workers of their evaluations by supervisors. In practice, welfare secretaries acted as intermediaries between the workers and managers, but their primary loyalty was to the latter group. Thus, Briscoe opposed legislative proposals that infringed too directly on managerial practices, such as safety inspections; moreover, she seldom, if ever, challenged supervisors' evaluations of workers, and tended to equate a proper moral atmosphere with an uncritical acceptance of managerial authority.

Each of Briscoe's activities encroached in some ways on the traditional power of foremen, but they were still able to retain many of their sources of power. This situation changed with the evolution of personnel departments out of the welfare secretary's role, which began just before World War I. A basic feature of personnel departments is that they are based on "scientific," rather than moralistic, evaluation of workers. For example, psychological testing to determine the suitability of applicants for a job is now widely accepted (Baritz, 1960). Elaborate job analyses and classifications of jobs and pay levels are also popular. But personnel departments have influence in other areas as well. Many personnel departments provide or arrange for counseling of workers and their families troubled by work problems or such personal problems as child rearing and marital relationships.

Each of these areas of personnel department operation has undermined the traditional power of foremen. The major criteria for hiring, firing, and disciplining are those of the personnel department, and the foremen's informal recruitment networks are unwanted. As with the rise of scientific management, the development of the personnel department means that the foremen's expertise, based on direct experience in supervising and counseling workers, is irrelevant; new criteria of assessment have been developed. Perhaps the best reflection of the irrelevancy of the traditional foremen's knowledge is the development of training programs for foremen, which show them how to direct and motivate their workers better. Not only is the knowledge of foremen devalued, but active attempts are made to eradicate it from the new factory.

In some ways the assumptions of scientific management and those of welfare programs are different, because the welfare workers are presumably concerned with the interests of the workers as well as managers, whereas scientific managers care only about productivity and efficiency. In practice, however, the two are quite complementary, because the primary loyalty of welfare workers is usually to the employer. Similarly, although scientific management developed out of the traditions of engineering and personnel work is based largely on industrial psychology, they share the assumption that scientific techniques are the best way of organizing and evaluating productivity and workers. Finally, both scientific management and welfare programs are keys to the development of *bureaucratic control* over both workers and managers (Edwards, 1979). Bureaucratic control is based on a hierarchy of jobs linked together through written rules which describe both the content of each job in the factory and its relation to others. Bureaucratic control is a unique way of coordinating work because it is based not just on routines created by machines or foremen, but on routines that have been planned by managers wishing to increase productivity and efficiency and to control the work process. Concomitant with the rise of job descriptions and routines is the development both of worker evaluations based on their conformity to the organizational rules and of other sources of information gathered and processed through the use of standardized forms.

The emergence of bureaucratic control is important in understanding the place of the labor union in the new factory. Although the image of union-management relations created in the mass media, business schools, and the like is that of conflict and divergent interests, this image is false. Most union-management encounters are highly routine and orderly sessions in which grievances are assessed in light of existing rules and agreements. On the shop floor, for example, everyday grievances are handled through a series of steps involving an assessment of both the accuracy of the workers' complaints and the legitimacy of them based on existing agreements (Spencer, 1977). Even if workers are accurate in portraying management practices as unsafe or arbitrary, their grievances are illegitimate if they cannot show that union-management agreements have been violated. But the shop floor is not the only area in which bureaucratic negotiations take place; indeed, with the rise of multinational corporations and international labor unions, the shop floor is becoming increasingly insignificant, as more and more agreements are negotiated at the national level by union officials and management representatives who have little knowledge about the concrete problems of their workers and managers (Aronowitz, 1973a, 1973b; Boraston, Clegg, and Rimmer, 1975; Mills with Schneider, 1948). Even at the national level the collective bargaining process is becoming bureaucratized. In the steel industry, for example, an Experimental Negotiating Agreement limits strikes to local issues, and even those strikes are restricted

(Bogdanich, 1974). In exchange for this protection from strikes, the companies gave each worker a bonus of $150. With the possibility of a national strike eliminated, it is difficult to characterize union-management relations in the steel industry as conflict-ridden; rather, routine bureaucratic bargaining is the principal feature of their relations. The bureaucratization of union-management relations is also evident during strikes, because the rights and obligations of each party have been previously negotiated. William Serrin (1973) offers a provocative example in his description of the reaction of Walter Reuther, former president of the United Automobile Workers union, to a strike of the Ford Motor Company in 1967:

> In 1967, as he trooped this line of pickets during the sixty-seven day Ford strike, Reuther asked a local union official where the pickets, warming themselves over fires, obtained their coal. They probably stole it from the company as workers did in the old days, Reuther said. No, the local man said, the coal came from the company. Mr. Ford has agreed to give it to them. A truck was sent through the picket line to pick it up. And the oil drums in which they build their fires? Reuther asked. They probably stole them from the company, like the union men did in the old days. No, Walter, the local union man said. The union and the company had an agreement: the company provided the barrels. After a long pause, Reuther spoke: "Karl Marx," he declared, "would never believe this" (Serrin, 1973: 152–153).

Thus, one of the ironies of the new factory is that although many of its basic features—particularly scientific management and welfare programs—were created to discourage labor union development, they have resulted in the incorporation of union personnel and negotiations into the ongoing processes of the new factory through the mechanism of bureaucratic control.

Thus far we have shown that the rise of the new factory is important because it has changed the way in which factory work occurs in time and space. The timing of work in the new factory is based on the orderly and coordinated activities of specialized workers, who are often linked by an assembly line or other machines. There is also much less movement of workers, because machines and specialized workers now transport materials from place to place. Finally, knowledge has been transformed in the new factory, because direct on-the-job experience is devalued, with scientifically gathered and bureaucratically processed knowledge taking its place. All of these changes have had important consequences for foremen, but they are also basic to understanding the social realities of the new factory to be discussed shortly.

But first we want to deal with the parallel changes that have occurred in the organization of office work.

The New Office

Like the new factory, the new office has developed over time. Beginning as a small, personalized, and relatively inefficient work setting, the office has become a large, impersonal, and efficiency-oriented operation (Benet, 1972; Braverman, 1974; Davies, 1974; Glenn and Feldberg, 1977; Lockwood, 1958; Mills, 1951). The similarity between the development of the new factory and the new office is perhaps best seen in the work role of the office clerk. During much of the nineteenth century office clerks held a respected position in the community because their jobs were clean and required a level of skill and discretion not common to other jobs. In addition, office clerks were often persons aspiring to their own businesses, and so they were seen as apprentices seeking to rise socially and economically. The fact that many clerks did not achieve their goal is less important than the fact that office work was seen as an avenue of social mobility.

The traditional office clerks combined several of the qualities of the master craftsmen in the early shoe industry and the foremen in the old factory. Traditional clerks were involved in a variety of work activities. For example, they kept the books and dealt with customers and clients. Their special knowledge and skill were based on experience gained on the job, not through formal schooling. Each clerk therefore did his or her job in somewhat different ways. The unique problems and practices of each office were also encouraged by these differences.

Finally, the traditional clerks worked directly with the office owners. This direct relationship provided them with opportunities to influence the owners' decisions, but it also allowed them to "borrow" respectability from the owners, who were often persons of influence in the community. In order to have their claims to high status taken seriously, it was necessary to associate with other gentlemen, and small, personalized offices offered such opportunities (Lockwood, 1958).

As with master craftsmen the foremen, traditional office clerks saw their influence and prestige decline with the rise of the new office. Indeed, the processes of mechanization and bureaucratization, as well as the creation of scientific management and welfare programs, are as important in the rise of the new office as in the factory. There is, however, at least one distinctive feature of the new office: unlike the factory, the new office is the work setting of large numbers of young women. Put differently, the new office may be dominated by male bosses and managers, but it is highly feminized at the lower levels where industrialization is most complete. The new office is thus unique, because sex-based values and practices are integral to understanding the social realities associated with office work, whereas they are less central to the everyday realities of most factories.

Initially, women office workers were young, single, middle-class individuals seeking short-term employment while waiting to get married (Benet, 1972; Richardson 1905/1972). When teaching and other respectable jobs became harder and harder to get, the office grew as an acceptable alternative because it was a clean work setting, unlike the factory. Women had a large impact on the office because they had few commitments in common with traditional clerks. First, the women workers were short-term employees who lacked a long-term concern for the success of the enterprise. Second most of these women lived with their parents and were not seriously concerned with their rate of pay. Finally, women held a generally degraded position in society. All of these differences threatened the status of male clerks. They asked themselves, if women can do the work, how skilled can it be? The clerks worried not just about their diminished prestige and possibilities for social advancement but about reductions in pay based on the women's willingness to work for little money.

Many of the traditional male clerks' fears were justified, because many did experience a significant reduction in prestige and pay. On the other hand, many took advantage of new opportunities and separated themselves from the female clerks. Both accounting and personnel management, for example, developed out of attempts by traditional office clerks to carve out special occupational niches that would separate them from the new female workers and provide them with other claims to respectability and higher pay (Benet, 1972). These opportunities existed because the feminization of the office work force was only one part of a more general process of office growth and development beginning in the late nineteenth century and continuing into the present (Barker, 1964; Glenn and Feldberg, 1977). Between 1880 and 1970, for example, the demand for clerical workers increased almost seventeenfold in the United States; accompanying this change was an increase in the percentage of female clerks from 4.3 percent in 1880 to 74.6 percent in 1970 (Glenn and Feldberg, 1977).

These figures reflect the extent to which the new office has emerged as a large, specialized, and hierarchical setting in which the general skills of the old office, learned through personal relationships, are absent. The new office evolved to its present state in much the same way as the new factory: through new sources of recruitment, the development of welfare programs, mechanization, scientific management, and bureaucratization.

As the new office grew, it became a major source of employment for women from a variety of backgrounds, who sought work for very different reasons from the original women clerks. Women from immigrant and poor families, for example, found that office work offered many advantages over domestic and factory work: it was certainly cleaner and it often paid better. The female work force thus became more diversified than in the nineteenth century. Out of this diverse work force emerged a group of women committed to careers as office employees, even though the chances for significant promotion were slim. These professional secretaries sometimes sacrificed marriage and families to pursue their careers (Benet, 1972). Even with changes in the composition of the female work force, however, the lowest clerical positions in the new office were filled primarily by young, single women with no long-term commitment to their employer. These women were considered desirable employees partly because they worked for much less pay than career-oriented persons, particularly men.

Women were recruited to the new office in a variety of ways, but two of the most important involved the development of new definitions of femininity and welfare programs. Employers encouraged these developments to some degree, but so did others acting independently.

The development of new definitions of femininity is best seen in the evolution of stories and advice of popular magazines (Davies, 1974). Prior to the turn of the century popular magazines often described women as physically and emotionally unequipped for office work, too concerned with their dress, grooming, and idle chitchat to put in a full day's work. Another popular claim was that the pace of office work was too demanding for the fragile constitutions of women. Finally, the magazines often described the atmosphere of the office as immoral; they were particularly concerned about women's inability to resist the illicit sexual advances of bosses and other men in the office. Beginning shortly before World War I, this imagery began to change. A new notion of femininity began to appear in popular magazines—that of the contented female office worker. The new woman was happy because the office offered her a unique opportunity to develop and express her natural abilities. Women continued to be seen as naturally passive and subordinate, but in different ways. The personal secretary, for example, was described as a woman with the unique opportunity to be a courteous, sympathetic, and loyal helper to her male boss: at work, she was to act like a wife. File clerks, stenographers, and typists, on the other hand, were described as contented because their work offered them a chance to use their natural dexterity to handle the tedium of routine jobs that they were so much better at than men. Their work may be boring, but they were thought to enjoy it (Barker, 1964).

Accompanying the evolution of new notions about femininity were developments in welfare work. The Young Women's Christian Association (YWCA) and a variety of other organizations concerned with the morality of young women emerged as responses to the influx of young, single women coming to the city for office jobs (Benet, 1972). These organizations frequently offered counterparts to the programs of the welfare secretaries in the factories. They provided libraries and reading rooms, clubs, and other opportunities for socializing; most important, they offered a moral atmosphere where counseling was available and where the young women's comings and goings could be monitored in order to minimize their chances of falling into sin. Employers often encouraged such organizations by making large contributions and referring new employees to them.

Although the recruitment of women to office work and the development of welfare programs were important, the mechanization of the office was a key development because large amounts of paper work could now be done in an efficient and coordinated manner (Baker, 1964). Symbolically at least, the most important machine in the new office was the typewriter, which became a major means of production. The typewriter was also important as a "sex-neutral" machine, which was not considered essential to the "men's work" of the traditional clerk (Davies, 1974). This meant that employers could hire female typists without worrying about protests from male clerks. The close connection between women office workers and the typewriter is reflected in the fact that only 40 percent of the stenographers and typists in the United States in 1880 were women, whereas by 1930, that figure was 95.6 percent (Davies, 1974).

But the mechanization of the new office involved more than the typewriter: adding machines, photographic and copying equipment, Addressographs and postage metering machines, and dictaphones have all been important in influencing the work of office employees (International Labour Office, 1960). An important feature of these machines is that they do only a limited set of activities. Today new machines that are capable of doing many work activities are being incorporated into the office. A particularly important machine is the electronic computer, which can do much of the calculating of the clerk, update customer accounts, and send monthly bills, among other tasks (Barker, 1964; Champion, 1967; Shepard, 1971). As the computer becomes adapted to more and more office settings, clerical work will change because some jobs will be eliminated and new, computer-tending jobs will develop. Another possible change is the development of night shifts for some office workers, because computers are operated continuously. In addition to large computers, the new office also includes smaller word-processing centers, which allow one or a few people to type, edit, and file materials that formerly involved many people.

Concomitant with the rise in the number of office machines has been the application of scientific management techniques and the development of bureaucratic control in the office. Both are consistent with mechanization of the work process because they create specialists. Thus, the individual in the typing pool who spends all day listening to a dictaphone and transcribing those messages into letters and reports is as much of a scientifically managed specialist as the factory worker who spends all day putting mirrors on cars. The typist is also tied to a location in much the same way as the factory worker on an assembly line.

But the application of scientific management techniques to the office is not limited to machine tending; it is evident as well in the flow of paper from desk to desk, where it is stamped, stapled, unstapled, paper-clipped, copied, and finally filed for posterity. Each of these steps involves a set of specialized activities that can be as routine, tedious, and isolating as machine tending. The mail departments of some large organizations offer proof of this statement. Workers spend much of their days in small cubbyholes surrounded by small boxes within which mail is sorted. Visual contact with others is extremely limited in the work setting, although communication can occur by yelling to others in the area—assuming, of course, that the supervisor is not around.

Although office work is generally not organized along an assembly line, the major techniques of scientific management still can be applied because other forms of conveyance are often used. Similarly, time and motion studies are less common in the office than the factory, but work is still broken down into small units which are coordinated by supervisors who plan the work flow. Certainly, the new office is based on a different type of knowledge from the old office, and this new knowledge reflects the influence of scientific management. As with the old factory, the old office was dominated by those with practical on-the-job experience. The most important knowledge in the new office is general knowledge created through "scientific" evaluation of the work process.

The creation of scientific knowledge is important, in part, because it is necessary to the development of bureaucratic control. Such control was difficult in the old office because of its small size and the idiosyncratic roles, relationships, and activities of the office workers. How does one evaluate an office using scientific and bureaucratic criteria when divisions of authority are obscure and the responsibilities of each worker are unclear? In the new office, such evaluations are possible because standardized forms exist for gathering information about workers. Sometimes these forms are direct attempts to measure the productivity of workers, and other times they are general assessments of the workers by their supervisors. In either case, these evaluations are bureaucratically processed, and they become a part of the workers' files which can be used for periodic assessments. In bureaucratically controlled offices, then, the "facts" about a worker's performance are found in his or her file and not necessarily on the job.

Table 3-1 • Sources of Industrial Realities

Work Setting	*Work-Related Timetables*	*Work-Related Communities*
Household and the Old Office	Diachronic: based on the discontinuous activities and demands of customers and coworkers in the office and household	Mixed: based on enduring relationships within the household and shifting relationships with shopkeepers and customers
New Factory and Office	Diachronic: based on the continuous demands and processes of the organization	Mixed: based on the organization of the work process and relationships to people outside the work setting; shifting work group membership and fleeting relations with others predominate

Consequences of Industrialization

We have considered two examples of industrialization in this section: the new factory and the new office. Each of these examples is different, but the general features of both examples are similar. Industrialization and its accompaniments—specialization, mechanization, and bureaucratization—undermined the traditional knowledge and authority of some workers. Traditional workers were replaced by persons with new, often more limited skills who could be linked with one another in efficient work routines. In addition, efforts to control and routinize certain work-related features of workers' lives have been made. Welfare programs and the bureaucratic routinization of union-management relations are important examples.

Industrialization has been accompanied by significant changes in the work-related timetables and communities of industrial workers. The sources of these changes are summarized in Table 3-1.

Within the household and the old office, time was experienced diachronically, but the personalized relationships of these settings and diverse activities of members made work a discontinuous process. This experience of time changed with the development of the new factory and the new office, where work flows in a continuous way and each worker does a limited set of routine tasks. Basic to the continuity of time and work in the new settings is the organization of work around machines, which are not fully controlled by workers and operate continuously. The assembly line and some computer operations are examples.

The work-related communities of industrial workers have also changed. In the household and the old office, the enduring relationships established by office and household members were the major source of community. In the case of the household these relationships extended to both the working and nonworking aspects of members' lives. This sense of community was reinforced by relationships with customers, shopkeepers, and others in the area, who identified a group of workers as belonging to the same office or household. In the new factory and office, work-related communities tend to be less enduring because membership in work groups shifts over time. There are, of course, exceptions to this pattern; in some work settings relationships do endure (Cunnison, 1966; Kornblum, 1974; Roy, 1952, 1959–1960). In addition community feeling among work group members may be encouraged by fleeting relations with outsiders, including employees outside one's department, union officials, customers, clients, and other nonemployees. The typists in a typing pool, for example, may spend little time together, but the fact that others identify them all as typists and treat them accordingly means that they have this minimal means of developing a consciousness of kind.

Because the concern in this section has been with the general historical development of industrialization, little attention has been given to the responses of workers. It is a mistake to assume that workers accepted industrialization passively; indeed, some of the most important labor conflicts in the history of the United States have involved workers resisting industrialization (Brecher, 1972; Grob, 1961; Hays, 1957). Still, though the account of industrialization given here is selective, it does accurately describe how the work situations of contemporary industrial workers have been transformed. It is within these situations that workers have created new social realities.

THE SOCIAL REALITIES OF INDUSTRIAL WORKERS

Because industrialization has not occurred in the same way in all factories and offices, it is not possible to describe fully here the many social realities of contemporary industrial workers. There are, however, some work situations which better reflect the general process of industrialization than others, and this section is primarily based on one such example—Riverside, an automated chemical plant in England. Although Riverside reveals many of the influences that shape industrial realities, there are other factors operative elsewhere that are equally important. We will discuss these other influences in this section as well.

Social Realities at Riverside

Riverside is a fertilizer plant that is one part of a large multinational corporation (ChemCo), a chemical concern (Nichols and Armstrong, 1976; Nichols and Beynon, 1977). The plant, considered one of the most progressive in England, earned its reputation largely because it is an example of a *process technology*—that is, it is almost fully automated. Another reason why Riverside is considered progressive is that ChemCo has developed a new management policy—the New Working Agreement (NWA)—which is viewed as a more humane and reasonable approach to management than the methods used in other plants. The NWA is an example of how bureaucratic control can be implemented within the contemporary factory, because it consists of a series of job classifications and descriptions used to determine the work responsibilities and pay scales of workers. Workers who are classified at the same level are allowed to rotate their jobs so that they do not become too bored with one set of activities. The NWA has also eliminated the old method of worker payment, which was based on both time and productivity: workers are now paid an annual salary. Finally, the NWA recognizes the right of workers to unionize, but it restricts most union activities to the national level, where almost all issues regarding pay and working conditions are negotiated. Managers and workers therefore find that most union-management activity is distant, mysterious, and unpredictable. However, the new union-management relationship is clearly visible at Riverside in some areas. The regular deduction of union dues from workers' paychecks by management is one illustration.

The Riverside plant is an important example of contemporary industrial work because it is highly mechanized and bureaucratized. It is also important because it is recognized to be a leader in the development of new management practices which take account of the needs of both managers and workers. An important assumption underlying this management policy is the belief that many old worker-management conflicts can be resolved through regular bureaucratic bargaining; certainly, the policy makers recognize no inherent and inevitable worker-management conflicts. To support this assumption, management points to the elimination of the old conflict over wages at Riverside. The NWA ended this dispute because it provides for some of the highest pay scales in any factory in England, and the company has committed itself to keeping worker salaries high. Looked at through the assumptions of top management and union officials associated with ChemCo, Riverside is like a family in which each person has a contribution to make, and any problems or misunderstandings that develop on the shop floor can be resolved through established channels. Looked at more closely, however, Riverside is a world of many actors who hold different, competing social realities based on the ways in which their work and the NWA affect the practical circumstances of their lives. In general, the world of Riverside can be divided into workers and management, but this division obscures the many differences within these categories. A more accurate division includes national and local managers, workers who are union officials, "scientific workers," and "donkey workers." We will begin with the latter two types of workers.

Donkey workers are those persons who make their livings by doing hard physical labor, such as loading bags of fertilizer. Although it is often assumed that these jobs will be eliminated with the full development of automated production, there are some tasks which machines cannot do as cheaply as human beings. It is a mistake, then, to assume that the donkey work at Riverside is a holdover from the previous form of organization or that it reflects the degree to which process technology is still unperfected. Indeed, managers at Riverside recognize the continuing need for donkey work and have attempted to deal with it by introducing *job rotation*. This means that workers in this category can divide their shifts by doing packing, loading, sealing, and similar activities. Although this arrangement offers the advantage of limiting the need for continuous work at one job, it does not really constitute a form of job enrichment, as management claims, because the workers have little opportunity for personal involvement and growth in these activities. As one worker states: "You move from one boring, dirty, monotonous job to another boring, dirty, monotonous job. And then to another boring, dirty, monotonous job. And somehow you're supposed to come out of it all 'enriched.' But I never feel 'enriched'—I just feel knackered [worn out]" (Quoted in Nichols and Beynon, 1977: 16).

Thus, "job rotation" and "job enrichment" are really new terms for describing work activities that have been a part of the factory from its beginning. But the notion of workers as scientists is new, though it too is somewhat of a misnomer. *Scientific workers* are not really scientists but machine tenders who spend workdays and nights watching dials and adjusting the various parts of the production process. Although less physically demanding, these activities are not enriching; rather, they are often boring because the workers have little to do most of the time and are placed in small control rooms where they are isolated from others.

Even more than the donkey workers, the scientific workers at Riverside are directly affected by the demands of the machines that make up the process technology. These workers, for example, must be constantly prepared to spot production problems, but they must also be available to work at all hours of the day or night. One of the benefits of process technology is that it is continuous; consequently, machine tenders must be available twenty-four hours a day. At Riverside this means that work schedules are continually shifting, because the company does not allow factory workers to have regular work routines, such as only days or nights. One of the problems faced by the workers, then, is adjusting to the constant shifts in their lives based on their work schedules, but they must also adjust to the need for continual production by being available for overtime and double shifts if needed. If someone is sick or does not show up, the scientific worker is expected to fill in on the next shift; indeed, it is possible for a Riverside worker to put in a full twenty-four hours at work. This can happen if the worker is scheduled for both a day shift and a late-night shift and the person scheduled to work between those shifts fails to appear.

The routine work activities and problems of donkey and scientific workers at Riverside are central to their social realities. These experiences give rise to feelings of resignation, cynical acceptance of work, management practices, and the union, and a noticeable emphasis on the financial advantages of working for ChemCo. This world view contradicts the underlying assumptions of the NWA, and it also runs contrary to the social realities of Riverside managers and union officials. An important part of management reality is the belief that scientific work and job rotation are enriching experiences for workers. Because managers are not in a position to observe or experience the activities of the factory workers, they continue to hold that view. Even when opportunities for communications are present, the practical circumstances of the situations often preclude a free exchange of information.

One example is the ritualized monthly appearance of Sammy Bell, a Riverside manager, on the shop floor. Supervisors and workers treat these visits as times to impress Bell with their smooth, efficient operations and not as times to present worker grievances. Another potential source of communication is the monthly meetings between some managers and worker representatives. However, managerial concern for reducing the disruptive potential of worker demands and grievances dominate these encounters. Again, Sammy Bell is a good example, because he is considered to be a master at handling worker representatives and young Riverside executives use him as a model. Bell, like other effective executives, uses all the resources of his office in order to control the flow of the meetings and thus manipulate worker representatives. For example, he offers the representatives coffee and snacks, compliments their good sense and maturity, and uses telephone calls and secretaries, who conveniently need letters signed, to disrupt the conversation when the subject of worker grievances is raised.

It is easy to attack such managerial practices as sinister, but to do so is to ignore the practical problems of the managers' work lives. Their pay and advancement depend on the productivity of their sections of the plant. An important factor in maintaining productivity is smooth, dependable operations; consequently, an important part of management's job is to placate workers by seeming to listen to their problems without taking them seriously. In addition, it must be recognized that many of the workers' most serious problems and complaints involve decisions made at the national level. The plant manager simply lacks the power to alter the organization of work so that boredom is reduced. Because most managers are successful in maintaining smooth working operations, there is little reason for change; rather, the forms and other indicators of plant success used by national company and union officials point to the effectiveness of the NWA and continuous process technology. Even the assumption that work at Riverside is enriching and humanizing is maintained, because the national leadership is not in a position to see or hear worker complaints.

The most important way in which workers voice their complaints is through disruptive actions on the shop floor. Sometimes they fight back by rigidly adhering to the rules, thereby placing supervisors at a disadvantage. When a supervisor asks a worker to do something at quitting time, for example, the worker refuses because it violates plant rules. But the most important way of expressing discontent is sabotage. Sometimes workers directly damage some part of the plant, but a more effective strategy is for them to make it appear to be the manager's fault.

Worker resistance can be very successful in achieving some of their goals. One Riverside manager, for example, openly called the workers idiots and treated them in dictatorial ways. The workers responded by reducing productivity in his area in the company: "Plants got mysteriously 'gunged up'. Storage pits ran dry. Wasteful emissions occurred. Valves leaked expensively throughout the night" (Nichols and Beynon, 1977: 140). The manager was ultimately fired because his performance was inadequate, as reflected on the bureaucratic forms and evaluations of ChemCo. The workers, then, are not totally powerless in dealing with managers, but even when they are successful in eliminating a hated manager, the message that national leaders receive is that the manager is incompetent. The bureaucratically created and transmitted message says nothing about the boredom of workers or their cynicism about job enrichment and humanization. Thus, national leaders continue to believe they are creating a modern, humanized work place despite the contradictory experiences and interpretations of workers.

The world of ChemCo is made up of multiple realities which are sustained by the segregation of workers from one another and managers from workers. Segregation makes it possible for each group to interpret the same events and actions in different ways. The multiple realities of ChemCo are also maintained by the differing sources of knowledge of each group. Donkey workers experience process technology as a series of bags of fertilizer that must be sealed and carried. Scientific workers experience it as a set of dials to be watched and levers to be adjusted.

Plant managers experience it as a set of problems that must be anticipated and controlled. Finally, national managers experience it as computer data on plant efficiency and effectiveness. Given the differing social circumstances and sources of knowledge, it is not surprising that each group interprets an act of sabotage differently. The scientific workers may consider it as a legitimate attempt to get even with management, while donkey workers see it as another job because they have to clean up the mess; on the other side, local managers may see it as a serious disruption of the continuity of production, while national managers interpret it as a dip in production figures and an increase in costs.

Because Riverside is a unionized plant, the ways in which different workers and managers interpret the union also reveal industrial realities. In general, plant managers treat the union as a potential source of disruption, and they seek to control it by encouraging "trustworthy" workers to run for union offices. They may also attempt to publicly discredit troublesome union officers, such as by calling them Communists. The workers experience the local union as a practical problem of everyday life as well, but for them the issue is representation. There are two major styles of union representation at Riverside.

The first is embodied by Alfie Grey, a man in his fifties who has been involved in the union movement for several decades. For Alfie the object of the union is to win the workers a fair wage and reasonable working conditions. In exchange, workers should give the company a fair day's work and stand behind the union at all costs. When disputes occur, whether with the company or the union, established procedures should be used. In sum, Alfie Grey holds a vision of the union and factory work which is based on years of effort to build a union and to acquire a secure job. So long as the union and job security are not seriously threatened, militant action is unnecessary and most worker grievances are looked upon as legitimate. Alfie's assessment of the union's "younger element" as primarily motivated by greed, not by a desire to do a good job, is a good reflection of his views.

The younger element, as Alfie calls them, is best represented by the point of view of thirty-year-old Greg Andrews. Although he has been associated with the union and similar movements in the past, he sees the union hierarchy and established union-management practices as major sources of the workers' problems. He also disagrees with Alfie about the most important rewards of work. For Greg, the appeal of work at Riverside is money, and Alfie's talk of job security and giving a fair day's work only obscures the fact that work at Riverside is a modern form of human sacrifice for which workers should be amply paid. Greg's style of union representation is the opposite of Alfie's. He almost never goes to union meetings, nor does he use established procedures for handling grievances about management or the union. Rather, he handles grievances by disrupting the usual routines of managers, workers, and union officials. Thus, he defends sabotage because it can be an effective way of cutting through bureaucratic "red tape" and dealing with a problem, but he also sometimes uses established rules and procedures to disrupt everyday routines. The company, for example, encourages workers to work overtime during the summer but offers little overtime in winter. Greg argues that the company should take account of the workers' needs and desires and schedule production so that workers can have more time with their families during the warm summer months. They could make up the lost production in winter when there is less time for family outings. In order to make this point, Greg has organized the workers in his section of Riverside to refuse all summer overtime. Since process technology is based on the contribution of all sections, their refusal eliminates overtime for almost all other Riverside workers as well. Thus, by using the bureaucratic right to refuse overtime, Greg disrupts the usual routines of Riverside.

Alfie and Greg represent two very different visions of labor union responsibility. Alfie's view reflects the problems and experiences of older workers and Greg's of younger ones. Both are respected and followed by some workers and hated by others. Workers see Alfie's style as too cozy with management, whereas they consider Greg's methods too personally costly for workers. Indeed, these reservations about Alfie and Greg are a good indication of the way most Riverside workers see the union: regardless of who leads it the union is basically irrelevant to the workers' lives so long as they have adequate wages and their lives are not too disrupted by its activities. Paying union dues may be a fact of life at Riverside, but the union should not take too much of the workers' time and energy, particularly time that can be spent in more meaningful activities away from work. Both Alfie and Greg are thus potential sources of difficulty because Alfie cannot be trusted to push for the workers' interests when that is necessary and Greg requires too much time and effort from the workers.

There are, then, several realities within Riverside and ChemCo. The realities of managers are not those of workers, and within both groups there are divergent viewpoints as well. Each set of realities is based on a somewhat different source of knowledge, because each group experiences the practical problems of everyday life differently. For most workers the key problems are the continuous flow of work within the plant, their isolation from others, the tedium of their jobs, and the irregularity of their working hours. All of these factors discourage the development of an enduring sense of community among workers. Except for the donkey workers, who sometimes work together in stable groups, and except for those special occasions when workers see their collective interests as threatened, Riverside workers come and go from work as individuals who are preoccupied with their personal, private troubles.

Other Influences on Industrial Social Realities

Although the remarks we have made about Riverside are generally applicable to other industrial settings, each setting is unique. At Riverside, for example, the skills associated with scientific and donkey work are not very important to the workers, but in other settings, such as in the automobile industry, among dock workers, in construction, and in the steel industry, skills are very important sources of community (Form, 1976; Kornblum, 1974; Herb Mills, 1976, 1977; Riemer, 1979). In addition to skills, such factors as the amount of worker isolation, company policies, and the ethnic and sexual composition of the workforce may also influence the social realities of workers.

Not all industrial workers are as isolated from one another as those at Riverside. In some parts of most factories and offices there are workers who have been able to create realities that are somewhat independent of managers' plans. Work-related communities and timetables may develop there which limit the impact of mechanization and bureaucratization. An example is offered by Donald Roy (1952, 1959–1960) in his descriptions of his job in a machine shop. The workers in the machine shop were shut in a room that allowed them little contact with others in the plant. In part, because these workers were so segregated, they were able to build a pattern of work and community that was unique in the plant. For example, they developed a shared notion of a fair day's work and restricted their production to that level. A more distinctive feature of this work group was the division of the day into a series of times when workers stopped their work and spent time talking and "horsing around." They broke for coffee time, peach time, banana time, fish time, Coke time, lunch time, pickup time, and window time. Banana time, for example, occurred at about the same time everyday when the workers stopped to eat a banana. Window time was when they all stopped to look out the window. The importance of those events is twofold. First, the workers created a timetable through their breaks that was imposed on that of managers. Second, the breaks gave workers a chance to build a sense of community that is largely absent in Riverside and similar settings.

Even within the new factory, then, workers may create alternatives to official timetables and work relations. Sometimes employers even aid in their development. Some of the early welfare programs were intended to encourage workers to build a sense of community among themselves and to identify with the company. A more recent example is offered by the New York Telephone Company, which fosters a sense of community through gifts and through its "culture of niceness" (Langer, 1970). Gifts are given on major holidays and as a reward for steady service to the company. The gifts grow in value the longer the period of service: two years of service may be worth a gold charm; forty, a diamond. These efforts at building loyalty are complemented by a general emphasis on informal, personal relations within the company. This culture of niceness is based on the belief that the telephone company provides a major service to the country. For this reason workers should be nice to customers and to each other. Being nice includes calling each other by first names, helping others with their work, and encouraging worker friendships. If successful, such efforts result in both loyalty to the telephone company and the development of enduring worker communities.

Although not always intended, management decisions about the composition of the industrial work force may also be important. Ethnic and racial divisions of workers on the job may aid the development of competing worker communities and realities. For many factory workers, these divisions end when they leave work, because they actively try to separate work from family and neighborhood life (Fried et al., 1973; Gans, 1962; Shostak, 1969; Wrobel, 1979). One exception to this pattern is the steel industry of South Chicago, where many workers live in neighborhoods surrounding the mills (Kornblum, 1974). For these workers it is not possible to separate work from family and neighborhood, because friendships and identities built in the local area are carried over into the mills. The connection between work and neighborhood is also evident in union politics, because many candidates campaign in the taverns and other institutions of the area. These campaigns are intense because each candidate's reputation within the union, mills, and neighborhood is on the line, and the winner is assured of respectability within both the neighborhood and the mills. Since workers are expected to publicly announce their choice for union representative before the election, their reputations are also vulnerable and this further intensifies the campaign. The social realities of steel work in South Chicago, then, are different from those of Riverside. Certainly, workers do not come and go as isolated individuals with little sense of community.

Another factor influencing the social realities of the industrial work place is the sexual composition of the work force. At Riverside the workers are male, but other factories employ many women and they dominate in most offices (Beynon and Blackburn, 1972; Cunnison, 1966; Lupton, 1963). The presence of women in the industrial work place is important because they may bring a different set of expectations, thoughts, and feelings with them. The women who entered the new office during its early stages are an example, because their work orientation was very different from that of the traditional male clerks. Because the practical circumstances of many women's lives, which include such responsibilities as bearing and raising children, are different from those of men, women bring a different set of concerns to the industrial work place. Sex-based stereotypes may accentuate such differences (Kanter, 1977a).

These stereotypes arise in part from cultural definitions of women. One reason that the feminization of the office was at first resisted was the cultural definition of women as weak and trivial creatures who could not handle the rigors of the office. The later justification of using women in the office relied on a new definition of women and office work, as propagated in magazines and other sources outside the work place. But the sex-based social realities of industrial settings are not just borrowed from the outside; they are also created in the work place. The early assignment of women office workers to the typewriter, for example, was a compromise with traditional male clerks, who wanted to protect their domain from female invasion. Because the typewriter was "sex-neutral," it could be assigned to women without upsetting the men. Over the years, however, this decision, which was originally based on the practical problems of everyday life in the new office, has been reinterpreted; the typewriter now has a symbolic importance as an indicator of women's place in the office. What has emerged is a tradition which accounts for the predominance of women in low-level positions and justifies the paternalistic relations that often exist between male managers and female clerks and typists. As with other traditions, this new office tradition is often experienced as common sense or a fact of life by workers themselves.

MYTHS ABOUT INDUSTRIAL WORKERS

Because an important part of the rise of the new factory and office is the development of management control, management theories are major sources of myths about industrial workers. Such theories generally draw on the themes of both scientific management and welfare work. An underlying assumption of most, if not all, of them is that managers are vital to the operation of the factory or office and therefore their decisions largely determine the success of the enterprise. Workers, on the other hand, tend to be treated as persons to be manipulated. In this section we will look at two management theories that are important sources of myths about industrial workers: scientific management and the myth of the new industrial order developed by Peter Drucker. Other important sources of myths about industrial workers are persons wishing to create social change. For example, myths often arise within social

Table 3-2 • Myths about Industrial Workers

Type of Myth	*Need for Work*	*Organization of Work*	*Rewards of Work*
Myth of Scientific Management	Based on material need and the economic self-interests of workers	Hierarchical, with close supervision and coercive control of workers	Income
Myth of the New Industrial Order	Based on material, psychological, and social needs	Hierarchical, stemming from rational planning, loose management control, and responsible workers with a managerial attitude	Income, personal achievement and prestige, feelings of belonging to a meaningful work group, and identification with the enterprise
Marxist Myth of the Alienated Worker	Based on material need, although it should be based on individual and social needs	Hierarchical, with close supervision and coercion of workers, in fact; ideally, egalitarian with workers in control	Income, at present, but personal and social rewards in an ideal future setting

movements of radical workers, which stress the need for workers to band together to fight their exploitative employers. Myths emphasizing social change are also created by radical theorists concerned with analyzing the organization and operations of modern economies as well as getting workers to create change. These two types of modern radicalism will be treated together here as parts of the Marxist myth of the alienated worker. Each of these myths is summarized in Table 3-2.

The Myth of Scientific Management

Because scientific management theory has been such an important part of the development of the new factory and office, it has been the object of much attention and criticism. Indeed, some of the most insightful analyses of this perspective have come from persons who disagree with it and who offer alternative management theories. Elton Mayo (1945, 1946, 1947), for example, was an early critic of scientific management. He claimed that it was based on a set of assumptions that form a kind of "rabble hypothesis" of human nature. Its major tenets are that (1) human beings in their natural state are disorganized, (2) the primary motive of all people is self-interest, and (3) human beings always make decisions by carefully calculating the advantages and disadvantages of each of their options.

Because the rabble hypothesis considers self-interest the dominant motive in human life, it directs management to deal with workers as individuals, not as members of groups. It also encourages management to deal with workers as if their only concern is with their incomes. Thus, according to the hypothesis, one of the best ways for managers to influence the output of workers is to manipulate the rate of payment for each item they produce. If workers are dominated by self-interest, they will increase their productivity when the rate per item of production is reduced. The hypothesis also fosters a belief in the need for closely supervising workers. Put differently, because workers are disorganized and continually pursue their own self-interests, the threat of chaos is always imminent. It is therefore necessary to develop strict supervisory practices that minimize the potential for chaos in the work place and in the larger society.

Douglas McGregor (1960) offers a somewhat different perspective on scientific management theory, which he refers to as Theory X. According to McGregor, the major assumptions of the theory are that most people (1) dislike work and try to avoid it, (2) have to be supervised closely and pushed constantly to do a good job, and (3) prefer to have little freedom or responsibility in their work. Theory X thus justifies the creation of work relations that are coercive and based on conflicts of interest. Coercion is necessary to offset the limitations of human nature: if workers really are lazy and dislike their work, then it is essential to manipulate them in order to get things done.

Each of these theories identifies different aspects of the myth of scientific management. First, the myth states that the need for work is based on the self-interested desires of workers to survive. There are no other human needs associated with work. Because human beings are self-interested, calculating, and opposed to work, it is necessary to build work organizations that are hierarchical and coercive. This is the second aspect of the myth of scientific management, and it justifies the creation of large bureaucratic organizations within which workers are constantly watched, evaluated, and pushed to work harder and faster. Finally, the myth of scientific management holds that because workers are essentially self-interested, the primary reward of work is income. It is not possible for industrial workers to derive other rewards, such as self-satisfaction, from their work. All of these aspects of the myth of scientific management justify the creation of a routinized and specialized work process in which workers spend their days doing tedious, uninteresting tasks for which their only reward is money. There is no need for managers to create policies that give workers control over their work, because the new factory and office are based on a bargain between managers and workers. It is human nature for workers to want only increased pay and security, and managers are willing to fulfill this desire in exchange for a day's work.

Managers who watch only the productivity figures of a company see much evidence from everyday life to support this view of human nature and industrial workers. Many workers seem to be concerned only with making a living and show little other interest in their work. It is also true that many industrial workers slack off when supervision and control are loosened. Thus, the belief in the need for coercion in the work place seems to be supported by everyday experiences. Finally, productivity can often be increased by offering workers a greater income. Productivity figures as well as observation on the job appear to bear out that fact. The vision offered by scientific management is thus not a fabrication of managers seeking only to justify their control over workers; it is an interpretation of everyday events and activities which provides managers with an understanding of industrial workers. Indeed, managers are not the only ones who hold this view; union officials who use the same everyday life experiences and interpretations accept the myth of scientific management because it justifies their emphasis on higher pay and more fringe benefits rather than changing the work process to make industrial jobs more interesting.

As with all myths, scientific management is an oversimplification. It provides answers to some questions but glosses over others. For example, this myth does not deal with the fact that workers in the new factory and office have little choice about the organization and rewards of their work. They are put to work in organizations that encourage a self-interested and calculating approach to work. Scientific management thus creates a self-fulfilling prophecy in which the assumptions that workers are lazy and only want money are borne out. The assumption that workers need close supervision to work efficiently also receives support within the organization that is set up. What the proponents of scientific management do not deal with is the possibility that a different set of assumptions might lead to a different type of work organization in which high productivity could be achieved without hierarchical and coercive controls.

A second problem with the myth of scientific management is that it does not take account of the ways in which workers resist scientifically oriented managers. One form of resistance is the strike, and workers historically have used this tool to protest abusive uses of scientific management theory (Nelson, 1975). Another form of resistance is the development of informal practices and standards which counter the influence of scientific management. For example, workers may establish their own standards of a fair day's work and resist further productivity even if it hurts them financially (Homans, 1950). Certainly Roy's description of time in the machine shop, cited previously, indicates a way in which workers can resist the monotony of industrial production. A more dramatic way for them to resist scientifically managed work routines is through sabotage. Riverside offers one example, but workers in other industrial settings use it too. In some offices and factories, workers purposely clog machines in order to get a break from their work, even if it costs them money.

Finally, the myth of scientific management does not take account of the many reasons why people work and how their work fits in to their total lives. Men and women, as well as full-time and part-time workers, often differ in the reasons they give for working, and consequently they do not respond in the same ways to the financial incentives of management and union officials (Beynon and Blackburn, 1972). Even persons within the same general category may be quite different in what they expect from work. A woman who is supporting a family, for example, is likely to respond to overtime opportunities differently than a woman who is working so that the family can buy some luxuries. Even the same person may vary in his or her expectations of work at different times of the year. At Riverside, for example, overtime is less desirable during summer, when workers want to spend time out of doors with their families, than in winter, when they feel there is less to do. Finally, this vision of work does not take account of the ways in which ethnic, neighborhood, and family traditions may affect workers' interpretations of work. Certainly, the steelworkers of South Chicago do not respond to the financial incentives of management as isolated individuals pursuing their own personal self-interests; rather, they interpret these incentives in light of a variety of obligations to themselves, their families, and their neighbors. The South Chicago example is also useful in seeing the variety of reasons why people work in factories and offices. Although many work primarily for the money, others combine that desire with an interest in maintaining ethnic or other social ties on the job. For these workers the need for work and its rewards are not as simple as the myth of scientific management indicates.

The Myth of the New Industrial Order

Because of the problems of scientific management theory, the new factory and office often added an emphasis on welfare work in the early days. The assumptions of welfare programs supported management's right to control the work place, but they did not support the views about workers offered by scientific management theories. Instead, they placed more stress on the social and psychological needs of workers. This early welfare emphasis has been picked up by a variety of analysts in this century, including Elton Mayo, who rejected the rabble hypothesis and stressed the need for building meaningful human relations in the industrial work place. One of the most popular theories in management circles today is that of Peter Drucker (1949, 1973), who offers a relatively sophisticated version of this theme in management theory—the *myth of the new industrial order.*

Basic to Drucker's argument is the belief that there is no fundamental conflict of interest between workers and management. The old days of hostility and mutual exploitation are gone, and it is necessary to build new forms of organization that satisfy the basic human needs of workers and the desire of managers for high levels of productivity. Both objectives can best be achieved in large corporations, which have the resources to rationally organize work and workers. A rational organization of work takes account of the workers' real interests and needs, which are more inclusive than simply a desire for money. More important than money are the desires to belong to a close-knit group of workers, to get along with the boss, to be respected by others, and to be given the opportunity to advance based on hard work and achievement. The first assumption of the myth of the new industrial order, then, is that workers need to work for social, psychological, and economic reasons. Should the economic reasons for work disappear, people would still need to work.

Drucker's belief in the existence of social and psychological motives for work, however, does not lead him to abandon all of scientific management theory; rather, he has modified it. The new industrial order is organized as a series of hierarchical organizations within which work is rationally accomplished and evaluated. But the object of rational assessment is to organize work for human beings, not machines. For this reason, Drucker argues, work should involve many different activities from which workers can derive personal satisfaction and build meaningful relationships with others. Satisfaction with work emerges as a direct result of the ways in which managers plan and implement the work process. Although the myth of the new industrial order rejects the scientific management scheme of rewards and punishments, it too assumes that managers are an industrial elite who must direct workers. Implicit in this claim is the belief that workers will shirk their responsibilities if they are not directed by effective managers.

The key to the proper organization of industrial work, then, is the creation of a responsible worker who does not have to be coerced by scientific management techniques. Workers are encouraged to be responsible when clear lines of authority exist to give them a sense of structure in their work activities. Equally important is the building of work groups and roles that give each worker a chance to become personally involved with others and with his or her work activities. Although management must always maintain the right to curb worker excesses and misjudgments, workers should have considerable control over the ways in which they do their jobs, Drucker maintains. To curb workers' tendency toward excess and misjudgment, a "managerial attitude" must be developed among them. Basic to this attitude is the recognition that they have a responsibility to their employer. The workers' main responsibility is the same as that of managers, although they may be paid less and have less respectable work. Workers and managers are thus engaged in a joint enterprise and, as with other teams, it is the obligation of the followers to accept the decisions of the leaders without question. The leaders, after all, are better able than those in lower positions to see the "whole picture."

Because the myth of the new industrial order defines the need to work as multifaceted, the rewards of work are also varied. Work should provide not only adequate income for workers but also opportunities for achieving personal prestige and advancement. Managers have to be open to the abilities and achievements of workers and to reward them appropriately. The personal rewards of work are also linked to its social rewards, because only within work groups is each person given the opportunity to display his or her abilities. Thus, a third major reward of work—besides income and prestige—is that of belonging, which includes identification with both one's work group and the larger organization. One of the benefits of developing a managerial attitude is that all workers can identify with the organization's successes, even if they are not involved in them.

This vision of the new factory and office involves two features that require special note. First, the myth of the new industrial order pictures workers as children who need to be guided from project to project because, although they are well intentioned, they do not always understand what the world is really like. Thus, they must be *made responsible*, and they must also be constantly reminded of management's (parents') better grasp of the situation. Similarly, although workers must be given the opportunity to make their own decisions and develop their abilities, managers must supervise and intervene when things get out of hand. Workers—like children—should also be encouraged to develop friendships among their peers. Unlike the myth of scientific management, which stresses the self-interested and calculating nature of workers, the myth of the new industrial order emphasizes the emotional features of workers. Both myths dehumanize workers because they fail to treat them as full-fledged human beings who are both calculating and emotional, but they do so in different ways. Both myths also justify managerial control, but for different reasons. Scientific managers wish to control workers who are intentionally in conflict with the aims of management, whereas managers who accept the myth of the new industrial order wish to control workers who shirk responsibilities because they do not know any better.

As with scientific management, the myth of the new industrial order is an oversimplification of the everyday operations of new factories and offices. Implicit in the myth is a vision of the modern industrial enterprise as a community of cooperative workers and managers. Riverside provides an appropriate setting for assessing this myth, because it is based on the principles of both progressive management and production. It is clear from the Riverside example that much of Drucker's theory is not achieved in practice. The NWA tries to meet the social and psychological needs of workers through job rotation for donkey workers, but that innovation consists primarily of moving workers from one boring job to another. Certainly the workers themselves do not see any significant opportunities for advancement or development of their individual abilities, because of job rotation. Rather, the majority of workers openly admit that they stay at Riverside because it pays better than other employers in the area.

Drucker's analysis of the organization of industrial work is also problematic. Although Riverside is a hierarchical organization, there is little cooperation between workers and managers. Nor do managers concern themselves with developing responsible workers with a managerial attitude. Rather, they treat workers as obstacles to be overcome, which usually involves manipulation rather than open discussion of the goals of the enterprise. In short, Drucker fails to recognize that even in progressive industrial settings, workers and local managers deal with a limited set of practical, everyday problems. Such general and abstract issues as building a managerial attitude or encouraging responsible workers may interest the highest levels of management, but they are of little concern at the plant level, where both managers and workers must deal with the mundane problems of their work.

The Marxist Myth of the Alienated Worker

Most of the important myths about industrial work reflect a management bias, because they are attempts to understand workers in order to control them, but there are also some myths which are antimanagement. The most important of these are Marxist-inspired theories, which stress the revolutionary potential of industrial workers and their present alienated condition. The *myth of the alienated worker*, as we will refer to this collection of myths, is made up of two parts: a description of present conditions and recommendations of what should be.

In general, Marxists believe that work is one of the most basic and important features of human life, because it is a creative activity through which workers grow personally and develop meaningful relationships with other workers and even nature (Marx, 1832/1964). Within capitalism, however, work is perverted by the employers' sole interest in making money. Thus, the need for work in capitalist society is ultimately reduced to making a living. The organization of capitalist work also reflects the employers' emphasis on the profit motive; large, hierarchical, and coercive organizations are built in order to more effectively exploit workers (Braverman, 1974; Marglin, 1974–1975). Work should be organized in more egalitarian and humanizing ways. The only way to accomplish this is to give workers ownership and control of enterprises. Finally, Marxist analysts of modern work claim that the primary reward of work is income, although work should be organized so that people also receive the rewards of personal and social growth.

Marxists thus tend to blame scientific management for most of the evils of industrial work and seek change to eliminate this dehumanizing way of organizing work. The fact that workers do not always see the need for change indicates the extent to which they are alienated from their work. They do not experience work as an important human activity but as something that they sell in order to make a living. Indeed, alienation from work is so widespread and so widely justified by exploiting employers that workers see that condition as natural; they feel they have no right to complain so long as they have a steady job. An important problem facing the leaders of Marxist-inspired social movements, then, is convincing workers that alienating work is not natural or human and they must organize to change it.

Anyone who has worked in a highly industrialized office or factory knows that much of the Marxist critique is useful in interpreting these work settings. It is difficult to develop a sense of personal achievement or to establish meaningful relations with others when workers are isolated in small spaces like the scientific workers of Riverside. Typists and file clerks are also often isolated, but more by the noise of the office and the requirement that their attention be constantly focused on their machines than by the physical setup of their work place. In such situations it is easy for workers to treat income as the only reward for work.

At the same time that Marxist theory is useful in interpreting the problems of industrial work, it is often applied in such a mechanical way that it becomes an oversimplification. Undoubtedly, many managerial decisions are based on the desire to increase both profits and control over workers, but not every decision. Managers also make decisions out of a desire to protect themselves from the uncertainties that surround them (Kanter, 1977b; Thompson, 1967). Indeed, a major problem in many new offices today is that managers have sometimes become so caught up in the trend to mechanize the office that they have purchased machines merely for the sake of owning more machines; now they must figure out how to use them more effectively in their offices, which may involve more expense if consultants have to be hired to assess the situation (Curley, 1980).

Oversimplification also results because Marx ignored the fact that the definition of profit, efficiency, and control can vary from situation to situation. One source of variation is the time span that is used. Two managers may come to very different conclusions because one sees profit in the short run and the other looks at it as a long-run goal. Generally speaking, those who apply Marxist theory in mechanical ways have a tendency to unskeptically accept managers' claims that they always make rational, hard-nosed decisions that are based on a systematic consideration of the "facts." The facts, however, are human creations and may therefore change from situation to situation.

In a similar way, Marxist analysts oversimplify the estrangement of persons from their work. Workers are seldom fully alienated from their jobs. When machine shop workers divide the day into banana time, Coke time, and window time, they are taking control of part of their workday, and they cannot be regarded as passive instruments of production that are manipulated by managers (Roy, 1959–1960). Similarly, the steelworkers of South Chicago do not fit the image of the alienated worker, because they interpret their work within the context of a variety of ethnic, neighborhood, and work group interests. To argue that these workers are alienated is to dehumanize them by denying the active ways in which they influence their work. When the myth of the alienated worker is taken to its extreme, then, it becomes the radical counterpart to the myth of scientific management: both assume that the values of self-interest and rationality always dominate the actions of workers and managers.

CONCLUSION

The definition of industrial work used in this chapter is broad, because there are many different industrial situations. All industrial settings share some basic features, however. All industrial work is organized around machines, workers are assigned specialized work roles, and they are evaluated bureaucratically. But despite these similarities, there are differences. Some work places are more mechanized or specialized than others. There are also important variations in the social realities of industrial settings based on the organization of work and such outside factors as ethnicity and sex. Finally, industrial work is associated with a number of myths which explain and justify the actions of managers and radicals. Three of the most important have been discussed in this chapter.

An alternative explanation is the humanistic approach. Basic to this approach is the assumption that industrial workers define their need to work in a variety of ways. Some work primarily for money, whereas others stress personal growth, prestige, or the opportunity to relate to co-workers. Indeed, it is possible to define the need for work through some combination of each of these factors.

A second feature of a humanistic approach to work is the recognition that both managers and workers are involved in the creation of work organization. Sometimes—for example, during contract negotiations—managers and workers form united fronts that do battle with each other over specific issues. At other times, however, managers and workers may differ radically with members of their own group. Thus, the policies of high-level officials at ChemCo are often transformed, if not contradicted, by the local managers at Riverside, who are trying to deal with their own everyday problems. Both Riverside and the steel mills of South Chicago also indicate the extent to which workers differ among themselves in their goals and their interpretations of the work world. There is, then, no single form of organization of the factory or office, because it is constantly changing in response to the interpretations and actions of managers and workers, who are themselves responding to a variety of influences and interests. If the humanistic approach is accepted, then the rewards of work must be seen as variable because workers and work situations vary so much. In brief, a humanistic approach to industrial work recognizes the existence of multiple social realities.

Many of the popular myths and other features of industrial work are being modified today in light of an international phenomenon known as the *enpowerment movement*. This movement supports greater worker control of the work place; indeed, in some cases workers have become the owners of the factories in which they work. The general nature of this movement and its implications for industrial work will be discussed in chapter eight. But because the movement seeks to change the organization of other types of work as well, we must first look at these other work forms.

Chapter Four

PROFESSIONAL WORK

Although there have been professionals and professional activities in England and the United States since at least the eighteenth century, the early professions bear little resemblance to those of today. In England, for example, the precursors of contemporary professions were the "liberal professions" of "divinity, physic, and law" (Reader, 1966). Indeed, the designation of these professions as "liberal" is useful in setting them off from their contemporary counterparts, because they represent a solution to a problem unique to that time—specifically, what to do with the younger sons of the gentry who were not needed on the family estates. One solution was to educate them in the liberal tradition of upper-class English society, which was mainly an exposure to the classics; upon completion of their schooling, they were then expected to take their rightful places in the world. Thus, the early English professionals were not trained to deal with the practical problems of religion, health, or law; rather, they were trained to be aristocratic gentlemen. While they received fees for professional services, their main sources of income were subsidies provided by the family, church, and state.

The pattern varied somewhat in the United States, although the early profesions were just as different from contemporary ones. The medical professionals of the colonies, for example, were private entrepreneurs who practiced medicine in openly competitive ways (Stevens, 1971). The common practice of training apprentices reveals the businesslike nature of that profession. The usual arrangement was for an aspiring physician to become apprenticed to an established physician, who would train the novice as a part of his ongoing practice. Such an approach to recruitment and training gave rise to three major problems (Stevens, 1971).

First, the practice of medicine in early America was not standardized, so that the quality and nature of medical treatment varied greatly. Apprenticeship merely added to the problem because it was an unstandardized training process in which the teachers typically emphasized their own idiosyncratic techniques and theories. A second problem was the lack of specialization in medicine. Again apprenticeship added to the problem because most teacher-physicians were "general practitioners" who treated whatever ills their patients had, which meant that apprentices primarily learned "general or domestic medicine." Finally, early medicine in the United States was intensely competitive because of the oversupply of physicians, a condition largely attributable to the uncontrolled nature of the recruitment and training process. Indeed, one of the most important characteristics of contemporary medicine in the United States is the low number of physicians relative to the general population, and this reversal of the earlier physician-population ratio is directly traceable to the professionalization of American medicine during the nineteenth and twentieth centuries. Similarly, because of professionalization, the aristocratic patterns of early English medicine are gone.

Although there are clear social, cultural, and historical differences between English and American medicine, the professionalization of both has resulted in a qualitatively different medical occupation from those that existed earlier. It is therefore possible to identify some underlying similarities between the two cases. These underlying similarities form the core of the professionalization process that has occurred in medicine and some other occupations, although they are not all equally professionalized. In the next section we will consider the historical process of professionalization, which will be followed by discussions of the social realities of professional work and myths associated with it. Before turning to these issues, however, it is important to define professional work.

The term "professional work" is not so easily defined as peasant or industrial work, because it is used in many different ways in modern society. Some people claim that a professional is a person who is paid for his or her work. Thus, we divide baseball players into those who are professionals and amateurs. The word is also often used to indicate the occupational and personal respectability of the worker. This vision of professional work has been important historically, because a major concern of those seeking professional standing has been to improve their own respectability and that of their occupations. Aspects of both of these popular uses of the term "professional work" are found in the definition used in this chapter, but they are not treated as the defining features of such work.

The definition of *professional work* used in this chapter stresses three features. First, it is organized around the provision of services to clients or customers. This characteristic separates professional from factory work, devoted to the manufacture of material goods. On the other hand, the definition includes a wide variety of services and work settings. The physician who works alone in a private practice and a social worker who works in a large bureaucratic organization, for example, are both engaged in providing services to others. A second feature of professional work is that members of the occupation claim to have special knowledge that allows them to better see and understand the problems of others. As one analyst notes, "They profess to know better than others the nature of certain matters, and to know better than their clients what ails them or their affairs" (Hughes, 1963: 656). Because professionals claim to know more than their clients, the professional-client relationship is not one of passively providing services to a customer who is always right. Rather, the professional takes an active part in determining the problem and its solution. Finally, professional work is distinguished by the occupational group's claim to special knowledge and the public's acceptance of it. Many occupational groups seek such recognition, but not all of them achieve it, and it is possible to lose recognition because of changing public perceptions and government policies (Jamous and Peloille, 1970; Ritzer, 1975). For this reason, the professionalization process is important, because it is the process through which occupational groups seek and maintain their professional standing.

THE TRANSFORMATION OF PROFESSIONALISM

Although the term "professional" has a long history, it has been used to describe a variety of kinds of people and work orientations. Over time, however, the concept of professional work has come to be related to the values of the urban middle classes. Today, many past assumptions about the unique knowledge of professionals are being challenged and new definitions of professionalism are arising.

Origins of Professionalization in England and the United States

The professionalization process in nineteenth-century England was initiated by the sons of traders, craftsmen, and merchants who were interested in two major goals (Reader, 1966). First, they were highly committed to their work, especially to providing a high-quality service to the public. Within the existing occupational arrangement of English society, however, middle-class workers were subordinated to the sons of the aristocracy, who were often more interested in maintaining their elite life styles than in serving the public. Given the professional training process and its emphasis on classical knowledge, even those professionals who were interested in providing the public with services had problems because they were largely incapable of supplying them. Indeed, the middle-class supporters of professionalization had previously taken advantage of this incompetence to carve out lower-ranking occupations that provided the services that the early professionals could not. A second concern of the middle-class reformers was to raise their own status. Because they could not compete with their aristocratic counterparts in demanding prestige based on birth, the reformers emphasized occupational achievement as the only legitimate basis for prestige. Thus, the professionalization movement combined a desire for public service with the desire for personal gain.

One of the major tools used by the English professionalizers was the establishment of "paper qualifications" for full professional recognition (Reader, 1966). These qualifications took three major forms: (1) formal educational requirements, (2) formal examinations, and (3) licensing. The establishment of educational qualifications was fundamental to professionalization, because it involved a direct challenge to the assumptions and practices associated with aristocratic training. As we mentioned above, the aristocratic professionals received a classical education, involving the study of classical languages, literature, and mathematics. The curriculum gave little attention to the literature on problems of law, medicine, or theology. It was assumed that this information could be obtained through personal study. The professionalizers, on the other hand, stressed a practical education organized around the problems of professional work. Thus, education was redefined as preparation for professional work, not for an aristocratic life style. Related to the professionalizers' demand for a change in the training process was their demand for the development of formal examinations and licensing as screening mechanisms to determine who should be accorded professional standing and who should be excluded. They succeeded in passing laws such as the Apothecaries Act of 1815, which gave the Society of Apothecaries power to set educational requirements for the profession, to examine for proficiency, and on the basis of examinations to grant or withhold licenses (Reader, 1966).

The professions in England, then, grew out of social movements against the aristocracy by middle-class workers who wanted to raise occupational standards and their own status. One of the most important developments of these movements was the rise of professional associations that were used not only to pursue the collective interests of the membership but to control the actions of members as well. Indeed, the associations acted as private governments in which licensing, though not a function of the state itself, was backed by the state's authority (Reader, 1966).

With the achievement of these successes, many of the reformers lost their revolutionary zeal. Not only did the new professionals become politically and economically conservative, but they consciously acted to emulate the life styles of the aristocrats they had fought so intently. This outcome is understandable, given the social backgrounds of the reformers and their goals. The professionalization movement was not initiated by people with a new vision for their society, but by those primarily concerned with improving the quality of the services offered in their occupations and with improving their own social positions. When these goals were achieved, the reformers had no reason to continue their political agitation for change, although their professional associations continued to engage in political activities to protect their newly acquired rights and privileges.

A similar pattern emerged in the United States during the nineteenth century, although the reformers were not acting against an established aristocracy (Johnson, 1974; Wiebe, 1967). As in England, the initiators of the professionalization movement here were middle-class people interested in improving the quality of human services and in improving their own social positions. Indeed, altruism and self-interest were so intertwined in the professionalization movement that it was necessary to reconcile their contradictions. One of the most important reconcilers, and one of the most ardent supporters of professionalization, was Mark Twain, who wrote many stories attacking the pursuit of money as a major human goal (Bledstein, 1976). However, if a person made money while being of service to others, then the immorality of pursuing wealth was decreased. Thus, as one commentator notes, "By portraying heroes whose professional code of behavior transcended a concern with payment for their services, middle-class culture prevented people from believing that they were working for mere money" (Bledstein, 1976: 43).

The professionalization movements in England and the United States, then, were similar, emphasizing social service and personal interest. They were also similar in their drive for licensing and other forms of occupational regulation. In both cases, this goal was achieved through professional associations that reflected the interests of both professional practitioners and educators. There is at least one other way in which the professionalization movements of the United States and England were similar and that is in their common acceptance of the basic tenets of the culture of professionalism. Burton Bledstein (1976), in his analysis of the development of higher education in the United States, offers the most comprehensive description of this culture. It is to this description that we now turn.

The Culture of Professionalism

The *culture of professionalism* stresses eight major themes that may be used to both justify professionalization and provide individual professionals and their associations with a way of seeing the world. Those themes are:

1. Individualism
2. The division of the world along intellectual lines
3. Control by the professional and client passivity
4. Alarmism
5. The correspondence between the public interest and those of the profession
6. Individual upward mobility based on competition and achievement
7. Professional, political, and social conservation
8. A professional way of life

Like their English counterparts, the supporters of professionalization in the United States rejected traditional and aristocratic standards for judging the moral and social worth of individuals. They believed in the radical idea (by nineteenth-century standards) that each individual should be independent and responsible for his or her own destiny. Such a value was clearly self-serving in the case of the English professionalization movement, because the reformers were interested in breaking down the old aristocratic traditions, but it was also a useful value for reformers in the United States to adopt. It helped justify such related professional concerns as the development of careers and the building of a distinctive professional life style.

Professionalization also fostered a division of the world along intellectual lines. It did this by emphasizing the need to approach the world through human reason and not through tradition. One consequence was a search for general theoretical principles that could become the basis for both understanding and controlling the social and natural worlds—an approach that contrasts with the perspective of craftspeople, who typically emphasize tradition and trial and error in their work. The development of a theoretical approach meant that not everyone has equal access to professional knowledge. Rather, the professional is an expert who understands aspects of life that are mystifying to others.

The emphasis on intellectual understanding of the world leads to a third element of the culture of professionalism—a belief in professional authority and client passivity. If professional knowledge were equally available to all segments of the society, then such a relationship would be unnecessary, but for a number of reasons, this is not the case. Consequently, it is necessary for the client to have faith in the professional and be passive in their relationship. This rule applies whether the client is an individual or the whole society.

One of the ways in which professional authority may be increased is through the creation of fear and uncertainty in clients. To be sure, individual professionals can cultivate client dependence by exaggerating their problems, but the tendency toward alarmism in the professions goes deeper than this. Alarmism is encouraged by the nature of the problems professionals deal with. They are usually problems which the public little understands and which individuals experience as crises. Death, illness, legal actions, and economic devastation, for example, are all events of individual importance and areas of professional work. The tendency to alarmism is also facilitated by the fact that professionals are given almost exclusive authority to identify problems in the society. Often the result is a general orientation which encourages professionals to see many human problems as needing their attention. Professional military personnel, for example, tend to see political and social events as threats to the security of the country that necessitate either immediate military action or a commitment to increased military preparedness (Abrahamsson, 1972). In part, this tendency reflects the immediate interest that professional military officers have in expanding military problems and organization, but the issue involves more than this. It also involves the development of a professional mentality that encourages professionals to see human conditions as problematic and cause for alarm.

Alarmism is thus related to the twin goals of improving social service and furthering self-interest that gave rise to the social movement for professionalization. These two factors are also related to the fifth element of the culture of professionalism: the tendency to treat the interests of the public and the profession as the same. The licensing and educational requirements that emerged from the professionalization movement, for example, were justified on the grounds that they increased the quality of service to clients, but they also increased the prestige and income of those who qualified as professionals. Sometimes the claim that public and professional interests correspond is obviously a sham. For example, in the 1890s physicians rejected a government effort to manufacture and give (free of charge) diphtheria antitoxin to the general public; instead, on the pretext that private enterprise's antitoxin was purer and more effective than the state's, they purchased the serum from commercial companies and sold it to their patients (Bledstein, 1976). In other cases, as with the educational and licensing efforts of the early professionalizers, the question of whether professionals are pursuing the public interest or their own is less clear. Because such cases exist, and because professionalism tends to foster alarmism, even public-spirited professionals are likely to see a correspondence between the interests of the profession and those of the public.

The sixth element of the culture of professionalism—the value placed on individual upward mobility based on competition and achievement—is also justified on other than purely self-interested grounds. The relationship between this value and the desires of middle-class reformers to increase their social and economic positions is self-evident. The English reformers clearly had an interest in changing the rules that relegated all nonaristocrats to subordinate positions, but so did the reformers in the United States. In both countries reformers encouraged this value by emphasizing the desirability of having a career. Indeed, the transformation of the word "career" in the nineteenth century illustrates the extent to which the emerging culture of professionalism emphasized individualism and upward mobility. Originally, the word referred to racing, particularly horse and falcon races. During the nineteenth century the term became associated with people who were in competition (or a race with) one another with respect to achievement. A career was something that an individual consciously chose and pursued over the course of a lifetime. The days in which a person such as Ben Franklin could dabble in a number of occupations and receive widespread respect and recognition were over. Now the respectable worker selected a line of work and stuck to it. In return, the professional could look forward to increased income and social standing both within the profession and the community. Indeed, it is within the context of this meaning of the word that the liberating impact of the professions must be seen: not only does professional knowledge require that the individual give up traditional ways of conceptualizing and treating problems, but the act of joining a profession may require that the individual give up old social ties and obligations. Professionalization thus requires the development of a new perspective, new skills, and new goals. All of these lead to upward social mobility and to liberation through personal achievement.

Although the blind pursuit of a career could be interpreted as nothing more than blatant self-interest, the professionalizers did not see it that way. Rather, they felt that society benefitted as well from their personal liberation through an improved quality of life. In exchange for that benefit, professionals deemed it appropriate that they should reap the social rewards of wealth, prestige, and power that other, less altruistic segments of the society enjoyed. Thus, self-interest and social service remain inextricably linked within the culture of professionalism.

It is evident from the types of services offered by professionals, particularly during the nineteenth century, that the public interest and the "proper life" are defined in very conservative ways. These are the seventh and eighth elements of the culture of professionalism. In part, the conservative tendencies of the professions show up in the ceremonialism of professional training and work. For example, professionals use titles in addressing colleagues in public, wear special clothing and insignia which separate them from other workers, and hold special ceremonial events (such as professional meetings and conventions) to encourage members to develop a sense of professional community based on their shared values and interests. But the professions are conservative in the deeper sense that professionals frequently lack interest in creating significant change. That conservatism arises because the culture of professionalism involves a commitment to values and interests that assume the legitimacy of the social institutions within which professionals work. Thus, efforts aimed at destroying or significantly altering existing institutions are often treated as radical and dangerous. The American Medical Association, for example, has historically opposed almost all changes in financing health care, from the early private insurance programs to recent government-financed programs (Rayack, 1967). Under some circumstances this tendency to preserve the status quo extends to the protection of life styles that are similar to those of professionals. In the 1890s, for example, physicians refused to quarantine their middle-class patients suffering from tuberculosis, whereas they readily quarantined the poor. It was assumed that disease thrived among the poor, who live in dirty surroundings, but respectable people could not possibly be carriers of disease.

The type of person and life style associated with professionalization also reinforced conservative tendencies. As noted above, the early professionalizers were liberated people who had been freed from the confines of traditional roles, relationships, and perspectives. But they were not free to become anything they wanted; rather, becoming a professional meant acceptance of the values of self-discipline, independence, self-reliance, and, most importantly, dedication to a career. Thus, the professionalizers were only liberated from the values and interests of traditional life. Not only were they tied to the values and interests of the emergent middle class, they were its best representatives.

The New Professional Model

We have seen that the rise of the contemporary professions has involved a process through which members of some service occupations consciously seek to improve both the quality of their services and their own social, political, and economic positions in the society. Those that have been most successful in these efforts enjoy great individual and collective prestige. The best example of a professional occupation is medicine, which is generally accorded high prestige in modern society. Indeed, medicine is often taken by members of professions and by sociologists studying them as the best-developed representative of the *professional model*. The term refers to a set of occupational characteristics which are assumed to be important sources of creating public and government support for the occupational members' claim that they should have the right to organize and control their work (Freidson, 1970, 1973; Johnson, 1972). Several characteristics have been identified in the literature on the professions, but one of the most influential papers argues that the professional model is based on a systematic body of theory, professional authority, sanction by the community, a regulative code of ethics, and a professional culture (Greenwood, 1957). Each of these characteristics is also consistent with the culture of professionalism.

The emphasis on a systematic body of theory is directly linked to the rational emphasis in the culture of professionalism. It is assumed that a central feature of professional work is the professionals' great insight into the problems of clients, an insight derived from absorbing the occupation's body of knowledge. The characteristic of professional authority derives from the professionals' special knowledge, which legitimizes their control over clients. The third characteristic of the professional model, sanction by the community, points to the importance of public and governmental support in maintaining professional control. Because of the professionals' greater knowledge and success in dealing with problem areas, it is argued that they should be allowed to police themselves and they should also be granted a monopoly in dealing with their problems. The fourth characteristic, a regulative code of ethics, is important because it acts as a check on potential abuse owing to the professional monopoly. It is claimed that the code of ethics sets standards for judging professional competence and for protecting the public interest. Another important check on the abusive potential of a professional monopoly is the culture found in professional work places and schools. This culture provides members with values, norms, and symbols for evaluating each other.

There are a number of problems with the professional model as it has developed out of the nineteenth century and is used today. Indeed, sociologists have provided a number of insightful critiques of the professional model (Daniels, 1973; Johnson, 1972; Leiberman, 1970; Ritzer, 1975; Roth, 1974). For the purposes of this chapter, however, the most important problem with the professional model is that it does not take account of the diversity and complexity of professional work. Many occupations which claim to be professions, such as social work and library science, are not thought of as prestigious by the public, nor are they seen as arising from a special body of knowledge. Establishing professional authority and obtaining community sanction are very difficult under these circumstances. Another source of diversity in the professions is the work setting. The problems and opportunities for solo practitioners are quite different from those of professionals working in large bureaucratic organizations. Indeed, each may offer differing pressures for violating the professional model. For the bureaucratic employee the pressure may come from administrators seeking organizational goals that violate professional standards. For the solo practitioner an important problem is satisfying clients who may want services that violate professional standards (Freidson, 1970; Rothstein, 1973). The authority of the professional is greatly undermined when clients who are the only source of livelihood threaten to take their business elsewhere.

Not only are professional work settings diverse, but the members of any profession seldom have the same interests or points of view; rather, the professions are made up of segments (Bucher and Strauss, 1961). Some segments may be opposed to professionalization, whereas others are for it. In police work, for example, many established, older officers find the current efforts at professionalization ludicrous, and they resist the testing and educational requirements ("paper qualifications") associated with it (Niederhoffer, 1969). Even within occupations where most members are committed to professionalization, there are segments which see the professional model differently and engage in conflict over their views (Bucher, 1962).

Finally, the professional model does not take account of the ways in which clients can influence professional decision making. Sometimes these efforts receive wide publicity. When women protest their treatment by gynecologists, parents protest teaching practices, or welfare recipients protest their treatment by social workers, clients are attempting—often successfully—to influence professional practices (Haug and Sussman, 1969a, 1969b; Piven and Cloward, 1977). But the influence of clients does not stop with organized groups; it can occur on an everyday basis as well. A problem facing many users of hospital emergency rooms is the long wait that they often must face before seeing a doctor and being treated. Regular users of these facilities may get quicker service because they have learned the work habits and classifications of the professional staff (Roth, 1972). For example, they know the time when the emergency room is least busy and come at those times. They also know that if they add a complaint about chest pains and other indicators of heart problems to their symptoms they will be given faster treatment and will not be punished for their ruse later.

In sum, the professional model has emerged out of the interests and interpretations of a segment of modern society—the middle class. Members have created an image of professional practice that stresses the homogeneity of professionals, their authority, their special knowledge, and their desire to place the public interest above self-interest. Although this image is an oversimplification, it is still presented to the public and students as an accurate reflection of the diverse settings and activities which make up contemporary professional work. The ways in which the model oversimplifies will become evident in the next section, which deals with some of the ways in which social reality is created within professional work places. Before turning to that issue however, we should summarize the differences between the old and new views of the professions.

The Old and New Professional Realities Compared

The move from the liberal professions to the contemporary professions was accompanied by changes in the sources of professional realities. Table 4-1 summarizes differences in the work-related timetables and communities of the two groups.

The most important feature of the liberal professions was their intimate connection with the British elite. Not only were professional workers recruited from the ranks of the elite, but they committed themselves to maintaining an aristocratic life style. For this reason, their work-related timetables are discontinuous, reflecting the variety of activities and commitments in the aristocrats' lives. Work was only one commitment, and it was often given a lower priority than other commitments. It was social standing and not work which was central to the identities of these professionals.

The contemporary professions are different in an obvious way because of the central position of work in the lives of modern professionals. The work-related timetables of contemporary professionals are based on activities in the work place and the continuous pursuit of a career. The pursuit of a career is continuous because, unlike horse and falcon races, there is no finish line for professional achievement. The timetables of work places vary based on the way in which these places are organized. Some professionals experience their work as a continuous flow of clients or activities, whereas others may experience their work discon-

Table 4-1 • Sources of Professional Realities

Historical Class of Professional	*Work-Related Timetables*	*Work-Related Communities*
Liberal Professions	Diachronic: based on the continuous processes of living out an aristocratic life style	Enduring: based on enduring relations with other members of aristocratic British society
Contemporary Professions	Diachronic: based on the continuous or discontinuous activities in the work place and the continuous process of pursuing a career	Mixed: based on varying relations with clients, the public, government officials, training schools, coworkers, members of one's professional segment, and members of professional associations

tinuously. Teachers, for example, often have the summer off from teaching and, although they may use the time to return to college, that is a different kind of activity from teaching. Theirs is a very different schedule from those of many social workers, physicians, lawyers, and nurses, who may have busy and slow times during the year but who are continuously involved in similar activities the year round.

The work-related communities of contemporary professionals are also quite varied. Unlike members of the early liberal professions, who had enduring relations only with other aristocrats, contemporary professionals have a wide range of relationships with others. Some professionals have fleeting relations with clients and colleagues, whereas others are involved in enduring relationships with these people. In general, the major sources of professional communities include relations with clients, the public, government officials, officials in professional schools, coworkers (professional colleagues and other workers), members of one's professional segment, and members of professional associations. Which of these relationships are enduring, shifting, or fleeting varies, but they may all foster a professional consciousness of kind.

Although the solo practitioner in medicine has historically been used as the model of professional practice, this type of professional is becoming atypical. Increasingly, professional work occurs in organizations where various types of professionals work together. With greater regularity, physicians, for example, are found working in clinics, various types of joint practices, and hospitals. Indeed, solo practitioners are often finding that their interests are quite different from those of the organizationally based professionals. These emerging features of contemporary professional work are important aspects of the social realities of such workers, and they are central to the discussion in the next section.

THE SOCIAL REALITIES OF PROFESSIONAL WORKERS

The social realities of contemporary professional workers are best studied through examples. Here we will present two that depict different aspects of professional work. The first example, Cedarview, is a residential treatment center for emotionally disturbed children (Buckholdt and Gubrium, 1979a, 1979b). It is generally regarded to be one of the finest centers in the city in which it is located, and it employs or uses as consultants a variety of professionals, including social workers, child-care workers, special education teachers, a speech therapist, psychologists, and a psychiatrist (Buckholdt and Gubrium, 1979a). Cedarview provides an opportunity both for observing the ways in which professionals use theoretical and everyday knowledge to create reality and for viewing the impact of clients on professionals. The second example looks at medical practice and, more specifically, at *health maintenance organizations* (*HMOs*), which are health-care programs intended to offer medical services that are more comprehensive, of better quality, and lower in cost than those offered in other medical practices. This example will show the ways in which professionals respond to government programs based on their self-interests. It will also point to the diversity of professional interests in many communities. The research from which this example is taken was a study of health care professionals' responses to HMOs (Miller, 1976; Miller and Warriner, 1980a, 1980b).

Social Realities at Cedarview

Although there are differences among the professionals who work at Cedarview, they share some general problems that set them apart from the children found there. It is possible, then, to describe Cedarview as made up of two major social realities: professional realities and client (children's) realities. Each of these realities arises out of different practical everyday problems and different types of knowledge. For the professionals at Cedarview three major problems help determine their social realities. The first is the maintenance of order within the school, the residences, and the other major settings of the treatment center. In part, their concern is similar to that of parents, teachers, and others who deal with children on a regular basis and assume that children need direction and discipline in order to get things done. However, at Cedarview the concern is heightened because the children are emotionally disturbed. They are therefore looked upon as potentially troublesome at all times and not subject to the same types of personal controls as other children. A second and related problem of the professionals at Cedarview is the evaluation of the children. Because the children are at Cedarview to be treated, two ongoing tasks for professional workers are the identification of each child's problem and the evaluation of the effectiveness of treatment programs. Finally, the professional staff must deal with the problem of justifying their programs, because funding for them is largely obtained from government sources and most of the children in the program are referred by the local welfare department. Should the government lose faith in the programs of Cedarview, it could be dramatically changed. The administration, for example, would have to seek alternative funding and find new sources of clients. For this reason, there is great concern for gathering numerical data which can be used to evaluate Cedarview's programs. Much of these data are created as the children are treated and evaluated.

The children at Cedarview have many characteristics in common. Most are boys, ranging in age from six to fourteen years, who come from low-income families. Most have come to the attention of welfare officials because teachers or parents perceive them as troublemakers who need help. Based on various files describing their troublemaking activities, they have been classified as emotionally disturbed and in need of help. A general feature of the social reality of the children, then, is their categorization as emotionally disturbed. But unlike the professionals, the children experience that reality as a label which has been applied to them, not as a general condition that afflicts them and others in society. Still, what the professionals think is important to them. Almost all the things which concern the professionals are of concern to the children because the decisions and actions of the professionals have a direct impact on the children's everyday lives. Certainly, the ways in which order is maintained and evaluations are done are critical to the children. In addition, the everyday lives of the children are affected by their relations with each other in school and the residential center, at play, and in other settings. These relationships are not experienced in the same ways by the children and professionals; indeed, many aspects of these relationships are hidden from the professionals.

Although the professional workers assume that emotional disturbance is a condition that exists independent of the interpretations of people, everyday life at Cedarview is largely organized around its discovery. The process of discovery involves regular negotiations among professionals about the activities of the children, who are sometimes able to influence the decisions and interpretations of the professionals. The process of discovering emotional disturbance also involves the major everyday problems of professionals and children alike. Emotional disturbance is not discovered independent of the desire of professionals to maintain order, evaluate children, and justify their programs—a fact best seen by looking at the ways social realities are created at Cedarview through the interpretation of tests and the "acting out" behavior of the children, in treatment, and during "staffings."

Because emotional disturbance is looked upon as a condition that can be discovered through "objective" tests, a great deal of professional work involves giving intelligence and achievement tests to measure the abilities of the children. The professionals assume that such tests yield clear-cut results under ideal conditions, though they do not think of Cedarview as ideal. Rather, they see a number of factors as sources of problems, the most important of which is that the children are emotionally disturbed and therefore incapable of always taking the exams properly. Consequently, they spend a great deal of time interpreting test scores. Various professionals often get together to interpret the same scores. Timmy is an example. Based on his high achievement scores a social worker recommends that he be discharged from Cedarview, but he is not discharged because other professionals interpret his high scores differently. The reinterpretation occurs in the following way:

> The teacher points out that the child's achievement scores, while high and improved from a year ago, "don't tell you what his real level really is because I know that from working with him on a daily basis in the classroom." She continues, "Why he got those unusually high scores, I don't know. . . . Maybe he cheated or something. That's not beyond him. You all know that. He's a real con artist." Several of those in attendance nod or comment on the child's deceitful cunning (Gubrium and Buckholdt, 1979: 129).

Ultimately, Timmy's achievement scores were changed to reflect a more realistic level. These scores were entered in his file, where they became a major source of knowledge and interpretation for others, such as psychiatrists and administrators, who often make their decisions based on the contents of the children's files.

Interpretation is also evident in the classification of the children's behavior as "acting out." This is a term which includes a variety of trivial and serious offenses, but all of them involve some degree of disruption of routine at Cedarview. Whether a disruption is interpreted as acting out or not depends on the point of view of the professional and the problems with which he or she must deal. An example is "being on the run." A child may be seen as being on the run any time that the professional staff does not know his or her whereabouts, whether the child leaves the Cedarview grounds or is simply missing while on the grounds. Being on the run is therefore a loosely defined term, since some children are missing for hours and not defined as such, whereas others may be treated as on the run even when they are hiding nearby. The everyday problems of professionals help to account for the looseness of the term. If being missing disrupts routines or makes the work of the professionals difficult in some other way, then the chances of being classified as on the run are greater. Reginald, for example, hid in the kitchen of his cottage and refused to come out of hiding to go to class when the cottage worker (Black) called to him and threatened to treat him as on the run. Ten minutes later he emerged from his hiding place, and this dialog occurred:

> REGINALD: Ha, fooled you. I was in there all the time.
> BLACK: The joke's on you. You're on the run. Now get to class.
> REGINALD: I ain't on the run. I was here, right in there.
> BLACK: Too bad. I gave you a chance, but you didn't take it.

REGINALD: Hell, that ain't fair. Now I may really go on the run and take Andre with me (Buckholdt and Gubrium, 1979a: 100).

The practical problems of everyday life at Cedarview, then, influence the way in which the behavior of the children is interpreted. If Reginald should actually leave the Cedarview grounds to get even with the cottage worker, then his file would indicate two episodes of acting out (emotional disturbance) without also noting the related conditions. Other forms of acting out are also treated and classified in this way. "Blowing up," for example, refers to children who seemingly go berserk and are totally out of control. Very often these episodes are preceded by conflicts among the children, and the child who blows up may simply be expressing frustration at being teased, being bullied, or having jokes played on him or her. The professional only sees the frustration, which appears to be totally irrational and indicative of the deep-seated emotional disturbance of the child.

It is possible, however, to overstate the professionals' power in dealing with the children. Certainly, the professionals do not see themselves as sinister. Rather, they see conformity to the rules and practices of the facility as an indicator of emotional health and classify children who do not conform as disturbed. Similarly, the professionals often temper their threats when they fill out files or make reports. Timmy's episode of being on the run, for example, was not reported by the cottage worker because it was too trivial.

From the viewpoint of the children, however, threats and use of authority are a major problem. They may give rise to feelings of injustice because the children feel abused. For example, Timmy, who assumes that his offense has been reported, may well cry injustice. But the children, far from being passive, can control their fates to some degree at Cedarview. They know, for example, which members of the staff will listen to complaints and which will not. They also know that many staff members forget to watch the clock when a child is told to stand in the corner. They can sometimes shorten their stay in the corner by pointing out that they have served their time before the time is up. As with the professional staff, the children are also human beings who attempt to deal actively with their everyday problems. In some aspects of life at Cedarview, however, children are excluded, and in these areas the interpretations of the professionals are more important. One example has already been noted: the interpretation of test scores. Children are also excluded from consultation during treatment and staffings.

The dominant treatment technique at Cedarview is *behavior modification*, which attempts to change specific observable behaviors through the use of rewards and punishments (Buckholdt and Gubrium, 1980).

Children who do what they are supposed to do receive points, which can be exchanged for rewards at other times. The actual giving of points is not so simple as that, however, because professionals often take account of a child's attitude. A child who conforms but has a "bad attitude" may thus not be given as many points as other children. The professionals also intervene to encourage an event. For example, children may be given large amounts of liquids so that they will have to urinate, and the professional sees to it that they use the bathroom. They can then be rewarded, although they did not really make a choice. Equally important are the evaluations of treatment programs. Behavior modification treatment requires baselining, that is, measurement of the behavior prior to treatment so that progress at a later date can be calculated. The baseline assigned a child is largely a matter of professional discretion, and it is not uncommon for a staff member to raise a baseline measure because the child was not "acting out" to the degree that the professional expected. The justification is that the professional knows what the child is really like from everyday life experiences with him or her. Finally, the behaviors selected for change are negotiated among the professionals. Teachers, for example, are reluctant to count anything which disrupts their classroom routine. In addition, the definition of behavior is problematic, because many behaviors are not so easily observed as the textbooks indicate. For example, what does teasing consist of? In one baselining effort at Cedarview, a child was defined as teasing "if he hits, touches, makes faces or negative comments, or does any namecalling involving other children" (Buckholdt and Gubrium, 1979a: 137). Using this definition, the professionals did not count a child as teasing when he made an obscene gesture at his teacher. Thus, treatment is not just a way of dealing with the children's problems, but a way of dealing with the everyday problems of the professional workers as well. Sometimes the major concern of professional workers is with protecting their usual work routines and at other times with creating standardized and "scientific" definitions of the behavior of the children.

A final area in which the social realities of Cedarview are created is in *staffings*. These are conferences of the professional staff which may involve a variety of people and issues. The most important feature of staffings is that they are occasions for building common professional definitions of reality. When Timmy's achievement scores were discussed and changed, for example, the discussion at the staffing resulted in a shared view of his ability and problems. Even the social worker who initially wanted him discharged ended up agreeing with the others at the staffing. Staffings are thus times of negotiation among the participants. Three of the most important features of this negotiation are "filling in," "realizing," and "glossing."

Filling in refers to the tendency of staff members to create links between different sources of information. Such links make sense of the information by imposing on it a broad theory or explanation. Because the theory is not entirely justifiable based on the information available, it often involves creating new facts about the child. *Realizing* occurs when the participants come to see (realize) the true nature of a case. The movement from considering possible explanations to realizing is most easily seen in the language of staffing participants. For example, an evaluation may move from talk about a child's possible manipulative personality traits to talk about his manipulative personality (Buckholdt and Gubrium, 1979a). But realizing is often threatened by the presence of contradictory evidence. Thus, a final aspect of the reality creation process in staffings is *glossing*, the practice of dealing with contradictory information by explaining it away as a unique case or by making it irrelevant in some other way.

Because filling in, realizing, and glossing occur within the context of the ongoing negotiation in staffings, it is difficult to appreciate their importance without seeing how they emerge in concrete situations. Jaber Gubrium and David Buckholdt provide an example in the following description of how one problem was realized, glossed, and filled in:

> Discussion [at the staffing] centers on Ronnie Bertram's eye contact. To have eye contact is to direct one's eyes at whomever one is interacting with and to maintain eye contact over the course of interaction. Children who cannot maintain eye contact are considered to be maladapted and are put on programs to improve it.
>
> A social worker addresses the staffers and asks whether Ronnie should be put on a program for eye contact, having prefaced this with, "You know, I've noticed something else about Ronnie when I'm working with him [in individual counseling sessions]. He doesn't seem to be able to look at me for more than a few seconds at a time. I don't know. What do you see here?"
>
> Ronnie's teacher responds first. She reports not having noticed any problem and that Ronnie is always very attentive whenever she addresses him. Indeed, she remarks, "I'd say he's among the most attentive kids in the class. I never have any trouble with him in that way. Yea, he's a mischief [maker] and gets carried away, but the eye contact thing . . . it's not there." The social worker, picking up on the teacher's reference to Ronnie getting "carried away," says, "That's what I mean—the getting carried away bit—he's just off somewhere talking to you, yeah, but really off the wall." Ronnie's teacher disagrees, "But I wouldn't call that poor eye contact. That's just fooling around. You can't really count that, can you?" The social worker looks puzzled and turns to the others, "Well I just don't know. I have this feeling. . . . What do the rest of you think?"
>
> At this point, staffers not only debate the question of existing eye contact, but also argue over whether the question was a rea-

> sonable one to raise in the first place. Varying opinions are expressed. Elaborate examples are presented where it is believed to be clear that poor eye contact is evident. These are challenged by different interpretations of the same examples as well as by the presentation of other examples where the same apparent behavior of a child "clearly" shows that there is no eye contact problem evident. Throughout their deliberations, staffers shift their attention many times between various layers of concern with the eye contact issue: debate over the degree of eye contact found in their individual experiences with Ronnie; negotiations over the legitimacy of using select experiences as a basis (data base) for judging eye contact; and deliberation over the meaning of eye contact itself.
>
> The staffing comes to an end with no resolution in sight. Several times, Ronnie's social worker interjects that some decision has to be made so that Ronnie can be put on a program if it's warranted. Finally, a childcare worker suggests, "Well, why don't we just take a vote." Everyone agrees and staffers are systematically polled. As the social worker proceeds to solicit opinions around the conference room, several staffers preface their comments with references to other staffers' opinions. For example, the teacher states, "You know, I really wasn't all that sure to begin with, but I can see what you mean [about there being a possible problem]. I guess I've been overruled. I'll go along with some kind of program. It can't hurt him, anyway." The social worker then concludes, "I guess that's it, then. Would it be fair to say that it's the informed opinion of the treatment team that a program to increase eye contact is indicated?" All agree. The social worker than asks, "From what most of you seem to be saying, I'd put his current eye contact at about two minutes out of a fifteen minute period. Let's see," she pauses, and then resumes, "that's about 12 or 13% eye contact. Does that sound about right to you?" The speech therapist responds, "Why don't you make it an even 10%? I really think that would be more accurate. His eye contact, I don't believe, is all that good." The social worker asks if that's all right with everyone, and they all agree (Gubrium and Buckholdt, 1979: 130–132).

This example is useful because it shows the extent to which realizing is negotiated. Not everyone agreed that Ronnie had a problem and an important part of the staffing involved negotiation of that issue. Whose interpretation of Ronnie's problem prevailed depended on the relative ability of staff members to gloss over contradictory information. Thus, the social worker glossed the teacher's interpretation by emphasizing the child's getting "carried away" and ignoring evidence of his attentiveness in class. Once the group realized that Ronnie had an eye contact problem, then the issue shifted to the extent of it. Here filling in is evident, because the number (10 percent) was created as a new fact to fill in the missing information in Ronnie's file about his eye contact problem. It was important to have some indicator of the extent of the child's problem since everyone now realized that he had an eye contact problem. In sum, Ronnie's eye contact problem was a socially constructed reality that emerged out of the discussion in the staffing. It might be changed at the next staffing, however, because it is also possible to realize that he does not have an eye contact problem. This process would also involve glossing and filling in.

There are, then, two major social realities at Cedarview. The first is that of the professionals who spend much of their time discovering and measuring emotional disturbance. For them the major sources of knowledge are the experiences of everyday life, theories about children and mental illness, and various types of tests. Because each of these sources of knowledge may lead to different conclusions and actions, the professionals fill in and gloss much of the time. For example, they simultaneously use psychiatric categories and treatments with behavior modification principles. The staff does not deal with the many contradictory assumptions underlying each of these approaches, because members "realize" that the children are emotionally disturbed and consider that each of these theories provides a different type of insight into the children's problems. In other words, the theories are important sources for filling in and glossing.

Simply because the professionals are able to gloss over the inconsistencies in these theories does not mean that the children do. Indeed, much of the children's social reality derives from the contradictions between the official claims of the professional staff and their everyday experiences. The children must deal with the ways in which being on the run and point-giving in behavior modification are negotiated and interpreted, and for this reason their social reality is more pragmatic and attuned to contradictions than that of the professionals.

It is important to recognize that Cedarview is not a snakepit where children are abused. The professionals are people committed to helping the children. The practices that may seem unjust to some observers arise from the problems of everyday life they confront. They are like all other workers in this respect. It is also important to recognize that Cedarview is not a unique professional setting. Rather, all professional settings involve negotiations and interpretation. Thus, biologists negotiate and create "scientific facts," television reporters negotiate and create "news," lawyers negotiate and create "cases," and physicians negotiate and create "illness" (Altheide, 1976; Freidson, 1970; Latour and Woolgar, 1979; Ross, 1970; Roth, 1972; Schlesinger, 1979). These professions may include some sinister and dishonest people, but they are less important than the everyday problems which professionals encounter. It is out of everyday experiences that professional realities are created and changed.

The fact that the importance of the everyday experience of professional workers is obscured within the professional model is evidence of how the model oversimplifies the complexities and diversity of professional work. One of the most important claims of the professional model is that members of the same profession are committed to similar goals and interests. We will test this claim by looking at the medical profession next.

Social Realities in Medical Practice

Just as the social realities of professionals and clients often vary, so professionals in different work settings often find that their interests differ. These divergent interests are often hidden from view because the conflict is limited to private places, the professionals are isolated from one another most of the time, or the conflict has become a routine, ritualized part of local professional life. Much of the conflict among medical practitioners occurs within their professional associations, which are not public bodies; often members tacitly agree that those conflicts be kept within the professional body. Similarly, the conflicts between physicians who work in small general practices and those in large multispecialty clinics are minimized by the limited number of occasions when they encounter each other. Finally, the ritualization of professional conflict can be seen in encounters between physicians who know each other well. For example, at hospital staff meetings a doctor who regularly expresses an unpopular opinion on a medical practice may be listened to politely by colleagues, who will then just as routinely dismiss his ideas and do as they please.

There are, however, occasions when the divergent interests of professionals come to light. An especially important occasion is during times of change when the prevailing standards of professional practice are seen as threatened. Many physicians consider recent U.S. government efforts to encourage the building of health maintenance organizations as such a threat. As we noted above, HMOs are intended to reorganize medical practice so that a higher quality of care can be provided at less cost (HEW, 1971; May, 1971; Rosser and Mossberg, 1974; Tessler and Mechanic, 1975; U.S. Congress, 1973–1974). More specifically, these programs emphasize preventive rather than curative medicine, comprehensive medical services so that the patients do not have to go from physician to physician in search of the appropriate services, and prepayment so that members know that their health-care needs will be provided for no matter what their cost. A major assumption behind these programs is that health-care costs can be reduced and the quality of service increased if physicians and patients have a financial incentive not to overtreat or seek overtreatment and if all health-care services and financing are coordinated within a single organization. The goal of reducing overtreatment and costs is linked to the emphasis on preventive medicine (because problems would be caught before they became serious) and the prepayment arrangement (because patient payments would go up with overtreatment and physicians would lose money if they overtreated). The goal of increasing the quality of medical services is related to the emphasis on comprehensive medical services, because it is assumed that a wider range of health-care needs could be dealt with in such organizations. In addition, supporters also claim that HMOs would provide better medical services to rural residents, the poor, and others who have not been given adequate medical services in the past. Finally, supporters argue that these organizations would increase the accountability of physicians to their patients, because the law requires that the decision-making boards and committees of HMOs include lay members (patients).

The degree to which the promises of HMO proponents can be realized in practice is a matter of great debate among those interested in improving the delivery of health-care services in the United States (Berkanovic et al., 1974; Goldberg and Greenberg, 1977; Greenlick, 1975; Kotelchuck, 1976; Luft, 1978; Saward, Blank, and Lamb, 1973; Saward and Greenlick, 1972). But these programs are of interest here for a different reason. They provide an example of how medical professionals interpret and respond to programs that may change the existing arrangement of professional services within communities. The source of much of the information we will cite here is a study of nine attempts at initiating HMOs within six communities in the Midwest (Miller, 1976; Miller and Warriner, 1980a, 1980b). For each of these attempts physicians, hospital administrators, health-care planners, and others involved in the provision of health-care services to these communities participated in considerable discussion and political activity. Indeed, partly because of the political activity of local health-care providers, many of the programs were not implemented. Even when the programs were implemented, they were not always successful, because the initiators often implemented their programs in such a way that the major aims of the HMO proponents were not realized. Most sponsors of the health-care program in this study used the HMO movement as an avenue for achieving their personal aims, and often this meant attracting patients from competing professionals. Thus, the everyday problem of making a living was basic to understanding how professionals perceived and initiated these government-sponsored programs.

Although the concrete disputes and details of each case are different, one of the cases is particularly helpful in seeing the ways in which professional interests diverge. This HMO plan was proposed for a five-county rural area of the Midwest. The largest town in the area has a population of about 10,000 people, and there are a number of smaller towns scattered within the five counties. In addition, a number of residents live on the many farms and ranches in the area. A major health-care problem of the area, then, was the large distances between patients and medical professionals and facilities. For this reason, one item in the HMO proposal was the development of helicopter services to isolated regions. The problem of distance was made worse by the number and quality of health-care professionals and facilities in the area. At the time of the study there were twenty-eight physicians in the five counties, but twenty of them were located in one county, and most of the twenty were located in one town in that county. It was also politically important that almost all the specialists were located in that town. In addition, of the seven hospitals in the area, only one provided skilled care, and it too was located in the town with the most physicians. Most of the other hospitals were places where persons with minor ailments and old people who could not get into nursing homes went. There were, then, some important health-care problems in this area, and an HMO might have provided a solution to some of them. But to limit the issue to how an HMO might have dealt with the health-care problems of the area residents is to oversimplify this case. The HMO plan was also proposed because it offered political and economic advantages to its sponsor.

The HMO plan was developed in a multispecialty clinic made up of twelve physicians located in the largest town in the area. An important part of the plan was the high degree of control by the clinic's physicians. The board of directors was to be made up of member physicians, other health-care providers in the area (e.g., hospital administrators), and members (patients), but the members were to be selected by the physicians. The most important day-to-day decisions of the HMO were to be made by the executive committee, which was to be made up of one physician, the administrator of the HMO (a clinic employee), and a member selected by the board of directors. On the surface, at least, the HMO was proposed as an extension of the clinic and its interests. The organization of health-care services supported this impression. Originally, the plan called for hospital services, but when the local hospital refused to renovate its facility, all hospital services were dropped from the plan. The plan also included physician services, although it called for no change in the practices of the clinic's physicians. It did, however, include area physicians (primarily general practitioners), who were to be paid on a fee-for-service basis for treating HMO patients. If these people then needed specialized medical attention, they were to be referred to the sponsoring clinic.

Largely out of fear, hospital administrators and area physicians responded very negatively to the plan. The hospital administrators opposed the plan primarily because they felt that the HMO physicians would refer all their patients to the hospital in the largest town. Although the administrators recognized that the HMO plan did not include hospital services, they felt that the clinic's physicians would still use the hospital closest to their practice. Even though the small hospitals offered few services, they still needed patients in order to survive. The past actions of the clinic's physicians increased fears. They had attempted, for example, to get the county government to build a new hospital that would make all of the other hospitals in the area unnecessary. Indeed, their proposal for the new hospital called for the appointment of an administrator with direct ties to the clinic. The hospital administrators thus saw the HMO plan as the most recent effort by the clinic's physicians to increase their control over the hospital services of the area.

The area physicians were also opposed to the plan. They saw it as another attempt by the clinic's physicians to gain control over all physician services in the area. They were particularly conscious of the referral requirement, and because of it, they unanimously refused to participate. The physicians also interpreted the HMO plan in light of the past. They noted, for example, that the clinic's physicians had once started a campaign to recruit new physicians to the area. These physicians would have been partially funded by the clinic, and they would have been placed in towns where they could compete with the established general practitioners. The clinic, of course, would have received all cases needing the attention of specialists. Another plan of the clinic's physicians was to encourage patients referred by area physicians to use the clinic for all their health-care needs. One aspect of this effort was to attack the competence of the area physicians, particularly the regular physician of the patient.

For a variety of reasons, including the negative responses of hospital administrators and area physicians, the HMO plan was never implemented. Rather, a new plan was developed in which specially trained nurses (nurse clinicians) were located in the various towns of the area. These nurses screened patients and determined who needed physician attention and who did not. If a physician was needed, then the patient was sent to the clinic. If not, then the nurse treated the patient. This plan offered a number of advantages to the clinic. There was less opposition to it by hospital administrators and area physicians, but it was also cheaper to operate and easier to staff. The clinic's physicians found it easier to recruit nurse clinicians than physicians, and the nurses worked for less money.

It is easy to conclude from this example that the clinic's physicians were greedy people who were interested only in money and power and, for this reason, they are not typical of usual professional practice. But such a conclusion neglects both the complexity of this case and its generality. The clinic's physicians were interested not just in money and power but in improving what they considered the area's inadequate medical services. They justified their efforts to build a new hospital on those grounds, and they admitted to deriding the competence of area physicians because they felt that those physicians were incompetent. To support their position, they pointed to a variety of mistakes made by the area physicians. They saw themselves, on the other hand, as the only real hope for developing adequate medical services. They noted, for example, that their clinic offered better technical services than most of the hospitals and that each physician there is required to return periodically to medical school for a year in order to learn new techniques and acquire new knowledge.

Within this Midwestern area, then, there were at least two social realities among physicians. The first was that of the general practitioners who had worked in the area for many years and developed steady clienteles and routine medical practices. Those physicians saw the clinic's physicians as greedy and power hungry. They felt that they were being unjustly attacked and feared that the attacks might be successful. The other reality was that the clinic's physicians, who saw medical practice from the viewpoint of highly trained and specialized professionals. They regarded the long-term attachment of the other physicians to the area as insignificant and emphasized the technical, as opposed to the social, aspects of patient care. In order to provide adequate care, the clinic's physicians thought it necessary to overcome the provincial interests and traditions of local physicians. Since the local physicians were unwilling to join with the clinic's physicians in order to improve their own skills and their services to their patients, then alternatives to them had to be found. The HMO and nurse clinician programs could provide such an alternative. Indeed, the clinic's physicians saw the response of local physicians to the HMO plan as one more indicator of their provincial and self-interested outlooks. Their emphasis on not being tied to the clinic and their fear of being run out of business were taken as proof that their most important concerns were with resisting needed change and making money.

In sum, the case shows both the diversity of social realities in different professional work places and the way in which public interest and self-interest are linked within professional segments. Both sides in this dispute can be seen as self-interested, and concerned primarily with protecting or expanding their respective clienteles. Both were also interested in power, because the local physicians wanted to be autonomous and the clinic's physicians wanted to coordinate medical services in the area. On the other hand, each of these segments also represented the public interest. The local physicians wanted to continue to provide the basic personal and general medical services that are badly needed in an increasingly impersonal world. The clinic's physicians wanted to provide the type of sophisticated medical care needed to deal with the health-care needs of contemporary patients. Both sides thus represented their own interests and those of the public, and both had readily available knowledge from everyday life to support their realities.

Although the specific details of this case may be unique, the political division of the professions is not. The professions are not the homogeneous bodies described in the professional model. Nor are they made up of self-sacrificing persons concerned only with serving the public: they are composed of human beings who are both public-spirited and self-interested. In part, the image of professionals as self-sacrificing derives from the conscious efforts of professionals to manipulate public opinion, but it is based on more than this. Much of the confusion of public interest and self-interest stems from a professional mentality that assumes that professional services are the most effective way of dealing with human problems. Thus, lawyers make decisions based on the assumption that the best solution to the problems of law is more lawyers; physicians, educators, psychiatrists, and social workers operate under similar assumptions.

The language of the professions, which stresses the helping and liberating aspects of professional work, support these assumptions (Edelman, 1974). The language encourages professionals to see the public's problems as "facts" which are real and not something to be questioned. Within every profession, then, there is a counterpart to the realizing that goes on in staffings. Every profession glosses and fills in to create a consistent social reality and definition of public interest. This use of language is evident in the two physician segments described here, but it is also observable elsewhere. Fundamental to the professions is the act of professing to know what the client and public need and an important part of professing is language. Professionals, clients, the public, and government officials may all be taken in by the claims and language of the professions and, for this reason, professional control and power cannot simply be reduced to the pursuit of self-interest or public interest.

Besides language, myths about professional workers may also obscure their full complexity. Two of these myths are discussed next.

MYTHS ABOUT PROFESSIONAL WORKERS

An important myth associated with professional workers is the professional model, which assumes that the professions are unique occupations because of the special knowledge and authority of members.

Table 4-2 • Myths about Professional Workers

Type of Myth	*Need for Work*	*Organization of Work*	*Rewards of Work*
Myth of the Professional Community	Based on material need and the desire to be of service to the profession and larger community	Based on the standards of the professional community, regardless of the specific work setting	Income and great prestige within the professional community
Myth of Self-Actualization	Based on the needs for physiological well-being, safety, belongingness and love, esteem, and self-actualization	Based on the satisfaction of all human needs, with self-actualization needs best satisfied in open, friendly settings where workers are secure, have opportunities to achieve, and may express their unique feelings and abilities	The meeting of all human needs, including self-actualization

When the work settings and relationships of professionals are considered, however, the uniqueness of the professions is difficult to justify. Some of the problems of the professional model have already been noted, and others are apparent from the descriptions of Cedarview and the case of the HMO plan. Both examples point to a variety of factors that shape professional work which the professional model does not take into account. The physicians' concern for their financial well-being and the Cedarview workers' desire to maintain order within the organization are examples. The Cedarview example is also important because it shows the extent to which the special knowledge of the professions is modified in practice. Professional knowledge is, then, only one basis for creating reality and making decisions in professional settings.

In addition to the professional model, there are several other myths about professional workers. Two of the most popular are the myth of the professional community and the myth of self-actualization. These myths, which will be discussed in detail here, are summarized in Table 4-2.

The Myth of the Professional Community

Although the *myth of the professional community* is implicit in the language assumptions of many officials in professional associations,

William Goode (1957) develops it best. He argues that the professions are communities that reside within the larger communities found in modern society, and, as such, they have many characteristics in common with other communities. The most important are the following:

1. Members share a similar identity.
2. Membership is long term and continuing because few members leave the profession.
3. Members share a set of values.
4. Members share a definition of professional and client roles.
5. Members share a language.
6. Members are controlled by the professional community.
7. The professional community has boundaries which are recognized by members of the community and the public.
8. The professional community controls recruitment and training so that new generations of competent professionals continually enter the community.

Although there are several problems with the myth of the professional community explicated by Goode, two are especially important. First, the myth assumes that the professions are distinct from other lines of work in having these characteristics. There are many worker communities in modern society, however, and not all of them are professions. The longshoremen of Portland, Oregon, for example, are not considered professional workers, and yet they have historically had most, if not all, of the characteristics listed above (Pilcher, 1972). The longshoremen's unique identity, language, values, and other characteristics are derived from the shared experiences of the workers in the work place and the union. The union is especially important because it controls the recruitment and training of longshoremen, as well as the hiring hall where jobs are made available to members. Indeed, the Portland longshoremen may be seen as more of a community than most professionals, who are often divided among themselves.

In fact, the second problem with the myth of the professional community is that it does not take account of the ways in which professionals are divided because of differences in specialization and work setting (Bucher and Strauss, 1961). Each professional segment may possess a unique identity, language, and set of values and may even be associated with different recruitment and training centers. The relationship between the clinic's physicians and the general practitioners discussed in the last section provides an example. In addition to divisions based on specialization and work setting, separate identities, values, and languages, professional segments may be divided in their views of their professional mission. For example, medical activists define the professional mission of medicine as working in cooperation with patients, nurses, and others to deal with the general health-care needs of modern society (Resnick, 1976). For these professionals, an important medical activity is lobbying for cleaner air and an improved quality of life for the poor. This vision of professional medicine differs markedly from that held by other segments, which limit medical activity to treating patients. The difference in vision is also evident in the activists' interest in expanding medical education to include courses in human development and other "nonmedical" areas and in their lack of interest in the conventional publications of medical associations and schools. Instead, they read such publications as *The Body Politic*, which emphasizes the political goals of the activist segment of contemporary medicine. Thus, the notion that the professions are homogeneous communities is best understood as a political claim made by professional associations, which often attempt to speak for the whole of a profession. In practice, the contemporary professions are too diverse to be truly represented by a single body.

Although the myth of the professional community overstates the uniqueness of the professions and the consensus found within them, professional communities do exist. The medical activists and other professional segments often possess many of the characteristics of a community. Such communities may be ephemeral or long-lasting, depending on the commitment of the members and the opposition of other professionals and the public. There are also occasions when the conflicts separating professional segments are set aside in order to deal with a common threat. In one community studied during the course of the HMO research, the researchers discovered that the physicians in one town had banded together to fight the creation of an HMO. They did this, in part, by letting it be known that any physician who went to work for the HMO would be treated as an outcast by other physicians and the local medical association. In another community, the physicians banded together to create an HMO plan of their own which would, if implemented, have given them control over the Medicaid services in the area. Medicaid is a program for financing health care to the poor, and a recurring conflict in the community in question was the state Medicaid agency's refusal to pay participating physicians at their usual rate. Professional conflicts were set aside in order to deal with this common problem. The myth of the professional community is not totally wrong, then, though it is an oversimplification. There are examples of professional communities, but they tend to be short-lived, because once a common problem is solved, old conflicts reemerge.

Although not fully explicated by Goode, the myth of the professional community is also based on assumptions which justify the professional claim to being unique and public-spirited. The need for work is explained by the myth as a response to the related desires of satisfying material needs and being of service to the professional community and the public. The myth treats the organization of professional work as based on agreed upon standards of competent practice found in the professional community. These standards are the written and unwritten "working codes" of ethical practice. Professionals consider them an important control over those in the profession who engage in ethically dubious practices in order to satisfy client demands. Indeed, often professional communities try to get such standards of competence enacted into law and enforced by the government. The standards are also used to judge the competence of professional workers in large bureaucratic organizations. Finally, according to the myth, the rewards of professional work are money and prestige within the professional community. The professional community accords the highest prestige to those who are most competent and who are most committed to serving the public and the professional community. Once again, the myth emphasizes the mixture of public interest and self-interest as the cornerstone of professional work.

Each of these claims is based on assumptions that are not always verified in everyday life. Individuals may select a professional line of work for various reasons, and service to the public and the professional community may not always be the most important. Some people select professional work because they enjoy doing it, and they have little regard for money or service to others; others select such work because it offers financial security not found in other lines of work (Harris, 1973). It is also true that a professional's reasons for working may change as he or she moves from the training stage to becoming a known and respected member of the profession (Becker et al., 1961; Bucher and Stelling, 1977).

The claim that the organization of professional work is based on shared codes and standards is problematic as well. First, it is difficult to identify a shared set of standards for any profession; rather, the standards vary from segment to segment and work place to work place. For example, much of the conflict between the clinic's physicians and local doctors in the HMO case stemmed from their differing standards of competent practice. A second problem with the claim is that it does not take account of the ways in which clients and employers may influence the organization of professional work. Professionals in solo practices who are directly dependent on clients for their incomes are particularly vulnerable to such influence (Freidson, 1970; Rothstein, 1973). For such workers, the standards of the professional community must be balanced against the more immediate problem of making a living. In a similar way, professional workers in large organizations often find that professional standards for organizing and doing work must be compromised because of the competing standards of employers (Robert Scott, 1970). The claim that hiring and promotion in bureaucratic organizations are based on professional standards does not take account of the diverse interests of employers and professional employees. Indeed, one study of engineers shows that the most professionally involved workers are often passed over when promotions into important decision-making positions are made (Goldner and Ritti, 1967). That happens because professional and executive concerns are often different.

Finally, the claims that the primary rewards of work are money and prestige and that prestige always accompanies competence in work and a commitment to service to others are problematic. The assumption here is that competence and service are visible features of professional work. Given the variety of work places where professionals are found, it is difficult to sustain this argument. A better argument is that prestige within one's professional *segment* accompanies competence in work and public service. Even this claim must be tempered, however, by the realization that much professional work is only indirectly visible to others. Thus, files, teacher ratings, and other indirect indicators of performance may be the only basis for judging a colleague. In addition to this problem, it must be recognized that all persons are not evaluated in the same ways within a profession. The sexual status of women, for example, is often an important factor affecting the ways in which their competence and commitment to public service are interpreted. Thus, the claim that a professional is very good "for a woman" raises doubts about her "real" abilities (Epstein, 1970; Kanter, 1977a). Finally, the claim that prestige goes to the most competent and community-spirited professionals does not take account of the ways in which prestige is actively cultivated by professional workers. One procedure is to become active in professional associations and community organizations, which give the person a chance to be noticed. It is not simply enough, then, to do a good job, because that aspect of professional work is not always seen and the standards for judging it are not always clear. Those who attain high prestige do much more; indeed, sometimes their striving for prestige and recognition means that they spend more time with the activities of the professional association than with their professional work.

The Myth of Self-Actualization

The myth of the professional community emphasizes the themes of community service and professional standards of achievement. But, as we have seen, the culture of professionalism also stresses the theme of professional work and life as a liberation from traditional knowledge and life styles and a commitment to a career and a professional way of life. The *myth of self-actualization* picks up the latter theme. Its chief exponent, Abraham Maslow (1954, 1965), emphasizes the ways in which work may be used to achieve human growth and fulfillment. Although this myth has been applied to many forms of work, it is most appropriately applied to the professions.

Basic to this view of work is a belief that human beings have needs that are ranked so that when one need is satisfied, another one becomes the primary source of motivation for an individual. Taken together, human needs form a hierarchy, and they account for the variety of motivations which people have (Maslow, 1954). At the most basic level human beings have physiological needs, that is, needs that must be satisfied for the individual to survive. The most obvious of these needs is for food, and when a person is hungry all other interests and motivations are secondary. When physiological needs are satisfied, the safety needs of an individual take priority. These are the needs a person has for security, stability, freedom from fear, and order. Once safety needs are satisfied, the needs for belongingness and love —that is, the desires to be a part of a group and to receive affection—dominate. In turn, when these needs are satisfied, they are replaced by the need to be esteemed, which includes the desire for achievement and mastery and the desire for prestige. Finally, the need for self-actualization emerges as dominant when all other needs are satisfied. Self-actualization is really a desire for personal growth and fulfillment, and its satisfaction requires that the unique, idiosyncratic features of the individual be taken into account.

According to Maslow, because the hierarchy of human needs is the basis for human motivation it is important for understanding modern work. In addition, Maslow (1965) argues that we should strive to achieve self-actualization for as many people as possible. Different types of work should be assessed in terms of the degree to which they encourage self-actualization. Implicit within this theory, then, is a vision of proper work. This vision is the essence of the myth of self-actualization.

The myth of self-actualization explains the need for work by reference to the hierarchy of needs. Thus, an individual's need to work changes as his or her needs are satisfied, though a person's ultimate need for work is self-actualization, when all other needs have been satisfied. The proper organization of work is one that recognizes the diversity of human needs. Workers should be paid enough to live comfortably, but they should also have secure jobs, feel that they belong to a meaningful group, have a chance to gain prestige through personal achievement, and be allowed to develop their unique characteristics and abilities. In order to achieve these goals, Maslow (1965) argues that it is necessary for administrators to operate from the set of assumptions constituting the *Eupsychian Management Policy*. The most basic of these assumptions are trust in the workers, belief in the right of workers to have all the information relevant to their jobs, belief in the achievement motivations of all workers, rejection of authoritarian leadership, and belief in the ability of all organizational members to get along with each other. Based on these assumptions, it is possible to build policies which will encourage self-actualization. This is the ultimate reward of work, although unenlightened administrators often settle for rewards that rank lower on the hierarchy of needs. When workers can achieve self-actualization in their work, selfish and unselfish goals are no longer distinguishable within the organization. Rather, the self-actualized worker receives satisfaction from helping others achieve their goals. In Maslow's words:

> Work transcends the self without trying to, and achieves the kind of loss of self-awareness and self-consciousness that the easterners, the Japanese and Chinese and so on, keep on trying to attain. S-A work is simultaneously a seeking and fulfilling of the self *and* also an achieving of the selflessness which is the ultimate expression of *real* self. It resolves the dichotomy between selfish and unselfish (Maslow, 1965: 7).

Through the development of self-actualizing work, it is possible to transcend the diachronic world of career and work place and enter a world with different rules and relationships. In this way, Maslow deals with the conflict between self-interest and public interest in professional work. It is his faith in the transcendent power of self-actualizing work that leads him to treat such work in almost a religious way as a means of "salvation" (Maslow, 1965).

In general, the theory of the hierarchy of needs underlying the myth of self-actualization is a very mechanical view of human beings and work. It is assumed that people move automatically from one need (motivation) to another with little thought or control over their actions. For this reason, the need for work and its rewards changes as the individual passes through various need levels. This vision of human beings and work does not take account of the ways in which social interaction gives human needs meaning. The members of the liberal professions in England, for example, would be classified as meeting their basic needs for survival, safety, belongingness, and esteem through their work, but not their need for self-actualization. They continued to work because it was an expected part of being an aristocrat. Further, Maslow would maintain, only with the development of the culture of professionalism created by the opponents of the liberal professions did self-actualization through professional work become possible. But Maslow's theory is flawed here, because the notion of self-actualization is not separable from the concern of the professionalizers for money, security, and prestige. Were Maslow's theory an accurate depiction of the professions, the concern for self-actualization should have developed only after the other professional needs were satisfied. Yet from the beginning the professionalization movement incorporated self-actualization claims.

Maslow's discussion of the organization of work is also flawed, because it does not take into account the everyday problems workers face. Cedarview, for example, is a work setting that meets most, if not all, of the criteria for a self-actualizing work place, but the extent to which self-actualization is achieved is unclear. Undoubtedly some of the professional workers believe that they are engaged in self-actualizing work. From the viewpoint of the children, however, it is difficult to believe that the professional workers simultaneously achieve selfish and selfless goals when the workers consistently emphasize maintaining order and control in their dealings with the children. In the children's eyes that concern reflects a selfish rather than a selfless goal, regardless of what the professionals may believe.

In sum, Maslow's theory reflects the social realities of only some professionals. Such professionals often believe that their work is self-actualizing because they feel that they are engaged in selfless work, a veiwpoint encouraged by several features of the culture of professionalism. Looked at from the viewpoint of a client or outsider, however, this claim appears to be self-serving, because it glosses over the contradictory features of professional work. Indeed, the claim to selflessness often can be interpreted as a public relations ploy to cover the "real" underlying motives of professionals—to attain wealth and power.

The Humanistic Approach

Because the myths of the professional community and of self-actualization are oversimplifications of the complex realities of professional work, a more humanistic interpretation is needed. Such an interpretation would point to the ways in which professionals, clients, and others in the work place create needs, motives, and realities. These created realities may arise from abstract theoretical schemes, but they may also reflect the problems of everyday life. To ignore the ways in which professional work is shaped by mundane problems and relationships that develop in life is to fall into the trap of dehumanizing clients and professionals. Clients are dehumanized because they are treated as mindless and passive receivers of professional services, and professionals are dehumanized because they are treated as saintly figures who have transcended the world of practical problems in which the rest of us live. Put differently, a humanistic approach to the professions rejects the elitist assumptions that make up the culture of professionalism, the professional model, the myth of the professional community, and the myth of self-actualization.

CONCLUSION

This chapter has dealt with the elites of the occupational world. The elite status of today's professionals derives in part from the aristocratic roots of professional service, but it is also based on professionals' efforts to convince the public that they deserve high social rank. For example, they have sought to raise their own status by comparing the effectiveness of professional and nonprofessional methods in dealing with the problems of clients (Freidson, 1970). Thus, physicians claim to be more effective in dealing with disease than folk healers. In other situations, members of the professions emphasize the uncertain or indeterminate nature of their work (Jamous and Peloille, 1970; Leiberman, 1970). If they are successful in this claim, professionals not only increase their occupational prestige but also are able to resist the efforts of others to control them by bureaucratizing their work. Finally, much of professional prestige is also engendered by officials in professional associations and training schools who project a public image of their professions as based on complex bodies of knowledge beyond the understanding of the general public (Larson, 1977).

Each of these claims is an oversimplification because it leaves out contradictory aspects of professional life and work. The claim to greater effectiveness must be tempered by the realization that a great deal of professional activity involves resisting development of alternative approaches to the profession's problem areas. Although resistance often involves a claim that the alternative is less effective than the present approach, that claim is not always easy to sustain. In medicine, for example, there is a long history of identifying most alternative forms of treatment, such as osteopathy and chiropractic, as forms of quackery, even though many of the techniques of these "quacks" have been incorporated into standard medical practice today. Similarly, the claim that all professional work is indeterminate glosses over the many professional activities that are highly routine and can be done by others with much less training. In Arizona, for example, lawyers have resisted the efforts of real estate agents to fill out preliminary sales forms on the ground that such activities constitute the practice of law without a license (Leiberman, 1970). Finally, the claim to highly specialized knowledge that is beyond the grasp of the public and clients ignores the ways in which professional knowledge is often kept from clients and public. This is done in obvious ways when the professional refuses to talk to his or her client about a case or when files are closed to client scrutiny, but it is also encouraged through the development of professional communication channels, such as professional journals, that are not easily available to the public and through use of a professional language not shared with the public.

As the flaws in professional claims come to light, clients, the public, and government officals will increasingly act to curb the freedom of professionals. Today, for example, many clients who wish to have more influence over the decisions affecting themselves and their dependents have organized protests (Haug and Sussman, 1969a, 1969b). Malpractice suits and efforts at public self-education are other indications of discontent. An example of the latter is the recent attempt by women to teach themselves about their bodies in order to better understand their physical problems and to deal more effectively with gynecologists. Some government programs and officials also have attempted to change professional practices by placing limitations on professional discretion. For example, sometimes officials review cases and, if overtreatment is detected, the professional is not paid for services that were not needed. But it is a mistake to assume that the sources of change are found only outside the professions. Much of the impetus for change derives from conflicts among segments of a profession as they each pursue their self-interests and their vision of the public interest.

In a general way, each source of change in the professions has contributed to the development of a movement to empower clients—a counterpart to the empowerment movement taking place in the world of industrial work. We will turn to this movement after dealing with other types of work in modern society.

Chapter Five

HUSTLING WORK

Although the word "work" is used here very generally, it more commonly depicts a limited set of activities and roles that are deemed legitimate ways of making a living. In the United States today, for example, people often use the word to indicate the possession of a job or occupation. Thus, we refer to working mothers as mothers who have jobs. Implicit in this usage is the assumption that mothers without jobs do not work. Depending on the context, the term "working mother" may also indicate a positive or negative evaluation of those in the category. We are not unique in making moral judgments about work; indeed, most societies have some general notions about what is and what is not legitimate work. In classical Rome, for example, legitimate work was limited to agriculture and large commercial ventures; other forms of work were reserved for less respectable persons (Tilgher, 1958). Indeed, an important driving force behind the organization of worker movements may be a desire to make laborers and their work respectable, as with the professionalization movement of nineteenth-century England.

An important consequence of the limited use of the concept of work is that many forms of making a living are relegated to the category of nonwork. Yet included in this category are a variety of people involved in many activities related to making their livings. Women prostitutes, for example, often refer to themselves as "working girls," but their work activities are obscured by the moralistic judgments of others who stress their deviance over their work. Similarly, drug dealers and other racketeers, strippers, thieves, and a variety of other persons involved in crime and deviance are also workers, though they are not generally regarded as such (Bullock, 1973; Miller, 1978). But the category of nonworkers includes other workers as well. Welfare recipients (including those receiving social security benefits) are often depicted as persons leading leisurely lives because their most basic economic needs are taken care of by the government. Yet observation of the life styles of those on welfare frequently shows that they engage in a variety of activities to increase their incomes (Stack, 1974; Bettylou Valentine, 1978). Finally, unemployed persons are usually relegated to the category of nonworkers. Yet the history of unemployment indicates that begging and scavenging increase during times of high unemployment (Garraty, 1978). Even during times of high employment, however, some people still beg for a living. The fact that begging and scavenging can yield an income for people is often obscured by our moralistic evaluations of those who engage in such activities as social problems.

In sum, modern society is made up of a variety of workers and work activities, and only some of them are taken into account in official measures of unemployment and the gross national product. One segment of the work force that is unaccounted for is the subject of this chapter. It is made up of people who spend their days and nights hustling in order to make a living (Caplovitz, 1970; Bettylou Valentine, 1978). Usually hustlers are looked upon as shady characters who can easily talk people out of their money or in some other way manipulate them. The pimp and confidence game operator fit the stereotype of the hustler. But this simplistic image becomes problematic when other hustlers are considered. Many former rural residents of Appalachia, for example, have recently migrated to cities such as Detroit, where full-time employment is not always available (Dow, 1977). One solution is to hustle for a living by buying and collecting old cars and fixing them up for resale. It is difficult to depict such people as shady characters. Nor can retired persons who seek odd jobs in order to supplement their social security checks or migrant workers who leave their homes to find summer work be described as manipulative types (Freidland and Nelkin, 1971). Yet both sorts of workers must hustle for a living. Finally, although collecting welfare is often treated by politicians and others as a simple process of filling out forms and receiving a check, being a welfare recipient often requires a great deal of time and effort because it involves dealing with the diverse and mystifying rules, procedures, and social realities of the social welfare bureaucracy.

Hustling for a living, then, is pervasive in modern society, and many different people and activities are included in the category. The most basic feature of workers who hustle for a living is that they do not have full-time conventional jobs; rather, they seek their livings in other ways. Sometimes they may work at low-paying, temporary jobs, but at other times they may do any number of other things to earn income. It is because hustlers do unconventional work that they are typically left out of official accounts of modern work and that outsiders often stress the immorality of their activities. For hustlers, however, a more important factor than their unconventionality is the uncertain nature of their work. They must be alert at all times to opportunities for making a living found in their environments. As a result, their histories reflect frequent job changes, and outsiders often describe them as unstable.

Hustlers are often looked at in contradictory ways by more conventional people. On the one hand, people tend to excuse the poor and deviant from blame because it is assumed that forces beyond their control have shaped their destinies. In medieval Christianity, for example, poverty was assumed to be a holy state that had been sanctified by Jesus, who accepted charity rather than to work in conventional ways (Garraty, 1978). On the other hand, many also believe that the poor and deviant are responsible for their fates and they deserve no sympathy or charity. One traditional resolution of this contradiction is to categorize the poor and deviant into those who are deserving of help and those who are not. In medieval Christianity the major criterion for distinguishing the worthy and unworthy poor was their level of righteousness. Although many of the assumptions about the nature of poverty and deviance are different today, the same contradiction exists and much public debate is still given over to the proper criteria for separating the deserving from the undeserving poor.

The purpose of this chapter is to explore this contradiction in modern society. We will begin with some of the ways "experts" have conceptualized the problem of poverty in the United States. Because conceptualizing the problem is seldom separate from efforts to solve it, much of the next section is a history of the rise of social work in the United States. Different societies have gone through differing historical processes, but almost all modern societies have had to confront the contradiction of excusing and blaming the poor and deviant in developing their social welfare practices. The second section of the chapter looks at two examples of hustling work found in the contemporary world. One is the Irish Tinkers, who have historically roamed the countryside begging and scavenging (Sharon Gmelch, 1975; George Gmelch, 1977). The Tinkers of today are becoming stabilized within cities and increasingly dependent on welfare for their livelihoods. The other example is taken from two studies of single-room occupancy hotels located in New York City and a city in the Midwest (Siegal, 1978; Stephens, 1976). These hotels are often filled with various types of welfare recipients, but more important is the fact that almost all of their residents must hustle for a living. That section balances the earlier one, because it looks at the social realities of the hustlers themselves and not just at the ways in which outsiders have seen them. The chapter concludes by looking at the ways in which the contradiction between excusing and blaming the poor for their condition is reflected in myths about poverty and work.

OFFICIAL IMAGES OF POVERTY AND THE POOR

Although the conditions associated with it may vary, there are few conditions in human history that are more pervasive and enduring than poverty. Looked at this way, the fourteenth-century French peasant who lived in fear of the devastation caused by crop failure and the Black Plague is not very different from many modern workers, who must deal with the equally uncertain world of fluctuating job opportunities and the possibility of being laid off. On the other hand, the ways that workers and officials view the uncertainties of work and poverty are considerably different. It is that difference which is of interest here, because the official images of poverty and the poor are often crucial to understanding the variety of programs devised to deal with the so-called unemployed.

Early Images of the Poor

For most historians the beginning of modern images of poverty and the poor is 1601, because it was in that year that the first English *Poor Law* was enacted. Since it only restated what was already common practice, the first Poor Law was not a major legal innovation. The law was important, however, because it gave official sanction to one vision of poverty and its solution, and it was a model for the development of similar laws and programs in the United States. The Poor Law of 1601 included two important features. First, it dealt with the issue of responsibility for helping the poor by identifying the family, the local community, and the government as major sources of aid. The family was to have the initial responsibility, but if it was unable to help, then the local community was responsible, although it could depend on the government for supplemental aid should the drain on its resources be too great. Second, the Poor Law distinguished between the deserving and the undeserving poor. Vagrant, beggars, and similar types of people were deemed undeserving, and the law called for their detention in the house of correction, where they were to be whipped and punished in other ways. The deserving poor—those seen as having a right to aid—were divided into three categories, with each receiving a different type of treatment. Needy children were to be apprenticed to tradespeople and others in the community, who could teach them work skills. The able-bodied poor were to be given work. The last category, the helpless, were to be given relief. Two types of relief were to be available: outdoor relief, which was aid given to a person who remained in his or her home, and indoor relief, which required that the poor person move to an institutional setting, such as a workhouse.

Generally, the Poor Law of 1601 established the imagery of the poor that dominated in the colonial, revolutionary, and early nationhood periods of American history (Axinn and Levin, 1975; Rothman and Rothman, 1972; Trattner, 1979). Both the family and community were responsible for their poor, although they could depend on the colonial treasury and later the government for aid when necessary. The methods for dealing with the poor were also similar to English practices. Needy children were apprenticed to farmers and tradespeople. Another method was for each household in the community to take in a poor family for a short period of time each year. This spread the burden of aid more or less equally among community residents, but it made for a very unsettled life for the poor, who had to move every two weeks or so. Still another method was to auction off the poor to the lowest bidder. That is, the bidder who was willing to accept the least amount of reimbursement from the community was allowed to house and work the poor. Often whole families were auctioned off at one time.

The Poor Law emphasis on deservingness and the willingness of the poor to work was also evident in the United States. Those who received aid from the community were expected to work if they could. Beggars, vagrants, and others who were deemed unwilling to work were considered to be undeserving, and they were placed in the same category as black slaves and American Indians. None of these people was allowed to receive aid, and often individuals were whipped, put in jail, or sent to the makeshift workhouses found in some communities.

This way of dealing with the poor was relatively effective as long as most people lived in small, stable communities. In such communities the everyday problems of the poor could be seen, and people's feelings about each other supplemented the religious, political, and cultural notions of charity then extant. Equally important was the ease with which the deserving and undeserving poor could be distinguished in such communities. But the small community was challenged by industrialization, urbanization, immigration, and the other features of nineteenth-century modernization (Rothman, 1971; Rothman and Rothman, 1972). These changes were accompanied by changing ideas about welfare. After all, how can one distinguish the deserving from the undeserving when the local population is so large that many residents are strangers? The influx of new people into many communities worsened the problem. The development of more effective transportation meant that persons from other parts of the country could migrate to industrializing and urbanizing areas. Just as important was the influx of foreign migrants, who brought languages, belief, and cultural practices which seemed to threaten many of the established residents. The new arrivals certainly did not have the sober, reverent respect for work that many of the long-standing residents professed to have. Indeed, although they expected to work, if it was not available, they expected relief, and they showed little of the self-deprecating humility and gratitude that others on relief had shown to their benefactors. These problems and fears gave rise in the nineteenth century to a new interest in developing alternative ways of providing aid to the poor and deviant.

Nineteenth-Century Images of the Poor

The most important solution to the problem of poverty proposed in the nineteenth century was the development of a variety of institutional settings for housing and "treating" the poor (Rothman, 1971). It was during this time, for example, that penitentiaries and asylums for the insane were created. There also emerged a renewed interest in the almshouse, or workhouse. This institution had existed since colonial days, but it was usually a makeshift operation that was used for punishing beggars and vagrants who would not leave the community when asked. In the nineteenth century a number of almshouses were created by transforming farmhouses and similar buildings in the city into institutional centers where the poor lived and, more importantly, where they could be observed in order to teach them desirable work and personal habits. Although the population of an almshouse was supposed to be divided into categories reflecting the Poor Law of 1601 (needy children, able-bodied poor, and the incapacitated), the usual practice was to treat all residents in the same way.

The intended organization of the almshouse reflects the extent to which it was created from the same assumptions as the penitentiary. Two of the most important assumptions were that the poor were idlers who needed rehabilitation and that their reform could only be achieved if they were removed from the community. Within the almshouse it was also assumed that a world of strict order based on quick and certain punishment and a rigid routine would rehabilitate the poor. Although some of these goals were achieved in the penitentiaries and insane asylums of the time, the everyday routines of almshouses seldom reflected such assumptions. Indeed, the almshouse was typically a miserable place where people idled away their time because there was no routine or any effort to rehabilitate by creating new work and personal habits. The most important features of the almshouse were the emphasis on order and punishment and the meager resources for sustaining life. The low priority given the poor in the nineteenth century accounts for the latter feature. Whereas the public and legislators tended to see criminals and the insane as victims of circumstances beyond their control, they were more likely to see the poor as victims of their own indolence. This view was often shared by almshouse workers, who showed little inclination to do anything other than punish troublemakers. Nineteenth-century reformers and officials apparently did not notice the irony of attempting to cure idleness by creating institutions encouraging it, because they continued to place immigrants and other idlers in almshouses until the turn of the century.

At the same time that the almshouse was emerging as a major public institution, private organizations also arose to deal with the problems of the poor. One of the most important was the *Charity Organization Movement*, which initially developed in England and became prominent in the United States after the Civil War (Lubove, 1973; Woodroofe, 1962). The leaders of this movement shared many of the assumptions of the proponents of the almshouse, but their programs of treatment were different. Indeed, the practice of casework, which was an important basis for the rise of professional social work and continues to be a major social work technique, can be traced to the early Charity Organization Societies (COS).

The formal beginning of these organizations in the United States was in 1877, when S. Humphreys Gurteen founded a Charity Organization Society in Buffalo, New York. The approach soon spread to other cities, and by the turn of the century there were few major cities without a Charity Organization Society. Although the organizations typically grew out of churches and were often led by clergy, they represented more than just religious interests. Indeed, the Charity Organization Societies best reflected the concerns of the emerging business interests of the post–Civil War period. Four of the most important interests were a fear of the revolutionary potential of the poor, suspicion of direct charity, faith in science, and belief in Social Darwinism.

Much of the fear of the poor's radical tendencies can be traced to the depression of the 1870s and the rioting that accompanied it (Trattner, 1979). The riots were often taken as an indicator of the underlying hostility of the poor toward the rich and the need to develop new techniques for eliminating class antagonisms. The concern aroused by the riots of the 1870s was reinforced by the established residents' suspicion of the poor immigrants, whose beliefs and practices were seen not simply as different but as a sign of underlying anti-American radicalism. Fear of the poor was also related to the COS leaders' belief that direct charity is dangerous and demeaning—dangerous because it does nothing to overcome the class antagonisms of the society and demeaning because it attacks the moral fiber of the recipient. Indeed, the most important effect of direct charity is the deterioration of the individual's incentive to work. Thus, direct charity encourages idleness and permanent dependency on others.

Besides fear of the poor and suspicion of direct charity, the Charity Organization Societies also had faith in the usefulness of science in administering organizations and treating the poor. The societies were operated in very businesslike ways and every penny was accounted for. In addition, casework developed largely because of the concern for the scientific study and treatment of the poor. Each family was carefully studied in order to determine the true causes of its poverty and whether family members deserved aid or not.

Finally, the Charity Organization Societies were influenced by the Social Darwinist philosophy that was popular in some circles at the time. Generally, the proponents of this philosophy argued that all societies go through a similar evolution and that competition is key to that evolution. Those who are rich, powerful, or otherwise in advantaged positions in society thus represent the most able and deserving persons: they are winners in the competition of life. The poor and powerless, on the other hand, are not only losers but have personal qualities that account for their lack of success. Social Darwinists argued further that any attempt to change the prevailing arrangement of society would disrupt the natural processes of competition and evolution. At best, charity helps the least fit to survive longer than they should, and, at worst, charity allows the unfit to attain levels of wealth and power that undermine the progressive evolution of society.

In sum, the Charity Organization Societies embodied the self-serving ideas and interests of a segment of the society that wished to forget the poor but felt it had to do something to control their dangerous tendencies. What emerged was a form of charity that stressed efficient administration, friendly visiting, and strict, often cruel, standards for separating the deserving and undeserving poor. The administrative emphasis of the Charity Organization Societies is evident in the rationale for their establishment. It was argued that there were too many charity organizations in existence and that they were giving away money indiscriminately. The Charity Organization Societies were founded to end the chaos and to put a stop to the unintended moral deterioration of the poor that such practices encouraged. Friendly visiting was an attempt by COS leaders to reduce class antagonisms. The friendly visitors were affluent volunteers who presumably went to the homes of the poor to talk, help them with their problems, and gather scientific information for studying the poor. It was assumed that if the poor and affluent could meet as equals, both would be improved: "The poor would realize that the rich were their friends rather than their oppressors, and the rich might benefit from the examples of courage and good cheer displayed by the poor" (Lubove, 1973: 14). In practice, the friendly visitors often increased the antagonism of the poor; instead of treating the poor as equals, they often treated them as sinners who deserved to be preached at. In addition to the friendly visitors, each Charity Organization Society had a full-time worker, who spend much of his or her time coordinating the friendly visitor program and making decisions about the poor's deservingness. The most important criteria for making these decisions were the industriousness and temperance of the poor. Any family that had an unemployed member or a known drinker was ineligible for the small amount of aid the workers handed out.

In many ways the Charity Organization Societies were private counterparts to the almshouses. Neither took seriously the idea that poverty and idleness might be related to the absence of jobs or seasonal fluctuations in employment opportunities. Both assumed that becoming successful was simply a matter of hard work and thus looked at the personal qualities of the poor as the ultimate cause of poverty.

These were not the only visions of the poor that existed at the time in the United States, however. Indeed, much of the criticism of the Charity Organization Societies came from persons who stressed economic factors as the source of poverty. One clergyman noted that using the moralistic criteria of the Charity Organization Societies as a standard for deservingness, Jesus and the twelve disciples would have to be classified as vagrants and therefore undeserving of aid or sympathy (Trattner, 1979). Perhaps the most important critics of the Charity Organization Societies were Jane Addams and other members of the *Settlement House Movement*. They were affluent people who rejected conventionality and moved into the slums with the poor. Based on their everyday experiences with the poor, they described a world of unemployment, low wages, overwork, and dangerous working conditions. Radicalism and immorality among the poor were treated as insignificant issues by these reformers. Thus, though they took different sides, both the Charity Organization Societies and the Settlement House Movement tended to think of the dilemma of poverty in terms of whether to excuse or to blame the poor.

Modern Images of the Poor

The conceptualization of the dilemma of poverty began to change during the latter part of the nineteenth and early twentieth centuries. The movement to professionalize charity work helped bring about the change. Both social work and contemporary approaches to dealing with the poor emerged out of this process (Wilensky and Lebeaux, 1958). The Charity Organization Societies themselves spurred professionalization, because members were tied together in various associations which provided them with opportunities to build a common identity and find collective solutions to their problems. The casework technique developed in the Charity Organization Societies also aided professionalization. This technique was elaborated and refined in the highly influential book *Social Diagnosis* by Mary Richmond (1917). Richmond argued that casework could be made truly scientific, and much of her book is a detailed description of how best to do casework. The book was an important reference for caseworkers, but it was also symbolically important because it was used to counter the popular claim that social workers had no special body of knowledge. Similarly, many Settlement House workers and others in social welfare agencies emphasized the need for formal education as well as practical experience in dealing with the poor. Some agencies arranged for college extension courses in social work areas and others opened their own schools of social work within their agencies.

But these were only the beginnings of the professionalization of social work. The full transformation of charity workers into professional workers was linked to several other developments, including the elimination of friendly visitors and other volunteers as major welfare workers, the incorporation of social work education into university curricula, the development of a variety of professional associations representing the diverse activities of social workers, and the incorporation of social workers into such professional settings as hospitals and schools. Each of those developments furthered the claim of social workers that they possessed special knowledge and skills that were both needed by the public and unavailable in other professions. In the long run, however, the two most important developments were the acceptance of a psychiatric vision of the poor and the Great Depression of the 1930s.

Although social workers had recognized the psychiatric approach to poverty and other social problems for many years, they remained committed to traditional casework methods. During and after World War I, the two approaches of treating the poor were combined, and the specialty of *psychiatric social work* emerged (Lubove, 1973; Woodroofe, 1962). Thus, the day of the friendly visitor who traveled to the homes of the poor to collect information and to comfort the poor ended. Now the proper treatment of the poor called for the services of a trained professional who worked in a clinic filled with the paraphernalia of science and professionalism. Accompanying this change was a changing conception of the causes of poverty. The old emphasis on moral criteria for judging the poor, which flourished in the Charity Organization Societies, was replaced by a vision of the poor as emotionally inadequate—a vision encouraged by Freud's belief in the unconscious as a major influence on human behavior. Social workers who accepted this view saw themselves not just as well-intentioned persons who offered charity and comfort, but as highly skilled experts who understood the true causes of clients' problems. Indeed, they often assumed that the problems of clients were so complex and deep-seated that it was impossible for clients to understand their own difficulties and motivations. Those seeking emergency financial aid, for example, often had to sit through the efforts of a social worker to go beyond their apparent problem to the true problem assumed to lie beneath (Woodroofe, 1962).

The adoption of a psychiatric orientation did not involve a complete break with the past, however. Indeed, this approach to the poor was only the most recent of many historical tendencies to blame the poor for their problems. If the problems of the poor are conceptualized exclusively as problems of individual inadequacy, then there is no need to deal with the environment in which the poor live. Thus such problems as unemployment and underemployment were treated not only as areas in which social workers had little influence but as areas totally irrelevant to the treatment of the poor. This position was most explicitly developed by Virginia Robinson, who argued that there is no reality external to the individual and therefore no objective environment to analyze and manipulate (Lubove, 1973). Rather, it is the job of the professional social worker to analyze the individual and restore him or her to good health.

Although not always intended, the assumptions of Virginia Robinson are evident in many social work settings today. For example, a basic assumption of the Cedarview staff (discussed in the last chapter) is that emotional disturbance is an individual problem. Consequently, little attention is given to the ways in which poverty or family relationships may influence the children's behavior. Equally important, little attention is given to the ways in which the environment of Cedarview may affect the children. Another important consequence of this individualistic conception of the mission of social work is that professionalism is often defined as technique: a professional social worker is a person who provides a service to the client, and any greater concern for the client, such as an interest in obtaining legislation to increase jobs or welfare payments, is deemed unnecessary. Indeed, in its most developed form, the argument for this style of professional service includes the claim that a truly professional relationship with a client requires that the social worker always remains aloof and uninvolved in the client's problem (Galper, 1975).

The introduction of psychiatry into social work is, then, important for several reasons. It provided social workers with a "scientific" basis for claiming professional standing. It reaffirmed the individualistic biases of many social workers and political officials, though giving them a new rationale. (The poor were no longer seen as immoral, only sick.) Finally, acceptance of a psychiatric approach to social work encouraged the development of a conservative view of professionalism, one that did not challenge the existing economic and political arrangement of the society.

Another basis for conservatism was the incorporation of social workers into administrative and policy-making positions in government. The major impetus for this development was the Great Depression of the 1930s; indeed, almost all of Franklin Roosevelt's attempts to deal with the problems of unemployment involved social workers to some degree. At first there was direct relief for the unemployed and later government-sponsored jobs such as those provided by the Works Progress Administration, which built many schools, roads, hospitals, and other public buildings (Piven and Cloward, 1971). The involvement of social workers in the Roosevelt administration is further reflected in the key roles played by Harry Hopkins, a presidential adviser, and Frances Perkins, the Secretary of Labor, in formulating the government's response to the Depression. Both of these political figures were social workers, and they encouraged the expansion of government investment in social welfare programs.

Thus, the beginnings of the so-called welfare state are found in the administration of Franklin D. Roosevelt. The *welfare state*, which is still with us today, is characterized by the proliferation of public welfare programs intended to benefit many sectors of the society. Among the beneficiaries are the recipients of social security, workmen's compensation, unemployment insurance, and Aid to Families with Dependent Children (AFDC). The underlying justification for such programs is the belief that the government has an obligation to ensure a minimum standard of living for all citizens. Although there is periodic debate about the extent of the government's obligation, all administrations since Roosevelt, both Democratic and Republican, have been committed to the welfare state. Indeed, well-publicized efforts to cut back welfare programs often obscure the fact that as offices are closed, the programs within them are moved into new departments. When President Nixon abolished the Office of Economic Opportunity in 1974–1975, for example, he eliminated only the office; its most important programs (Community action programs, community legal services, and Head Start) were continued within new departments (Axinn and Levin, 1975).

The incorporation of welfare programs and social workers within the sphere of government responsibility has important implications for the poor. One of the most important is the bureaucratization of welfare services. Although the treatment given the poor in the early colonies and by COS volunteers was often demeaning and unnecessarily harsh, bureaucratic welfare also involves problems. Of special importance is the way in which cases and statistics are created and used within modern welfare departments (Altheide and Johnson, 1980; Street, Martin, and Gordon, 1979). Indeed, the vision of the poor as sinners is replaced in bureaucratic agencies with a vision of them as human material which must be processed in an efficient and orderly manner. Bureaucratic procedures and rules have come to replace temperance and righteousness as the major criteria for distinguishing the deserving from the undeserving poor. In addition, single-room occupancy hotels, residential treatment centers, and similar settings are the contemporary counterparts to the almshouses of the nineteenth century. It is within these institutional settings that we place those who are deviant, idle, or otherwise deemed threats to the social order (Elman, 1966; Scull, 1977).

The emergence of the welfare state, then, has not signaled the end of the concerns first articulated in the Poor Law of 1601; indeed, the concerns have only been redefined and implemented differently. Many private welfare programs, some of which continue to practice a kind of friendly visiting, are still in existence. Migrant workers in New York, for example, often have to endure the visits of local volunteers, who bring their secondhand clothes and their self-serving questions, such as "Well, why do you think it is, son, that colored people just don't seem to want to work hard; that they have such low motivation?" (Friedland and Nelkin, 1971: 279). Many of the earlier concerns about allowing the poor to remain idle and unproductive are also evident in recent government programs for the poor.

One popular program is the *sheltered workshop*, which is a place where persons who are unable to compete for jobs in the larger society are often sent (Macarov, 1980). It is assumed that such people are handicapped due to age, physical or emotional disorders, or lack of skills. The sheltered workshop gives such "unemployables" an opportunity to work at unskilled, often monotonous, jobs, which presumably make them better workers and less dependent on the public dole. In practice, sheltered workshops pay very little money and, therefore, reduce dependence on public relief very little. The goal of improving the work skills of the sheltered workers is also undermined often by the demand of local employers and unions that the workshops not produce goods which compete with local businesses and jobs. The option often selected is to produce toys, knickknacks, and similar items, the production of which does little to improve the employability of the workers. Further, the products are often openly marketed as items made by the handicapped which the public should buy for charitable reasons, not because the items or the workers who produced them are worthy. Another hindrance to the effectiveness of the workshops is the expectation that they pay much of their own way. Given that expectation, a worker's productivity may become an important criterion for being admitted to the program and for remaining in it.

Perhaps the most important indication of the continuing interest in distinguishing the deserving from the undeserving poor is the periodic call to make willingness to work a requirement for receiving welfare. Agricultural areas have used this criterion to require welfare recipients to take low-paying farm jobs during the busy planting and harvesting seasons (Piven and Cloward, 1971). When all of the work is done, the people are then returned to the welfare rolls. The Work Incentive Program, initiated in 1967, also uses this requirement and has even extended it in the past few years (Axinn and Levin, 1975). With the exception of a few people, the program requires that any adult or out-of-school child receiving AFDC payments must be available for work or job training. This requirement effectively negates the original intent of the AFDC program, which was to encourage women with small children to remain in the home as full-time mothers and housewives.

Both the sheltered workshop and the Work Incentive Program reflect the continuing dilemma that work and welfare pose for modern society. On the one hand, the old, young, handicapped, and deserted are treated as deserving poor, but on the other hand, we have difficulty giving up the notion that everyone should have a conventional job. For this reason, the history of legislation dealing with the poor points to a pattern of vacillation, as old programs and laws are negated by new ones based on different standards of deservingness. Current welfare laws and regulations are thus riddled with contradictions. As the number of welfare programs has increased, for example, there has also been a conscious attempt to keep benefits low enough so that the poor still have an incentive to work. Thus, persons on social security are expected to live on incomes that are considerably below those of their working years, even though retirement is often forced upon them. This problem is exacerbated by other regulations limiting the amount of money that recipients can officially earn to supplement their social security benefits.

The Effects of Official Images on Hustling Realities

The financial inadequacy of most welfare programs together with the moralistic and bureaucratic restrictions placed on such programs are experienced by the poor as practical problems of everyday life. They may resent their treatment and the assumptions others make about them, but a more important and pressing problem is making a living. Their involvement in the diverse activities that constitute modern hustling is a response to that problem. Two examples of hustlers will be discussed in the next section, but before turning to them it is necessary to look at the ways in which the historical processes discussed here have affected the social realities of hustlers. Table 5-1 summarizes those effects.

Because there are many different welfare and hustling settings, it is not possible to describe them all here. The two identified in Table 5-1 are composite types. The first, termed "indoor relief," refers to welfare settings where people are institutionalized, such as almshouses. Within such institutions time is organized diachronically, and work is supposed to occur as a regular and continuous feature of organizational life. This ideal is often not achieved, however. For example, in the nineteenth-

Table 5-1 • Sources of Hustling Realities

Welfare Setting	*Work-Related Timetables*	*Work-Related Communities*
Indoor Relief	Diachronic: based on continuous and discontinuous work activities of the institution	Enduring: based on enduring relations inmates develop with each other and with the institutional staff
Outdoor Relief	Diachronic: based on the discontinuous nature of activities required by welfare organizations and by other sources of making a living	Mixed: based on varying relations with welfare officials, coworkers and members of the public

century almshouse the poor spent almost all of their time in idleness. Thus, the timetables of institutionalized workers may be discontinuous. Because indoor relief is based on the centralization of the poor in an institution, there is little contact between the public and the inmates. For this reason, the work-related communities of indoor relief may be thought of as enduring and based on the regular encounters of individuals with institutional staff and other inmates.

The social realities of outdoor relief are different because this welfare setting allows the poor to remain at large. Time for persons not confined to institutions is experienced diachronically, but the problems of dealing with welfare rules and procedures often means that their income is discontinuous. The supplementary work that hustlers do also gives rise to a discontinuous experience of time, because few hustles last a long time. Indeed, the poor are often thought of as present oriented (i.e., subject to synchronic time) because of their welfare and hustling experiences, and that orientation is usually considered pathological. Because of the variety of settings and activities in which recipients of outdoor relief may be found, their work-related communities are mixed, based on their enduring, shifting, and fleeting relations with welfare officials, coworkers, and members of the public.

Because Table 5-1 gives a picture of composite types, the complexity of hustling work is obscured. Although hustlers generally have a diachronic view of life and work, the uncertainties of their existences often mean that they place high priority on immediate needs and opportunities, which could be described as a synchronic view. Moreover, the distinction between indoor and outdoor relief is not always easily maintained, because there are many contemporary institutions that have qualities of both. The sheltered workshop is an example, because the poor are gathered within this institution for work, but they are allowed to return to their homes when it is done. Single-room occupancy hotels also have many features of indoor relief, but they are not usually operated by welfare officials, nor are the residents monitored in the same way that residents of almshouses were. There are, then, a variety of intermediate settings between indoor and outdoor relief, although both extremes continue to exist. Social security is a widely recognized form of outdoor relief, and prisons, mental hospitals, and residential treatment centers are important places for institutionalizing the contemporary poor and deviant.

THE SOCIAL REALITIES OF HUSTLING WORKERS

Because no single example could adequately demonstrate the essential features of hustling and welfare realities, we will deal with two of them here—the Irish Tinkers and the residents of single-room occupancy hotels. The Irish Tinkers show how economic disruptions may give rise to a roving population that evolves a culture and way of life based on begging, scavenging, and similar "marginal" economic activities. They also provide a useful example of the impact of urbanization and welfare on such free-floating groups. The residents of single-room occupancy hotels are mainly the poor and deviant. They live in these hotels, which are clustered in the low-income areas of many cities, because the rents are cheap and welfare officials often place them there. The single-room occupancy hotel, then, represents an intermediate type between indoor and outdoor relief and the social realities of the residents reflect both settings.

Life among the Irish Tinkers

Originally the word "tinker" was applied to the tinsmiths who traveled the Irish countryside in search of work (Sharon Gmelch, 1975, 1976; George Gmelch, 1977). The word refers to the sound that the tinsmiths' hammers make as they pound tin. Their itinerant style of work was necessary because few of the small rural villages could support a full-time tinsmith. The original population of tinkers was later increased by the addition of other craftspeople, such as tailors, weavers, thatchers, chimney sweeps, and peasants who had been driven from their lands because of crop failures and the exploitative practices of landlords and the government (George Gmelch, 1977). These various groups form the nucleus of the *Irish Tinkers,* who over the course of many years developed a unique way of life based on their nomadism. Although poverty and finding sufficient work continue to plague the Tinkers, they cannot be described merely as a band of roving craftspeople and peasants. They have become a distinct ethnic group, which is viewed in antagonistic and romantic ways by different segments of Irish society.

The unique life style and outlook of the Tinkers can be traced to their diverse ways of making a living. Indeed, until they began to settle in urban areas in the 1950s, the Tinkers were an important part of the Irish rural economy. They were willing to take short-term jobs that offered no future employment, such as farm work during harvesting season. They also provided services that were not always available in rural villages, including tinsmithing and cleaning chimneys, but also often peddling and horse trading. As the men traded, the traditional Tinker women sometimes told fortunes and they always begged. The people supplemented these economic activities by collecting discarded objects which could be resold (scavenging), hunting and snaring, and stealing, particularly stealing fruits and vegetables from the fields.

The Tinkers could support themselves through these activities because they were willing to accept a low standard of living and because they constantly moved about the small regions that they worked. Thus, when one village no longer offered customers, employment, or other sources of income, the Tinkers moved on to more promising villages. This nomadic style was encouraged by the organization of Tinker life around a horse-drawn wagon and the nuclear family. The wagon was both a home and a business, because it carried the personal belongings of the family as well as items to be sold and traded. Indeed, the two types of items were often not distinct, since almost everything owned by a Tinker family was potentially salable. Even the horse pulling the wagon was available, if a good offer was made. The center of Tinker social life was the nuclear family, which provided its members with their only enduring relationships. Sometimes two or three families traveled together, but such arrangements were usually filled with conflict and, consequently, membership in the traveling group was constantly changing. The importance of the nuclear family is apparent in the absence of any great commitment to a clan or other large family unit. Except for funerals and other special occasions, the center of Tinker life was the nuclear family, and every member of the family made a contribution. Even infants were used to elicit sympathy and make begging easier.

But the traditional Tinker way of life was made up of more than just family and work. A unique language and way of seeing the world were also characteristic. An important part of the Tinker world view was a belief in the joys of rural and itinerant life, as opposed to the more conventional pattern of settling in one place. That view made the Tinkers objects of suspicion among the settled rural residents, who often told their children stories of how they would be given to the Tinkers if they misbehaved and who also blamed almost all vandalism on the Tinkers.

The Tinkers were not blameless in their relations with the settled population. Tinker men were very good horse traders, and they often took advantage of farmers. They also did damage to fields and crops when they let their horses loose to graze in available fields and when they stole fruits and vegetables. Admittedly, though, some farmers did overreact to the Tinkers by shooting at them and falsely accusing them of crimes. Thus, the nomadic life style of the Tinkers gave rise to relations outside the nuclear family that were filled with conflict and suspicion.

The traditional Tinker way of life changed in the 1950s when Ireland began to modernize and rural life was transformed. The old services of the Tinkers were no longer desired, because plastic utensils were now available and new transportation channels made it easy for rural people to travel to towns and cities where the number of household items for sale greatly exceeded the number Tinker peddlers could offer. The mechanization of farming also meant that the demand for seasonal workers and horses was eliminated as tractors and other implements took the place of both people and horses. Finally, the traditional Tinker way of life was undermined by the systematic killing of most of the rabbits in rural Ireland. Although they were a major destroyer of crops, the rabbits were also an important source of food for the Tinkers. No matter how unprofitable the day had been, a Tinker family had been able to depend on hunting rabbits to tide them over. With their disappearance, a major source of sustenance was gone.

The changing circumstances of rural life forced Tinkers to turn to cities in order to look for new ways of making a living. But the Tinkers were not just pushed into the city; they were also attracted to it because it offered new sources of income. The most important attractions were the easy availability of welfare payments from the government and private charities, the abundance of scrap metal and other materials for collecting and reselling, and the advantages of begging in densely populated areas. Although each is consistent with Tinker tradition, all of the attractions have also been sources of change.

Tinker men have become highly skilled urban scavengers and traders. They travel the city in horse-drawn carts and trucks seeking old mattresses, furniture, deposit bottles, clothing, rags, and metal items such as worn-out pots and pans, appliances, bicycles, and the like (George Gmelch, 1977). The Tinkers have also aroused suspicion among city residents, because the residents know that many of their scrap items are worth more money than the Tinkers are willing to pay. The residents are not always aware of which items are valuable, however, and much of the Tinkers' negotiations are attempts to manipulate the residents into making the wrong assessment. As one observer notes: "They may feign disinterest in items which would actually be of value to them, bargaining enthusiastically for a relatively worthless object; only later to return, seemingly with reluctance to the desired object" (George Gmelch, 1977:66). The urban Tinker scavengers have also developed new skills in dealing with the buyers of used metal. Because the price of a metal object is based on its weight, the Tinkers have developed ways of increasing the weight of their goods. For example, they put dirt or molten lead inside radiators. These attempts at cheating by the Tinkers are often counterbalanced by the buyers' attempts to take advantage of Tinker illiteracy by misreading scales and receipts. The tradition of horse trading, then, continues in the urban Tinker world, although horses are no longer the object of trade.

The Tinker women also continue their traditional begging activities. Indeed, the urban setting has allowed women to become an increasingly important part of the Tinker work force, because many of the traditional male sources of income have disappeared and begging is more profitable in the city than the country. There are two types of Tinker begging: street begging and door-to-door begging (George Gmelch, 1977; George Gmelch and Sharon Gmelch, 1978; Sharon Gmelch, 1975). Each type of begging requires a somewhat different strategy. Begging on the street is based on a fleeting encounter in which appearance is vital. Thus, street beggars wear tattered and dirty clothes, carry a young child, and, most important, use facial expressions to communicate their forlorn circumstances. Very often Tinker women work in teams so that when one person finds a donor she can signal to the other person who is also seeking charity. When the usual strategy is not effective, Tinker women sometimes follow pedestrians and talk to them in loud voices. By creating a scene, the women focus attention on the pedestrian, who gets unwanted attention and appears to be a callous miser. The pedestrian will often give in to get out of the limelight.

Door-to-door begging also involves the use of a child and wearing old clothes, but this encounter is less fleeting than begging on the street. For this reason, door-to-door beggars must develop a story to tell the house dweller. The story usually involves several related themes. First, the beggar appeals to the "Christian mercy" of the resident and her need for a little help. She continues by describing how she only wants a donation for the benefit of her children, who do not deserve their fate. Often the beggar's current difficulty is explained by reference to her husband's illness or, if the resident feels sympathy for only the wife and children, by his frequent drunkenness and desertion of the family. A very important person in door-to-door begging is the child, because if he or she is adorable, then the donations are usually larger. Indeed, one especially attractive and playful child in a Dublin Tinker camp was shared by all the women. There is at least one more way in which door-to-door begging can be different from street begging: some women develop patronesses who give only to that beggar. These women take a special interest in a Tinker family and are willing to make frequent and generous gifts. In addition, the patronesses often give advice or help when the family is in trouble with the police or welfare officials, and they may even lobby to change legislation affecting Tinkers. The strategy for dealing with patronesses is, then, different from the one for dealing with others, because the patroness is interested in the truth about the family. She has already committed herself to giving, regardless of the family's situation. For this reason, a visit to the patroness is without dirty and tattered clothes or appeals to religion or sympathy for the children. In this way the urbanization of the Tinkers has given rise to routine begging styles and relationships.

The most important change in the Tinker life style, however, is the relationship Tinkers have developed with welfare officials in the city. On the one hand, welfare offers the Tinker family a steady and secure income, which can be supplemented by begging and scavenging. In fact, many males eagerly await their eighteenth birthday because they are then eligible for unemployment assistance. On the other hand, the Tinkers are losing much of their resourcefulness and independence as they become more dependent on public and private charity. Indeed, an important new activity of Tinker women is keeping social workers contented so that these sources of income will not be threatened. Besides supplying income, welfare officials have also played a key role in trying to settle the Tinkers in conventional housing. Although the Tinkers have become urbanized, they have tended to live on the outskirts of the city in wagons and makeshift homes. This arrangement makes it easy to move when a conflict in the campsite becomes too intense or if a family wishes to return to the road for a time. The placement of Tinkers in permanent housing eliminates these options, and it limits the family's ability to store scrap materials, keep horses, or beg in the neighborhood, since neighbors object to these traditional Tinker practices. In addition, Tinkers are sometimes scattered in the resettlement, so that old relationships and practices are destroyed. Many of the failures of settlement programs can be accounted for by the loneliness and sometimes blatant ostracism that often accompanies placing a single Tinker family in a neighborhood.

There are some advantages to the settlement efforts, however. Most important are the amenities of a settled life—electricity, indoor toilets, and kitchen appliances, for example. These benefits make settlement especially attractive to Tinker women, who have the major responsibility for housekeeping and child care. In addition, some Tinkers see settlement as a solution to the problems in many Tinker campsites of conflict and drunkenness, which have increased as the scavenging activities of the men have decreased in importance. Not only do the men have less to do in the city, but the most important work of the family is being done by women. Indeed, this pattern is likely to continue into the future, because most Tinker men have great difficulty obtaining and keeping conventional jobs. Male unemployment is partly accounted for by the prejudices of settled Irish people about Tinkers, but it also reflects the difficulties the men have in giving up their traditional life style. Simply put, many Tinker men find conventional jobs boring, they resent their authoritarian bosses, and they lack the conventional knowledge, including basic literacy skills, that would enable them to get ahead.

The future of the Tinkers is unclear. It is possible that this ethnic group will disappear as the men and women take on conventional roles and life styles. Such a change would require that Tinkers develop new sources of knowledge and a new perspective consistent with settlement and competition for conventional jobs. The past urbanization of the Tinkers, which significantly eroded old work skills and values stressing nomadism, supports this outcome. But another possible outcome is that the Tinkers will become permanent welfare recipients. If that occurs, the Tinkers will also be eliminated as an ethnic group, though their life style will be different from that of conventional Irish people. For example, hustling will become a necessity, as it is for most welfare recipients worldwide. Some insight into how important hustling is to welfare recipients and the possible future of the Tinkers is offered next.

Life in Single-Room Occupancy Hotels

Although the poor have lived in low-rent hotels for a long time, the government has officially sanctioned this style of life only since the rise of the welfare state. Some hotels are now important places for locating the old, poor, and handicapped who do not need other forms of institutionalization, such as placement in hospitals or nursing homes. One consequence of this development is that a variety of people who provide services to the poor have become dependent on the government for their livings. Put differently, the welfare state does not undermine private enterprise so much as it offers new opportunities to entrepreneurs who provide services to the poor. Another consequence is that the poor are concentrated within a small area, which encourages the development of a distinctive way of life based on their common problems. That way of life has been the object of much theorizing, and one of the most important of those theories will be discussed in the next section.

Here we will look at two examples of *single-room occupancy hotels* (*SROs*). One example is taken from a study of several SROs in New York City (Siegal, 1978) and the other from a study of the Guinevere Hotel in a large Midwestern city (Stephens, 1976). SROs are hotels that have low rents and offer more or less permanent residency to their occupants. For the residents the hotel and the surrounding area is their neighborhood, and their rooms are their homes; indeed, SRO residents sometimes refer to their rooms as their houses. By any standard of assessment, the world of the SRO resident is depressed. At the Guinevere Hotel, for example, the average weekly rent for the 108 permanent residents is $20.59 per week, and most residents live in a bedroom with no bath. The hotel provides a once-a-week maid service, and some rooms also have television (Stephens, 1976). The rooms are small and dingy with the only cooking facility being a hot plate that is sometimes provided by management. A communal kitchen is available, but the lack of security and cleanliness in the hotel makes it easy for food to be stolen or to spoil. For this reason many SRO residents eat every meal in neighborhood restaurants, while others buy small amounts of groceries each day. In winter the need for a daily trip to the grocery store is decreased, because some items can be kept cool by placing them outside on windowsills.

The crowdedness and dinginess of the rooms is also characteristic of the rest of the hotel, which is usually poorly lit and dirty. In addition, the hotel is often permeated by a concern for security. For example, some hotel personnel make a conscious effort to keep nonresidents out, and mirrors which allow the clerk to watch the entire hotel lobby are everywhere. The most striking feature of most SRO hotel lobbies, however, is the caged enclosure through which business is transacted. One observer describes such enclosures this way: "In some hotels, the precautions are so elaborate as to include electronically operated doors, bullet-proof glass with a narrow opening, set at right angles to the base panel, through which mail or communications can be passed, or thick plexiglass carousels to move material between tenant and management. . . . Prominently visible from the outsider's perspective is an armamentarium of baseball bats, taped pipes, nightsticks, heavy clubs and even firearms, hanging in mute anticipation of any sort of trouble" (Siegal, 1978: 59–60).

The SRO world is built on uncertainty and squalor, which are reflected in almost all aspects of SRO life. Both are evident in the physical conditions of most hotels and the emphasis on security. But the uncertain and squalid nature of SRO hotels goes deeper than this: it pervades the various relationships found there. For residents, it is a continuing struggle to maintain personal dignity in light of the various threats in their environments, including assaults on their person administered by muggers and assaults on their dignity administered by those who are supposed to help them. In the process of providing services that are intended to reduce the squalor and uncertainty of SRO life, caretakers often introduce new problems into the lives of the residents. Two of the most important sources of aid and problems for SRO residents are hotel managers and welfare officials.

A fundamental feature of SROs is that they provide income for hotel personnel, and for this reason many of the most important events in the residents' lives occur because of the desire of hotel personnel to protect or increase their incomes. In some hotels, for example, the manager collects the residents' social security and other welfare checks and hands them over only when the rent is paid. The manager usually cashes the checks and gives residents what is left after the rent is paid. To gain the authority to do this, the hotel manager must convince welfare officials that a resident is incompetent and needs help in dealing with financial matters. If welfare officials agree, a resident's check will then be made payable to both the resident and manager. Thus, the resident cannot cash his or her check without the endorsement of the manager, who demands that the rent be paid in exchange for the endorsement (Siegal, 1978). Another technique to force rent payment is the "lockout," in which a plug is placed in the keyhole of the resident's room. It is impossible to remove the plug without a proper key, and, consequently, the manager can force the resident into paying the rent or risk never seeing his or her belongings again.

Economic considerations are also important in perpetuating SROs as dirty and deteriorating places, because improving these hotels is often not economically feasible from the viewpoint of managers and owners, who are often small-time operators. Indeed, if an extensive renovation occurred, rents would probably increase beyond the residents' ability to pay. In some cases an SRO may be owned by an investment group, which buys a hotel and holds it until its market value increases significantly, and then sells—often to another investment group. In the interim, the investor makes some money from the rents and has little incentive to make improvements in the hotel, since it would not increase the hotel's market value very much and the margin of profit would be reduced. Even the manager hired by the investment group has little interest in improving the hotel, because his or her income is usually based on the hotel's total profit. Thus, improvements in the hotel would also reduce the manager's income.

But money is not the only uncertain feature of SROs, and it is not the only consideration of hotel personnel. They are also concerned with the maintenance of order and security. Their concern is partly related to the crime-ridden neighborhoods in which SROs are located, but it is also based on the assumption that the residents are potentially troublesome. Some managers cultivate a network of informants among the residents, who exchange information for small favors managers dispense. Other residents are hired as desk clerks, security guards, porters, and maids, and a part of their job is providing the manager with information about the goings-on of the hotel (Siegal, 1978). Finally, SRO hotel managers attempt to control trouble by exchanging information about residents. A tenant who has been thrown out of several hotels, for example, is likely to find that he or she has great difficulty in getting into other hotels because word has spread.

Despite these efforts, trouble does develop in SRO hotels, and when it occurs the manager may use hotel personnel to restore order. Indeed, security guards are major figures in the lives of SRO residents, because they are a regular source of physical threat. In addition, hotel managers often cultivate a relationship with police officers, which makes it possible for the managers to use them to control residents. The managers, for example, provide the police with information about cases and may even inform them if a wanted person is in the hotel. In exchange, the police are often willing to intervene in disputes within the hotel. These disputes may include major confrontations involving criminal acts, or they may involve petty quarrels over hotel matters in which the police often have no legal right to intervene. Equally important, the police almost always accept the hotel managers' accounts of incidents. Practically speaking, then, the managers have the law on their side in dealing with hotel residents.

The relationship between managers and residents is not totally conflict-ridden or based on economic and security concerns, however, because the managers may develop personal relationships with some long-term residents and allow these people to violate hotel rules or even be late with their rent. In addition, the hotel managers' concern for safety and security is not just self-serving, since it is also a service to residents who wish to live in an orderly and safe world. Another service that hotel managers provide is watching for illness and accidents among the residents. At the Hotel Guinevere, for example, the manager continually tells his employees to watch for residents who might be sick in their rooms and unable to alert others. Similarly, hotel managers usually accept responsibility for notifying the families of persons who die in their hotels and for planning the burials of those who have no relatives.

The relationship between hotel managers and residents, then, cannot simply be reduced to the claim that managers exploit the residents. There is no doubt that managers sometimes use and control the residents in unethical, if not exploitative ways, but they also provide services that are unavailable from other sources. In addition, managers are usually willing to overlook the criminal activities of permanent residents. Some of the women in SRO hotels, for example, use prostitution as a means of increasing their incomes, and so long as they do not attract the police or the other residents' rent money is not being spent for their services, then most managers choose to ignore it. Similarly, illegal alcohol and other drugs are easily available in most SRO hotels, because hotel employees seeking to supplement their incomes often provide them. Finally, the notion that managers exploit residents overlooks the ways in which residents attempt to manipulate the managers. Getting the rent is often a problem for managers, who must deal with residents who are very good at feigning forgetfulness or other reasons for nonpayment. Similarly, many residents are involved in a continuing attempt to get their managers to bend the rules for their special case.

The picture of SRO hotels as places where managers exploit residents is unbalanced; instead, SROs should be looked upon as places where practical, self-interested people attempt to control their fates. The residents are as likely to use others as are the managers. The utilitarian perspective of residents is evident in their relations with social workers who come to the hotel to help residents. The residents and social workers define the word "help" differently. For the social workers help is the same as treatment, and financial aid is only a small part of their attempt to remold the individual. For the residents, however, help is money, and the other activities of the social workers are seen as unnecessary and bothersome. But the residents also recognize that their welfare checks are partially dependent on the reports of social workers, and so they tolerate this intrusion into their world.

Besides dealing with social workers who visit the hotel, residents must also confront the welfare bureaucracy, which they experience as a distant and mysterious force in their lives. Whether it is the Veterans Administration, the Social Security Administration, or a local welfare agency, SRO residents must cope with the variety of bureaucratic rules and procedures that make up the contemporary welfare state. Equally important, they must deal with the language of bureaucracy, a language they seldom understand. As Harvey Siegal notes:

> The arrival of an official looking, windowed envelope evokes fear and anxiety in most; they wonder "what do they want now." Since many SRO'ers find it difficult to understand the communication, which is invariably written in bureaucratese, it is ignored. Subsequent letters generally receive the same treatment and the SRO'er is then shocked if the stipend that he is used to receiving fails to arrive (Siegal, 1978: 80).

The next step in getting the stipend reissued is also mysterious, because it typically involves a hearing at which more rules, procedures, and bureaucratese are found. Because of these problems, most SRO residents feel powerless in the face of welfare agencies, and few attempt to acquire the knowledge necessary to manipulate these organizations to their advantage. Rather, most quietly acquiesce to what they perceive as greater power, or they futilely resist through a public display of bravado such as the threat of a lawsuit.

A major reason why SRO residents have so much difficulty with the welfare bureaucracy is that they live in a highly personalized world, and the world of welfare officials is impersonal. The residents' ability to manipulate personal relationships is evident in their dealings with hotel personnel and social workers who come to the hotel. Residents regularly use both of these types of people to achieve their ends. The personalized nature of the SRO world is also reflected in relationships among residents. Although the residents place a high premium on privacy and autonomy, they are willing to join groups in order to solve some of their problems (Siegal, 1978). In some SRO hotels, for example, alcoholics and other addicts establish "helping pairs" so that the intoxicated person is not totally at the mercy of muggers and others. Similarly, some SRO hotels have "quasi-family" groups, in which a woman gathers a number of men around her. Although they live in different rooms, the woman cooks the men's meals and collects their various welfare payments, including their food stamps. She uses some of the money to buy food and gives some of it back to the men in small amounts according to their needs. The world of SRO residents is not, then, simply controlled by outsiders, for the residents themselves develop their own ways of dealing with the squalor and uncertainty of their lives.

Another important way in which SRO residents attempt to control their lives is by hustling for extra money. Prostitution, cited earlier, is an example. Indeed, hustling is sufficiently widespread that various types of hustles are ranked differently by residents (English and Stephens, 1975; Stephens, 1976). The major criteria for distinguishing hustles are the profitability of the hustle, its regularity and dependability, and the degree of personal control enjoyed by the hustler. A respectable hustle is one which is regular, yields a good profit, and allows the hustler great independence and control. Developing a respectable hustle is often a problem for SRO residents, because, based on their age, they are excluded from many of the most profitable and dependable areas of deviant work. Racketeers, for example, often refuse to hire old hustlers, because they assume that these people are undependable. A respectable hustle in SRO circles, then, is often considered to be a marginal and disreputable enterprise by others. Examples of such hustles are begging, shoplifting, small-time conning operations, and small-time attempts to procure young girls for prostitution and other crimes.

Perhaps the most respectable hustle is working as a "capitalist," that is, a person who has built a regular business on the fringe of a conventional event or place (English and Stephens, 1975; Stephens, 1976). Included in this category are those who sell flowers, food, or balloons and other novelties at baseball games, festivals, fairs, and on street corners. The SRO residents consider such selling a good hustle because, compared to other alternatives, it is profitable and dependable, and it allows for personal autonomy. Having a respectable hustle does not mean, however, that the work is easy or without risks. For example, the capitalist must invest in his or her stock and hire others to help sell it. In addition, most shopkeepers charge a fee for allowing novelty stands in front of their stores, and many hustlers feel that they must buy police protection from the street rowdies who may steal the hustler's money or damage his or her goods. The police are bought off by giving the patrol officers small items to take home to their children. The ability of the hustlers to control these uncertain features of their environment is limited, however, by the attitudes of shopkeepers and local statutes. In some cities, such as New York, street peddlers are required to buy a license and the police, responding in part to pressure from local shopkeepers who fear competition, regularly hassle them to see their licenses. Failure to have a license results in confiscation of the hustler's goods and payment of a fine for their recovery.

Although their investment is not large by the standards of most business, the capitalist hustler often has more than $200 tied up in stock, workers, fees, and other expenses needed to do a day's work. Whether the capitalist recoups the investment is quite uncertain, because the conditions for successful selling cannot be guaranteed in advance. Bad weather, for example, is a serious problem, as are children and others who may damage the merchandise without buying anything. The capitalist hustler also works in a highly competitive business, and much of his or her success depends on finding dependable workers and a good location for selling. These uncertainties are increased by the irregularity of many public events. During some times of the year, there are several events each week, but at other times the capitalist hustler is fortunate to find one or two a month.

Because of the uncertainty of the capitalist hustle, the workday starts with great pressure on the hustler and the workers to sell. Indeed, the workers are not allowed to take a break from selling without permission from the hustler. On bad days everyone may work all day without a break. On good days, however, the pressure to sell is reduced as the capitalist begins to make a profit. The hustler may then signal the workers to take a break, and he or she may even buy them a bottle. In addition, the hustler may feel free to leave the stand and go visit other capitalist hustlers in the area. The pace of work is thus linked to the success of the hustle, and because the capitalist hustler does not expect to make a fortune ($100 in profit is considered to be a very good day), he or she is willing to reduce the pace of work when the expenses are covered. Still, any money that is made from the hustle is helpful in supplementing the small, sometimes uncertain, incomes provided by the various welfare agencies of modern government.

Evaluation of Hustling Realities

The purpose of this section has been to look at the social realities of welfare recipients as opposed to those of welfare and government officials. It is evident from the two examples cited here that work does not cease when people receive welfare benefits; rather, life on welfare often involves efforts to find supplemental sources of income through economically marginal activities that are shunned by others seeking higher incomes and greater regularity in their work. Looked at one way, marginal workers provide services to the larger society that would otherwise be left undone. Tinker scavengers and beggars, for example, collect a good deal of scrap metal, old clothes, and other items that would not be recycled without them. The capitalist hustler selling ballons and other novelties also enhances the festiveness of many public events. Similar claims could be made about the social contributions of migrant workers, who take low-paying seasonal jobs, and Appalachian migrants to the city, who recycle cars. What this vision of hustlers fails to note, however, is that hustlers do not see themselves or their work as providing a needed service to the society: they are simply trying to make their livings, and their activities reflect the opportunities available to them. Indeed, hustlers may even resent the degraded and uncertain nature of their work. The capitalist hustlers, for example, are often willing to sing, dance, and tell stories to children in order to get customers to buy their goods, but in private they are contemptuous of the public's insatiable desire for the junk they sell.

A similar schism often exists between those who provide and those who receive welfare services. Although welfare services have historically been justified as serving the "real needs and interests" of the poor, the recipients do not always share this perception. Rather, they are ambivalent about welfare benefits, which include some desirable features (particularly money) but also entail costs. In the past the costs were that the recipients had to expose their life styles to the public and be scrutinized by self-serving champions of an intolerant morality. Today the costs are more likely to be subjection to secular treatments, such as psychiatry, and to bureaucratic handling of problems. But these changes should not obscure the many remaining continuities.

The continuing dilemma over whether to blame or excuse the poor means that they seldom receive benefits that fully meet their needs, and, consequently, they are often forced to work for a living while on welfare. In addition, welfare benefits are still tied to the intrusion of welfare officials into the recipients' lives. Moreover, welfare policies continue to encourage the poor to abandon life styles that are deemed unconventional, if not threatening, by welfare officials. The efforts of early charity workers in the United States to get the urban immigrants to abandon traditional beliefs and practices are mirrored today in Ireland, the United States, and other Western countries, where a major concern of welfare officials is to encourage various types of gypsies, such as the Tinkers, to settle in one place and to take conventional jobs (Kornblum and Lichter, 1972). A final continuity is the proliferation of explanations about the causes of poverty. These explanations, which tend to be created by the nonpoor, are the subject of the next section.

MYTHS ABOUT POVERTY AND WORK

Although hustling has a long history that predates the rise of the welfare state, it has become institutionalized in the contemporary world because of the various problems and opportunities associated with welfare services. A unique feature of hustling, however, is that it is not recognized as work by the general public, welfare officials, or most theorists, who continue to see the poor as unemployed. In their view, then, identifying the causes of the poor's "idleness" is an important task. Those who blame the poor tend to concentrate on their inadequacies, and those who excuse them tend to stress the inadequacies of the society. In practice, it is difficult to separate these two causes of poverty.

There is no doubt that an important cause of poverty is the absence of enough well-paying and secure jobs. Regardless of their qualifications, some people are going to be stuck in undesirable jobs or without conventional employment at all. Indeed most government officials do not treat full employment as an important goal because it is seen as inflationary (Garraty, 1978). The unemployed, then, are expected to bear the burden of keeping down the costs of living for other people. But a case can also be made for tracing poverty to individual motivations as well as social conditions. Many of those who became Tinkers during the nineteenth and early twentieth centuries, for example, took conventional employment when it became available, whereas others chose to remain itinerants. Thus, both points of view are partially verified by human experience.

In what follows we will consider two myths about poverty and work. The first is a theory that blames the poor for their plight by claiming that they are dominated by a culture of poverty that keeps them from achieving. The other argues that poverty is largely a consequence of the organization of society and that we have reached a stage of economic and social development in which it is not necessary for everyone to work. Both myths are summarized in Table 5-2.

The Myth of the Culture of Poverty

In some ways the myth of the culture of poverty is an updated version of the point of view that gave rise to the nineteenth-century almshouse and the Charity Organization Societies. Both of these early approaches to poverty and work assumed that the poor consisted of

Table 5-2 • Myths about Poverty and Work

Type of Myth	*Need for Work*	*Organization of Work*	*Rewards of Work*
Myth of the Culture of Poverty	Based on material need, the need to integrate the poor into "mainstream" institutions, and the need to improve the emotional health of the poor by encouraging organization and self-discipline	Conventional employment that makes the individual self-sufficient and requires that he or she be organized and self-disciplined	Income and the satisfaction of being a conventional, healthy, self-sufficient person
Myth of the Leisure Society	No need for most people to work	Ideally, fully mechanized work overseen by a small worker segment of the population	Few or none for most workers; values stressing the rewards of leisure must be adopted

many able-bodied people who were voluntarily idle. A similar assumption about the poor underlies the *myth of the culture of poverty,* although the cause of poverty is no longer directly linked to the morality of the individual. Rather, the myth claims that long-term abject poverty gives rise to a culture that discourages achievement and encourages continuing dependence on welfare. The culture of poverty is not just a set of ideas, however; it is a total way of life, which includes ideas justifying dependence and roles and relationships which inhibit the development of self-sufficiency (Lewis, 1966a, 1966b; Ryan, 1971; Valentine, 1968, 1971; Van Til, 1976). This way of life is transmitted from generation to generation so that a more or less permanent underclass of poor people exists in modern society.

The imagery of the myth of the culture of poverty, then, is different from that implicit in justifications of almshouses and the Charity Organization Society. The earlier approaches envisioned the poor as "bad people," whereas the myth of the culture of poverty sees the poor as part of a "bad culture." The most basic features of this bad culture have been identified by Oscar Lewis, who argues that poverty is sustained by "the relationship between the subculture and the larger society; the nature of the slum community; the nature of the family, and the attitudes, values and character structure of the individual" (Lewis, 1966a: 21). In general, Lewis describes the poor as living in a world of social institutions which are different from those of others in society. The poor, for example, have only minimal involvement with political and educational institutions, whereas they are highly involved with welfare institutions and such legal institutions as the police, the courts, and jails. The institutions of the nonpoor are seen as encouraging self-sufficiency, whereas those of the poor encourage dependency.

Slums and the slum family life also encourage dependency. Both are seen as highly disorganized and based on values that are different from those of other segments of the society. In part, the disorganization of slums stems from the practical problems of living in densely populated areas with poor housing and little employment. But slum disorganization also arises from the ways in which people interpret and respond to these problems; for example, the tendency of the poor to forgo official marriage ceremonies and to simply live together and their tendency to live only in the present with no regard for the future encourage disorganization. The poor family also contributes to the disorganization of slum life because it is unstable and places little value on children. Rather, children must compete for the scarce emotional and material resources in the home, and they are initiated into sex at an early age. Both the poor neighborhood and family, then, are seen as providing individuals with experiences and values which discourage self-sufficiency and encourage dependency.

The most important feature of the culture of poverty is its impact on the individual, who is seen as qualitatively different from others in the society. The person raised in the culture of poverty is almost exclusively oriented to the present and unable to defer gratification. He or she also has low self-esteem and feels powerless and inferior in most situations, although men may deal with these feelings by projecting an image of themselves as superior and extremely masculine. The person who is socialized into the culture of poverty, then, sees the world as molded by fate rather than individual action. This vision of the world encourages the acceptance of poverty and dependency. For this reason, Lewis claims that a major technique for eliminating the culture of poverty is psychiatric treatment, because it attacks the deep-seated personality traits which keep people poor.

When applied to the relationship between work and poverty, this argument takes two general forms. One argument is that the lack of future orientation by the poor leads them to value the spontaneous pleasures of street life and to reject conventional work (Banfield, 1968). Although proponents often associate the present orientation of the poor with pathological individual and family characteristics, they see little hope in rehabilitating the poor as long as they live in poverty. Edward Banfield, for example, concludes that the culture of poverty will disappear only when everyone is affluent, because the conditions of life in poverty help undo any change created through treatment. The other argument about work in the myth of the culture of poverty is less pessimistic about the possibilities of transforming the poor without significantly changing the society. The proponents of this view emphasize the personal and emotional aspects of poverty, and they describe the poor as "inhibited from their work," as opposed to rejecting it outright (Robinson and Finesinger, 1957; Tiffany, Cowan, Tiffany, 1970). For these people, the solution to the problems of poverty and unemployment is counseling and other forms of treatment which attack the sources of the individual's avoidance of work.

Although they may give lip service to the need to develop more and better jobs, in practice most agencies that deal with the poor and unemployed stress the personal deficiencies of their clients. Social scientists who have observed educators on Indian reservations in the United States refer to this notion as "vacuum ideology" (Wax and Wax, 1971; Wax, Wax, and Dumont, 1964). The educators assume that the children have grown up in a cultural and intellectual vacuum in which both the ability and desire to do well in school have been undermined by parents and community. The students' lack of interest in classes, then, can be explained away as a reflection of the overwhelming problems facing teachers and administrators. Similarly, proponents of the myth of the culture of poverty tend to blame the victim of poverty and injustice while excusing welfare agencies and job counselors from blame (Ryan, 1971). This self-serving argument is implicit in treatment programs, where it is assumed that the poor and unemployed are sick or otherwise handicapped. It is also evident in other programs which are presumably designed to give the unskilled opportunities to acquire skills. In practice such programs are often based on a vacuum ideology which assumes that the poor have little desire to work. A supervisor in one such program recently noted that the problems of the trainees involved more than the lack of job skills; they are also "about a quart low on attitude" (personal communication). The language used in other programs may vary, but the message is often the same: the poor and unemployed are undisciplined, present oriented, and uncommitted to the moral value of hard work. Thus, the problems of poverty and unemployment are really caused by the deficiencies of individuals and not by inadequate vocational training or insufficient job opportunities.

The myth of the culture of poverty, then, legitimizes conventional work. The need for work is justified on the ground of material need, but it is also important because work ties the individual to the "mainstream" institutions of the society, which encourage self-sufficiency. In addition, conventional work is an important source of emotional health and well-being. The proper organization of work is defined as conventional employment, which makes people self-sufficient and helps them organize their lives around self-discipline. Finally, the major rewards of work are the income that is earned and the personal and social rewards that come from being a self-sufficient and productive member of the society.

In many ways, the assumptions of the culture of poverty are consistent with those of the culture of professionalism discussed in the last chapter. A fundamental characteristic of both arguments is that conventional work is important for human development and particularly for attaining control over one's life. This is assumed to be as true for dishwashers as surgeons. The similarity of the two views should not be surprising since the major creators and proponents of the myth of the culture of poverty are professionals seeking to understand and explain poverty. Indeed, many of the critiques of this perspective point to the ways in which it reflects and serves the interests of professionals and others who wish to control the poor and unemployed. A complete review of all such criticism is not possible here, but basic assumptions of the myth deserve further note.

A major problem with the myth of the culture of poverty is the limited definition of work found within it. Work is treated as conventional employment, and most of the hustling of the Tinkers and the SRO residents is regarded as nonwork and as evidence of their immorality and dependence. The arrest rates of hustlers, for example, are interpreted as an important indicator of how dependent they are on the state for their livings. The possibility that the arrest rates might indicate the active ways in which such workers are attempting to control their destinies by seeking illegal sources of income is ignored. Similarly, the high number of welfare recipients among hustlers can be interpreted as a sign of dependency or as one more way in which they actively manipulate social workers and others to carve out a living in a world of limited opportunities. Looked at from the viewpoint of the everyday lives of hustlers, then, it is difficult to maintain the usual distinctions between work and nonwork and dependency and self-sufficiency. Indeed, it is possible to treat the person who slavishly hangs on to a low-paying, monotonous, powerless, but secure job as more dependent than the hustler, who can make a living in a variety of ways. In other words, lack of interest in some kinds of conventional work may be a sign of rationality and not disorder.

Other assumptions of adherents of the culture of poverty myth also reflect their moralistic interpretations of the everyday lives of the poor and unemployed. The claim that the poor are present oriented, undisciplined, and disorganized is an example. That claim ignores the ways in which hustlers are organized and make investments in the future. The capitalist hustler, for example, is just as future oriented, organized, and disciplined as other entrepreneurs who must buy merchandise, hire a sales force, find a location for doing business, and convince the public to buy their products. The predictability of the begging styles and routes of Tinker women also suggests that these workers plan their lives. The regular sharing of the cutest children in order to elicit greater public interest and donations further reflects the extent to which Tinker women treat begging as a rational, organized activity that requires planning. To be sure, there are also examples of lack of foresight by hustlers, as when Tinker women sometimes dump unwanted items on the lawns of those from whom they have begged, but that slip does not separate them from others who dump chemicals and other waste products into rivers and lakes with little regard for future consequences.

Underlying the myth of the culture of poverty, then, is a moral perspective which assumes that conventional employment is better than unconventional work. Those who do not have conventional jobs or live conventional life styles are assumed to be both qualitatively different from others and a problem requiring social intervention. In this way the issue of poverty and work is transformed into a problem of individual deficiency, and the nonpoor do not have to take responsibility for the poor. As with the early charity workers, modern social workers see little need to rethink their interpretation so long as the practical circumstances of the lives of hustlers and other poor people are ignored.

The Myth of the Leisure Society

An alternative to the myth of the culture of poverty is the *myth of the leisure society,* which has most recently been restated by David Macarov (1980). This view is also very moralistic and accepts the legitimacy of the welfare state, but instead of stressing the need for providing social services to eliminate unemployment, supporters want to increase the number of unemployed.

Central to the myth is the belief that we have reached the point in modern society where most human work is unnecessary. Many jobs are nothing more than contrived positions that keep people employed while they idle away their time by producing trivial goods and services. In addition, automation and other forms of mechanization promise to eliminate many jobs in the near future. A major reason why the mechanization of work has not proceeded further is because short-sighted government, business, and union officials resist it in the name of protecting jobs. Our emphasis on jobs results from our stubborn clinging to an outdated view of work as a morally desirable activity. Although this belief can be traced to some of the most important developments in modern history, such as industrialization and the rise of Protestantism, it has little relevance in the contemporary world of abundance, where there is no longer a need for everyone to be employed.

The persistence of the belief in the necessity and morality of work has important consequences for members of modern society. On the basis of that belief, for example, we continue to condemn welfare recipients, who are depicted as lazy people because they refuse to take low-paying, insecure jobs. As a result, our welfare policies not only fail to provide the poor with an adequate income but entangle them in bureaucratic rules and procedures which needlessly complicate their lives. Among the bureaucratic policies with which the poor must deal are sheltered workshops, the Work Incentive Program, and other programs which periodically force the poor to do degrading and meaningless work in order to satisfy the consciences of government and welfare officials.

But the worship of work in modern society also affects those who hold or aspire to conventional jobs. Indeed, it is as corrupting for them as for welfare recipients. Thus, millions of college students try desperately to acquire the proper certification for jobs that promise little challenge or room for personal expression. In addition, the unemployed suffer terrible personal insecurities, because they assume that all full-fledged adults (particularly men) must have a job of some type. The corrupting influence of the modern worship of work also can be seen in the high priority government officials give to creating and maintaining often useless jobs. A major argument for maintaining unneeded military installations and for giving financial aid to faltering private corporations, for example, is that too many jobs will be lost without them. Yet, few people argue that the products of the workers are really needed or even wanted.

Perhaps the best reflection of the corrupting influence of the worship of work is the paradoxical relationship between how people feel about work in general and their jobs in particular. Recent research indicates that many people are highly critical of their jobs and have few hopes of finding fulfilling work, but they continue to believe that, in general, conventional work is normal and moral. Indeed, the gap between the desires of workers and their actual experiences may help account for the vehemence with which conventional workers condemn welfare recipients. Because conventional workers see them as persons who have escaped the pains of conventional jobs, welfare recipients often become the scapegoats for those who cannot deal with the meaninglessness of their own work.

Unlike the myth of the culture of poverty that implicitly legitimizes conventional work, the myth of the leisure society rejects conventional work and attempts to justify the development of a new society in which human worth is based on leisure activities. It does this, in part, by pointing to the lack of need for most work, its corrupting organization, and the few rewards that can be derived from it. In addition, Macarov (1980) points to emerging conditions which will discourage work and increase unemployment, the number of people on welfare, and the leisure time of all people. Among these developments are the continuing reduction of work hours, an increasing population of aged people, and the elimination of jobs based on technological developments, particularly automation. Trends such as these will ultimately force people to reassess their values and to develop a society in which only a small segment of the population actually works.

For many workers the myth of the leisure society is a pipe dream which has little to do with the circumstances of their work. The workers at the Riverside plant described in chapter three, for example, are unlikely to find Macarov's prediction very reasonable. They know that automation often results in new forms of tedious, uninteresting work, rather than increased leisure and control over one's life. Someone, after all, must watch the dials, adjust the levers, and carry the materials produced in automated work places. Similarly, Macarov does not fully consider the many service occupations that are not easily automated because of the complexity of the work or the expense of automating them.

It is hard to deny, however, that many of the trends identified by Macarov are occurring and offer a challenge to past interpretations of work, leisure, and welfare. Certainly, a new image of old age and retirement has emerged in the last several decades—one stressing the joys of leisure and freedom from work. Where the analysis may err is in the claim that the ultimate outcome will be a revolution in values and a new world of leisure for all.

It is equally plausible to argue that work will continue to be important, but for different reasons. Both the contemporary feminist and the empowerment movements, for example, argue that all work should be liberating and self-actualizing. Rather than rejecting work, these movements are attempting to redefine and change it. If they are successful, the worship of work and the condemnation of the poor and unemployed are likely to continue.

Whatever the future of work and welfare may be, Macarov offers an alternative to the myth of the culture of poverty. Rather than pointing a moralizing finger at the poor, he points it at a society which refuses to come to terms with the reality he sees—one that defines most work as unnecessary and current welfare practices as indefensible.

CONCLUSION

If the chapter on professional work dealt with the elites of modern work, then this chapter has dealt with its dregs. They are dregs because these workers are generally viewed as the most degenerate segment of the modern work force. But tempering this view is another that excuses the poor from blame and looks for the causes of their plight in the organization of the society or in a plan of God. More impressive than the rise of new treatment techniques and bureaucratic agencies is the persistence of this contradictory view of the poor in modern society. Because the public cannot make up its mind on the roots of poverty, government policy concerning the poor and unemployed continues to be confused. The problem promises to intensify in the future as the number of persons eligible for social security and other forms of welfare increases in relation to those who have conventional jobs and must support these programs. A fairly safe prediction is that many who today look forward to a leisurely life of retirement will find themselves hustling for a living.

Chapter Six

HOUSEWORK

Although Thorstein Veblen (1899/1953) wrote *The Theory of the Leisure Class* for other reasons, he gives a description there of housework and housewives that other popular accounts still reiterate. Veblen's major concern was to describe the unique way of life developing within the middle class of the late nineteenth century. Central to this way of life was the unending pursuit of wealth and the advantages associated with it. But the mere accumulation of money was seen as insufficient, because a truly wealthy person was one who could afford to spend his or her money on objects and activities that were unrelated to subsistence. One example is the purchase of expensive items of art, which may enhance the beauty of a home but contribute little to meeting basic needs for food and shelter. Luxury items were thought desirable because they could be displayed conspicuously so that others could both enjoy them and recognize the great wealth of the owner. In short, instead of simply amassing wealth, the leisure class was also concerned with conspicuous consumption and conspicuous waste.

One important indicator of wealth was the employment of servants, who took care of much of the most basic work around the house, such as cleaning and child care. Servants could also be dressed in brightly colored, highly adorned, sometimes revealing costumes, which were assumed to reflect the employer's great wealth. Thus, even when the employer was busy making money, the servants continued to act as conspicuous symbols of his or her social position. Veblen calls these substitutes for the wealthy the "vicarious leisure class," but servants were only one part of it. Another segment of the vicarious lesiure class was made up of the wives of wealthy men because, although they enjoyed many of the advantages of wealth, they did not actually own it. Rather, they were allowed to use what was earned by their husbands. Equally important, wives—like servants—were public symbols of the family's wealth; indeed, conspicuous consumption and waste were full-time activities for many of these women. Their activities included art collecting, volunteer and philanthropic activities, and the presentation of an image of beauty and refinement. The wives of the wealthy, for example, spent great amounts of time and energy finding the most fashionable clothes to wear and trying to remain as slender as possible. In sum, the leisure class was based on a vision of the "good life," and one part of it was a definition of femininity and womanhood. A proper woman was one who was attractive, well dressed, and devoted to economically meaningless activities.

For most people joining the lesiure class was an unrealistic dream, because they would never have the great wealth needed to achieve that way of life. Still, historically, the vision of the good life the leisure class pursued has been an important symbol for many men and women who are not wealthy: they have simply modified the vision to take account of their own financial limitations. An important indicator of success for some men and women, for example, is for the wife to be a full-time housewife. This arrangement tells the world that the husband is a "good provider." The counterpart of the husband as a good provider is the wife as consumer. Although all families cannot afford to purchase expensive art, they can imitate the division of the household into male workers and female consumers found within the leisure class. This cultural assumption about the roles of males and females has contributed a great deal to the general devaluation of housework in the United States and other societies. The leisure class obviously gave little value to housework because they relegated it to servants. Other households modified this assumption, although the consequence was the same. Today it is often still assumed that people who are freed from the constraints of holding a job have little more to occupy their time than did the women of the leisure class. After all, with all of the appliances and other conveniences of the modern household, how long can it take to cook, clean, and do the other simple tasks that make up housework?

Men unable or unwilling to see the contributions of women are not the only ones to hold this assumption; it is also apparent in the writings of some feminists who associate liberation with jobs outside the home. In the highly influential book *The Feminine Mystique*, for example, Betty Friedan (1963) describes housewives as women suffering from a problem with no name. The problem is the assumption made by both men and women that marriage, children, and housework are the keys to feminine fulfillment. Housewives make this assumption despite the fact that they often feel unfulfilled and guilty because they have not achieved the cultural goal they assume other housewives have achieved. Instead of questioning the premise, however, they blame themselves as inadequate. Part of the solution to the problem, according to Friedan, is to come to terms with the inherent limitations of marriage and housework:

> The first step in that plan is to see housework for what it is—not a career, but something that must be done as quickly and efficiently as possible. Once a woman stops trying to make cooking, cleaning, washing, ironing, "something more," she can say "no, I don't want a stove with rounded corners, I don't want four different kinds of soap." . . . Then, she can use the vacuum cleaner and the dishwasher and all the automatic appliances, and even the instant mashed potatoes, for what they are truly worth—to save time that can be used in more creative ways (Friedan, 1963: 342).

Although perhaps not intended, writings such as Friedan's have also contributed to a vision of housework and housewives that is as incomplete as that of the wealthy men who dominated the earlier leisure class. The increase in the working hours of housewives since 1925, for example, is often ignored or explained away as attempts by housewives to keep busy because they have nothing else to do. Historical research indicates, however, that the introduction of washing machines and other appliances into the home has been accompanied by the introduction of new sources of work, such as more clothes to wash, and new standards of work quality (Bose, 1979; Cowan, 1974; Vanek, 1974). Thus, the contemporary housewife may not have to do all of the backbreaking work required of women in earlier times, but she is not free to devote herself to full-time leisure either.

Another problem with the new vision of housework is that it fails to take account of the economic contributions of housewives and others in the household (Burns, 1975). Proof of their contribution can be secured by comparing the costs of eating in restaurants or paying a maid with the costs of using an unpaid housewife. But there are also other, less obvious ways in which household members do work of economic value. Painting, wallpapering, tending the lawn, raising a garden, canning, and making and repairing clothing are all ways in which household members contribute to a family's livelihood. The fact that some of these activities are undertaken as hobbies because they are inherently satisfying should not obscure their economic importance. After all, we do not tell people who enjoy their jobs that they are not working for a living.

A final problem with analyses such as Friedan's is that they do not take account of the diversity of ways in which family life and housework are experienced. There is little doubt that many women feel confined and unfulfilled by their work and position in the family, but other women are quite happy as housewives (Lopata, 1971). The wealth of the family, the presence or absence of children, the presence or absence of a spouse, and relationships between the adults living in the household are obvious factors accounting for some of the differences. In addition, the degree to which a housewife is involved in a network of family and neighbors who can help with crises and listen to problems is also important, because the isolated housewife must deal individually with a variety of problems that others share (Bott, 1957). Another factor accounting for the ways in which housewives assess their work is the stage in the life cycle through which they are going (Lopata, 1971). The practical circumstances of life for a young mother trying to care for small children on a limited budget are very different from those of a middle-aged woman whose children have families of their own and whose husband is at the financial peak of his career. Both situations involve problems and satisfactions, but they are different and therefore contribute to the ways in which different housewives see themselves and their work.

It is impossible to deal fully in this chapter with the diverse circumstances surrounding housework. A full treatment would require that the work lives of servants as well as housewives be considered (Erlich, 1974; McBride, 1976). In addition, husbands, children, and others may also contribute to the household. For the purposes of this chapter, the discussion will be limited to the most numerous and important household workers—women. Some are full-time housewives and others also have jobs outside the home, although their jobs will be treated as secondary to their housework. We will look first at some important historical processes that have shaped the contemporary image of housework. That discussion will be followed by a look at the way different types of families experience the social realities of housework. Finally, some of the most important myths about housework and housewives will be discussed.

Before turning to these topics, however, we should make explicit two major assumptions of this discussion. First, although some analysts (Berk and Berk, 1979; Oakley, 1974a, 1974b), prefer to treat housework as a somewhat separate issue from the general relations within the family, we will not do so here. It is not useful, for example, to separate women's feelings about washing clothes from their feelings about their children and husbands, because women—like men—are often willing to endure many boring and even painful activities if they feel they are contributing to the general good of the family. Indeed, an important reason for the increased working hours of contemporary housewives is the change in the demands and expectations of others in the household. A better question than how a woman feels about washing clothes is what being a housewife means to her and how she feels about the activities and obligations that make up this social role.

A second assumption underlying this discussion is that the work of housewives, as opposed to servants and other paid workers, is not an occupation; rather, it is qualitatively different from what is normally called a job (Miller, 1980). One way to separate housework from other kinds of work is to compare them according to their level of industrialization (Bernard, 1974). When housework is considered in this way, it has little in common with fully industrial work, such as a high level of technological development or an extensive division of labor. More important reasons for treating the work of the housewife as unique, though, are its unpaid status and the fact that it is not separable from the many obligations associated with being a wife and mother. A man may be expected to get a job and support his family, but how he does his job is treated as a separate, nonfamily matter. The work of the housewife is different both because it is defined as nonwork within a world where social worth is often measured by income and because the manner in which the housewife does her work is a matter of great concern to the whole family. Indeed, the uniqueness of the housewife's work role is implicit in the many descriptions of the woman who fills that role as always loving and nurturant, and willing to sacrifice her interests for those of others. This image is very different from that of other successful workers, who are often described as aggressive, determined persons who allow nothing to deter them from achieving their goals.

If, as some people suggest, the work role of the housewife is changed so that she is paid and the job of maintaining a home is distinguished from other aspects of being a wife and mother, then this assumption would have to be abandoned. At least in the present the chances of these changes occurring are not great.

OFFICIAL IMAGES OF HOUSEWORK AND HOUSEWIVES

Feminists, government officials, religious leaders, and others interested in defining the proper place for the family and housewives in modern society are reviving an issue that has occupied the attention of a variety of people since the beginning stages of industrialization. Because the people who have dealt with the issue have looked at housewives from many different perspectives, the official images that surround this work role are varied and often contradictory. In this section we look at some of the most important of these official images and their consequences for housewives. First, however, it is important to consider the social and economic origins of this role.

Origins of the Modern Housewife's Role

According to most analysts, women became full-time workers in the home only after the onset of industrialization (Easton, 1976; Catherine

Hall, 1974; Kanter, 1977b; Oakley, 1974b; Women's Work Study Group, 1976; Zaretsky, 1976). Most preindustrial work was done in the home, where every member of the family made a contribution to the production process. In the textile-producing household, for example, the father and sons did the weaving while the mother and daughters did the spinning, cleaning, carding, and other preparatory activities for weaving (Oakley, 1974b; Smelser, 1959). With the rise of factories, many of these activities were done by machine and, more importantly, work was removed from the home and family. At first, the shift of work to the factory had little impact on the family, because the husband, wife, and children took employment in it; indeed, family ties were sometimes strengthened in the factory, because brothers, sisters, aunts, uncles, and cousins often worked side by side. But over time, women and children were pushed out of the factory and into a world of their own.

Contributing to this change was the enactment of legislation limiting, if not prohibiting, the work of women and children. Although such legislation was typically justified on humanitarian grounds, it also served the interests of many adult men, including both workers and managers. Another reason for the separation of work and family was the elimination of many family activities and responsibilities through the development of welfare programs within the factory (Kanter, 1977b; Nelson, 1975). The establishment of libraries, clubs, recreational facilities, and programs of relief for injured workers, for example, undermined old family obligations and ties by making the worker dependent on the employer, not the family. Finally, the separation of work from family was encouraged by the rise of new ideas about the nature of women and childhood. The new image of children stressed their vulnerability and their need for full-time maternal attention (Ariès, 1960; Kett, 1977). The new vision of femininity was based in part on the new emphasis on the importance of child care in women's lives, but it was also based on the belief that work outside the home was unhealthy for women and encouraged immorality. Factory workers, for example, were said to have more illegitimate children than women who stayed home. Similarly, according to late nineteenth-century medical theory, a college education destroyed women's reproductive capacity by causing their uteruses to atrophy (Ehrenreich and English, 1975). Lending support to these claims was a new conception of the natural division of labor in the family: by nature, a husband had to provide for his wife, who was naturally inclined to take a supportive role in the household.

This historical account of why women were forced out of the factory and other work places stresses economic factors: women's employment was simply inconsistent with the demands of industrialization. There is much evidence to support this view. Factory managers, for example, found workers with wives and children to support to be more docile and dependable than those with working wives who could tide the family over while the men looked for other work. Similarly, many male workers wanted women banned from their work places because women were willing to work for less money than they. The result was an artificial separation of family from work and the rise of the notion that home is a retreat from the "real" world. For women the change meant the assumption of the primary responsibility for maintaining the home, raising the children, and sustaining the husband, who was seen as the only worker in the household. It also meant becoming isolated figures whose work was devalued and who were segregated from the valued world outside the home. The real world of meaning and contribution was, in the words of one writer, a "world looked at through the window over the kitchen sink" (Oakley, 1974b: 59). In recent years new economic realities are changing this picture. The modern economy is increasingly organized around office work, and women offer an inexpensive source of labor for doing the routine, clerical work of the office (Glazer-Malbin, 1976; Women's Work Study Group, 1976). Economic shifts are once again influencing the history of housework.

In a very general and crude way this economic explanation is an accurate portrayal of the rise of the full-time housewife. In many ways, however, it is too simplistic and does not take account of the many contradictions and subtleties of human life and history. For example, it does not deal adequately with the historically strong demand for women workers in some industries, even during the time when many women were becoming full-time housewives. The industrial economy is not a monolithic entity that affects everyone in the same ways (Pleck, 1976); rather, it is made up of the diverse, sometimes irrational, decisions of employers and workers. For this reason, it can be said that the economy both encourages and discourages women's work outside the home. Similarly, the separation of work from family life cannot be accounted for exclusively by industrialization (Pleck, 1976). The children of farmers and craftspeople during preindustrial times also took jobs working for other people when the household could not provide adequate work. In addition, simply because work occurs in the household does not mean that everyone works together. It is possible to divide work into that of men, women, and children so that each of these groups is isolated from the others. Finally, the economic explanation of the evolution of housework does not take adequate account of the ways in which women, responding to the practical problems of their everyday lives, have created a work role for themselves as housewives. When the work of the housewife is considered, the assumed separation between work and family does not seem as clear-cut as many analysts claim. Rather, the worlds of work and family are intertwined.

To understand the interconnection between these two worlds, as well as the image of women and housework, the model that should be kept in mind is not the wife of the factory worker but the wife of the more affluent man who could afford to be the sole supporter of a family. Women in this position were important because they had the time, money, and other resources needed to create a vision of housework as a career—one based on rational and scientific principles—and to impose it on others.

Housework as a Science

In eighteenth- and nineteenth-century England the wives of affluent merchants and others did not work outside the home because women were seen as cleaner and purer than men; to work in the world of men would spoil their femininity (Davidoff, 1976). Their role, then, was to remain in the house where they would watch over their servants and children, making sure that high levels of cleanliness and order were always maintained. Within the household, these women were active in shaping the daily life of the family and, just as important, the image of the modern household. Their most important contribution was to turn the household into a rational world where planning and specialization prevailed. They attempted in the home what their husbands were attempting to do in their factories and businesses. As with the rationalizers in other work settings, these women believed in careful budgeting of household expenses, precise scheduling of laundry and other household chores, and the creation of household specialists assigned to different tasks and areas of the house. Thus, cooks, gardeners, nursemaids, and housemaids began to appear in the homes of the affluent at this time. In addition, affluent women encouraged the earlier trend of dividing the house into specialized rooms for eating, sleeping, entertaining, and cooking. The development of these specialized areas further contributed to the sense of order and control which was the most important feature of these households.

But the concern for building highly organized households extended beyond England and the internal arrangements of each household. There were also attempts to share and disseminate information about housework; indeed, much of the English housewife's concern for budgeting and organizing can be traced to the many housekeeping books which were published at this time. To encourage the building of rational households in the United States, various social movements arose, and their efforts culminated in the establishment of *home economics* as a profession (Ehrenreich and English, 1975; Strasser, 1978). The symbolic beginning for home economics, or "domestic science" as many of the founders called it, was the Lake Placid Conference of 1899. Among the participants at this conference were members of Charity Organization Societies, Settlement House workers, educators, and a variety of other people concerned about the disintegration of the family. This was a problem of great urgency and importance to those gathered at the conference, because they were the wives of the newly affluent middle class who were being forced to carve out a new life in the home, where their status and obligations were uncertain. Put differently, they worried about the "domestic void" which they saw in their lives, and the Lake Placid Conference and later activities were attempts to fill that void (Ehrenreich and English, 1975).

The women who met at Lake Placid were not just affluent; they were well-educated and socially conscious people who were concerned about the world in which they lived. Indeed, they took as their major goal the encouragement of "right living" for all, and the center of a proper way of life was to be the home, where the physical and moral health of the family could be maintained. Implicit in the rise of home economics, then, was a desire to create a new and respectable role for the housewife. Ironically, one outcome was the development of a profession which offered women careers outside the home as educators, researchers, journalists, and consultants. As with other professions, home economics arose from an amalgam of self-interest and public interest. This is evident in the efforts of the early home economists to impose their notion of right living on the immigrant poor, but it is also evident in their emphasis on germ theory, scientific management, and the need for higher education for housewives. By emphasizing these issues, the domestic scientists sought both to improve the quality of family life and to develop careers for themselves as teachers in colleges and universities and as advisors to housewives.

The popularization of germ theory was an event of great symbolic importance for the domestic scientists, because it provided them with a major justification for full-time housework (Ehrenreich and English, 1975). Housewives were defined as persons protecting the health of the family by keeping the home clean and free of germs. At a practical level, this claim had some appeal because disease and early death were a problem in the late nineteenth and early twentieth centuries. Indeed, the interest in disease and germs was complemented by the new vision of children as vulnerable and needing constant attention from their mothers. In practice, however, the emphasis on germ theory had relatively little impact on disease and death rates, because the primary enemy of the domestic scientists was common household dust, which is not a major cause of disease. Still, dust and germ theory were elevated to symbols that could justify the new role of the full-time housewife. The competent and loving housewife was defined as a woman who kept her house spotlessly clean and who paid particular attention to areas where dust might accumulate. Indeed, one of the most important tools for fighting dust and disease was the "damp duster," which, unknown to the domestic scientists and the housewives who listened to them, was a more likely source for germs than dust because the damp duster provided a warm, moist environment for bacterial growth.

A second major point emphasized by the domestic science movement was the need to turn the household into a rational place where planning and efficiency prevailed (Ehrenreich and English, 1975; Strasser, 1978). To achieve these goals, the movement turned to the model of scientific management developed by Frederick Taylor for organizing industrial work. Work in the rational household was to be planned and organized in the most efficient ways possible. Sometimes planning meant drawing an elaborate map of the house in order to schedule work to minimize steps and wasted time; at other times it was simply figuring out the most efficient way to peel potatoes or wash the baby. In addition, the truly competent housewife was expected to keep extensive records and files on the costs of food, clothing, and other items regularly consumed in the household. This information could be used to invest in new "labor saving" appliances, which would increase the efficiency of the household by relieving the housewife of some of her most time-consuming work. The assumptions implicit in the adaptation of scientific management to household centers were thus twofold: (1) that housewives could create a career that involved building their homes into retreats from the outside world; and (2) that a truly modern and rational housewife could not operate without the latest appliances.

The third major emphasis of the domestic scientists was education—a troublesome point, because higher education was an important male privilege that men wanted to preserve. Indeed, several popular theories were developed to point out the undesirable consequences of providing women with higher education, including claims that it would ruin their health. The domestic scientists countered that a modern housewife required an awareness of many of the subjects studied by men, though for different reasons. For example, the competent housewife was described as a woman needing a basic knowledge of chemistry, anatomy, and related subjects in order to be a good cook and look after the health of her husband and children (Ehrenreich and English, 1975). Similarly, the housewife's taste in home decoration could be improved through some experience with artistic and literary classics. Thus, women were not in the university to compete with men; rather, they were there to learn how to build better homes for their families. Hidden beneath this claim, however, was another concern: the desire to create departments of home economics which would offer careers outside the home to the domestic scientists and would make their work and themselves more respectable. Thus, the self-interests of the domestic scientists were combined with the more general interest of middle-class women in higher education to give rise to a variety of undergraduate and graduate programs in home economics during the early part of the twentieth century. The blending of self- and public interest was perhaps best reflected in Julia Lathrop's plan to use housewives with home economics degrees as auxiliary researchers. They would study their own families and provide this information to the educational professionals, who would use it to expand the knowledge base of the profession (Strasser, 1978).

Like other attempts at professionalization, the domestic science movement was torn by conflict, and it had many qualities of a moral crusade. Not all of the women in the movement, for example, were committed to the emphasis on buying new household appliances. They were skeptical that these items really could save time or money. Other women were bothered by the subordinate position assigned to many women in the rational household. Charlotte Perkins Gilman, for example, supported the rationalization of housework because she felt that eventually it would lead to the transformation of housework into an industry that would take care of the household for women (Strasser, 1978). Child-care centers, cleaning services, and cooking services would eventually develop to replace the housewife, who would then be free to join her husband in the world of jobs outside the home. This, Gilman believed, would result in better service in the home and eliminate the parasitic and unequal relationship that inevitably results when a woman is dependent on a man for her income. The home economics movement, then, included different viewpoints and was filled with conflict.

Nevertheless, those who accepted the basic tenets of the movement were thoroughly convinced of the morality of their mission, and they were quite willing to impose their views on others. The notion of right living, for example, was frequently applied to the immigrant poor who were almost always found wanting (Ehrenreich and English, 1975). Indeed, because the supporters of domestic science were also often Settlement House workers and Charity Organization workers and volunteers, instruction in right living was often combined with charity. In its least demeaning form, right living was simple instruction in the basic principles of thrift and home maintenance, but it also often took other forms, which reflected the deeper moralistic and political concerns of the reformers. For example, the immigrant poor were often seen as potential sources of socialist movements, and it was assumed that one condition encouraging this tendency was the centralization of the poor in large tenement buildings, which were seen as almost communistic. One reason for the domestic scientists' emphasis on single-family home ownership, then, was a desire to disperse the poor and thereby combat their radical tendencies. But if right living could not be fully achieved by moving the poor to separate homes, then it could be encouraged in the tenements by instructing the poor in proper etiquette. Middle-class domestic scientists assumed that a major problem in the relations between the rich and poor was the unrefined demeanor of the poor; they believed that by teaching the poor how to behave, an important source of class conflict could be eliminated.

A major change in the late nineteenth and early twentieth centuries, then, was an extension of the notion of right living and of the full-time role of housewife to women who would never have a house full of servants. This change was due in part to the altered circumstances of the affluent, who were experiencing increasing difficulties in finding women to work as domestics. Many young women who might have worked as domestics found the office a more profitable and glamorous work place. Thus, many affluent women found themselves doing increasing amounts of housework. This change in work arrangements was accompanied by a shift in ideas about right living. Domestic scientists began to believe that right living required a private home in which the family members have control. Since a home filled with servants offered little privacy and limited family control, domestic scientists adopted the notion that it was better to do the work oneself. This new conception of the household and housewife also made it possible to apply the principles of right living to other, less affluent, servantless homes. The emphasis on scientific housework has remained a central feature of home economics, as is evident in some recent textbooks which stress scientific management principles and ecological housework (Percivall and Burger, 1971; Steidl and Bratton, 1968).

Housework as a Craft

The period between World Wars I and II was to witness the full justification of the servantless home. It was during that time that a number of household conveniences, such as electricity, modern bathrooms, and canned foods, were made available to the general population and that leading women's magazines concentrated their attention on the problems of the housewife (Cowan 1976; Ewen, 1976). The magazines also provided their readers with a somewhat new conception of what constitutes right living. The most general change was a shift in the image of the proper housewife; instead of a scientist, she was now seen as a craftsperson. Housework was no longer just something that needed to be done in the most efficient manner possible, but instead was a form of self-expression and social contribution. Commenting on the change, one sociologist notes: "Laundering had once been just laundering; now it was an expression of love. The new bride could speak her affection by washing tell-tale gray out of her husband's shirts. . . . Diapering was no longer just diapering, but a time to build the baby's sense of security." (Cowan, 1976: 151). Both housework as science and housework as craft are images that make the housewife a respectable worker, but the nature of their respectability is quite different. The scientist is an aloof, objective worker, whereas the craftsperson is a personally involved worker seeking fulfillment.

Although cooking and cleaning were important craft activities for the housewife, her most important activity was child care, because the physical and emotional health of the child was assumed to be directly traceable to child-rearing techniques. This belief was based in part on Freudian theory and its emphasis on childhood experiences as significantly affecting mental health, but it was also related to the concern for popularity and "fitting in" so often voiced by this segment of the population. It was important to create healthy and popular children, which could be done by proper parental discipline and guidance, but also by the housewife carrying out her mundane household chores. Thus women's magazines described scuffed shoes, improperly ironed clothes, and inadequate breakfasts as legitimate topics for worry by housewives. Indeed, two of the most important emotions for housewives were embarrassment and guilt. A woman should feel embarrassed when her home is not properly maintained and guilty when her children and husband fail to be as popular or successful as they should be. These emotions were not only central to the advice of the women's magazines, but they were effectively used by advertisers to sell such disparate products as toilet bowl cleaners, slenderizing equipment, and ballet lessons for the children.

Perhaps the most inventive advertising technique of this time was the linking of feminism and women's liberation to the consumption of household goods, because an important problem facing advertisers and manufacturers at this time was the tendency for women to hang onto old habits and practices (Ewen, 1976). By linking consumption with liberation, the self-interests of the advertisers and manufacturers could be obscured by their appeals to the broader issues of equality and freedom. An obvious example of the link made between the two was a campaign by the American Tobacco Company in 1929 that encouraged women to smoke cigarettes while marching in New York City's Easter Parade in order to protest the inequality of women. The cigarettes were described as "torches of freedom" symbolizing the full liberation of women; the desire of the tobacco company to open up a new market for their product was never mentioned. Advertisers also linked liberation with the purchase of household goods. Toaster manufacturers, for example, declared that buying their toaster freed women from the drudgery of having to watch and turn the toast before it burned. Precisely how this convenience contributed to the liberation of women was left unexplained, although it was clear from the advertising message that no fully liberated woman could live without a toaster. Similar claims were made for other household appliances such as vacuum cleaners.

The period between World Wars I and II, then, was a time when the notion of the full-time housewife was further extended to the general population. The work role of housewife was described as both socially important and a source for self-fulfillment for women.

New Images

After World War II the popular media continued to to stress the image of housework as self-fulfilling. But not all women were equally committed to seeking fulfillment in gourmet meals, shiny dishes, or their children's popularity. Certainly, the many women who had to take full- or part-time jobs outside the home in order to provide for their families could not reasonably expect to live up to the ideal then prevalent. It is also safe to assume that their failure to do so was another source of guilt for many of these women.

In more recent years the image of the contented housewife has been challenged. Friedan's discussion of the housewife's problem mentioned earlier is one of the most important of these challenges, but there have been others. Much of the femininist emphasis on expanding job opportunities for women is predicated on the belief that full-time housework is unfulfilling for many women. Similarly, although the popular media continue to present an image of the contented housewife, some advertising depicts the "truly fulfilled woman" as a person who has a challenging job outside the home and still finds the time and energy to be an exciting wife, a good mother, and a tidy housekeeper.

Thus, new images of being a housewife are being created, and, like their predecessors, these images are part of more general images about being a woman, wife, and mother and about right living. The new images are also similar to the old ones in that they reflect the moral and social interests of only a part of society. The image often found in contemporary literature and advertising of the woman who has a professional career and lives in affluence with her adoring and well-scrubbed husband and children is as foreign to the poor woman of today as finger bowls and other features of refined etiquette were to the poor at the turn of the century. These women live in a world of continuing scarcity where a job is something one takes primarily to pay the bills and housework is something that never seems to get done.

At the outset of this chapter the paradox of contemporary housework was noted: while labor-saving devices have been introduced into the home, the working hours of full-time housewives have increased. The main reason for the increase in working hours has been the rise of new images about housework and housewives. New standards of child rearing, cleanliness, and nutrition have expanded the obligations and concerns of the full-time housewife. It is no longer sufficient to maintain a *house;* the housewife's work involves the diverse activities associated with maintaining a *home.* These include getting rid of the dirty ring around the bathtub and attending PTA meetings, soccer matches, and recitals. Not all women experience the housewife's paradox in the same ways, however; rather, depending on the everyday circumstances of their lives, housewives experience the burden of housework differently. It is these circumstances that are most important in shaping the social realities of housewives. We will turn to these realities next.

THE SOCIAL REALITIES OF HOUSEWIVES

Although the images of housewives and housework created by reformers, advertisers, and others usually depict the family in the same way, not all families are alike. Differences among families are partly accounted for by the wealth of the family, the ages of the children, and similar factors which limit the options of husbands and wives. But they are also accounted for by the choices which men and women make about their lives and relationships with others. Thus, the statement that affluent husbands do more housework than poor husbands oversimplifies reality because that statement does not take account of the ways in which affluent and poor men interpret themselves and their situations. During the Great Depression of the 1930s, for example, the unemployment of the husband and the need for wives and children to take jobs outside the home challenged many family arrangements. How quickly and effectively families adjusted to this problem varied, however, depending on the extent to which the husband rigidly adhered to a vision of himself as the sole provider for the family (Modell, 1979). Families differ in other ways as well, depending upon how members respond to one another as the circumstances of everyday life change.

The relationships among family members are not the only key to understanding differing family realities, however. Relatives outside the household, neighbors, friends, and coworkers may also be important in helping families interpret what a proper family life is. For this reason, it is possible to classify families and their work arrangements based on the social networks to which the families belong (Bott, 1975). If the classification scheme is thought of as a continuum, at the extremes there are two general family types: one belongs to a very loose-knit network, in which persons outside the home play only an indirect part in the day-to-day activities of the family members, and the other belongs to a very close-knit network, in which relatives, friends, and others are actively involved in the work and relationships of the household. There are, of course, a variety of intermediary types which belong to networks that vary in their degree of closeness. In addition, it is possible to classify families based on the degree to which the husband and wife share the same network because they may belong to different close-knit networks.

For purposes of this discussion, we will consider the two extreme types of networks and the degree to which the husband and wife share the network as most important. Our interest is limited to a consideration of how networks affect the ways in which housework is defined and experienced. In general, the more close-knit the network outside the household, the more likely a husband and wife are to divide the household into "men's work" and "women's work" (Bott, 1957). The reason is that the husband and wife are likely to belong to different networks which have formed around different activities and interests.

Consider the example of the Newbolt family. The husband belongs to a network of friends who are former schoolmates, coworkers, and persons involved in the leisure activities that occupy much of Mr. Newbolt's time (Bott, 1957). Mrs. Newbolt, on the other hand, belongs to an equally close-knit network made up of her children and neighbors and relatives who are primarily linked by their common interest in housework, husbands, and children. The center of Mr. Newbolt's social network, then, is recreation, whereas family and work are central to Mrs. Newbolt's network. The fact that the two social networks to which the Newbolt family belong are oriented toward different activities is important, because these networks sustain an arrangement of housework that is also divided. Thus, Mr. Newbolt is responsible for some household repairs, but the bulk of housework, including tending the children, is defined as Mrs. Newbolt's rightful obligation.

In families belonging to loose-knit networks, the circumstances for defining "men's work" and "women's work" are different. The members of these families must take greater responsibility for the operation of the household, because they have fewer people outside the home to help them. Thus, the family within the home defines the divisions of housework, although the definitions that emerge may vary. Simply because husbands and wives in loose-knit networks must take greater responsibility for the housework does not mean that the work is equally divided. The housework may indeed be evenly shared, but it is also possible that the wife will be stuck with all or most of it. Indeed, research indicates that despite their rhetoric of egalitarianism, affluent, suburban families most often choose the latter possibility (Berheide, Berk, and Berk, 1976).

The social networks within which families are embedded are, then,

Table 6-1 • Sources of the Social Realities of Housework

Family Type	*Work-Related Timetables*	*Work-Related Communities*
Close-knit Network	Diachronic: based on the regular and irregular processes of the household	Mixed: based on the enduring ties with some network members and fleeting ties with others
Loose-knit Network	Diachronic: based on the regular and irregular processes of the household	Mixed: based on the enduring relations among family members, and the shifting relations with persons in the family's social network

important in understanding how housework is defined and accomplished. They are also important in creating the social realities of modern housework, which are summarized in Table 6-1. The work-related timetables for housework are basically the same for both close-knit and loose-knit family networks, because housework is based on a variety of continuous and discontinuous processes. It may be possible to reduce some of the unpredictability of housework by carefully planning and dividing it between husband and wife or between the wife and members of her network, but it is not possible to plan for children who track in mud, spill glue, or for some other reason make it necessary to wash the floor before it is scheduled to be cleaned. Similarly, a broken washing machine cannot be taken care of routinely in a home where the work force is one person and there is no maintenance department. There is, then, a certain level of unpredictability and discontinuity in the work of most housewives.

Some important differences do emerge, however, in the work-related communities of housewives. In a family belonging to a close-knit network, the housewife's community is based on enduring relations with others who live in close proximity and have deep personal ties to one another. An example is the mother-daughter relationship, which is often the most important link in the close-knit network. In addition to the enduring relationships, a sense of community may also be encouraged by shifting relations with persons who are nearer the margins of the housewife's social network, such as neighbors and shopkeepers. The communities that develop for families in loose-knit networks are different, because the most enduring part of communities are relationships among household members. But, in addition, relationships are often cultivated with people who are involved with the family from time to time. Thus, casual acquaintances and friends do have a definite though irregular impact on the family and its work.

From these sources the social realities of housework are created and they can be quite different for urban and suburban housewives. Though both have often been the major objects of attention of advertisers and writers in women's magazines, the images presented of them in the mass media often vary significantly from the images those housewives have of themselves. In what follows we will explore the experience of being a housewife first and then discuss some of the major problems housewives in traditional nuclear families confront. At the end of this section we will briefly consider the extent to which the experiences of relatively affluent urban and suburban housewives can be generalized to other housewives.

Being a Housewife

Although the popular media write a great deal about housewives and manufacturers and retailers are constantly surveying their buying tastes and habits, relatively little academic research has been done on the experience of being a housewife. One exception is the ten-year study by Helena Lopata (1971) of 1,000 housewives living in Chicago and its suburbs. Lopata's research provides a useful starting point for considering this work role, because it clearly shows that all housewives are not witless dunces who can speak only of babies and laundry, as they are sometimes stereotypically depicted. Rather, housewives are quite varied.

Lopata found seven major types in her study. Three of them—the *husband-oriented* wife, the *child-oriented* wife, and the *house-oriented* wife—give primary attention to one aspect of their lives and work and place less stress on other aspects. The *life-cycle* and *family-oriented* types, on the other hand, offer a more comprehensive vision of being a housewife. The life-cycle type changes her focus as the family situation changes; the family-oriented type refuses to give priority to either the family or work (that is, she refuses to separate cleaning the house from her obligations as a wife and mother). The other two types of housewives focus their attention outside the home. The first, the *self-directed* woman, places greatest emphasis on her personal development as a woman. She may be a full-time housewife, but her major concern is not with home and family as they are typically defined; rather, her obligations to the family include active participation in community affairs or other activities. The second, the *career-oriented* woman, actively seeks out the roles of jobholder, wife, and mother to bring meaning and fulfillment to her life.

Lopata's classification is useful not only because she recognizes many different types of housewives but also because she emphasizes the changing circumstances of their work lives. Just as industrial and professional workers experience their work differently at different times in their lives, so the primary orientations of housewives may also vary, depending on the practical circumstances of family life. Indeed, the work situations of housewives often vary more than those of other workers, because the social and economic circumstances of the family may change dramatically from the time a child is born to the time he or she finally leaves home. The "career" of the housewife, then, is not separable from the life cycle of the family, and each stage in the cycle offers the housewife new problems and opportunities and new ways of defining herself and her work. Lopata distinguishes several stages.

Although becoming a wife and housewife may initially entail important problems, such as learning to cook or dealing with marital disputes, the early years of marriage impose fewer constraints on women than later ones. Part of the reason is that the husband and wife often hold jobs which allow them to maintain important relationships outside the home. That pattern changes as children are born, because many women give up their jobs and become full-time housewives. Even those who continue their jobs, however, usually must deal with the responsibilities and limitations of having children—a phase in the family's life cycle known as the *expanding circle* stage. The housewife experiences new problems then, and they are often exacerbated by the husband's increased involvement in his work outside the home. The problems of the woman with small children are thus not just limited to the increased amount of cooking and cleaning that she must do. She must also deal with the isolation from other adults that concentrated child care sometimes requires.

For many women the zenith of their lives as housewives is the *full-house plateau* stage, when all of the children are born but are still living at home. Great demands are placed on the housewife' time, but many satisfactions are characteristic of this stage. The children are now old enough to be interesting companions, and their activities may also be a source of stimulation for the housewife. In addition, the children may be required to help with some of the housework, and the woman's desire to try her hand at gourmet cooking or similar activities is more likely to be appreciated by the family at this stage. Perhaps the most important change is the opportunity for the housewife to become involved outside the home in a job, community activities, or a club.

The full-house plateau stage is followed by the *shrinking circle* stage, which begins when the first child leaves home and ends when the woman is alone. For many women this is a difficult phase in life, for they feel worthless without children to care for. For others, however, it is a time to develop new interests, relationships, and definitions of themselves by taking on a job, learning a new hobby, or becoming active in community affairs. An equally important change often occurs in the husband-wife relationship, because the husband is often at the top of his career at this time and does not have to spend so much time at work. In addition, the higher pay of the husband and the absence of expenses associated with children means that husband and wife now have the financial means to travel, buy a new house, or do other things which were impossible before. Because most women live longer than their husbands, the final phase of the shrinking circle stage is often widowhood, which involves new adjustments and definitions of self. Not only are old routines altered by the death of the husband, but relationships with friends and family are changed. For some women this is a time of greater personal difficulty, but others adapt to the change by redefining their goals and expectations about themselves.

An important factor affecting the ways in which women experience the various stages of the family's life cycle is the wealth of the family. It is easier for women with greater income to find new interests after losing their children and husbands than it is for the poor. Another important factor is the woman's social network. How others define the role of grandmother or widow may influence the way the woman sees her options. Indeed, a child often sees the changes made by parents after he or she has left home as incomprehensible and expresses opposition. Besides a woman's social network, an equally important factor in how she experiences the life cycle is her own interpretation. She may be husband-, career-, child-, or self-oriented at various times in the life cycle, depending on how she defines herself.

Housewives' interpretations of themselves as women, wives, and mothers are important, because other sources—including advertising, popular literature, newspapers, and many television shows directed toward women—are always creating images of what "right living" and a "good wife, mother, and homemaker" should be. At times, the images conflict, as when some TV shows stress the housewife's obligations to herself as a woman and others stress the need to sacrifice for the good of the family. But housewives are not helpless pawns; typically they pick bits and pieces from a number of images and incorporate them into the definitions they construct of themselves. Lopata (1971) confirmed this when she asked housewives how they learned about their work roles and found that they cited many sources, including books, magazines, newspapers, television, school, mother, husband, friend or relative, doctor, and trial and error. Even women who use the same sources often use them differently. Some women read the newspaper only for recipes, for example, while others read it to get ideas about cleaning, sewing, and decorating.

In sum, the work world of housewives is quite diverse and reflects the varied circumstances of their lives. It also reflects the great extent to which housewives are free to organize and define their work. Their freedom may be limited by a husband, and children, but housewives still have more control over the organization of their work than many assembly-line and low-level bureaucratic workers. Despite their diversity, however, housewives share some general problems.

Major Problems of Housewives

In a general sense, the problems of housewives arise from the contradictions between the images of marriage, parenthood, and housework their culture offers and the way women experience being wives, mothers, and homemakers. For example, the culture may emphasize that assuming these roles is the cornerstone to full femininity and fulfillment but ignore the practical, everyday realities of dealing with a grouchy husband, sick children, and a backed-up sink. The general devaluation of housework in most modern societies only adds to housewives' problems. Large numbers of housewives today indicate that they would like to have at least a part-time job outside the home (Ferree, 1976; Komarovsky, 1962; Rubin, 1976). Although part of the reason is the desire for some level of financial independence from husbands, the low level of prestige associated with being a housewife is also responsible.

In addition to these general problems, housewives also face more specific dilemmas which arise in the course of their work lives. The most important of these problems involve relations with children; the fragmentation, monotony, and isolation of housework; and the absence of clear standards for judging their work.

In many ways the problems of child rearing are the most difficult for many housewives because mothering has become a central feature of their roles. This development has been encouraged by new definitions of children as vulnerable and by the belief that proper child care is one of the family's most important responsibilities. Juvenile delinquency, for example, is explained frequently by reference to the child-rearing practices of the parents, and since the mother has the major responsibility for raising the children, she often receives the greater part of the blame. The importance associated with mothering may also be increased by the new emphasis on getting along within the family. Thus, parent-child conflicts require active resolution and are not treated as the natural conflicts that arise between parents and children based on differing interests.

In practice, mothering and child-rearing are filled with conflicts of interest (Lopata, 1971; Oakley, 1974a, 1974b; Piotrkowski, 1978). Children often require attention that disrupts the routines of their mothers. Frequently they must be supervised so that time mothers could devote to other activities is taken up with watching the children. Children also increase the workload of their mothers by requesting favors and by creating messes around the house. Put simply, much of the energy of the housewife is directed toward child care, and although mothers may find satisfactions in it, they also encounter a number of frustrations and problems. Adding to these frustrations is the housewife's belief in the ideology of patience, which defines the proper mother as an eternally patient, loving and supportive person (Piotrkowski, 1978). Thus, the housewife sometimes interprets feelings of resentment toward children and the desire to be alone as signs of inadequacy as a mother, and her feelings may inspire guilt, which children and others in the society may manipulate. The housewife's problem with child rearing, then, involves more than boredom; it involves the way in which women define motherhood.

Although less emotion charged, the housewife's problems with the fragmentation, monotony, and isolation of her work are also related to a contradiction in modern culture (Oakley, 1974a). On the one hand, the home is described as a haven of good cheer and emotional support for all family members, but the work of the housewife is not always very inspiring. Ironing, dusting, and washing dishes are repetitive activities that few women find exciting or fulfilling. In addition, housewives experience many of their most basic activities as isolated or fragmented bits of work that are not obviously related to the other activities that make up housework. Although making the beds and washing the dishes may be central to housework, for example, their connection to each other or to some general work plan is not self-evident. As with other workers in monotonous and fragmented work settings, housewives often feel frustrated in their work. One study comparing the feelings of factory workers, assembly-line workers, and housewives, for example, found that of the three work groups, housewives experience their work as the most monotonous and fragmented (Oakley, 1974a). Seventy-five percent of the housewives complained of monotony, and 90 percent complained of work fragmentation. These figures compare with 41 and 70 percent for the factory workers and 67 and 86 percent for the assembly-line workers. The problems of monotony and fragmentation are often intensified by the isolation of many housewives, particularly those with small children. As one housewife stated in an interview, "I could be murdered here and no one would know. When the milkman comes, it's an event" (Quoted in Oakley, 1974a: 91). For many women, then, the home is not so much a haven as it is a workhouse where they must do boring, repetitive work with little meaningful adult interaction.

A third problem shared by many housewives involves the absence of generally shared standards for adequate housework (Oakley, 1974a). Rather, the standards of most housewives are derived from their social networks as well as from their own interpretations of what constitutes enough work. Looked at one way, this is advantageous because the housewife is free to develop her own standards and she can alter those standards to take account of the practical limitations of her life. But the absence of shared standards can also be a problem because the woman who desires to be a conscientious housewife is often confused about what is required to be truly conscientious. Children, husbands, parents, neighbors, friends, advertisers, and experts of various types all have different, and sometimes contradictory, ideas about what housewives should do with their time. This problem is made more intense by the ways in which others take for granted much of the most basic work of the housewife. Indeed, many housewives claim that they get more attention when they fail to wash clothes than when they do their work conscientiously (Oakley, 1974a). The development of useful standards of competence, then, is complicated by the fact that many of the features of competent work are likely to go unnoticed by others.

One response to the uncertainties of housework standards is to adopt the most extreme standards. Others in the housewife's social network may encourage such a response, but it may also arise because of the isolation of the housewife and the nature of her work. For housewives the workday does not end so long as there is work to be done. What they fail to recognize is that housework is always incomplete and undone. Jill Duffy, who works an average of 105 hours per week in her home, is an example of this extreme response (Oakley, 1974a). She constantly cleans, cooks, and rearranges her cupboards. Indeed, she feels that her standards are slipping now that she has a second child, because she only changes the children's clothing once a day as compared with twice a day before. But Jill has been able to maintain her standards in other areas. She sweeps and dusts her bedroom every day, and she never allows her husband's dirty clothes to accumulate. She states, "When my husband takes his shirts off *I wash them straight away*—like he wears two shirts on Sunday and I wash them as soon as he takes them off" (Oakley, 1974a: 109).

For many people, Jill Duffy is indicative of the way in which some women develop a pathological orientation to their work. What such an explanation often fails to note is that this style of doing housework is a practical response to Jill's everyday problems. She is isolated in her home with her children, and her husband spends very little time there. Thus, housework is one of the few activities available to her, and since she enjoys most of her work, Jill's seemingly pathological attachment to a clean and orderly household is understandable as a rational response to her problems and opportunities. For different reasons, other housewives who place a high premium on cleanliness and order are also best understood as persons dealing with their everyday problems. In some neighborhoods, for example, the great stress placed on cleanliness may reflect a close-knit network of family and friends who share similar standards of housework (Gans, 1962; Wrobel, 1979). In this case, cleanliness and order do not indicate isolation but involvement in a meaningful group.

Housewives in Other Family Settings

Although the urban and suburban housewives discussed here are somewhat diverse because of differences in ethnicity, income, location, and similar factors, they do not represent the full range of social conditions associated with housework. Most of the research on housework, for example, looks at families in which both the husband and wife are present. We know little about the ways in which single men and women go about their housework. Similarly, the practical circumstances of housework may be quite different in single-parent families, where the father or mother must maintain a home and hold a job. The practical problems this situation presents may mean that the family's standards for housework are reduced, that the children may take greater responsibility for doing the housework, or that maids, relatives, or others outside the family take an active part in maintaining the household.

The problem of being a single-parent family is exacerbated when the family also lives in poverty. In response, single-parent poor families sometimes develop social networks that act as a buffer between the family and the threats to it which exist in the outside world (Mithun, 1973; Modell, 1979). Carol Stack (1974) offers one example of such a network in her description of life in The Flats. The Flats is a section of a small Midwestern city which is populated largely by very poor, underemployed black men and women who have migrated there from their homes in the South. Life in The Flats is extremely precarious because the residents hold jobs that are low-paying and insecure, and many are dependent on the local welfare department for part of their income. Unexpected expenses, such as those occasioned by a severe illness or accident, can have devastating consequences for a family in The Flats. Ironically, unexpected wealth may also result in problems, because the local welfare department usually cuts off aid until the money is spent. When one couple received an inheritance of $1,500, for example, they were denied food stamps and medical coverage for their children for four months.

Over the years a way of life has emerged in The Flats to help the residents deal with these uncertainties. The center of the way of life is the *domestic network*, which is made up of relatives, neighbors, and friends who can be depended on for help when it is needed. An important part of the network of aid is the practice of *swapping*, through which goods are redistributed to those in need. Unlike other forms of swapping, however, the residents of The Flats do not worry about completing the exchange immediately; rather, the person who gives up an item today knows that he or she can depend on the other person to reciprocate when it is needed. As one Flats resident explains:

> My TV's been over to my cousin's house for seven or eight months now. I had a fine couch that she wanted and I gave it to her too. . . . I don't ever expect nothing back right away, but when I've given something to kin or friend, whenever they think about me they'll bring something on around. Even if we don't see each other for two or three months (Quoted in Stack, 1974: 41–42).

In addition to couches, television sets, and similar items, the residents of The Flats also swap their children, because it is sometimes necessary to house the children temporarily in someone else's home. Thus, one way of paying back a relative or friend is to take her children while she returns to her home town for a funeral or to visit a sick relative.

Life in The Flats, then, is very different from the way of life depicted in women's magazines and advertising. For women in The Flats, housework is not separable from the problem of keeping the family together and solvent. The domestic network is central to maintaining the household, because it is a source of money and other resources that are more readily available in more affluent households. But the residents of The Flats are not unique; other housewives facing similar problems often develop networks of aid. Peasant wives who cannot depend on their husbands for help in the house, for example, often develop social networks for companionship and help. The emphasis on relatively affluent urban and suburban families in the literature of sociology, then, has obscured the diverse ways in which rural and very poor housewives experience, conceptualize, and deal with their housework.

Finally, the organization of housework within households where both the husband and wife have outside employment deserves further study. The developing body of literature on dual-career families suggests that the demands of two careers severely limit the time and freedom of family members (Holmstrom, 1973; Rapoport and Rapoport, 1976). Sometimes families in this position hire someone to take over much of the housework. These families also redefine their obligations to each other and others in their social networks. Dinner parties and similar events, for example, are less frequent in these families than in those where the wife is a full-time housewife. Similarly, a wife in a dual-career family is less likely to take an active part in the social activities associated with her husband's career. Some corporations assume that the executive's wife will act as a hostess for cocktail parties and attend other corporate events. Women who have careers of their own are recognized to have less time for such activities, and their absence is frequently understood by others, whereas the absence of a full-time housewife would be seen as a problem (Kanter, 1977a).

In dual-career families, then, housework is frequently organized and defined differently than in other households to take account of the demands of each person's career. In part, the redefinition is possible because the income level of the family is great enough to make hiring a housekeeper and frequent meals in restaurants feasible. But dual-career families include more than those where both spouses have professional jobs. Equally important are families in which both the husband and wife work to meet their basic expenses and have little or no money left over to pay for a housekeeper or meals in restaurants. Although husbands in these families may be more willing to help with the housework than their counterparts whose wives are full-time housewives, the bulk of the housework is typically shouldered by the women, who often return from their jobs to face several more hours of work (Walshok, 1979).

In sum, the everyday circumstances surrounding modern family life are quite diverse, and for this reason the ways in which housework is organized are varied. Public accounts of housework and family life seldom fully recognize this diversity; rather, they typically hold up one or a few examples as the "normal" family. In part, the moralistic assumptions of the producers of the public images account for this tendency, because they assume that there is one best way for the family to be organized. Although the images may vary in their details, they are contemporary efforts to preach "right living" to those who are seen as deviating from the norm. Advertisers have an economic interest in projecting an image of right living because it helps them sell their products, but others also have a self-interest in creating such an image. Much of the analysis and theorizing about the family in the social sciences, for example, can be understood as an attempt to create a vision of the family that justifies either the status quo or dramatic social change. Because these theories oversimplify the diversity of modern families and housework, they are myths. We will turn to a few of the major myths about families and housework next.

MYTHS ABOUT HOUSEWORK AND HOUSEWIVES

No social institution receives more popular and academic attention than the family. The popular media regularly survey its health, and we are periodically told that it is in a crisis situation. Indeed, occasional efforts to redefine the notion of family to include a broader range of relationships, such as those of unmarried or gay couples, are often opposed in highly emotional ways. One reason why issues affecting the family raise such emotions is that many people see it as a fundamental unit of society; changes are thus seen as threatening. Many theorists have built formal explanations which also place family relations at the center of modern society. Included among these theorists are those who want to justify the status quo and those who wish to encourage radical social change. In this section we will consider three myths about housewives and housework: the myths of separate worlds, the egalitarian family, and the exploitative family. These myths are summarized in Table 6-2. Each represents a different way in which the assumption that the family is a fundamental unit of society may be used to explain the work and family situations of housewives.

The Myth of Separate Worlds

The *myth of separate worlds* is a theoretical counterpart to the popular belief in the division of life into "men's work" and "women's work." Both assume that such a division is basic and necessary. The popular version considers the division as the outcome of natural differences between the sexes: women are emotional and nurturant, whereas men are aggressive and competitive. The academic version is different, because the sexual division of labor in modern life is explained as the result of social needs rather than the differing constitutions of men and women. In sociology this perspective is most evident in the writings of Talcott Parsons (1949, 1951; Parsons and Bales, 1955).

Central to his approach is the belief that modern industrial society is made up of a number of institutional worlds which are largely unconnected. Each institutional world is organized around the accomplishment of a limited number of objectives, and although individuals may be involved in several institutional worlds, their roles and relationships in each are quite different and do not overlap. One basic division in modern society is the separation of the occupational world from that of the family. The major objective of persons in the occupational world is achievement, which requires the unemotional and calculating pursuit of self-interest. In the world of the family, however, close emotional and nurturant ties are most important, because the main objectives of family life are socialization of the young and meeting the personal needs of family members.

The division of the world into work and family is necessary because modern society has evolved specialized institutions that are more effective than other institutional forms. Thus, society is treated as having needs which men and women are socialized from childhood to fulfill. Those needs are the reason that little girls are encouraged to play house

Table 6-2 • Myths About Housework and Housewives

Type of Myth	*Need for Work*	*Organization of Work*	*Rewards of Work*
The Myth of Separate Worlds	Based on the needs of modern industrial society, which require a separation of male-occupational and female-family worlds	Responsibilities for meeting the emotional and socialization needs of family members fall solely on the housewife	Sharing of the husband's social status and the satisfactions derived from close emotional relations in the family
The Myth of the Egalitarian Family	Based on the need to maintain the household, raise the children, and meet the emotional needs of family members	Housework responsibilities shared by family members	Increased individual choice and expression, fuller and more human relationships, and increased responsiveness to the social environment
The Myth of the Exploitative Family	Based on the unequal relationship between men and women as well as the need to maintain the household, raise the children, and provide emotional support	Responsibilities are sexually segregated, leaving housewives with isolated, monotonous, and dehumanizing work which keeps them from achieving self-actualization.	No real rewards, although housewives are encouraged to believe that inferiority to men, child-rearing, and close emotional relationships are rewarding

and little boys are encouraged to be aggressive and seek achievement. In adulthood divisions are further encouraged by the development of sexually segregated roles, which ensure that basic societal needs will be met. One of the most important divisions occurs in the family, where the husband has a job and the wife remains at home. To involve both the husband and wife in the occupational world would be very risky, because the unemotional and calculating attitude of the occupational world may intrude on the world of the family and the emotional and nurturant needs of its members would go unmet.

In sum, the myth of separate worlds justifies the notion of men's work and women's work by arguing that sexual segregation is necessary for maintaining modern life. Thus, housework, which is primarily organized around the emotional and personal needs of family members, is needed to maintain the existing organization of modern society. The work of the housewife is not comparable to that of her husband because he is a calculating, self-interested worker who is primarily concerned with rational goals, such as profit, efficiency, and power. She must forgo a rational household in the interests of meeting emotional needs. As a corollary, the myth also claims that more rational techniques for socializing the young and dealing with emotional problems must be developed in specialized, therapeutic institutions outside the home (Lasch, 1977). To attempt to incorporate them into the housewife's role would create personal and institutional contradictions that could not be resolved. Finally, the myth claims that one of the most important rewards the housewife receives for her work is sharing her husband's occupational achievements, because her income and prestige are increased when her husband receives a raise and promotion. Another major work reward is the intrinsic satisfaction that accompanies close emotional and nurturant relationships. These rewards may be supplemented to some extent by female-based sources of prestige, which come partly from rational achievement in such settings as women's clubs, community organizations, book clubs, and the like. However, these sources of work rewards are much less important than those deriving from the husband's occupational position and relationships in the family (Parsons, 1949: 271).

Parsons' theory obviously justifies the maintenance of a world in which women are dependent on men for their incomes. In addition, the myth has three other problems that deserve special note here. First, this view of housewives and housework is based on an incomplete grasp of the range of family situations found in modern society. The myth does not account, for example, for the persistence of single-parent families, within which one person must meet the family's income and emotional needs. Indeed, one of the most important reasons that female-headed families persist among some welfare recipients has been government policy requiring that adult men be absent from the home. There are, then, institutional as well as personal reasons for alternative family arrangements which contradict the fundamental needs of society. If modern institutions are truly organized to meet the needs of modern society, this situation should not exist.

A second problem with the myth is that it ignores the many rational features of housework. The woman who regularly clips coupons from the newspaper or shops at several stores to keep the family's food bill at a minimum is acting in as rational, calculating, and self-interested a manner as a man who regularly seeks ways of cutting business costs in order to increase company profits. Indeed, the myth ignores the many ways in which home economists, specialists in child-rearing, and others have encouraged housewives to adopt rational techniques in doing their work. Whether this advice is heeded or not is better explained by the circumstances of housewives' lives than by reference to an abstract set of societal needs. The related assumption that work outside the home is always based on rational and self-interested motives is also problematic, because it does not take account of the fact that human beings develop close emotional relationships on the job. These relationships include more than the sexual affairs which often dominate the gossip of the work place. They also include friendships which may develop in work groups—friendships that workers often consider in deciding about accepting alternative employment that may offer more pay or other rewards typically classified as rational rather than emotional.

Finally, the myth does not take account of the ways in which occupational and family experiences overlap (Kanter, 1977b; Piotrkowski, 1978). The overlap can be seen at a very simple level when one considers the impact of a bad day at the office on the family, which must suffer through its outcome. Similarly, anger, frustration, and anxieties in the home may affect performance on the job. The overlap of family and occupation is also evident in the ways some jobs intrude on the family. Many women and men regularly bring work home from the office, which cuts into family time. In addition, the so-called full-time housewife often is expected to aid her husband at social events sponsored by his employer (Kanter, 1977a). How the wife performs on these occasions may affect her husband's occupational success. Thus, a housewife may not simply borrow her social standing from her husband; rather, she is an important reason for his success.

The myth of separate worlds, then, is an oversimplification of the many social realities of housework. It also justifies an institutional arrangement in which women are relegated to the home and to sustaining others. The rationale is not that the home is the natural habitat of women, but rather that women are socialized in such a way that they desire to meet this societal need. Presumably, male and female roles could be reversed with no great damage to the society so long as the occupational and family worlds are kept separate. This is, however, only one way of looking at the relationship between the family and societal needs. Other myths explaining this relationship exist.

The Myth of the Egalitarian Family

Another approach to explaining the link between family and society argues that societal needs are changing so that the old, male-dominated family will eventually become too burdensome to maintain and it will be replaced by a family where equality prevails. This is the *myth of the egalitarian family*. If the myth of separate worlds is a conservative theory which justifies the male-dominated family, the myth of the egalitarian family is a liberal theory which justifies the reform of the male-dominated family.

For theorists who support the egalitarian myth family reform is not just a good idea but an inevitable consequence of changes occurring in modern society (Bennis and Slater, 1968; Young and Willmott, 1973). Generally these changes stem from the decline of the old family in which stability and permanence were basic features. But the changes in the family accompany many other changes in modern society. Fewer and fewer people now hold a single job or even live in the same city for a lifetime; a new, more flexible family arrangement is essential because of these developments. Similarly, new family arrangements are encouraged both by the rise of suburbs, which are populated by family-centered people who are less controlled by their parents than their urban counterparts, and by the spread of feminist ideas, which stress the need for women to have equal legal rights and equal opportunities for education and employment.

The ultimate outcome of recent changes in society is the rise of the *egalitarian family* in which husband, wife, and children share power and responsibility. This family type is already evident in some sectors of modern society, and proponents of the myth assume that eventually it will become the dominant type as the changes encouraging equality become more widespread. The egalitarian ideal is embodied today primarily in the middle-class family in which one or both of the spouses are employed as professionals, managers, and the like. In such families employment and other experiences encourage an openness to new types of relationships which are more egalitarian and flexible. In addition, these families have less interest in maintaining traditional roles and values which subject children to the arbitrary power of parents; rather, children are encouraged to develop flexible and egalitarian relationships with their peers and adults, including their parents.

The myth regards the changing circumstances of modern life as important for housework. Although the need for housework as a way to maintain the household, raise the children, and meet basic emotional needs will persist, new means to meet this need will evolve. Housework will be shared by all family members, and it will not be the major responsibility of the housewife. Encouraging this new work organization is the wife's employment outside the home, which gives her less time for housework than the full-time housewife. In addition, the men and women of these families share new ideas about the role of the father in child-rearing. No longer is his responsibility limited to supporting them financially and acting as a disciplinarian; he is expected to take an active role in meeting their day-to-day emotional needs. Changing ideas about the father's role not only encourage more equitable relations between husbands and wives and fathers and children but free wives for alternative activities and relationships outside the home. They will also result in the development of new rewards for household workers. The most important are the rewards of increased individual choice and expression for all family members, the development of fuller and more human relationships in the family, and an increased ability of all members to respond to the opportunities in the family's environment.

The myth of the egalitarian family is based on the assumption that recent social changes require changes in family structure. If families do not become more flexible, they will not be able to respond to the changing social environment. This assumption oversimplifies the diverse environments in which modern families exist. The steelworker in South Chicago, the coal miner in southern Illinois, and the automobile worker in Detroit are all examples of workers who have been little affected by changing social conditions that might encourage development of the egalitarian family (Kornblum, 1974; Lantz, 1958; Wrobel, 1979). In fact, in industrial settings, work, family, and neighborhood are often very stable, and it is difficult to find even the beginnings of the changes that are assumed to affect other sectors of the society. Many industrial workers live their entire lives within the neighborhoods in which they were raised and they devote their lives to working for one company—a company that may also employ their fathers, brothers, uncles, and cousins. The major source of change in these jobs is an occasional promotion, which rarely requires that the family move to a new city or neighborhood. Stability and permanence are further encouraged by ethnic and religious ties, which bind neighborhood residents to traditional institutional practices. What proponents of the myth of the egalitarian family fail to recognize is that changes in one part of modern society may have little or no impact on other sectors, in which institutions are built based on the unique circumstances of the everyday lives of the people in those sectors.

A second problem with the myth is that it assumes that close-knit family networks necessarily give rise to unequal relationships and that loose-knit networks encourage equality. Close-knit networks, the myth's proponents argue, are based on sexually-segregated groups which maintain the traditional distinction between men's and women's work. Under such an arrangement the woman is usually saddled with the bulk of the housework while the man is free to pursue leisure activities after work. But sexual segregation leading to female oppression is not an inevitable feature of close-knit networks. It is just as possible for close-knit networks to stress equality and shared housework. Even those close-knit networks that are based on a clear division of men's and women's work are not necessarily dominated by the husband. In dividing the world along sexual lines, families in close-knit networks may also divide responsibility and power so that women control some aspects of family life and men other aspects. In other words, the egalitarian theorists do not take account of the ways in which all family members regularly negotiate their relationships and responsibilities; rather, they assume that certain types of social relationships are inevitable in each form of family organization.

Even within the loose-knit, middle-class family, which is presented as the prototype of the emerging egalitarian family, there is contradictory evidence that true egalitarian relationships are evolving. Although the husband in the dual-career family does tend to do more housework than the husband in a family with a full-time housewife, the contributions of the husband and wife are not equal. The conclusion that the egalitarian family is inevitable is based on a selective interpretation of existing data, and theorists who come to this conclusion often gloss over contradictory evidence. For example, despite the increased contribution of husbands in dual-career families, one study has shown that the full-time working wives worked an average of 63.3 hours at their jobs and at home, whereas the full-time housewives averaged only 45.5 hours (Young and Willmott, 1973). On the basis of this evidence, it is just as plausible to argue that the new middle-class family may give rise to new forms of inequality rather than equality.

In addition, proponents of the myth of the egalitarian family often overlook the ways in which dual-career and egalitarian families may become locked into routines that make flexibility and responsiveness to the environment difficult. It is difficult for a husband or wife to move across the country in pursuit of a better job, for example, when the new location offers few employment opportunities for a spouse. Similarly, taking account of the various desires and interests of all family members may lead to creation of a rigid schedule of responsibilities which leaves little room for flexibility in family relationships. In some situations, at least, the family with one dominant leader—be it the husband or wife—may be more flexible and responsive to the environment, because there are fewer interests to satisfy and, therefore, fewer obstacles to overcome. Put differently, egalitarian theorists fail to see that equality and flexibility do not necessarily go hand in hand, and they oversimplify the ways in which men and women interpret and respond to changing social conditions. No form of social organization seems inevitable when the impersonal forces of evolution are looked at through the eyes of the diverse human beings who experience them.

The Myth of the Exploitative Family

Both of the myths discussed thus far stress the ways in which the family is shaped by social needs and forces, though one is conservative and the other liberal. There is at least one more way in which to conceptualize the family as the product of social forces. This is the radical vision, which treats the family as inherently unequal and exploitative. The family is seen neither as a haven of good cheer and emotional support or a source of hope for a new, more humane, and equitable society: it is an institution which must be eliminated in order to build a better way of life. This is the *myth of the exploitative family*.

The myth combines the feminists' concern for the unequal position of women in modern society with the Marxist concern for the ways in which all workers are exploited. Thus, proponents pay particular attention to the ways in which the modern economy is organized so that housewives are an unpaid labor force which provides free services to employers (Benston, 1969; Dalla Costa, 1972; Mitchell, 1966). The most important of these services are childbearing, child-rearing, and sustaining men so that they may be dependable employees. The problem of unequal relations between men and women, then, is not separable from the more general problem of economic inequality in modern society. One of the best developed of the arguments supporting this myth is presented by Ann Oakley (1974b), whose research concentrates on the history of housework and the problems of contemporary housewives. Oakley's analysis is the basis for this discussion, although it is consistent with the most basic claims of other radical theorists.

Central to Oakley's perspective is the belief that housework involves more than just maintaining a household, looking after the children, and meeting the husband's emotional needs. In addition, housework is a necessary feature of modern society because it is one of the most important supports for male dominance, which is essential to maintaining a sexist society. Unlike other forms of domination, however, male domination goes unnoticed because of the ways in which girls are raised and the close personal relationship between husbands and wives. The socialization of girls into the traditional female roles means that they accept subordination as a natural feature of being a woman: it is a fact of life. The family further supports subordination by fostering the assumption that women will find happiness and fulfillment in their housework. Indeed, to admit to boredom or unhappiness is to both challenge prevailing assumptions about the nature of women and to call into question the ability of one's husband to provide an adequate home for his family.

Housework is needed in modern society, then, and both men and women are frequently unable to see the many ways in which it dehumanizes housewives. This claim is supported by research that indicates that many housewives find little joy or satisfaction in their work. Equally important is the belief by Oakley and others that self-actualization for workers should be a major goal of modern society and that this can be achieved only when all work is interesting, rewarding, and occurs in meaningful work groups. They reject the claim that although washing dishes may be boring, women achieve some satisfaction in knowing they are serving their families; self-actualization emerges only from the act of doing work and not from the general conditions associated with it. Thus, the claims about the many rewards of housework reflect the recognized and unrecognized interests of those who have power. When these claims are stripped away, it is clear that there are no real rewards associated with housework.

The alternative to the existing arrangement of housework is a new society in which the sources of sexual inequality are eliminated. One of the most important is the family, the social institution which most directly exploits women through the husband-wife relationship and through traditional socialization practices that prepare girls for inferiority. The new society must be organized so that men and women can be equals both at work and in their personal relationships with each other. The way to do this is to make housework the domain of paid domestic workers. These male and female workers would occupy a different role from the housewife, even the housewife who is paid, because their jobs would not be based on sexual subordination: the relationship would be that of employer and employee and nothing more. In addition, such domestic work could be organized so that isolation and boredom are minimized and self-actualization encouraged. Another feature of the new society might be paying men and women for raising their children, since they are providing a basic service to the society. Whatever the specific details of the new society, the major point is that the family made up of a husband, wife, and children fosters inequality and must be abolished.

In some ways this vision of the family suffers from the same problems as the myths of separate worlds and the egalitarian family. All oversimplify the range of family relationships and arrangements in modern society. Even if it could be demonstrated that all families are exploitative, the nature of that exploitation and its consequences cannot be treated as the same. The pampered wife in the leisure class may be used by her husband to achieve his desire to be recognized as a wealthy, respectable man, for example, and this may be interpreted as a type of exploitation, but her situation is quite different from that of the peasant wife who may be asked to work in the fields all day and then do housework at night. Thus, a fundamental problem with the radical critique of the family and household is the tendency to overgeneralize and ignore the variety and subtlety of the issues which are raised. An example is the claim that the family must be abolished because it necessarily socializes girls into subordinate roles and relationships. This claim fails to acknowledge that no matter how important early socialization is, human beings are not slaves to their childhoods. Indeed, the radical feminists themselves are an example of how women can break out of conventional roles and develop alternative desires and ways of life. If it is possible for women to overcome their childhood training, then it may also be possible to build a more equitable family.

In a similar way, the proponents of the myth of the exploitative family hold to a vision of self-actualization that is very narrow and does not take account of the variety of ways in which human beings give meaning to their lives. Oakley claims, for example, that "an affirmation of contentment with the housewife role is actually a form of antifeminism, whatever the gender of the person who displays it. Declared contentment with a subordinate role—which the housewife role undoubtedly is—is a rationalization of inferior status" (Oakley, 1974b: 233). The housewife who states that she is content in her work role and relationships may be taking an antifeminist position and she may even be justifying her inferior position with the family, but neither of these interpretations negates her claim to contentment: they merely point to some of the consequences of her stand.

In sum, the radical vision of the family and housework is a myth because it is a theoretical perspective which forces the diversity and richness of everyday life into predefined categories which reflect the interpretations and interests of its theorists. The myth's most obvious oversimplification is the claim that a more equitable world would relegate housework to specialized domestic workers, which would free housewives from their isolation and make housework more self-actualizing. The details of how housework could be made less alienating are not explained. Certainly some of the isolation might be reduced by organizing housework as a group activity, but clothes would still need to be washed, floors scrubbed, and ironing done. The presumption seems to be that paid work is less alienating than unpaid work, and yet radical analysis of factory workers provides evidence to the contrary. How this contradiction could be resolved is of less interest here than the failure of this myth and others to take account of the ways in which human beings interpret the worlds in which they live. Thus, human beings are not simply shaped by forces in their environments but act to shape them. When theorists speak of society's needs, an inevitable process of evolution, or the inherently exploitative nature of a social institution, they deny the ways in which human beings have created the societies, evolutionary processes, and institutions to which these theorists attribute so much power. They also fail to take seriously the options for change and innovation that persons within society or institutions may create.

CONCLUSION

This chapter has dealt with a form of work that is frequently devalued by men and women alike, even as they glorify motherhood and femininity. The unpaid status of housewives and their frequent description of themselves as "just housewives" provide evidence of the work's devalued status. So too do the attempts of domestic scientists and others to improve the image of housework by making it both a science and a source of respectability for women. Despite the best efforts of these reformers, the social standing of the housewife is little better today than at the turn of the century. Even feminists who claim to speak for the interests of all women often operate from Charlotte Perkins Gilman's assumption that the full-time housewife is a parasite and that true liberation and equality require that housework be turned over to domestic services so that housewives can pursue careers of their own. At the same time, the feminists' vision is countered today, as in the past, by alternative visions which simplistically stress the joys of motherhood and being a self-sacrificing wife.

Which of these visions of femininity and the housewife's role women adopt depends on the practical circumstances of their lives. These circumstances include the wealth of the family, its location, the presence or absence of a close-knit network, and the life-cycle stage being experienced by the woman. Indeed, these life circumstances are likely to discourage the full acceptance or rejection of either of these visions; instead, most women are likely to use parts of each vision to create their own unique definitions of themselves and their families.

Chapter Seven

COUNTERCULTURAL WORK

With the exception of some types of hustling work, all of the kinds of work considered to this point are conventional ways of making a living, because they are seen as legitimate by most people and they do not involve a rejection of the assumptions and practices of major social institutions. In this chapter we will consider several ways in which the conventional organization of work is challenged in alternative communities and social movements, which often give new meaning to work as they attempt to build a better world. These communities and movements have a long history in the United States and other industrialized countries, and they are central to the countercultural tradition.

The term "counterculture" is often used today to depict a narrow range of youth life styles which involve some degree of opposition to conventionality. Thus, rock singers who espouse the values of individualism, self-expression, and hedonism are sometimes presented as typical members of the contemporary counterculture. Often ignored are the facts that these values are widely shared by others in modern societies and that these exemplars of the counterculture are also highly committed to the conventional goals of wealth and fame. The countercultural tradition is not limited to the life styles of the young and it certainly predates rock music; indeed, the beginnings of this tradition are the same as those of modern society as a whole (Miller, 1980; Veysey, 1973). The reason is that the countercultural tradition is a reaction to the social, moral, political, and economic effects of modernization, particularly the consequences of industrialization and the rise of markets as the major centers for distributing goods, services, and workers.

In this chapter the *counterculture* includes those groups which reject to some extent modern values and practices and adopt an alternative perspective. Spontaneous and short-lived movements, such as wildcat strikes to increase wages or to reduce the speed of an assembly line, are excluded from this discussion because they are not organized around an alternative vision of modern work and life (Ash, 1972; Gusfield, 1970, 1973b). On the other hand, the Industrial Workers of the World (the Wobblies), a socialist labor group involved in strikes and efforts at sabotage during the early part of the twentieth century, are typical of the American counterculture, because the Wobblies were dedicated to the overthrow of private business interests and the establishment of a worker-controlled economy (Brooks, 1964; Pelling, 1960). Unlike most wildcat strikers, the Wobblies did not see their mission as merely obtaining a higher wage or slowing down the assembly line: they were engaged in a struggle to transform the world, and strikes and sabotage were only one part of that struggle.

The counterculture, then, is at least partly made up of the many *social movements* that have emerged during modern times. Some of these movements, such as the Wobblies and other socialist movements, have been politically and socially radical, but others have been conservative and their members have sought to achieve a utopian vision of the past. Another important part of the modern counterculture is the *alternative community*, which attempts to create an alternative way of life (Zablocki, 1971). Unlike social movements, which try to change the world, alternative communities withdraw from the world to achieve what members consider a better way of life. An example is offered by the Icarians, a group of nineteenth-century French workers who found their work transformed with the rise of the factory. Instead of fighting to change the world in which they lived and worked, as the Wobblies did, these people chose to withdraw from that world and create a new society in which equality and sharing would prevail (Cabet, 1848; Wheeler, Hernon, and Sweetland, 1975). Thus, the Icarians migrated to the United States, where they founded a number of communities that disregarded the changes occurring in the outside world and preserved old relationships and skills.

There are, then, two major components of the modern countercultural tradition, and each points to a different feature of the tradition. Social movements stress the counterculture's critique of conventional beliefs and practices, whereas alternative communities point to new ways of organizing life. In practice, most social movements and alternative communities include some features of the other, because it is difficult to criticize conventions without developing some type of alternative vision and it is difficult to set up an alternative way of life without criticizing the conventional beliefs and practices that community members reject. Thus, the main difference between social movements and alternative communities is one of degree, with some countercultural groups placing more stress on criticizing conventionality and others on building an alternative to it. For this reason, it is important to begin this discussion of work in the counterculture by considering which conventional beliefs and practices members of countercultural groups accept and which they reject. Following that, we will discuss the ways in which work is organized and given meaning within countercultural groups and the ways in which work may be changed as these groups become established in modern society.

THE SOCIAL REALITIES OF THE COUNTERCULTURE

Because one part of the counterculture involves a critique of conventional beliefs and practices, a useful beginning is to look at some basic modern beliefs and assumptions. One such listing is offered by Peter Berger (1977), who states that modern society is dominated by a belief in abstraction, futurity, individuation, liberation, and secularization. Each of these beliefs is observable in the major social institutions of modern society, and they affect the lives of individuals as well. For example, individuals often experience these beliefs as dilemmas which require some type of resolution. For some people the resolution takes the form of resigned acceptance of conventionality, but others seek a deeper understanding and resolution. For the latter, the resolution to modern dilemmas may be to seek a new life in social movements and alternative communities. Thus, it is important to consider each of the major modern dilemmas in some detail. But countercultural groups do not just criticize and reject aspects of modernity; they also embody values and goals that point to a better way of life. These are the organizing myths of the counterculture. They are important both for understanding the diversity of groups that make up this segment of modern society and for classifying them. In this section we will consider the modern dilemmas against which countercultural groups react, the organizing myths that give them an identity, and the way their alternate views of reality can be used to classify the groups.

Modern Dilemmas

The *dilemma of abstraction* involves the tendency of modern institutions to be separated from the everyday realities of ordinary people's lives. Decisions made in government, corporations, and other impersonal organizations are important forces shaping our lives, and yet few of us understand, much less have great control over, these mysterious forces. Another indication of the modern tendency toward abstraction is the way in which we treat institutions as social entities having needs which are more important than those of individuals. Indeed, it is paradoxical how social institutions that presumably exist to serve human needs have in practice become vehicles that serve the interests of institutional elites. Abstraction poses a dilemma precisely because, although abstract institutions increase general human control over the world, they reduce the control and understanding of most people.

One reason that human beings lose control over abstract institutions is that these institutions are based on a unique view of the world—that of the expert, who approaches the world as an aloof, unemotional technician concerned only with a limited set of technical problems and not with the larger problems of our age. Thus, physicians act as "body scientists" whose sole concern is with a patient's liver or heart, not with the whole person or those industrial conditions that foster physical ailments. Similarly, high-level managers develop measures of corporate profitability, effectiveness, and efficiency that are used to assess the performance of workers. Contributions made by workers which are not detectable by the manager's indexes are treated as nonexistent. In sum, people feel powerless in dealing with abstract institutions because only a few people understand the principles on which they operate and their goals often seem arbitrary and nonsensical.

The *dilemma of futurity* is similar to the dilemma of abstraction in that both lead to absurdity. The former dilemma arises because of the emphasis modernity gives to the future. In general, modern societies are highly future oriented because an important cultural assumption found in all of them is that decisions and actions taken in the present can affect the future; indeed, as rational beings humans are the only creatures that can understand and control their future. It is not hard to find an example of future orientation: parents often advise their children to save their money so that they can enjoy a better future. Within this perspective, the present is an investment in the future.

Another important example of future orientation is the modern concept of a career. Embodied in this concept is a concern for increasing one's prestige, wealth, and power in the future. The present job of the careerist is always a stepping stone to another more attractive one. The dilemma arises because, in Berger's words, "futurity means endless striving, restlessness, and a mounting incapacity for repose" (Berger, 1977: 74); thus, the careerist is always discontent with the present and seeking a more desirable future. When taken to its extreme this view becomes absurd because the individual can never achieve contentment or fulfillment so long as there is a future that looks more exciting, challenging, and rewarding. The dilemma of futurity, then, involves finding a proper balance between the present and the future.

The basis of the *dilemma of individuation* is another tendency carried to extreme—the tendency of modern society to focus on individuals and their pursuit of self-interest. In contrast, in other societies, meaningful groups—such as families, tribes, and villages—dominate life, and group interest takes precedence over individual interest. The term "self-interest" is often used in a disparaging way to indicate a callous or greedy perspective, but such usage obscures the pervasiveness of this value in modern society and the variety of circumstances within which the pursuit of self-interest is seen as legitimate. One indication of the pervasiveness of self-interest and individuation in modern society is the tendency of young people to terminate many family and neighborhood ties when they begin their careers. Careerism is an individual journey which frequently requires relocation outside one's home town or home neighborhood and the adoption of a life style that is different from that of one's past (Sennett and Cobb, 1972). Although it is possible to share the financial rewards of career success with parents and friends, it is not possible to make them a part of one's career.

In general, individuation is related to the processes of futurity and abstraction. The emphasis on self-interest in careers is one example of the link between futurity and individuation. A link between abstraction and individuation can be found in the modern notion of individual rights, the cultural and institutional means by which individuals can hold abstract institutions accountable. Put differently, modern rights are individual, and for this reason they do not take account of the special needs of each person in modern society; rather, they act to define what rights all persons may claim in dealing with each other and with the organizations and institutions that shape their lives. Because individual rights are institutionalized, people may experience them as another set of abstractions that control their lives. Indeed, so long as organizations and institutions do not abridge institutionalized individual rights, individuals may be unable to claim any further rights. One of the fundamental contradictions of modern society, then, is that as individual rights are scrupulously protected, the needs and desires of individuals are often ignored.

The dilemma of individuation arises from the tendency of modern life to be increasingly organized around discrete individuals and their interests. Ironically, this emphasis on extreme individualism may become oppressive, because it places the major burdens of life on each individual and discourages the development of group solutions to common problems. What those who adopt an extreme individualist position fail to see is that the self-interests of individuals may be better served in groups which provide their members with mutual aid and a sense of purpose beyond themselves. One reason why extreme individualists do not see this consequence of individuation is that they associate individualism with liberation, which is the basis of another dilemma.

The origin of the *dilemma of liberation* is the desire of people to be free from the constraints of tradition. To be liberated is to free oneself from the confines of old ideas, roles, and relationships and to create new ones that provide individuals with more opportunity to grow and to express themselves. Modern women, for example, are encouraged to free themselves from the narrow confines of the traditional family, and children are encouraged to achieve greater respectability and wealth than their parents. At the heart of the dilemma of liberation are the dilemmas of abstraction, futurity, and individuation, because liberation is treated as synonymous with involvement in a world of abstract, future-oriented institutions in which individual interests take on more importance than the interests of groups. This is a world that is often as constraining and frustrating as the traditional world from which the individual has become liberated.

Because much of tradition is grounded in sacred explanations and practices, it should not be surprising that the *dilemma of secularization* in modern society is the final one with which we are concerned. In a wide variety of institutional settings scientific research and secular theories have come to replace sacred beliefs as the primary bases for decision making and human action. Even religious officials reflect this tendency, because they increasingly use knowledge taken from psychology, sociology, biology, and other secular disciplines to counsel their followers. The emphasis on secularism in modern society is also evident in the world of work, where the secular rewards of money, power, and prestige are actively sought. Even those workers who claim to be seeking more enduring rewards from their work typically betray their secular assumptions when they assert that personal growth and self-actualization can be achieved only in this world. Thus, central to the dilemma of secularization is the identification of the major source of meaning in life. While extreme secularists claim that all meaning can be found in this world, their critics note that the major rewards offered by this world are the ephemeral ones of money, power, and prestige and the mixed blessings of abstraction, futurity, individuation, and liberation.

Although all of the modern dilemmas identified by Berger are evident in some areas of modern life, they are also denied in other parts. Just as we live in a world of large, abstract institutions, such as corporations, universities, and government, many of us also live in a world of smaller, more personal, and controllable institutions. Included in the latter category are various community groups and associations, such as bridge and garden clubs, and other centers of sociability, such as churches and taverns. Similarly, the modern dilemmas of futurity, individuation, liberation, and secularization are obvious in some areas of modern life but absent in others. The critics of modern society, however, tend to emphasize their pervasiveness. Thus, they consciously create myths which oversimplify modern life and justify their oversimplifications on the ground that they have identified the most important problems and processes of modernity. They have, in other words, identified the essence of modern life.

Mythmaking is not limited to formal academic theories such as Berger's, for it is also evident in the analyses of members of the counterculture. Indeed, the less formal critiques of different groups found in the contemporary counterculture recognize each of the modern dilemmas discussed here. An important difference between the critiques of countercultural groups and others, however, is that members of the counterculture do not always reject all aspects of modernity; rather, they reject some parts and accept others. The contemporary community of Twin Oaks provides an example. The members of this community believe that through careful planning and the rational use of rewards and punishments, a better world can be created (Kincaide, 1973). Within this community, then, the modern values of secularization and liberation are accepted, but the tendencies toward abstraction and individuation in modern life are rejected. Other groups in the counterculture, such as the Church of the Cosmic Liberty, accept the modern values of individuation and liberation while rejecting secularization (Damrell, 1978).

One way of understanding the diversity of the modern counterculture, then, is to classify the different social and alternative communities based on their critiques of modernity. This approach would provide insight into those features of modern life that these groups see as problematic, but it would not provide us with a full understanding of the counterculture. The reason is that besides rejecting some features of modernity, these groups also embody an alternative vision of life. In other words, they are based on alternative realities, and these realities are the key to understanding both the diversity of the contemporary counterculture and the ways in which countercultural groups give meaning to their work. The alternative realities of which we speak are the organizing myths of countercultural groups; combined with the counterculture's critiques of modernity, they are used to justify the alternative way of life.

Organizing Myths of Countercultural Groups

Basic to the organizing myths of countercultural groups are their visions of the future. For some groups the future will be a time when a new, more equitable, or humanitarian way of life will exist on the earth, but other groups reject this vision and argue that the real alternative to modernity can be achieved only when each person leaves behind the constraints of earthly life and enters a spiritual world. For the latter, then, the object of life on earth is to prepare the individual for entrance into a spiritual state.

Whatever their content, the countercultural group's organizing myths are important because they provide members with a sense of direction and purpose in their everyday activities. It is sometimes difficult, for example, to see how weeding the garden or washing the dishes is important in changing the world, but such a link is made within countercultural myths, which claim that mundane activities such as these are basic to creating revolution, establishing God's kingdom on earth, or achieving new states of spiritual consciousness (Kanter, 1972).

The organizing myths of countercultural groups are also important because they justify a social organization that is seldom fully equitable. Indeed, one of the ironies of social and alternative communities is that as they preach the coming of a more equitable and humane world, they are often organized as oligarchies in which decisions are made by the group's elite while other members are expected to unquestioningly follow. Often the explanation for this paradox is that full equality and humanism are unachievable in the present world, where threats to the group abound. Once such threats are overcome, however, the contradictions of the social movement or alternative community will be resolved. Thus, the organizing myths of countercultural groups are important because they embody each group's critique of modernity, point to a future state toward which the group is striving, and justify its existing organization and practices (Gusfield, 1973a).

As in more conventional groups, the contradictions found within countercultural groups are not always recognized or, if they are recognized, are treated as irrelevant in everyday life. One reason is that the problems of everyday life seldom involve serious philosophical questions; rather, they are the immediate problems of deciding who must scrub the floor or milk the cow. The problems of everyday life, then, are typically experienced as problems of a different order from those associated with defining the mission of the group. Even when everyday problems are raised and their link to the group's mission is questioned, the contradictions between the goals of the group and its practices are often glossed over, because the questioning occurs within a ceremonial context within which consensus and consistency are given priority over dissension and contradiction. Put differently, the question implicit in most ceremonial events is how a practice fits with a stated mission, and it is further assumed that everyone in the movement or community is similarly committed to the group's mission. Just as weddings, funerals, and Fourth of July celebrations are times when conventional people ignore their conflicts and choose to proclaim their unity of purpose, so ceremonial occasions in countercultural groups, such as religious services or the celebration of the harvest, are treated as times for proclaiming the group's unity and the propriety of its mission.

Just because countercultural groups gloss over their contradictions does not mean that they are more hypocritical than conventional people or that they are unthinking. Such a conclusion is unwarranted because these groups often go to great lengths in order to live in accordance with their beliefs. In the nineteenth-century alternative community of Oneida, for example, members were expected to meet occasionally to criticize each other's commitment to the community and its goals (Carden, 1971). The justification for this practice was that since the Oneidans were attempting to build a perfect community on earth, mutual criticism could be used to achieve personal insight and greater perfection. The fact that mutual criticism involved all of the members of the community except its leader, John Humphrey Noyes, does not appear to have been perceived as a problem, since community members assumed that Noyes had achieved a higher state of perfection than others. Thus, he was free to criticize others while remaining immune from their criticisms. The point is that although countercultural groups are often highly conscious of their beliefs and actions and go to great lengths to practice their beliefs, the contradictions between myth and everyday life are still evident in these groups. The reason is that human life cannot be reduced to a simple moral or philosophical code.

An important problem facing members of countercultural groups, then, is developing work activities and meanings which are consistent with their general beliefs about the world. This is often a serious problem because work is seen as a necessary but mundane feature of life which is given lower priority than other, more inspiring activities. In a later section we will consider how six contemporary countercultural groups have solved this problem. In general, however, the solution to the problem is linked to the general world views of these groups. It is therefore important to consider these world views before dealing with the specific cases. Finding a way to categorize these world views is the task we will undertake next.

A Typology of Countercultural Realities

As we did with conventional realities, we can begin to understand and to classify the general social realities of countercultural groups by looking at their conceptions of time. Chapter one discussed the three major ways in which time may be conceptualized. To review, those who treat time diachronically see it as a continuous process in which past, present, and future are linked. The diachronic conception of time is the dominant one in modern society, as is evident in the general acceptance of the value of futurity, which assumes that actions taken in the present have consequences for the future. In contrast, those who subscribe to the synchronic view of time reject the link between past, present, and future, because they live in a world in which only the present exists. The past is not only gone, but it is irrelevant, and the future can only be known when we experience it as the present. One cannot assume that decisions and actions occurring in the present will have any impact on the future. Finally, those who view time apocalyptically live in a world where the present is irrelevant, because their attention is directed toward a new world which will be achieved in the future. For some the new world will be far removed from this life; it will be a spiritual realm in which worldly concerns and problems are absent. For others, the apocalypse will occur on earth. A new social order based on greater equality, peace, spirituality, or some other general value will arise. In either case, those who subscribe to the apocalyptic conception of time are seeking to transcend their everyday life experiencies, although they must take some account of this world as long as they remain in it.

Each of these conceptions of time can be the basis for building an alternative reality or a countercultural group. For example, those groups that treat time synchronically or apocalyptically emphasize the present and transcendence, and they do not interpret the values of futurity and liberation as they are typically interpreted. Groups based on a synchronic conception of time reject the notion that present and future are linked, and they treat liberation as being free to fully experience the present. Members of apocalyptic groups reject the notion that the future of this world is important or that true liberation can occur without transcending this world. The synchronic and apocalyptic conceptions of time may also be used as bases for rejecting the modern values of abstraction, individuation, and secularization, although they may also be made compatible with these values.

Because the diachronic view of time is widespread in the conventional practices of modern society, it is more difficult to see how this conception of time could be used as a basis for building a countercultural group. It is important to recognize, however, that acceptance of diachronic time does not necessarily lead to the adoption of other conventional values. Simply because a person believes that the present and future are linked does not mean that he or she is highly future oriented or believes that liberation from traditional constraints is desirable. Similarly, the values of abstraction, individuation, and secularization do not necessarily derive from a diachronic view of time. The modern counterculture, then, is made up of a number of groups which differ from conventional society in their conceptions of time and in the assumptions about life they make. Those holding synchronic and apocalyptic views differ more than those holding a diachronic view of time.

Even within countercultural groups subscribing to the same gen-

Table 7-1 • Typology of Countercultural Realities

	Modes of Organizing Time		
Value Stressed	DIACHRONIC	SYNCHRONIC	APOCALYPTIC
Sacred	Diachronic-Sacred (Hutterites)	Synchronic-Sacred ("The Farm")	Apocalyptic-Sacred (International Society of Krishna Consciousness)
Secular	Diachronic-Secular (Kibbutz)	Synchronic-Secular (Hippies)	Apocalyptic-Secular (Symbionese Liberation Army)

eral view of time, differences may arise because the groups' critiques of modernity and their visions for a better life diverge. Thus, any of the central values of modernity could be used in further distinguishing countercultural groups, but one of the most important is the value of secularization. Unlike the values of abstraction and individuation, which countercultural groups generally reject in favor of seeking to build more personal and group-centered worlds, the acceptance or rejection of the value of secularization is not so clear-cut. Some countercultural groups accept a general secular world view (although they may reject some specific features of secularism, such as scientific research or some secular theories), while others hold to a sacred view of the world. Although it is a crude approach, classification of countercultural groups based on whether they emphasize secular or sacred principles is still valid. Combining this classificatory scheme with the differing views of time found in countercultural groups, it is possible to build a typology of countercultural realities.

This is done in Table 7-1, where six types of social realities are presented: diachronic-sacred, diachronic-secular, synchronic-sacred, synchronic-secular, apocalyptic-sacred and apocalyptic-secular (Miller, 1980). Each of these social realities is associated with a different kind of countercultural group. Apocalyptic-secular groups, for example, tend to be revolutionary because they wish to transform this world, whereas apocalyptic-sacred groups tend to be oriented toward transcending this world and achieving new states of spiritual consciousness. For the purposes of this chapter, one example of each type has been selected for more extensive consideration. Each of the groups noted in Table 7-1 will be discussed next, then we look at the relationship between the social realities of these countercultural groups and their work.

WORK-RELATED REALITIES IN THE COUNTERCULTURE

Like other countercultural groups, each of the social movements and alternative communities that will be discussed in this section accepts an organizing myth which justifies its rejection of conventionality and offers an alternative. The myth is usually sustained by a variety of ceremonial practices stressing the uniqueness and unity of the group. When the myths and ceremonies are applied to the practical problems of everyday life, particularly work, the contradictions between belief and practice can be easily seen.

Equally important, the myths and ceremonies are used to justify the diverse work-related communities found in social movements and alternative communities. In this section we will consider six countercultural groups—one representative of each of the types mentioned above—and the ways in which they organize and justify their work. The descriptions presented here are the basis for the more general discussion in the following section.

Diachronic-Sacred Reality and Work in the Hutterite *Bruderhof*

The *Hutterites* are a conservative Protestant community which emerged as one part of the Anabaptist movement in sixteenth-century Europe (Bennett, 1967; Hostettler, 1974; Hostettler and Huntington, 1967; Peters, 1965). Although all of the groups in the movement were opposed to infant baptism (hence the name Anabaptists), they differed in many other respects. Of the surviving groups today, the Hutterites differ significantly from other Anabaptist groups, such as the Amish, the Mennonites, and the Society of Brothers (Hostettler, 1968; Redekop, 1969; C. Henry Smith, 1957; Elmer L. Smith, 1958; Zablocki, 1971). Much of their distinctiveness derives from the influence of Jacob Hutter, the initial leader of the community who guided the group through a time of disorganization and uncertainty. One of the most important influences of Hutter was his belief that Christian principles require a communal life in which the most important community resources are shared and private property, extreme privacy, and other practices encouraging individualism and secularism are avoided.

Although the Hutterites have long since left Europe for Canada and the United States, where many unique colonies, or *bruderhöfe,* have grown up, they continue to practice communal living and remain committed to the most basic religious principles of their early history. Two of the most important of these principles are the belief in agriculture as a way of life and belief in work as a basic feature of living a moral life. As with work, the Hutterian dedication to farm life is based on a conviction that this way of life is most pleasing in God's eyes (Peters, 1965). More basic and general than their emphasis on agriculture and work, however, is the Hutterite belief in the existence of a universal and divine order within which each living creature has a place. Indeed, the emphasis on knowing one's place in the world is important, because, as John Hostettler notes, the divine order is organized as a hierarchy of relationships and responsibilities within which some have the moral right to rule over others:

> God is lord over man, man over woman, parent over child, and the older person over the younger. Human beings have power over animals and are "lord of the same." Human beings may rule over material things, inventions and machines and use them as long as the proper relationships and functions are observed, but they may not change the order of God (Hostettler, 1974: 143).

The most important concern of the devoted Hutterite and the central organizing myth of his or her community, then, involves maintaining the divine order in a world where individualism, materialism, secularism, and hedonism prevail. This concern is reflected in all aspects of Hutterite life, where simplicity, practicality, orderliness, and communalism are stressed (Bennett, 1966). Although each Hutterite family has its own apartment, for example, it consists basically of sleeping areas, because meals are prepared and served in the community's kitchen and dining hall and most leisure activities occur outside the home as well. Orderliness and communalism are also apparent in Hutterite work, which is organized as a series of interconnected activities which culminate in church services on Sunday. The workweek of Hutterite women, for example, is as follows:

> On Monday the women do the family washing at the community wash house at the time assigned to them. They wash, in rotation, beginning with the oldest women and ending with the youngest, moving up one turn each week, Ideally, a women does all the washing for her family and finishes the ironing and the mending on Monday. In some colonies the women try to polish their floors every day, but if they are unable to do this, they polish them on Tuesdays and Fridays. During the summer the school girls pick peas for the kitchen on Tuesday mornings. On Wednesday, Thursday and Friday the women hoe the garden and pick vegetables. Women with small children wash again on Thursday. Friday is a major cleaning day. . . . Saturday morning all of the women roll buns, and the unmarried girls scrub the school house so that it will be ready for the Sunday services. On Saturday afternoon everyone bathes, hair is combed, and beards are trimmed. Everything must be in order and everyone must be clean for Sunday (Hostettler, 1974: 158–159).

Within the world of the Hutterites, then, time is organized diachronically because the past, present, and future are interconnected within the divine order, and it is the responsibility of each individual to live in accord with that order. But the divine order involves more than just the organization of work routines, for it also requires a set of hierarchically organized work roles and responsibilities that reflect the universal hierarchy decreed by God. At its simplest level, the hierarchy of Hutterite work maintains a clear division between men's work and women's work: men are responsible for the community's agricultural activities and women for cooking, cleaning, sewing, and similar activities. But the hierarchy of Hutterite work is based on more than just sexual divisions; age and religious position are also important (Bennett, 1967).

At the top of the hierarchy are the leaders of the community. Some of these people may hold community offices, but a more general characteristic of members of this group is that they are all older men who have little impact on the day-to-day work activities of the community, although their support is necessary in order to change its general economic policies. Indeed, these men often see themselves as protectors of tradition, and they are typically skeptical of the new ideas presented by younger men seeking to deal with the practical problems and opportunities of their work. Below the leaders are the other men and women in the community, who are divided into separate hierarchies. For younger men, the highest-ranking positions are agricultural management roles, which involve full-time attention to one facet of the community's economy. These men plan the work in their areas and take general responsibility for seeing that it gets done. On occasion, managers may work as laborers in other areas, but they do this only when labor is in short supply and there is a great need. A more typical pattern is for each manager to use the community's laborers, who are men with no managerial roles. These men are available for a wide variety of work, depending on the decisions of the managers and the older men at the top of the hierarchy.

The work hierarchy for women is less involved than for men, because they have fewer managerial positions and they are not allowed to participate in elections and policy-making activities, as are men. At the top of the female hierarchy is the head cook, who is in charge of all food preparation. She is elected to office by the adult males, who may presumably use any criteria they wish in making their decision, although it is likely that in practice many men consult with their wives on this matter. The selection of the head cook is important because she is the leader of the women's domain within the community—a domain centering in the kitchen and other food preparation and storage areas. Indeed, the women have sufficient control in these areas that they may ask the men to leave or make it known that they are in the way (Bennett, 1967). Below the head cook are the specialized women workers (the garden, school, and kindergarten women) and the other women who are available for a variety of work responsibilities.

The organization of Hutterite work, then, reflects the hierarchical arrangements that are found in the divine order. Most important are the ways in which men dominate women and older people dominate younger people. Further justifying this work arrangement are a number of ceremonial practices, such as the selection of leaders. It is claimed that elections reflect the intervention of God in the community's affairs, because God influences the decisions of the voters so that the most deserving, capable, and religious people are selected.

One consequence of this organization of work is that it encourages the development of a number of work-related communities within the larger community of believers. Such communities form around the division between men and women workers, but they also result from the divergent interests and problems of male laborers, managers, and the community's elite. Indeed, the Hutterite emphasis on not attaching honor to community offices and the tendency to equate pride with sickness can be understood, in part, as efforts to minimize the potential conflicts of interest in their organization of work.

Ultimately, the most important factor inhibiting conflict is the Hutterite practice of dividing when the community approaches a total population of 150 people. As long as the community is small, it is possible for people to know each other personally and to live communally, but it is assumed that this becomes impossible when the community exceeds 150. Colony expansion reduces conflict, because it helps to maintain a world of personalized and intimate relationships. Equally important, colony expansion provides a means for advancement by those at the bottom of the community's hierarchy. The colony literally divides itself in half by attempting to populate both the mother and daughter colonies with the same types of people. Thus, with colony division the second minister becomes a first minister, some managers may become elders or chief executives, and some laborers may become managers. The fact that most colonies divide about every fourteen years means that new opportunities are available for each generation (Bennett, 1967; Hostetler, 1974).

The practice of colony division is also important because it supports the Hutterite emphasis on the necessity of work within the divine order. Those who join the new colony face a difficult struggle: they must build a new community, and although they are aided by the mother colony, they are expected to be as self-sufficient as possible. The mother colony is affected as well, because many of the community's human and financial resources are depleted in the division, and it is necessary to replenish them before the next division. Thus, the need for work is a continuing reality of everyday life in Hutterite communities.

The Hutterites are one example of the way in which a sacred world view can be combined with a diachronic perspective to create an alternative to a conventional life style. Although they are diverse in many of their beliefs and practices, the Hutterites and other countercultural groups which fit in this category share a tendency to sacralize their work; that is, they treat work as activity that is important both for meeting basic needs and for achieving a sacred way of life (Poll, 1962). Within this perspective, work itself is not sacred, but it is an avenue for achieving a sacred state. Indeed from the Hutterites' point of view, the glorification of work in itself would be another form of idolatry, which would rival that of the secular materialists who dominate conventional society and whom the Hutterites reject.

Diachronic-Secular Reality and Work in the Kibbutz

Unlike the Hutterites, members of the kibbutz are committed to a secular point of view and they treat work as a highly valued end in itself. Put differently, kibbutz members believe in the "religion of labor," which was preached by A. D. Gordon during the early part of this century in Palestine. According to Melford Spiro, central to this philosophy is the belief that work is a "uniquely creative act, as well as an ultimate value. Through labor . . . man [becomes] one with himself, society, and nature" (Spiro, 1970: 13).

The *kibbutz*, a center where mainly agricultural work is carried on, has a long history in the Middle East. It has been particularly important as a center for building and preserving a Jewish way of life in this part of the world. The first permanent kibbutz, for example, was established in 1910 (Criden and Gelb, 1974; Leon, 1969). The political, religious, and economic importance of such settlements (called "kibbutzim" in the plural) increased when the drive for the establishment of a Jewish state began to develop in earnest, and they have continued to be important as the state of Israel has grown. During the years preceding the establishment of Israel, the kibbutzim were rural outposts which could be used for military purposes as well as places for locating immigrants and for producing food. The importance of the kibbutzim in providing such military services has, of course, diminished since the growth of the modern Israeli military, but these communities are still important in the social, political, and economic life of Israel.

Although the close ties between the contemporary kibbutzim and the Israeli government might seem to contradict the classification of these communities as part of the counterculture, they can be so classified because the early movement to establish these communities was based on a rejection of many features of conventional life and a vision of an alternative world. The kibbutz of Kiryat Yedidim, for example, was established by young migrants from Poland who were disillusioned by their treatment at the hands of non-Jews in Poland and by the Jewish traditions preserved by their parents (Spiro, 1970). In seeking alternatives to conventionality, these young people turned to the European youth movement and they were especially impressed by the ideas which arose in the German youth movement after World War I. In this movement the founders of Kiryat Yedidim encountered the idea that a truly happy, courageous, and liberated life required a return to the country, where it would be possible to live in concert with nature while also achieving more equitable and meaningful relationships with other people. This movement was also important because it provided a rationale for rejecting the urban life style which sustained conventional Jewish practices in Polish cities. The youth movement's emphases on a return to nature, simplicity, and equality were combined with a general commitment to Zionism, and a belief in the necessity of establishing a Jewish nation. The commitment of the young people of Kiryat Yedidim to the religious implications of Judaism was very limited, however, because they rejected their parents' religion and hoped to establish a Jewish state based solely on secular and socialist principles.

Initially, at least, the kibbutzim were countercultural groups which rejected some aspects of modernity and held an alternative vision of a proper human life. For the founders of Kiryat Yedidim the appeal of the Middle East was that it offered both a chance to build a new life in the country and a chance to build a Jewish state based on their own values, not those of their parents. Not all kibbutzim were like Kiryat Yedidim, however. The fact that these communities were established by persons coming from very different countries and experiences precluded such uniformity. For this reason, some kibbutzim place more emphasis on maintaining religious tradition than others. Even so, the kibbutzim share some basic characteristics that distinguish them from other communities in Israel. One of the most basic of these characteristics is the emphasis on communalism. Like the Hutterites, kibbutzim members stress group over self-interest and the elimination of private property, but there are some differences (Cohen, 1972; Criden and Gelb, 1974; Orbach, 1968; Leon, 1969; Spiro, 1970).

One of the distinguishing features is an emphasis on age and sex equality, because an important aspect of the life that kibbutz founders rejected was the tendency of women and children to be economically dependent on men. This dependence often got in the way of developing more meaningful and egalitarian family relations. Within the kibbutz, then, women are not economically dependent on their husbands, because they are recognized as workers who earn their share of the food, clothing, housing, and other items provided by the community. Conventional child-parent problems are dealt with by having the children raised together in a center which provides for their basic needs. As a result of this arrangement parents and children can use their time together to develop more egalitarian and less coercive relationships.

The historical roots of the kibbutzim are also apparent in the ways in which work is conceived and organized in these communities. Most generally, work is given great value as a reflection of one's commitment to the community and it is treated as a source of personal satisfaction. Thus, persons seeking to join a kibbutz are evaluated, at least in part, on their willingness to work hard and get along with coworkers (Criden and Gelb, 1974). But all forms of work are not of equal value in the kibbutz; rather, agricultural work, in which the person deals directly with nature, has been most prized historically. This evaluation of work stems from the value commitments of the founders of the kibbutzim and the practical circumstances of trying to carve a community out of the countryside. Although working with one's hands, as opposed to intellectual work, continues to be prized in the kibbutzim, the changing circumstances of kibbutz life have eroded some of the value placed on manual labor.

One reason for the changing evaluation of work is that many of the kibbutzim founders are now too old to spend all day at hard physical labor, and this development has encouraged a reevaluation of old assumptions. More important than age, however, has been the emergence of the kibbutzim as major suppliers of food and other products to urbanites and others living in Israel. No longer can the members of a kibbutz be satisfied merely with producing enough food for themselves; now they are expected to produce a surplus of goods. To live up to this expectation, kibbutzim members have had to build factories (Fine, 1973). Besides meeting the increasing demands of the Israeli population, such factories are a source of work for the old and new members who are not needed in other areas.

The tendency for the kibbutzim to increase agricultural production and build factories has had important implications for Israel, where the kibbutzim have emerged as a major political and economic force. Indeed, members serve in high government posts, where they speak for the interests of other kibbutz members. In addition, the kibbutzim help shape the policies of the Histadrut, which is the agency responsible for the Israeli economy (Fine, 1973). The expansion of kibbutzim production has also had important implications for people working in these communities. The early goal of achieving full work equality by rotating tasks so that everyone does similar work has been abandoned in some communities, where specialized professional and craft workers now help to increase production (Vallier, 1962). Similarly, the goal of work equality between men and women has been compromised by the new emphasis on production. The result has been that men dominate in the areas of agricultural and factory production, and women tend to be relegated to cooking, cleaning, child care, and similar "service" activities.

These changes have led to the development of a new form of work organization to replace the old arrangement of shared work. The new organization also reflects the kibbutz's emphases on equality and democracy, but these values have been redefined to take account of the large and specialized organization of work developing in many contemporary kibbutzim. Today the most important sources of work-related communities are the various work branches, which are specialized areas within which kibbutz members work. At Kiryat Yedidim, for example, the eight major work branches are dairy, field crops, vegetable gardens, fishery, fruit orchards, flocks, poultry, and fodder (Spiro, 1970). Each of these areas is the responsibility of a branch organizer, who coordinates the other workers. There is great emphasis on democracy within each work branch and, for this reason, the branch organizer is not described as "a foreman giving orders to subordinates, but a comrade leading a team of equals" (Leon, 1969: 69). Above each work branch are several other governing and administrative units, within which decisions are made. Although community members theoretically have influence at each of these levels as well, in practice these units are often dominated by administrative specialists who, because they must deal with a number of community interests, are often unable to deal effectively with the problems of individuals. For this reason, the work branch is emerging as a major community within the kibbutz, because it is through the work branch that individuals can express their desires and needs. If work branch members are able to get their case through the administrative level of the community, they will have it decided by the General Assembly. This body is made up of all adult members of the kibbutz, most of whom belong to other work branches and may have special interests which conflict with those of others. Thus, a new form of decision making is emerging in some kibbutzim based on the communities of interest that emerge within the work branches and the conflicting interests of the General Assembly (Leon, 1969).

In sum, the kibbutzim were initially created as alternative communities intended to build a new way of life dedicated to communalism, Zionism, and a romantic view of work and nature. As these communities have grown and the state of Israel has changed, they have become linked to the urban world which they initially rejected. They have undergone changes in the way they organize work, which has given rise to new work-related communities and new conceptions of work and democracy. These changes point to the way in which countercultural groups interact with others in their environment and are influenced by them. Indeed, one of the ironies of the counterculture is that as social movements and alternative communities achieve success, they also create social conditions which encourage conventionality. This outcome is most likely to occur with countercultural groups like the Hutterites and the kibbutzim members, because they view time diachronically and thus share some similar social realities with conventional groups. Reconciliation with outsiders is more difficult in movements and communities that view time synchronically, as we shall see next.

Synchronic-Sacred Reality and Work on "The Farm"

The Farm is an alternative community located in Tennessee and organized around the charismatic leadership of Stephen Gaskin, who has blended a variety of religious traditions, ranging from Eastern mysticism to Western Judeo-Christian beliefs, with a synchronic view of time to create the group's organizing myth (Stephen Gaskin, n.d., 1977; John Hall, 1978). Most basically this myth consists of the claim that the world is an integrated whole which cannot be broken into discrete parts, such as work, family, and religion, as conventional life styles try to do. The world is integrated because God is inseparable from this world; indeed, God is found in every person, animal, plant, and inanimate object in the world. As Gaskin puts it, "All you have to do to meet God is to understand that you are a corner of it," because God is the universe within which all life occurs (Stephen Gaskin, n.d.: 86).

This view of God and the universe is consistent with a synchronic conceptualization of time, because God is in the present. People do not need to spend their lives worrying about an afterlife; indeed, such a concern is one of the many ways in which conventional people become slaves to a future that may never come to pass. Similarly, Gaskin believes that people who dwell on the past or think that rational planning is needed to eliminate the uncertainties of life are unrealistic, because their preoccupation with the past and future means that they lose contact with the present. When the present is lost, it is impossible to live in concert with God and the universe; a sacred life is therefore impossible. A truly sacred life requires each person to "hang out in the here-and-now." As Gaskin notes, "It is healing. When you're in the here-and-now, accept it as reality. Don't think about it or run it through your mind-filter when it's coming in. Accept it" (Stephen Gaskin, n.d.: 30).

The combined emphasis on living in the present and living in concert with the universe is important in understanding life on The Farm. Residents are encouraged, for example, to practice natural birth control—abstaining when it is possible for the woman to conceive—and "spiritual midwifery," through which community residents and parents take responsibility for the birth of children rather than allowing physicians and hospital employees to transform this spiritual event into a secular routine (Ina May Gaskin, 1978; Nofziger, 1978). The emphasis is also important in understanding work on The Farm. Gaskin preaches that residents should reject the popular notion that the right to human life is related to holding a job or working hard; rather, we should all work as hard as we can, because it is a part of living in the universe. Working is part of being alive and not a justification for life. In a similar way the residents of The Farm reject most forms of modern work, which are seen as antagonistic to the processes of the universe rather than in harmony with them. Evidence of the way in which conventional work is antagonistic to the universe can be found in the pain and sacrifice that many industrial and professional workers must endure in order to make their livings and the pain that they knowingly and unknowingly inflict on others. From the beginning, then, an important question facing Gaskin and the other leaders of The Farm was what type of work constitutes "right livelihood," or how they could work in concert with the universe. They found several answers:

> The first thing we got into was farming, because we thought farming was guaranteed good karma. It *must* be okay to farm. Then we thought, "What other kinds of things can we do that are also right vocation[ally] and for mankind?" Well, if it's good to grow food, it must be good to truck it, to distribute it and get it out to the people. So those are related good karma industries (Stephen Gaskin, 1977: 68).

As with the Hutterites and the founders of the kibbutzim, the members of The Farm do not treat work there as a separate issue from the community's general goal of building a better way of life. On the other hand, residents must deal with the seeming contradiction of emphasizing the present as the only reality while having to organize their work. They reconcile this conflict by organizing the community's work within several specialized areas resembling the work branches of the kibbutzim (John Hall, 1978). Each member belongs to a work group which meets each morning to arrange the day's activities. Primary responsibility for coordination rests with the crew leader, but once the work for the day has been arranged, each of the work groups proceeds at its own pace. It is at this point that the synchronic perspective of "The Farm" is important, because everyone is expected to take an active part both in accomplishing the work and in relating to others in the group. The duty of each work group member, then, is to create a communionlike atmosphere in which enjoyment of the present and concern for living in concert with the universe, particularly with others in the work group, take precedence over other concerns (Hall, 1978). Those who undermine the achievement of communion by becoming too involved in their work or by showing too little interest in it are chastised for not "hanging out in the present."

Thus, work on The Farm is given meaning within the larger organizing myth of the community. Gaskin regularly interprets this myth at the Sunday morning religious services, in which all members of the community participate. It is during these ceremonies that Gaskin clarifies the community's mission and attempts to give direction to its future and to the lives of his followers. Equally important in understanding the meaning of work on The Farm is the way in which the specialized work groups act as work-related communities. These communities are the means by which life is evaluated within the present. Work groups that are filled with conflict are a serious problem, because it is impossible to create a communionlike atmosphere within them. If work group members are incompatible, then the work itself is meaningless and just as illegitimate as the work of conventional people, who also regularly violate the most basic principles of the universe.

Although there are some similarities in the organization of work in the Hutterite colony, the kibbutz, and The Farm, a major difference is The Farm's synchronic conception of time. Because of this view of time, it is impossible to justify monotonous, unsatisfying work by pointing to a future state in which life will be better. The work-related communities of The Farm are also affected by the synchronic conception of time: it is difficult for them to develop into enduring interest groups when community members are expected to pay attention only to the present. A more likely outcome is for these communities to exist only while the work lasts and to break up at the end of each day. Indeed, this outcome is encouraged by short-term work-oriented parties held in the evenings, which bring together people from different work groups, and by the constant blurring of the distinction between work and play in all groups. As John Hall notes "What is done is to be accomplished with a sense of enjoyment, and any feelings of ascetic self-sacrifice, self-righteousness, or the like are usually challenged" (John Hall, 1978: 149).

Synchronic-Secular Reality and Hippie Work

Like the residents of The Farm, members of *hippie communities* live in a synchronic world in which the distinction between work and play is blurred. The reasons for the blurring of these aspects of life are quite different, however, because members of The Farm live in a sacred world, whereas the hippies live in a secular one based on the desires and perceptions of each individual (Cavan, 1972b; Richard Mills, 1973; Partridge, 1973). Put differently, the primary organizing myth of hippie communities is the belief that we live in a psychic world, and the ultimate source of all social realities is the vision that each individual chooses to adopt in dealing with his or her environment. Sherri Cavan describes the psychic world this way:

> The psychic world is an attitude, a perspective, a particular choice of how to order and arrange the elements of the physical world. Thus, any particular "picture" one has of the physical world is dependent upon where one chooses to stand to look at what there is to see; how one chooses to arrange such "states of affairs" (Cavan, 1972b: 62–63).

Although social reality consists of the choices individuals make within the present, those choices can be assessed in terms of their consequences for nature and other human beings. Some visions are highly incompatible with the processes of nature and hippies reject most of them. Similarly, some visions divide people from each other while others bring them together. A hippie community exists, then, because each member has freely chosen a vision of the world that is similar to the visions of others, and the community will exist as long as everyone chooses to see the same world (Cavan, 1972b; Richard Mills, 1973). At its most general level, the hippie community is made up of all people who subscribe to this world view. In practice, however, hippies spend their everyday lives as members of small, bandlike groups within which members share a vision of the world (Partridge, 1973). It is within these groups that the general principles of hippie philosophy are put into practice.

An important and well-publicized tenet of the hippie philosophy is the claim that each person should do his or her "own thing," which means that each person should choose to do those things which are personally enjoyable or meaningful. This tenet is often interpreted as a call for stopping work and spending life in the pursuit of pleasure (French and French, 1975). But such an interpretation oversimplifies hippie reality, because it assumes that all hippies see work as drudgery. Although hippies see most conventional work as unrewarding and reject it, some forms of work do offer the individual an opportunity for self-expression and thus can be pursued. This belief is reflected in one hippie's explanation for why he worked so hard preparing for a rock concert:

> I mean everybody's happy to work, and I worked my arse off. I mean some days when we were putting that festival together I was working fourteen hours a day, and nothing would induce me to work fourteen hours a day if I didn't want to. I was thoroughly enjoying myself. . . . *It's not a fact of totally not working, it's a question of doing it when you feel like it, how you feel like it and to what extent you feel like it* (Quoted in Richard Mills, 1973: 119–120, italics in the original).

Legitimate work, then, is work which allows for self-expression and control. Because most conventional jobs are highly routinized and controlled, they are incompatible with hippie philosophy, and they are taken only when there are no options available to the individual. One reason that many hippies can avoid these jobs is that the general hippie community is partially made up of economic enterprises which offer alternative means of livelihood. Playing in a rock band, producing a rock concert or festival, and dealing in drugs are obvious examples of how the hippie life style provides opportunities for work (Richard Mills, 1973). An important characteristic of each of these forms of work is that it combines making a living with a hippie ceremony or practice. Rock music and the use of certain types of drugs are important means of self-expression and discovery in the hippie community, and important ways of building a hippie consciousness of kind are rock concerts and festivals, which bring together the diverse people and groups that make up this segment of the counterculture.

But the hippie economy extends beyond rock music and drugs. It includes a variety of manufacturers, salespeople, and entrepreneurs, who supply this community with commonplace and exotic items (Cavan, 1972a). The most respected of these workers are the hippie craftspeople, who produce items for drug use, clothing, tools, and art objects. Such items may be sold directly to the public, as when hippie craftspeople set up booths on the street, or they may be sold by merchants in the hippie community. The most important factor accounting for the high prestige of craftspeople is the belief that the crafts involve work that is interesting, allow for self-expression, and are organized so that the worker is free to set his or her own pace and to work in harmony with the natural and social environment of the community. In other words, hippies see the crafts as free from the many restrictions associated with conventional work. The other major work roles in the hippie community are also ranked based on these criteria.

Below the craftspeople are the nomadic peddlers and scavengers, who have great control over their lives but few opportunities for self-expression. Less respected than the peddlers and scavengers are the "hip merchants and entrepreneurs" who operate permanent businesses within the community. Because of the nature of their businesses and the great financial investment that they have made, those workers often emphasize conventional business goals, and they therefore come into conflict with others in the community who reject such beliefs and practices. In San Francisco, for example, there is a hippie publishing firm known as The Co., which publishes and distributes underground comic books (Cavan, 1972a). Although this enterprise is clearly different from conventional publishing houses, because it provides its workers with food and lodging in place of salaries and promises them a share of the profits when the business is a success, there are still conflicts within The Co.: workers often emphasize their immediate desires and needs, whereas the head of the enterprise is more future oriented. Finally, there exist a number of conventional jobs that are acceptable to hippies because they allow personal freedom or self-expression. An example is working as a postal carrier, because the worker is unsupervised and free to establish his or her own routines during much of the day (Cavan, 1972b).

Hippie work is thus evaluated within the present, and efforts to justify it by pointing to future career advances are rejected. The high value placed on the crafts and art derives from the fact that these forms of work can be organized to be highly rewarding in the present. The hippies' synchronic conception of time is also important in understanding their work-related communities. They tend to be short run because of shifting memberships; persons who lose interest in their work or in the other workers have little justification for remaining in the group. Nevertheless, relationships within these work-related communities may be highly intense, because everyone is very involved in his or her work. Unlike members of The Farm, hippie workers are not likely to be chastised for being too involved in their work; rather, such involvement is interpreted as a sign of individual expression and fulfillment. This feature of hippie philosophy points to another reason why these work-related communities tend to be shifting: communities exist only as long as workers choose to share similar visions and interests; when one or more workers choose to become so personally involved in work that they exclude others, the work-related community disintegrates, although it can be rebuilt in the future. Indeed, this tendency is encouraged by a hippie philosophy which places highest priority on the individual and not the community.

The individualistic and present-centered reality of the hippies directly conflicts with the social realities of apocalyptic countercultural groups which seek a new world based on transcendence of the present. We turn to these countercultural groups next.

Apocalyptic-Sacred Reality and Hare Krishna Work

Although the deep historical roots of Krishna worship in India are sometimes stressed in analyzing the contemporary *International Society for Krishna Consciousness* (*ISKCON*), or the *Hare Krishna* movement as it is more popularly known, this countercultural group is quite different from the earlier groups found in India. For this reason, it is best to treat ISKCON as primarily an American movement which began in 1965, when A. C. Bhaktivedanta Swāmi Prabhupāda arrived in the United States (Judah, 1974a, 1974b). The following year a temple was established in New York City, and many other temples and settlements in different parts of the country have been established since.

Central to ISKCON reality are a rejection of the individualistic, secular, and materialistic tendencies of modern life and an acceptance of Krishna consciousness as a transcendental reality toward which everyone should strive (Judah, 1974a, 1974b; Bhaktivedanta, 1969). Only by total devotion and surrender to Krishna can the individual hope to achieve salvation and eternal bliss, because both are contingent on leaving this world of mundane and profane pleasures and entering the world where Krishna lives and plays. Few people achieve a state of full Krishna consciousness, and, consequently, they are reincarnated after their deaths. There is, then, only one escape from this life and that is full Krishna consciousness.

The achievement of full Krishna consciousness involves a number of stages of development, during which the individual grows, gains insight, and establishes new relationships with Krishna. Initially, Krishna consciousness consists of a peaceful feeling, but that is replaced by more direct ties to Krishna until finally Krishna and the devotee are joined in a relationship of mutual love. Each stage requires that the devotee surrender him- or herself to Krishna by doing "loving service," which gives Krishna pleasure (Daner, 1976). For those at the higher levels of Krishna consciousness, loving service may involve continuing religious activity, but for most devotees the requirement of loving service means that they must deal with the mundane secular world that surrounds them. In addition to taking part in various religious ceremonies, devotees at this level must go into the world to recruit members and engage in what Bhaktivedanta (1969) calls "fruitive work": they must make a living. The center for these activities is the temple, where devotees live and worship.

Life within the Krishna temple is austere and highly routine. Gambling, the use of intoxicants such as alcohol, tobacco, coffee, and marijuana, and sex outside of marriage are banned. The daily routine of the temple also shows the single-minded devotion of members to achieving Krishna consciousness. Members rise at 3 A.M. to engage in several hours of religious activity (Judah, 1974a; Daner, 1976). When these activities are completed, the devotees leave to recruit new members, sell their literature, and do other work. The devotees return at noontime for lunch and then go out to their duties in the afternoon. Upon returning in the evening, devotees still face several hours of religious activity before going to sleep at about 9:30. The central figure in the temple is the president, who has achieved the highest level of Krishna consciousness of the temple residents; for this reason, he (it is always a man) has the responsibility of guiding the development of the others. The temple president is also in charge of the mundane features of temple life, such as making decisions about buying a truck, giving permission for a member to visit a sick friend or relative, and making the daily work assignments (Daner, 1976). Because of their subordinate spiritual and political positions, temple members are not free to openly challenge the president's decisions, although he often takes account of member preferences in making his decisions.

The world of the ISKCON temple is a highly organized one, in which there are clear lines of authority and clearly defined schedules of activity and rules for members to follow. This organization is seen as consistent with the larger goal of helping each devotee achieve higher stages of Krishna consciousness. Work is an integral part of the developmental process, because it is a type of loving service. Whether the devotee is asked to solicit donations, sell incense or literature to outsiders, or to work at household tasks, he or she is expected to treat such activities as sacred and requiring serious attention (Daner, 1976; John Hall, 1978). Those who question routines and the decision-making rationales of community elites often receive a reply that is similar to the paternalistic response of parents to naive children's questions. An example is the following exchange between a devotee and a supervisor on a Krishna farm.

DEVOTEE: I'm tired of working on the road. Why can't I do milking? That's what I'm most qualified to do.
STRAW BOSS: Sometimes Krishna asks you to do other work so that you don't become conditioned to one material plane mode.
DEVOTEE: Yes, but I'm getting conditioned to road work if I'm getting conditioned to anything.
STRAW BOSS: Do you want to become Krishna-conscious?
DEVOTEE: Yes, of course.
STRAW BOSS: Then you must accept Krishna's authority in doing devotional service to him (Quoted in John Hall, 1978; 155).

In sum, the apocalyptic and secular reality of ISKCON encourages members to seek ultimate meaning in a transcendental state that they can only partially achieve in the present. At the same time, they are expected to involve themselves in some aspects of the mundane world which they seek to escape. This contradiction is resolved by treating work and other everyday activities as types of loving service to Krishna. Thus, work is taken account of by the movement's organizing myth, and relations between devotees and the temple president support this view. The temple is also important because it is the center for the development of work-related communities. Generally, these communities include everyone in the temple, although, in practice, smaller communities may develop because some members tend to work together regularly. The potential for the smaller work-related communities to become major interest groups is limited by the power of the temple president to reassign workers and by the devotees' primary concern for attaining a transcendental state, rather than changing this world.

Apocalyptic-Secular Reality and the Work of the Symbionese Liberation Army

Members of apocalyptic-secular movements and communities share with ISKCON a primary concern with transcending the present, but the new world they wish to enter will be built in this world. One example is the *Symbionese Liberation Army* (*SLA*).

The SLA was a revolutionary movement that was organized to destroy the existing social order and to replace it with a new one based on equality, an equitable distribution of wealth, and humane relationships (John Hall, 1978). It was perhaps best known for its kidnapping of Patti Hearst. Because the SLA was at war with conventionality and not seeking to escape it, the everyday actions and attitudes of its members must be understood as attempts to further the movement's cause while dealing with the practical problems of their lives. Within this movement, finding safe and dependable transportation and housing was an important problem, because members had to move regularly to avoid the police. Similarly, making a living was a problem for the SLA, because holding conventional jobs meant that members had to settle down or in some other way give more priority to their jobs than they wished. In addition, few conventional jobs allowed the worker to express his or her radical political views at work, a special problem for people in social movements like the SLA who cannot compartmentalize their lives in this way.

Work within apocalyptic-secular movements like the SLA is defined in terms of the general goals of the movement and the practical problems of achieving those goals. For the SLA an important type of work was robbing banks, because this provided the movement with money and it also furthered the cause of destroying conventional institutions. Related forms of SLA work involved training in the use of firearms and in self-defense: both types of training were essential in achieving the aims of the movement. Within the SLA, then, the act of working and the justifying ceremony were not separate, because every action by the revolutionary has significance for building a new social order. Indeed, it was the inability of SLA members to separate any aspect of life from their cause which accounts for the absence of work-related communities within the movement; rather, the movement itself was a work-related community. As John Hall states, within the SLA and other apocalyptic sects, "life itself becomes apocalyptic work" (John Hall, 1978: 149).

An Overview of Countercultural Work

Because of the diversity of countercultural groups and their conceptualizations of legitimate work, it is useful to end by summarizing the major points of difference. These are presented in Table 7-2, which notes each countercultural group's primary organizing myth, work-related communities, and their myths legitimating work.

Each of the organizing myths assumes that human life is orderly and that, although the conventional order is based on the wrong principles, it is possible to specify an alternative order in which the real interests of human beings are served. The sense of order is basic to defining the group's mission, and it is also important in understanding how countercultural groups define, organize, and justify their work. Thus, Hutterite communities maintain a vision of a divine order, the kibbutzim of a democratic order, The Farm of a natural order (living in accord with the universe), the hippies of a psychic order, ISKCON of a (spiritually) transcendental order, and the SLA of a revolutionary order. Some of these organizing myths include a belief in hierarchy, which can be used to justify inequality in work, whereas others stress the importance of work equality and finding satisfaction in the work activity itself and in the work group. This difference is important in understanding the types of work-related communities found within countercultural groups and their significance for everyday life. Within some countercultural groups the work-related communities can become enduring interest groups, but this possibility is inhibited in other groups, where assumptions about time and the organization of work are different. Finally, each countercultural group's myth about work varies. Within some groups work is a major source of personal growth and expression, whereas other groups define work as less important than other activities. In none of the countercultural groups, however, is work treated as nothing more than a way of making a living.

One obvious conclusion to be drawn from Table 7-2 is that the counterculture is diverse and it is difficult to make generalizations about it. At the same time, some generalizations about work in the counterculture can be drawn. We turn to these next.

EVERYDAY REALITIES AND THE INSTITUTIONALIZATION OF WORK IN COUNTERCULTURAL GROUPS

The discussion to this point has concentrated on the official images of work found in countercultural groups. Although they are important in grasping the diverse ways in which work can be interpreted, these

Table 7-2 • Summary of Work-Related Realities in the Counterculture

Countercultural Group	*Primary Organizing Myth*	*Work-Related Communities*	*Need for Work*	*Organization of Work*	*Rewards of Work*
Hutterites	Divine Order	Mixed: based on enduring relations with others of similar rank, sex, and work specialization	Based on material need and the need to live in concert with the divine order	Divinely sanctioned hierarchy, based on sexual, religious, and age divisions	Living in accord with the divine order
Kibbutz	Democratic Order	Mixed: based on enduring relations with work branch members and shifting relations with others	Based on material need and the need to be a creative part of the community	Complex division of labor, reflecting personal desires and the community's commitment to high productivity	Satisfaction derived from one's work and from making a contribution to the well-being of the kibbutz and Israel
The Farm	Natural Order	Fleeting: based on the immediate work group and its activities	Based on material need and the need to live in accord with nature	Flexible division of labor, based on personal desires, the collectively defined needs of the community, and relations within each work group	Satisfaction derived directly from one's work activities and relations with coworkers and from living in accord with the universe

Hippies	Psychic Order	Fleeting: based on the immediate work group and its activities	Based on material need and the desire to "do your own thing"	Allowance for a variety of types of work, ranked by the degree to which they allow for self-expression and personal control	Income and the possibility of "doing your own thing"
ISKCON	Transcendental Order	Enduring: based on the enduring relations in the temple and other settlements	Based on material need and the need to do loving service for Krishna	Flexible work arrangements, based on personal desire and the preferences of the temple president and other leaders	Doing loving service to Krishna and achieving Krishna consciousness
SLA	Revolutionary Order	Enduring: based on the enduring relation within the group	Based on material need and, because work is inseparable from political action, the need for a new social order	Flexible work arrangements, based on the collectively defined needs of the group	Satisfaction derived from making a contribution to the revolution

images seldom reflect the full complexity of work in the counterculture. Just as factory, office, and household workers sometimes find the interpretations and justifications of bosses and other elites to be hollow sounding, if not fully self-serving, so the low-level worker in a social movement or alternative community may find that his or her everyday experience calls into question some of the group's beliefs and goals. Both the ISKCON devotee who must do road work rather than milking and the woman in the kibbutz who finds herself in the kitchen because productivity is given higher priority than worker satisfaction point to the way in which everyday experience may contradict the claims of elites. It is important to recognize, then, that conflicts of interest may develop in social movements and alternative communities, and although they may be denied when dealing with outsiders, these conflicts may give rise to reassessment and change in the group's way of life. In other words, work is institutionalized within countercultural groups in a way that is seldom anticipated by the founders. New and unintended developments may pose problems for some members, but they are also a source of vitality and change.

At the same time that we should be skeptical of the claims of some countercultural members about the harmonious and utopian worlds they have built, we should also recognize that these movements and communities are based on principles different from those associated with conventional jobs. Many workers in the counterculture, for example, receive no direct monetary payment, such as a wage or salary; rather, their basic needs for food, clothing, and shelter are provided in a communal setting. With the exception of hippies, each of the countercultural groups considered here is of this type. One consequence of such an arrangement is that the responsibility for the livelihood of each member is shared by all members of the group. That arrangement of work and its rewards discourages the individualism often rampant in conventional jobs and encourages the development of a consciousness of kind, which is basic to the survival of countercultural groups.

Similarly, the conventional ranking of work roles is often altered in countercultural groups, where work is assessed based on different principles. The extreme emphasis on the importance of work as a creative activity in the kibbutzim does not include all forms of work; rather, the religion of labor is primarily concerned with manual work. Within the early kibbutzim, at least, the person who worked in the field enjoyed higher status than a physician or a full-time administrator. Other groups discussed here share this assessment. Both the Hutterites and members of The Farm place great value on farm work, and they treat most industrial and professional work as inconsistent with the divine order and the basic processes of the universe. Perhaps the most unique of the countercultural groups are the hippies, SLA members, and ISKCON people, because they value begging, scavenging, or crime more than many business activities. More than the other groups, they have turned the prestige rankings of conventional work upside down.

The relationship between work and the life cycle is also different in many countercultural groups. The conventional view is that a career consists of a series of work stages offering the individual greater opportunities for income, prestige, and influence in life. The notion of having a career is largely absent from the counterculture, although the individual may be encouraged to seek advancement in other ways. Within ISKCON, for example, each member is encouraged to increase his or her Krishna consciousness, but success in this area is related only partially to work accomplishments. Indeed, the Krishna devotee who advances spiritually will find that he or she is expected to be less involved in work rather than more. The tendency for apocalyptic movements and communities to link success with nonwork is seen most dramatically in revolutionary groups like the SLA. Because revolutions are thought of as built on the personal sacrifices of revolutionaries, one sign of success in life may be martyrdom. The traditions of revolutionary groups are filled with stories of the ways in which brave and dedicated members were killed while fighting for their cause. Politically and symbolically, these traditions are often more important to the success of apocalyptic movements than effectiveness at robbing banks. Martyrdom is also more likely to guarantee the individual a place of immortality in the history of the movement than is being effective at leafleting.

The relationship between work and the life cycle is also different in synchronic movements and communities, because work is exclusively evaluated in the present. The idea that it is all right to hold a boring or exhausting job in the present because it will eventually lead to a better job is quite foreign to synchronic workers, who see no necessary connection between the present and the future. The work orientation of both the residents of The Farm and the hippies reflects a noncareerist view, because living in concert with the universe and "doing your own thing" are incompatible with the future orientation and voluntary subordination of immediate desires that are basic to careerism.

Even within diachronic movements and communities, which are based on a vision of time that is more consistent with the future orientation of careerism, there is a tendency to deemphasize personal achievement. In the Hutterite *bruderhof*, for example, leaders who take pride in their achievements are sinners who are unlikely to be reelected; similarly, when a leader gathers a following of devotees, it is assumed that a spiritual sickness has consumed the community and a complete reassessment of the community's mission and activities is required (Bennett, 1967). A proper attitude is one which stresses humble commitment to the divine order and the realization that the achievements of life are attributable to God, not individuals. Individualistic and careerist tendencies are also countered in the kibbutzim by rotating some leadership positions, by holding leaders accountable through elections, and by making them regularly appear before the community to answer questions about their decisions and activities. Perhaps the most creative approach to this problem is found in the Society of Brothers, also an Anabaptist group based on a diachronic-sacred reality (Zablocki, 1971). It is possible within communities established by the Society to be demoted from positions of influence and leadership, if others in the community feel that the leader has become corrupted by individualistic concerns. The possibility of demotion occurring is increased by the high visibility of the leaders in these small, highly personalized communities. But demotion is not permanent, and for this reason some leaders spend much of their lives achieving leadership positions only to be demoted and to begin the process again by returning to a life that is more in tune with the sacred and anti-individualistic beliefs of the community.

The uniqueness of countercultural groups also is reflected in their uses of modern machinery and other technical devices. Although some groups reject mechanization outright, most integrate some technical features into their ways of life while being careful to limit their disruptive potential. An obvious example is the SLA's openness to new firearms and other devices which could be used to better pursue their cause. The adoption of modern technological devices is also apparent in the hippie acceptance of electric musical instruments and the sophisticated equipment that goes with them and in the use of modern printing presses and other materials by The Farm and ISKCON in order to better transmit their messages to the outside world. The Hutterites have also found that modern farm machinery is helpful in making their land more productive and the process of accumulating resources for the division of the colony easier. At the same time that these groups accept some features of modern technology, they attempt to control it by using it for purposes that are clearly consistent with their aims. The Hutterites, for example, require that investments in new machinery be approved by the leaders of the community, who are quite concerned with protecting the traditional Hutterite way of life. One of the most inventive approaches to adopting new technology is found in some Amish communities, which have adopted a noncommunal life style that is in other ways similar to the Hutterite way of life. In these communities the motors of farm implements are sometimes removed so that they must be pulled by horses, which work at the slower pace traditionally favored. In this way, modern technology is transformed to fit into a countercultural way of life.

But technology is not always so readily adopted; indeed, the history of the kibbutzim suggests that alternative communities can be easily undermined by too easy an acceptance of modern tools. Although it is an overstatement to claim that the kibbutzim have lost all of their unique characteristics, they are an important example of how alternative communities can change and become "conventionalized." The critical factor is not the willingness of community members to adopt modern technology, but the relationship between the community and the outside world. The close ties between the kibbutzim leadership and leaders in the Israeli government have encouraged an attitude of accommodation by kibbutzim members. They have been willing to sacrifice some of their community goals in order to respond to the demands of the government for greater productivity. The important lesson to be learned from the kibbutzim, then, is that countercultural groups do not exist independently of their environments; rather, the problems and opportunities present in the conventional world significantly influence their goals and activities.

For kibbutzim members the environment poses problems because they live in a world of political, military, and economic uncertainty. The problems found in the environments of other countercultural groups are seldom so dramatic but are still important. Two key features of the Hutterite world view, for example, are communal property and the desirability of living a simple life unencumbered by modern distractions. Thus, historically the Hutterites have banned radios, decorative items for the home and body, and other modern luxuries. Despite the ban, such items can be found almost everywhere in the Hutterite environment. The usual solution to this problem has been termed "controlled acculturation": the community leaders condemn the modern items and practices until they become widespread, at which time a new policy is announced and the forbidden items are brought out of hiding (Eaton, 1952). Indeed, the willingness of Hutterite leaders to bend in the face of public pressure is an important reason that these communities have persisted despite the many intended and unintended threats in their environment. Adaptation is also important in understanding the changing nature of Hutterite work. Although both horses and machinery are used in agriculture, the contemporary Hutterite who drives a tractor all day and uses other modern equipment is involved in a very different kind of work than was his earlier counterpart, who worked the land with horses and his hands. Similar changes accompany other decisions to accept modern inventions and practices, because change offers fresh opportunities for developing new Hutterite traditions and new forms of work. As one *bruderhof* member notes, "If they [the Elders] ever decide to let in radios, I am going to see to it that we make them ourselves. That's the Hutterian way" (Quoted in Bennett, 1967: 278).

A full understanding of the changing organization and meaning of work in countercultural groups, then, must include a consideration of the impact of the conventional world on these groups. The outside world has just as great an impact on synchronic and apocalyptic groups as it has on diachronic groups, because as these movements and communities develop economic ties to the outside, they are often faced with the dilemma of altering their perspectives or losing desired sources of income. The hippies who work at The Co., for example, face the dilemma of living each moment to the fullest while facing publication and distribution deadlines. As workers at The Co. deal with this problem, it is likely that new definitions of work will emerge. One possible outcome is that The Co. will become less individualistic and more community oriented, perhaps like the kibbutz. Should this occur, work may also be redefined as an obligation to the community, and its primary reward will be carrying out this duty, not the immediate pleasure the work brings. Another possibility is that The Co. will sacrifice most of its hippie philosophy and become a conventional business dealing in a specialized and unconventional product. Successful hippie rock bands and promoters may also face this consequence (Richard Mills, 1973).

Perhaps the best example of how work in the counterculture changes as movements and communities develop and are influenced by the conventional world is the case of the *Unification Movement*, or the *Moonies* as they are commonly known (Lofland, 1966; Bromley and Shupe, 1979). The movement is a conservative (Korean-based) religious one, led by the Reverend Sun Myung Moon, who wishes to restore God's kingdom on earth by uniting all world religions into a single movement. Central to the social reality of this movement is an apocalyptic conception of time, because the world will be transformed when God's kingdom is reestablished on earth. Its apocalyptic character is important in understanding the blending of work and religion in this movement. An example is the mobile fund-raising teams (MFTs), which were put together to spread the movement's message, seek recruits, and raise money. All these tasks are interconnected and given religious meaning. Thus, success at fund raising has been taken, in the past at least, as one indicator of a member's spiritual growth, and for this reason members once sought donations with a missionary zeal that is characteristic of few social movements. The financial success of the movement attests to the effectiveness of this approach, but just as important is how the Moonie notion of "heavenly deception" emerged as a consequence of the movement's blending of work and religion. The term refers to the untrue statements Moonies sometimes made to potential donors about their beliefs, affiliations, or the uses to which the donations would be put. These statements were not defined as lies, because they were made in the name of a religious cause which represents God and the true interests of all people. As with other movements, like the SLA, this apocalyptic movement considers work inseparable from the larger goal of transforming the world. Thus, the conventional notion of truthfulness was seen as irrelevant.

As the Unification Movement has grown, it has encountered considerable opposition from religious, governmental, and other officials representing conventional interests. One source of conflict has been the use of MFTs and the more general issue of funding the movement by donations. At the same time, the leaders of the movement have developed a new vision of its place in history and the present world. During the early years the movement claimed that the millennium (the ultimate transformation) would occur in 1967, but leaders later reinterpreted the prediction to mean that the foundation for the millennium would be laid by 1967, but the full transformation would not occur until later (Lofland, 1966). More recently, the early predictions have been reinterpreted as purely symbolic and not intended to be taken literally (Bromley and Shupe, 1979). Reinterpretation of the timing of the millennium has been accompanied by the leadership's desire to reconcile differences with critics and to become a respected religious denomination holding a position similar to that of the Mormon Church. This change is important for work in the Unification Movement, because, as the members move away from a vision of themselves as crusaders seeking to transform the world in the near future and as they find areas of accommodation with their critics, the old emphases on soliciting donations in public and "heavenly deception" are being replaced by a concern for building stable conventional life styles. Evidence of this trend is found in the development of fishing and fish-processing enterprises in several New England states and in Louisiana in recent years (Bromley and Shupe, 1979). Such enterprises make it possible for members to combine their religious beliefs with a stable life style organized around conventional families and careers. These changes also reflect the way in which accommodation with the conventional world undermines an apocalyptic perspective and encourages a diachronic one. In sum, it is evident that the Unification Movement is developing a diachronic-sacred reality, which will have important implications for the way in which work is organized and given meaning.

The institutionalization of work within countercultural groups is a multifaceted process. Work can be defined and organized in diverse ways, and the conventional world can affect the meaning these groups give to work. Looked at one way, the institutionalization of work points to the futility of attempts to create utopian alternatives to modernity, because they are doomed to failure. But such a conclusion is unwarranted because it is based on the same naive assumption of many founders of these movements and communities: that it is possible to build a static, utopian world in which the injustices of the present world are eliminated and people can develop to their full potential. That view is naive because it overlooks the dynamic and changing nature of human life owing to its constant reinterpretation through everyday experience. A better conclusion is that countercultural groups reflect one part of modern life, and those that change by reaching some accommodation with the outside world point to the way that general values and the practical circumstances of daily life can combine to give life direction and meaning. Change within these groups is thus not a sign of failure or death, but a sign of life and vitality.

CONCLUSION

This chapter has dealt with a segment of modern society that sociologists and others interested in the diversity of modern work frequently ignore. The general assumption is that countercultural groups are insignificant, deviant cases which can tell us little about the nature of modern work. In other words, these groups are dismissed as the fanatical fringe. One of the purposes of this chapter has been to counter this assumption by showing that countercultural groups are as much a part of modern society as are more conventional groups and that their initial development or their later changes cannot be understood without looking at their relationship with conventional forces. These groups arise out of the contradictions and dilemmas of modern life, and their later development is significantly influenced by the problems and opportunities presented by the conventional groups and individuals found in their environments.

When the work of countercultural groups is considered, it is clear that only a limited range of possibilities is available through conventional work. The tendency for conventional work to be organized so that each individual is primarily responsible for his or her own livelihood is absent in many countercultural groups, where everyone takes responsibility for the well-being of the community or movement and its members. Many countercultural groups also reject the conventional tendency to evaluate work based on careerist assumptions and to forgo enjoyable work in exchange for enough income to pursue meaning in leisure and consumption; instead, they stress the importance of finding pleasure and meaning in the present. Indeed, the ability of conventional people to compartmentalize their lives into work, play, family, politics, and religion is one of the most important criticisms made by counterculturalists, who frequently try to blend these aspects of life in order to give their work a more general meaning.

Countercultural groups are important, then, because they represent an often ignored part of modern life and they point to modern dilemmas and alternatives to conventionality that are obscured when only conventional workers are considered. Such groups are also important because many of them have a long history of trying to organize work in more equitable and satisfying ways. That concern is now emerging as well in conventional circles, where a variety of experiments are under way to give power to workers and others who have had little power in the past. Indeed, the kibbutzim and similar countercultural groups have been used as models for developing some of these experiments. Thus, just as countercultural realities are affected by conventional forces, so conventional work realities are being reshaped by social movements and alternative communities.

Chapter Eight

EMPOWERMENT: AN EMERGING REALITY

Although countercultural groups are an important source of change in modern society, they are not the only source. In addition to members of these social movements and alternative communities, there are others who accept the basic tenets of modernity but seek to reform some aspects of modern life. Many, perhaps most, of the men and women who identify with the contemporary feminist movement are of this type, because they see the problem of sexism as a condition which can be resolved largely within the institutions that prevail today. To achieve economic equality, for example, they suggest opening new job opportunities for women while combating discriminatory hiring and promotion practices, not constructing a new social order based on a different set of organizing principles.

Various reform movements are also dedicated to changing the conception and organization of work today. Both opponents and proponents of such movements frequently reject characterization of their activity as reform because they prefer to see the changes that are advocated as revolutionary in their consequences. A critical test, however, is the extent to which a social movement is based on a critique of modernity and a vision of an alternative way of life. Reform movements are based on a limited critique of modernity and a vision of how to make modern institutions operate better.

The human relations approach to management in the 1930s and 1940s, which arose to challenge Frederick Taylor's assumptions about scientific management (see chapter three), is one example of a reform movement dedicated to changing work. This approach developed out of a series of studies conducted at the Western Electric Company in Hawthorne, Ill., in the 1930s. The studies purported to show that high rates of productivity are based on more than the reorganization of work into small, simple steps and the linking of each worker's pay to his or her productivity; just as important are relationships within work groups and those between workers and managers (Roethlisberger and Dickson, 1939). These findings were important because they were used by Elton Mayo (1945, 1946, 1947) to partially justify a new approach to management that he saw as revolutionary. Mayo believed that the *human relations approach*, as he termed it, was based on a new vision of human life—a vision which rejected the rabble hypothesis and its assumption that human life can be reduced to the pursuit of self-interest by isolated individuals. The alternative vision assumed that it is human nature to desire to live and work in groups which provide their members with a sense of meaning beyond the self-interested pursuit of money and other rewards. As evidence of this belief the Hawthorne studies showed that fast workers often helped slower ones reach their production quotas even though the fast workers received no pay for their help and that workers set informal production limits that were below their capabilities. Both practices indicate the way in which workers subordinate their self-interests to the interests of the work group.

Although Mayo's criticism of scientific management and his vision of human nature might have supported a radically different approach to work, perhaps like that of the kibbutzim founders, Mayo was not a revolutionary. His belief that managers had to act as an administrative elite to lead workers belies his revolutionary rhetoric. He used the desire of workers to belong to meaningful work groups not as a means to secure greater equality between workers and managers but rather as a way to further managerial goals of increased productivity. His work led to reorganizing workers into cohesive work groups and to managerial training to create the impression among workers that management genuinely cared about their well-being and that their ideas were taken into account in making executive decisions. Such a policy was thought to serve the best interests of society because it would result in increased productivity and the best interests of workers because they were relieved of responsibility for dealing with the complex issues involved in managerial decision making. The human relations approach thus treated workers like children who needed to be led by manager-parents to do what was best. The new work groups were thought of as similar to children's peer groups, and the new managerial training was a way of giving workers the feeling that they were appreciated and important. Instead of being a revolutionary approach, then, the human relations approach was an effort at the reform of management theory and practice.

An important contemporary movement that is also sometimes described as revolutionary is made up of the diverse interest groups committed to the goal of *empowerment*. The most general goal of these groups is to alter the distribution of power in work settings so that those who have been powerless in the past are given more opportunities to control their destinies. No longer, it is argued, should factory and office managers be allowed to evaluate and direct their subordinates arbitrarily, nor should professionals be allowed to make important decisions without consulting clients. Empowerment is thus a concept that takes in a wide variety of groups and issues. A partial list of the supporters of empowerment include feminists seeking to improve the position of women in work places and in their dealings with professionals; client groups seeking to curb the arbitrariness or evasiveness of professionals; industrial workers who want to protect or gain greater control over their jobs; government officials concerned with developing new ways of protecting the public interest, socialists and others committed to a new social order who are willing to settle in the short run for reforms that are consistent with their goals; and even some professionals and managers who see empowerment as a way of improving their services, making themselves more accountable to others, dealing with the problems of low morale and productivity, or dealing with high rates of turnover and absenteeism. The number of different interest groups supporting the general goal of empowerment reflects the breadth of this movement and the potential for conflict and division within it.

Despite the diversity of groups and interests associated with empowerment, it is possible to specify very broadly the major assumptions that underlie the movement. As with the assumptions of the human relations approach, those associated with empowerment could be applied in such a way as to encourage radically new approaches to work. A basic thesis of this discussion, however, is that this outcome is unlikely because the sponsors of the movement see it primarily as a way of dealing with a limited set of practical problems that they wish to solve. Thus, they seek reform, not revolution. The main features of the empowerment movement will be discussed in greater detail next. Following that, there will be a discussion of three solutions which the empowerment movement proposes to the problems of workers and clients. The chapter will conclude by returning to the general nature of the empowerment movement, its consequences for the everyday lives of workers, and its importance as a major work-related social reality of the future.

BASIC FEATURES OF EMPOWERMENT

In some ways the empowerment movement is a contemporary version of the movement to introduce human relations practices into industrial settings. Both, for example, are based on a critique of the assumptions of scientific management and on alternative visions of human nature. Both are also sometimes justified on the ground that they will result in higher profits through increased worker productivity and decreased costs stemming from absenteeism, turnover, and sabotage. There are, however, some important differences between these movements. Most obviously, the empowerment movement seeks to reform a broader range of work activities than human relations, which was limited to factory settings. The empowerment movement includes office workers, the clients of professionals, and garbage collectors in addition to factory workers. The underlying assumptions of empowerment also differ from human relations, because proponents of empowerment believe that people want to find direct satisfaction from their work and not just from their work groups. Douglas McGregor (1960) explicates the major assumptions of this movement in his *Theory Y,* which he proposes as an alternative to the Theory X, the philosophy of most contemporary work settings (see chapter three). Theory Y makes six basic assumptions:

1. Depending on the conditions surrounding it, work may be experienced as enjoyable or as drudgery. It is not an inherent characteristic of human beings to dislike their work.
2. Close supervision and punishment are not the only ways to motivate people to work hard. They may also be motivated by their desire to control and express themselves through their work.
3. Workers are not necessarily antagonistic to the goals of managers. They will work toward those goals if their needs for self-expression and self-actualization are also met.
4. Most people want and seek responsibility. The apparent avoidance of responsibility by some workers is a learned response to the authoritarian nature of their work settings. It does not reflect human nature.
5. Most people, when given the chance, are able and willing to be creative workers.
6. The typical job allows workers to use only a small portion of their creative and intellectual capacities.

Unlike advocates of the human relations approach, who concentrated only on the relationships among workers and their feelings about management, the proponents of empowerment argue that work must be reorganized so that all of the persons involved may find satisfaction in it. It is no longer sufficient to locate suggestion boxes where low-level employees work, to sponsor company bowling teams, or to employ personnel specialists to placate disgruntled workers; indeed, such practices make the work situation worse because they divert attention from the real problems of modern work. Those problems are that too many people have routine, monotonous, and dead-end jobs and that too many clients of professionals are processed within human service organizations as though they were nonhuman materials in factories and offices. In both cases priority is given to such goals as productivity and efficiency, and the feelings and aspirations of workers and clients are ignored.

Still, the proponents of empowerment are unwilling to fully challenge the existing organization of work. They argue that self-actualization is possible through reform, because there is no fundamental conflict of interest between workers and managers and clients and professionals. All people would be willing to work for conventional goals if they were given a chance to take an active, responsible part in their achievement. The fundamental problem facing managers and professionals, then, is to develop new modes of operation which encourage workers and clients to contribute their special knowledge to the work process and which reward them for caring about their work. More than just lip service, which gives workers and clients the illusion of power, must be paid to these new modes of operation; power actually must be redistributed more equitably through work activities and relationships. It is only in this way, the proponents of empowerment argue, that the physical, emotional, and social adaptations of powerless workers which undermine the achievement of higher productivity and greater efficiency will be eradicated. The empowerment movement, then, attempts to link a humanistic concern for clients and low-level workers with the conventional managerial concern for productivity and efficiency.

Instead of settling for a vague expression of general values or desirable future goals, proponents of empowerment point to a variety of contemporary trends to support their view. Warren Bennis and Philip Slater (1968), for example, claim that the same forces of change that will give rise to the egalitarian family will also affect the world of work outside the home. Old hierarchical relations between bosses and workers will increasingly be replaced by egalitarian relations. Work teams will be given responsibility for solving a limited set of problems, and when that set is solved, the members will be reassigned to other teams. Few other proponents of empowerment share Bennis and Slater's view that such a development is inevitable, but they do believe that it is the best way to solve some of the most important problems of modern work.

Other supporters of empowerment claim that the trend that gives the most impetus to the movement is the new set of expectations that highly educated and minority workers bring to their work. Beyond an adequate income, those workers believe they have the right to interesting work. Indeed, the problems of high rates of absenteeism and turnover among these workers will continue as long as such work expectations are unfulfilled.

Support for empowerment can be found not just in contemporary trends but in current research findings, such as a government-sponsored report on the problems of work in the United States (HEW, 1973). The report endorses the empowerment movement and states, for example, that many of the most important physical and emotional health problems in the United States are related to the unnecessarily stressful and demeaning circumstances of much of our work—problems which result from the unequal organization of work. In addition, the report notes that work satisfaction is the single most important factor accounting for human longevity, ranking above such factors as genetic constitution and life style. Thus, according to the proponents of empowerment, since the evidence indicates that there are serious problems with modern work, a solution based on empowerment must be implemented.

THE EMPOWERMENT SOLUTION

The empowerment movement proposes solutions both to the problems of factory and office workers and to those plaguing professional-client relations. It is important to note that as the proponents of empowerment analyze the problems of modern workers and develop solutions to them, they are also redefining the meaning of work as a social reality. Some aspects of this redefinition are generally recognized by empowerment advocates, but others are not so likely to be seen or given serious discussion by them. In a later section of this chapter we will raise some of these less recognized issues and discuss their possible consequences for workers, clients, and the general public.

The Reform of Factory Work

Clearly the area in which the notion of empowerment has been most widely applied is factory work. In this area empowerment advocates have developed various models for implementing their ideal. Two of the most important are the *West German model of codetermination*, through which workers have been given representation on the supervisory bodies (boards of directors) of major West German corporations, and the *Scandinavian approach*, which concentrates on building new types of work organization which allow autonomous work groups to arrange their work as they see fit (Hunnius, Garson, and Case, 1973; Jenkins, 1973). One reason that these models of empowerment in the factory are important is that they are well-established approaches which demonstrate that empowerment is possible. They are also important because they reflect the variety of ways in which empowerment has been defined in different countries and industries.

Different models have evolved partly because nations have varying philosophies and traditions associated with work and democracy and partly because the interest groups involved in the empowerment movement and the practical problems facing these groups are dissimilar. In West Germany, for example, the British initiated codetermination after World War II in the steel and coal industries in order to break up this industrial power base of Nazism (Jenkins, 1973). The British were encouraged in this direction by West German labor union officials, who wished to increase worker control and who argued that codetermination would be an effective way of monitoring management and its tendencies toward Nazism. In Scandinavia, on the other hand, the empowerment solution emerged out of the concern of some people with the high level of factory worker alienation and the concern of others for extending the traditional Scandinavian principles of social democracy to the work place.

Although it is not so well developed in the United States as in West Germany and Scandinavia, the empowerment solution has also been used here to deal with the problems of low productivity and high absenteeism and turnover. A pet food plant in Topeka, Kansas, for example, redesigned work to allow for autonomous work groups which specialize in one area of the production process (HEW, 1973). The members of each group are allowed to make their own decisions about how the work is done and who does it. Worker versatility and job rotation are further encouraged by payment based on the number of different jobs a worker can do. One result of this change in work organization is that the plant now employs 70 workers to do the same work as 110 workers before the change. Another way in which the empowerment solution has been used in the United States is to save enterprises which are deemed unprofitable by management. For example, the Vermont Asbestos Group and South Bend Lathe were taken over by the workers when the previous owners found them unprofitable (Zwerdling, 1978). By purchasing the enterprise, the workers protected their jobs and became their own employers, thus increasing their power in relation to management. Finally, some factories in the United States have been built from scratch based on the principles of empowerment. One of the most important is Olympia Veneer, which is a plywood cooperative in Olympia, Washington. This cooperative was founded in 1921 by a group of lumberjacks, carpenters, and mechanics who were out of work (Bernstein, 1976; Zwerdling, 1978). Today there are sixteen plywood cooperatives located in the northwestern region of the United States.

Outside of the United States, one of the most interesting and important efforts at empowerment of factory workers is found in Yugoslavia where officials have attempted to both empower workers and to make factory managers accountable to the local community. Because of the breadth of the *Yugoslavian approach,* it deserves a more detailed discussion.

This approach to empowerment was initiated in the 1940s when Marshal Tito, the leader of Yugoslavia, broke with the policies of Stalinist Russia and began to develop a new vision of communism (Blumberg, 1968). Although Tito's dispute with Joseph Stalin involved a number of issues, much of his concern was with the assumption that there is only one way in which to achieve a fully communist society. Tito not only disagreed with this view, but felt that the Russian approach had a number of disadvantages. Most important, he was skeptical about the Russian policy of eliminating private property by bringing it under the control of the government. Although the Russian leaders claimed that the government was representative of all the people and it therefore had the right to control property in the public interest, Tito and his followers pointed to the potential for exploitation inherent in such concentration of power. Certainly, workers can be exploited as much by government as by private employers and, although a recurring theme of Russian policy had been that the state would eventually disappear as the workers took increasing control over their society, a large and powerful government is better able to resist such a takeover than is a less centralized and powerful one. Indeed, Tito believed that a large, centralized, and powerful government gives rise to a new type of exploiter—the bureaucrat—who continues to control the production process and the workers who are part of it (Blumberg, 1968).

The Yugoslavian approach to workers' self-management evolved from this general concern, but it also included two other commitments (Wachtel, 1973). First, the Yugoslavian leaders were committed to *social ownership,* a concept which rejects both private and government-owned property and accepts instead the right of all people in a society to own its property and of those most directly involved with it to make decisions about its use. In the area of factory work the principle of social ownership leads to a policy of worker control, because they are most directly involved with the property that makes up the factory. The second, and related, commitment of the Yugoslavian leaders was to minimizing government interference in the planning process of organizations. This commitment is the basis for the Yugoslavian policy of *market socialism,* which rejects the right of government planning agencies to decide the types, amount, or quality of products produced in each factory. Market socialism allows the workers in each factory to decide for themselves what they wish to produce and how they wish to produce it. At the same time, they are not protected by the government from failure; rather, workers who commit themselves to making products for which there is no demand must face the consequences of their decision, because their pay depends on the profitability of their enterprise. The national government's role in the operation of factories is generally limited to forecasting the future needs of the country and the various industries within it.

Because of the great amount of self-determination found in Yugoslavian factories, each is unique to some degree. It is possible, however, to specify the general characteristics of these factories, which is done in Figure 8-1.

An important assumption underlying the Yugoslavian approach is the belief that the traditional factory is organized so that those who create policy and those who implement it are different people holding differing interests. One consequence is that management policy seldom takes account of the needs and desires of workers, and for this reason workers seldom implement policies in the way they were intended by managers. Thus, a vicious circle of suspicion and hostility is inevitable in factories where workers are excluded from managerial activities. The solution found in the Yugoslavian factory is to involve workers in all aspects of factory operation. Figure 8-1 shows that the general membership is involved both at the top, where decisions are made, and at the bottom, where they are implemented.

The general membership may influence factory policy in four major ways (Adizes, 1971). First, it may call a referendum on important issues involving the long-run operation of the factory, such as plant relocation, consideration of a merger, or a disagreement between the workers' council and workers. A second way in which the general membership influences policy is through *Zbors*, or general meetings. In these meetings policies of the factory are discussed and voted on; the rules of the factory are discussed, changed, or eliminated; and members of all governing units are elected or recalled.

The third way in which the general membership influences factory policy is through its connection to the various work, or economic, units and councils of the factory. Because many Yugoslavian factories are large, it is difficult for the general membership to take an active part in the operation of each department or division. For this reason, the factory has been divided into a series of interrelated work, or economic, units as a compromise with full worker self-management. Although these units vary somewhat in organization, they are similar in that all emphasize self-management by the members of the units (Hunnius, 1973). In addition to their influence within work units and economic councils, factory workers within a given unit or council can also influence policy by asking the general membership to delegate responsibilities and authority to the unit or council. In one factory, for example, the general membership allowed the economic councils to schedule vacations, make

Figure 8-1 • The Formal Organization of a Yugoslavian Factory

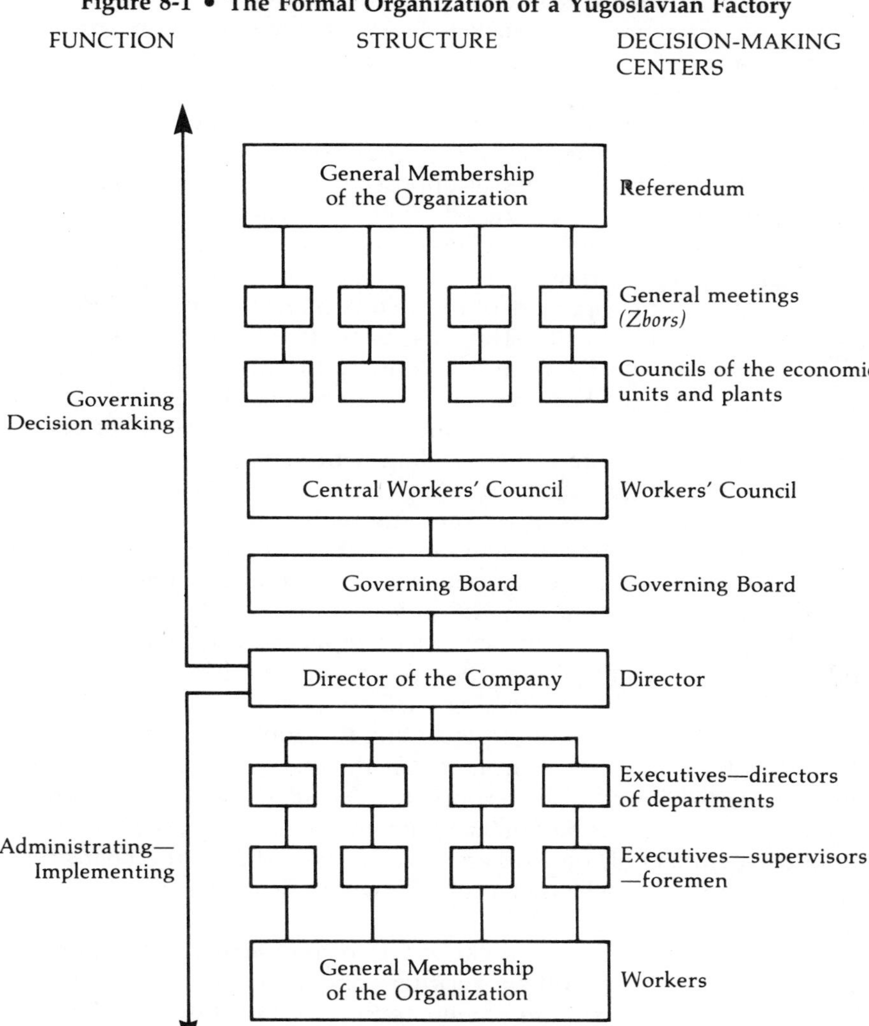

Source: Ichak Adizes, *Industrial Democracy: Yugoslav Style* (New York: The Free Press, 1971): 34.

decisions about firing and hiring, and determine the proper allocation of funds (Adizes, 1971).

The fourth major way in which the general membership influences factory policy is through the election of the workers' council, which is more directly involved in the decision-making process of the factory than the general membership. Because the workers' council is a representative body of the workers, it has the right to influence policy in a large number of areas. In practice, however, the workers' council acts much like a board of trustees in other organizations, because its primary duties are the selection of the major executives within the factory and the approval of the major policy recommendations of the director of the company, such as new rules, pricing, and how much of the organization's profits should be invested as opposed to being returned to workers as dividends (Kolaja, 1965). In addition, the workers' council is the ultimate source of appeal and decision making concerning grievances within the factory. Although the workers' council has the potential to shape the day-to-day practices of the factory management significantly, it seldom does so in practice. The reasons are that the factory managers demand sufficient flexibility and autonomy to administer the organization on an everyday basis and the governing board, which is elected by the workers' council, assumes most of the responsibility for representing the workers' interests in dealing with managers.

Just as the workers' council is like a board of trustees, so the board of governors is like an executive committee within the board of trustees, because it is a small body made up of members of the workers' council and it acts as an intermediary between the workers' council and the factory management. The general policies approved by the workers' council, for example, may not have clear implications for management, and it is part of the job of the governing board to clarify these policies so that the aims of the workers' council are carried out. Similarly, the board may aid management in presenting its problems and recommendations to the workers' council. It can do this, in part, because the members of the board of governors meet regularly with management and are more likely to be familiar with management's problems than are other members of the workers' council. In addition, the board typically has some limited powers of its own to deal with financial and personnel issues (Kolaja, 1965).

Completing the formal organization of the factory is the director of the company and the other executives and supervisors linked to the director. In some ways these administrators are like those in other factories, because they are also responsible for the day-to-day operation of the organization and they are accountable to the various policy-making bodies in the factory—in this case, the governing board, the workers' council, and the general membership. In other ways, however, the role of the director is different from that of his or her counterparts in other organizations. Perhaps the most important distinguishing factor is the extensive involvement of workers in all aspects of the factory. Within other, more traditional organizations the autonomy of the executive is often increased by the fact that the members of the board of trustees and others who have power over him or her are absent from the work place most of the time. Even though the chief executive may be accountable ultimately to the board, his or her accountability is limited to those areas that can be assessed through reports and similar organizational measures. It should not be surprising, then, that much attention in traditional organizations is directed toward rates of profit and productivity, whereas other areas of organization life—areas that are not easily measurable—are more likely to be given lower priority. In the Yugoslavian factory, however, the workers have the right to hold all executives accountable, which means that all administrators are constantly surrounded by people who are able to judge many aspects of their performances. Because they are more visible to their evaluators, the executives and supervisors in the Yugoslavian factory have less autonomy than their counterparts in more traditional factories.

In addition, the autonomy of the executive and supervisory personnel is affected by rules and regulations which limit their authority. The director's role, for example, is typically defined so that he or she has no direct authority to implement decisions by commanding or ordering other people; rather, all such decisions are ordered through the various administrative bodies made up of the workers (Adizes, 1971). The same is true for other executive and supervisory personnel. The foreman, for example, does not have the right to punish or fire workers; rather, as Ichak Adizes notes, "He can make a complaint, but the verdict will be given by the disciplinary committee of the Economic Unit" (Adizes, 1971: 46). Finally, the autonomy of the executive and supervisory personnel is limited by the possibility that they may be turned out of office by the workers at the next election. Indeed, the great limitations managers face in the Yugoslavian factory are important in understanding the tendency of some managers to develop similar work practices and orientations as low-level workers in other factories (Jenkins, 1973). They complain of feeling powerless, and they are apathetic about their work. In the Yugoslavian case, at least, the empowerment of low-level workers has its costs for managers.

While the factor director in Yugoslavia is more accountable to the workers than those in other countries, he or she has some influence on the workers and their councils because of the relations the director has with important organizations in the factory's environment (Abrahamsson, 1977). Important outside organizations include the local community, sociopolitical organizations, and interest groups within the community. Each of these may attempt to influence the policies established by the workers, but this influence is channeled through the administrative offices of the factory. Thus, the director and other administrators have access to knowledge and people that the workers do not.

In many ways, the most important of the outside influences is the local community or commune, which is also largely a self-governing group in Yugoslavia. Although the factory and the commune intersect in a variety of ways, their interdependence becomes most obvious during times of conflict and crisis. One conflict involves the degree to which the factory should be independent from the community. This is an important problem, because the factory and the commune are made up of many of the same people who have a stake in seeing that the interests of the two are served. The factory obviously contributes to the maintenance of the community by employing its residents, but the commune is also important to the success of the factory. The commune, for example, often supplies investment funds needed for starting a factory and subsidizes those factories which cannot pay their workers a minimum wage (Wachtel, 1973). In addition, the commune is responsible for the debts of its factories that go bankrupt. The desires of local community leaders concerning the factory, then, cannot be ignored easily; rather, they are important in factory decision-making processes, and the influence of managers is increased by their position as intermediaries between the workers and community leaders.

After the communes, the two most important outside organizations are sociopolitical—the League of Communists (Communist party) and the labor union. Although the party has had greater influence in the past, its primary activity today is defined as "education" (Kolaja, 1965; Wachtel, 1973). It works to communicate broad government policies to the workers, thus shaping general worker perspectives (Wachtel, 1973). In addition, the party has some indirect influence over executives, because most of the higher-ranking executives belong to the party. The labor union's role in the factory is also limited, because many of the traditional activities of the labor union are eliminated when the workers manage the factory (Kolaja, 1965). For this reason, the Yugoslav labor unions act as advisory boards only and are most involved in decisions about worker pay, such as what percentage of the factory's profits should be reinvested as opposed to being paid to the workers (Wachtel, 1973).

Finally, there are local interest groups that seek to influence the decisions made within the factory. These groups tend to be concentrated in public service areas, such as health care, education, cultural activities, child care, and social assistance, which are highly dependent on the factory for funding (Abrahamsson, 1977). As with most aspects of work and community life in Yugoslavia, outsiders do not determine the factory's contribution to the community; rather, the factory negotiates taxes and other contributions to the commune. Central to the negotiation process are managers who speak for the workers and thereby gain access to information not available to the workers—information which can be used to extend their influence over the workers.

The Yugoslavian factory, then, exists in an environment that is both supportive and evaluative. That is, the commune, sociopolitical organizations, and interest groups share a concern for keeping the factory in operation but are also in a position to hold the factory management accountable for the achievement of the general goals of the empowerment movement. Because of the close economic ties between the factory and commune, for example, the workers' council must answer to the representatives of the commune in making decisions about the wages, prices, production goals and similar issues. Unwise or inappropriate policies adopted by the workers' council or other bodies within the factory can be resisted in theory by representatives of the commune who may act as an external check on the factory management. Thus, the Yugoslavian factory is similar to other modern work places in that it is also characterized by political relationships and struggles, although the participants, rules, and relationships are different in the Yugoslavian factory.

In sum, the Yugoslavian model of empowerment goes beyond the codetermination plan of West Germany and the autonomous work group plans found in Scandinavia and the United States. Empowerment there is part of a general commitment to building a socialist way of life in which the national government plays a restricted role in the everyday lives of citizens. The objective is to build a world in which such institutional settings as work, the commune, and education will be the dominant forces in people's lives. It is assumed that these institutional settings are the places where workers and other citizens can exert the most control over their lives. The result is a country that tolerates a wide range of work and community settings reflecting the problems, interpretations, and negotiations of workers and residents. In encouraging this diversity, the Yugoslavian government implicitly takes the position that diversity based on local control is more important than attempting to achieve a uniform state in which all of the most important tenets of socialism are realized. The sponsors of this program are, then, reformers, not utopians.

The Yugoslavian empowerment model has long-range implications for the development of factories in Yugoslavia. We will deal with some of these implications in a later section, but it is important to consider some other examples of empowerment first.

The Reform of the Office

One of the areas offering great promise to proponents of empowerment is the office, where a variety of workers are engaged in a number of routine tasks which could be rearranged into autonomous work groups similar to those developed in factories. Despite its promise, the office has been much less affected by the empowerment movement than the factory. One important reason for the lack of interest in the office may be the large number of women who work there—women who occupy the lowest positions and are often seen as unqualified for more challenging work or uninterested in achieving positions of power. One proposal for empowering office workers is found the analysis provided by Rosabeth Moss Kanter (1977a) of Indsco, a multinational corporation. Kanter focuses initially on office politics.

Although the term "office politics" is widely used, it typically describes relations among executives who are struggling to preserve, if not expand, their power and prestige within the office. This conception of office politics is too restricted, however, because it does not take account of the often subtle political relationships between bosses and secretaries and among secretaries. These are political relationships because they are an integral part of the bargaining process associated with success in the office. Thus, the secretary who intentionally or unintentionally fails to inform her boss of an important meeting may have as much impact on his career as the other executives who are competing with him. But the political relations between bosses and secretaries are not limited to the ways in which secretaries shape the careers of bosses. Equally important is the way in which bosses shape the careers of secretaries. Indeed, it is the latter feature of this political relationship that is crucial to understanding how the practical circumstances of office work and sexist assumptions combine to encourage practices which limit the secretary's potential for independence and advancement.

At Indsco widespread uncertainty among executives encourages the restriction and control of secretaries (Kanter, 1977a). The executives—primarily men—are locked into a competitive situation in which the winners are promoted and the losers are left behind. But the criteria for promotion are not clear to the competitors, because those making promotion decisions are also uncertain about their positions. An important consequence of the pervasive feeling of uncertainty at Indsco is a desire by executives to construct small, safe worlds around themselves in which they can feel secure. Only by discouraging competition and encouraging emotional ties to the executive do they think they can derive such security. Indeed, loyalty to the boss often is given highest priority by bosses in evaluating subordinates.

The everyday lives of executives at Indsco, then, are filled with feelings of uncertainty, and when these feelings were combined with the executives' assumption that women are more nurturant and less self-interested than men, they justify the development of practices and relationships which give priority to the desires of the boss. The result is a world in which each boss thinks of his secretary as "my girl"—a woman totally committed to the boss' success based on her personal attachment to him. For this reason few bosses worry about finding new, more challenging, and better-paying jobs for their secretaries; rather, when job announcements are sent to their offices, they throw them in the wastebasket. In this way the secretary's career is made dependent on the decision-making criteria of the boss—criteria that seldom include an assessment of the secretary's work skills and potential apart from her personal relationship with the boss. Bosses respond to secretaries who complain about their lack of opportunity in a very negative way. Such secretaries are often seen as overly aggressive and therefore not good workers, or their complaints are taken to indicate that they feel unloved by the boss. In the first case, the boss refuses to recommend his secretary for advancement because she lacks the required attributes, and in the second case he sends her flowers. In neither case is she likely to achieve her goal of advancement.

In the world of office politics, then, the ultimate loser is not the executive who is left behind because he has been outmaneuvered by others, but the capable secretary who has not been given a chance to compete because her skills have gone unnoticed or they have been evaluated as very good "for a woman." According to Kanter, proponents of the empowerment movement must concentrate on this person to make him or her a dignified worker who is respected by others, has interesting work, and has the resources to do the job properly. In developing a solution to the low-level office worker's problem, however, it is important to recognize that it is multifaceted. It includes the worker's lack of access to opportunity and positions of power, but the fact that most low-level office workers are women also complicates the problem. Thus, an adequate empowerment solution for low-level office workers must take account of opportunity, power, and people. Each of these factors is central to Kanter's model for empowering office workers, which is summarized in Table 8-1. According to the model, changes in all three are needed to reduce the impact of uncertainty and sexism on the low-level office worker's career.

The variable "opportunity" refers to the chances for achievement and/or personal growth that workers have within organizations. A change in the organization's opportunity structure must involve a serious analysis of the avenues for advancement and development of alternative avenues where they are needed. In addition, reformers must realize that competence is not a fair measure for advancement so long as everyone does not have an equal opportunity to compete. This realization leads to two general policies for change: (1) greater access to rewardable skills must be provided to low-ranking workers and (2) greater recognition must be given to the skills that many low-ranking workers already have. Concerning the latter, many secretaries possess highly developed and varied skills that could be of value in managerial positions, but the typical evaluation procedure for secretaries fails to

Table 8-1 • Empowering Office Workers

Alterations in the Distribution of:		
Opportunity	*Power*	*People*
1. Job descriptions 2. Performance appraisal 3. Career review 4. Job posting 5. Job redesign 6. Job rotation 7. Project management 8. Job enrichment 9. Decentralization 10. Flexible working hours 11. Counseling for managers	1. Flatten the hierarchy 2. Open communication channels and publicize system knowledge 3. Extend sponsorship	1. Batch promotions and hiring 2. Concentration of minorities within the organization 3. Provision of role models 4. Development of a minority network 5. Flexible organization structures 6. Training for managers 7. Support programs for minorities

Source: Adapted from Rosabeth Moss Kanter, *Men and Women of the Corporation* (New York: Basic Books, Inc., Publishers, 1977): 264–287.

take account of these skills; rather, too often the secretary's competence is evaluated in light of her boss' achievement in the organization. Within such an arrangement the secretary has skills and competence only if her boss does.

Beyond these general considerations, opportunity structures in offices can be reformed through the implementation of the eleven specific policies noted in Table 8-1. First, organizations must develop detailed *job descriptions* of what low-ranking office workers actually do. With such descriptions, it is possible to identify skills that have previously been ignored, but it is also possible to develop new criteria of competence based on the worker's performance, not that of the boss. Related to job descriptions are *performance appraisals,* which are regular reviews of job performance by workers, their immediate superiors, and others in the organization who may influence the career chances of the worker. Such appraisals would not be counseling sessions in which the boss tells the subordinate how much he or she is needed and loved; rather, they would be serious discussions of the strengths and weaknesses of the worker's performance. The meetings might also include a *career review,* in which the worker's long-range goals are considered along with how best to achieve them. Such reviews would involve a discussion of the worker's effectiveness in his or her present job, a consideration of new skills that might be needed for future advancement, and a discussion of the avenues of advancement within the organization that are most likely to meet the worker's desires. A worker might discover, for example, that although he or she likes a current job, it does not offer the long-range opportunities of a job in another department. Thus, the worker might seek a job change that in the short run offers few advantages but in the long run is more likely to lead to the worker's goal.

The next three changes are intended to reduce the worker's dependence on his or her boss. *Job posting* requires that all job openings in the organization be made public so that anyone may apply for them. At Indsco and in other offices, much of the advancement of secretaries is blocked by bosses who refuse to make such jobs known. Job posting eliminates this source of control, as does *job redesign*. Although job redesign may take a variety of forms, its most important consequences for low-ranking office workers is to eliminate much of their dependence on others. One aspect of job redesign for secretaries is the "decoupling" of the boss and the secretary so that the secretary is evaluated independently from the boss. Thus, a secretary could be promoted without her boss. Another aspect is the development of new rewards for bosses who are effective at helping their secretaries develop skills that make them promotable. In other words, it is possible to design jobs so that helping others is rewarded and the subordination of others is discouraged.

One way in which relations of subordination could be discouraged, according to Kanter, is through *job rotation*, in which the office worker moves from job to job, although he or she may not move up. Not only does job rotation decrease some of the dependency inherent in subordinate-superordinate relations, but it provides low-ranking workers with the opportunity to develop new skills and to grow as people. Thus, even if such opportunities do not result in career advancement, workers may still find them desirable. The same is true for *project management*, which refers to the development of short-run work groups put together to deal with a limited set of problems. Once the team's goals are achieved, it is disbanded and the workers return to their old jobs. Such work teams offer a flexible way for organizations to deal with many problems, but they also can be used as forms of job rotation and as bases for job redesign. Put differently, work teams may be used to demonstrate that secretaries can work effectively as equal members of a team and they do not have to be relegated to the job of taking notes and getting coffee. At the same time that the work of low-level employees is diversified, it should be improved as well. This is *job enrichment*, which is defined as the practice of adding new skills and other requirements to low-level jobs so that workers have more opportunity to feel challenged by their work.

In order for many of the above changes to occur, it is necessary to implement policies to *decentralize the organization*. Such policies would emphasize the need to spread the decision-making process within the organization. One way in which to achieve decentralization is through project management. Another is to spread decision making among a variety of permanent organization units—such as departments—that have previously been dependent on those above them. From the point of view of empowerment advocates, however, the method is less important than the fact that decentralization opens avenues to meaningful achievement that are closed when only a few officials at the top make all the important decisions in an organization.

Merely to open new avenues of achievement is insufficient, however, because many low-ranking workers are at a disadvantage in competing on the job. Women with families, for example, are often caught in the dilemma of having to choose between the demands of their work and those of their family. In order to give such workers an equal chance in the work place, it is important to implement programs that allow for *flexible working hours*. Such programs require that the worker still contribute the same number of hours as in the past, but the employer no longer has the right to specify the precise time when work gets done. The employer may specify, for example, that work must be done between the hours of 6 A.M. and 11 P.M., Monday through Saturday, but leave it up to the worker to arrange his or her own schedule within those times. The point is that many of the problems that have confounded male and female workers in the past are really unnecessary ones that have resulted from the inflexible assumption that work and family obligations can be separated. The result has been that those people who take primary responsibility for the family—usually women—are placed at a disadvantage in their work.

The transformation of the organization to increase opportunity involves more than creating alternatives for the low-ranking and powerless; it also requires that the problems of superiors be addressed. Specifically, there is a need to create new incentives and criteria of evaluation for managers, neither of which can be achieved through the implementation of a policy developed at the top and handed down in an arbitrary manner. Rather, it is necessary to *counsel* or *train managers* in new techniques of management which emphasize and reward the manager who effectively teaches and facilitates the achievement of his or her subordinates. Unfortunately many managers have been trained in a tradition that emphasizes the undependable and childish nature of subordinates, and they work in environments where the delegation of authority is unrewarded. Thus, training managers in new management techniques must be accompanied by the development within offices of new evaluation procedures which are based on nonauthoritarian assumptions about workers.

Besides broadening the opportunity structure, offices must also work for the redistribution of power. Three changes in power are stressed in Kanter's model of empowerment. First, it is necessary to *flatten the hierarchy* of the organization so that power and authority are less centralized. Flattening the hierarchy increases the discretionary power and autonomy of workers, and for this reason the chances of achieving worker dignity are increased. In addition, workers in a more decentralized organization are less likely to face the problem of being accountable to their superiors while not having the power to do their jobs properly. Still another advantage of flattening hierarchies is that superiors can be freed from many of the most time-consuming, unrewarding, and conflict-ridden duties related to supervising subordinates. In a more decentralized office, the subordinate is held directly accountable for his or her actions, and the superior is therefore free to concentrate on more interesting and important tasks.

The second change in the distribution of power is to *open the communication channels of the organization and publicize system knowledge.* Knowledge about the operation of the office is an important source of power, because those who have it can take advantage of opportunities and perhaps even manipulate situations to their advantage. When such knowledge is regularly denied to some members of the organization, they are made powerless. By publicizing knowledge about the organization, everyone has a greater opportunity to compete based on ability.

The third and final change in the distribution of power involves *extending sponsorship* to include low-ranking office workers. The typical pattern for advancement in large organizations is through sponsorship by a higher-ranking official, who keeps the person being sponsored informed about new opportunities and protects him or her from attacks by others in the organization. Although the sponsorship procedure can be seen as inherently unfair, Kanter does not reject it; rather, she claims that it is unfair primarily because everyone is not given an equal chance to have a sponsor. In extending sponsorship to low-ranking workers, it is important not to give the impression that the person being sponsored is somehow undeserving; rather, sponsorship of low-ranking workers must involve the same commitment by the sponsor as does sponsorship of higher-ranking workers. This requirement is particularly important when a woman is sponsored because her authority can easily be undermined by a sponsor who is insecure or too solicitous. Kanter believes that the sponsor should consciously resist "watching women more closely than men, thinking of women managers or professionals as an 'experiment' that must be monitored, or reviewing the decisions of women more frequently than usual." She would also discourage "protective" actions that prevent women from solving their own problems: "It makes a woman look weak and powerless to have a man take over for her in emergencies or crises" (Kanter, 1977a: 280).

A final area of reform involves the distribution of people within offices. In part, the unequal distribution of people that exists today reflects past assumptions and practices that channeled different kinds of people (particularly men and women) into different parts of the organization, but it also reflects some of the problems that have arisen from more recent efforts to open the organization to minorities. The major problem is *tokenism,* the practice of placing minority members in highly visible jobs in departments dominated by nonminorities. A common result is that the minority worker is made insecure because of his or her visibility and becomes isolated from other minority workers who share similar problems and interests. It is therefore necessary to develop policies and practices which encourage minorities to find collective solutions to their problems and thereby increase their power within the office.

An important first step is to stop introducing minorities into new areas one at a time; rather, organizations should develop policies of *batch promotion and hiring*. Related to this recommendation is a second which encourages *minority clustering within the organization*. This is not to say that the organization should be divided into sections filled with only men or women. The purpose is to prevent women and other minorities from being spread so thin within the organization that they have little meaningful contact with each other. The third recommendation is that organizations should provide minority workers with *role models* to emulate. Although this recommendation may sound like a new burden for management, the fact is that most high-ranking managers already consciously present role models of success and respectability to their workers. They do this formally through such events as training sessions and informally through the creation and projection of an image of the "up-and-coming" worker. Such role models are often a problem for minority workers, because characteristics that cannot be emulated by minority workers are included in the role. A black man cannot become white, for example. The problem is more difficult for women, because both women workers and superiors do not always want the woman worker to have all of the social and personal characteristics of the male role model, but they are not always certain what an appropriate female role model would be like. For these reasons, it is important for high-level managers to provide realistic role models for their minority workers. If no such people exist within the organization, then it may be necessary for workers to look at successful people in other organizations.

The fourth recommendation is that organizations create *minority networks,* through which minority workers can share their problems and seek common solutions. Such networks are most effective if they involve serious, rather than just social, activities. A useful way of developing them is through project management, in which minority workers interact in teams to develop solutions to serious organization problems. Such work groups could also be a way to use *flexible organizational structures* to deal with the problems of minorities in organizations. In order for minority networks and flexible organizational structures to be effective, however, managers must be informed of the special problems of minorities in large organizations. Such *training of managers* will not only increase their sensitivity to minority problems, but it will provide them with insight into how everyday situations and events within the office can be changed to make them less problematic for minorities. Finally, organizations need to build *support programs for minorities* which allow them to communicate their problems to managers and to develop meaningful solutions to them.

In sum, Kanter's recommendations for empowering office workers stem directly from her analysis of Indsco and her assumptions about work and workers. The basic cause of the problems facing workers is not their personal inadequacy but unnecessarily rigid and authoritarian work settings. The result is an uncertain and a sexist world where low-level workers are often asked to sacrifice their career goals to protect their bosses. The empowerment solution is intended to eliminate uncertainty by making the criteria of evaluation explicit and publicizing basic knowledge about the organization. The most important aspects of office sexism would be solved by allowing women to join men in work groups where they are equal, by encouraging the sponsorship of women into better jobs, and by developing new policies and practices which take account of the special problems of women. Based on these changes, Kanter argues that the work of low-level office workers will become dignified.

The Reform of Professional Work

Although many occupational groups have been successful in achieving high levels of respectability and autonomy for members, which therefore qualifies them as professions, their social standing is nevertheless occasionally threatened by competing occupations, the government, clients, employers, the general public, and even competing segments within the professions. Indeed, a great deal of time and energy is expended within professional associations to combat threats and thereby protect, if not expand, the sphere of control of the professions. One obvious ploy in protecting professional control is to depict competitors as self-interested persons who are quacks and who, unlike members of the profession, place money and prestige above the greater public good. Another strategy, as we mentioned in chapter four, is to argue that the work of professionals is so complex that it is beyond the grasp of the ordinary citizen and government official. A related claim is that efforts by government and other outside officials to evaluate the professional work must be resisted because such work cannot be reduced to a set of technical routines; rather, the competent professional is described as a person who develops an almost intuitive ability to understand cases—a skill that cannot be evaluated properly by outsiders (Jamous and Peloille, 1970). Physicians, nurses, social workers, teachers, lawyers, and other professionals speak, for example, of developing a "feel" for their work that cannot be communicated to others or organized into routines; to do their jobs right they must be left alone.

The relationship between the professions and outsiders, then, is an area ripe for conflict and bargaining, because the social, political, and economic position of any profession largely depends on the willingness of outsiders to respect its members and to allow them to work unimpeded. Seldom, however, is an entire profession challenged by outsiders; rather, specific professional practices or segments are typically the issue of contention. Both homeopathic and psychoanalytic treatment techniques, for example, were introduced into American medicine in the nineteenth century by middle-class patients who refused to continue to endure the painful treatments prescribed by most physicians (Rothstein, 1973). Both homeopathy, which involves giving patients small doses of drugs to encourage the body to heal itself, and psychoanalysis, which primarily involves talk and little manipulation of the body, were appealing because they required little patient discomfort. Those treatment techniques were introduced into medicine mainly through physicians who worked alone and practiced general medicine. Such physicians could not easily resist their patients who threatened to take their business elsewhere unless homeopathic and psychoanalytic treatments were used. Once the practices became widespread among physicians, they were incorporated into the general practice of medicine. In this way, the profession of medicine adapted to the demands of clients.

The revolt of clients continues to be an important challenge to the power of contemporary professionals, who pay too little attention to the problems of their clients and impose their social and moral views on them in the name of professional service. In some cases even the general expertise of professionals is challenged by clients (Haug and Sussman, 1969a; 1969b). Elements of client revolt are evident in the efforts of women to change the unnecessarily cold and insensitive practices of some gynecologists, the efforts of parents to gain some control over the content of instruction offered their children in school, and the claim of some welfare recipients that social workers are merely bureaucrats with no special knowledge or right to greater prestige than others. In addition to clients, the contemporary professions are also under some pressure from the government, which requires regular reviews of professional practices and justification of those that are unusual. Moreover, the employers of professionals may affect professional work by introducing new considerations into the professional-client relationship. An example is the military psychiatrist whose diagnosis of the patient is limited by the rules and procedures of the military bureaucracy and the degree to which soldiers are needed: during crises strict diagnoses are encouraged, so that fewer people are hospitalized or discharged (Daniels, 1969). Not all professions are equally affected by the influence of employers, but increasingly professional work takes place in bureaucratic organizations, which suggests that employer demands will remain an important external influence on professionals.

One conclusion some have drawn is that the professionalization process that gave rise to the modern professions has ended and we are entering a time of deprofessionalization, during which the professions will gradually lose their unique characteristics and high social standing (Haug, 1973). This conclusion is difficult to sustain, however, because throughout the history of the professions there have been forces that have sought to control them. Clients have been an important source of resistance, but so have government officials, who historically have created some policies which support the professions and others which restrict them (Tabachnik, 1976). Indeed, even segments within the professions have from time to time rejected conventional notions of professionalism and sought to redefine it so that clients and others have more power. The result of such conflicts has not been the elimination of the professions but a continuing redefinition of the rights and responsibilities of professionals to their clients and the public.

It is within this context that the current efforts to empower clients must be understood. Empowerment will involve a redefinition of the rights and responsibilities of professionals and clients—a process best described as reform and not revolution, because the proponents of empowerment do not wish to create a new world devoid of professionals. Rather, they wish to alter only those aspects of professional practice which they see as problematic. The most important problem, in their opinion, is that current professional practice discourages professionals and clients from cooperating to achieve a jointly defined goal. The extreme emphasis on professional control of the client in contemporary professional education and the related pressure exerted by government and employers to gain control encourage a relationship in which the professional and client have become adversaries as each seeks to achieve separate ends (Cloward and Piven, 1976; Fischer and Brodsky, 1978; Galper, 1975; Perrucci, 1973; Resnick, 1976). Empowerment, then, is an attempt to increase the client's power and to build a cooperative relationship between professionals and clients.

Although professional power is manifested in a number of ways, one of the oldest reflections of such power is the record of the professional-client encounter kept by the professional (Wheeler, 1969). Indeed, because of the assumption that the client is ignorant and helpless to deal with his or her problems, it is common for the professional to treat the record of their encounter as confidential and private property. One reason that professional records may be a problem is that they are not intended to give a balanced picture of the client. Because the purpose of such records is to provide a description of the client's problem, the professional may unintentionally create a general picture of the client that is inaccurate and extreme. For example, professional records are often filled with catchwords that allow the professional to categorize the client and his or her problems. Such categorizations are not necessarily an accurate depiction of the client's problem, but they are useful in the development of treatment approaches. Although this practice may create problems in the professional-client relationship, a more serious problem emerges when the records are made available to others who have had no contact with the client. Indeed, professional records are often requested by decision-making bodies that wish to look at "objective" information and evaluations in order to make more informed decisions. When used in this way, professional records are treated as sources of indisputable fact rather than as partial and subjective assessments by a person who is looking at only one aspect of the client's life. The consequences of this practice, however, can be very important for the client. As one observer notes:

> I recently saw school district officials refuse to offer public education to a seven-year-old child whom none of them had met, simply on the basis of one psychologist's written report that the "hyperactive" and "borderline retarded" child could not benefit from public education. This child has been illegally, and, I think, unjustifiably excluded from school for five months, all because the written word has been attributed more importance than the child himself (Biklen, 1978: 21).

Professional records are accorded such authenticity because it is assumed that the professional is an aloof observer who is concerned only with describing the client's problem. Such an assumption overlooks the political nature of the professional-client relationship and the factors outside the professional-client encounter that affect it. As noted above, the professional typically dwells on what is wrong with the client and not with how he or she is effectively coping with life. Similarly, such records often involve little recognition of the impact of treatment organizations on the client and his or her problems. Indeed, if treatment organizations do not provide the full services they are supposed to, the client may be held accountable for the organization's failure. In some human service institutions, for example, showers, baths, and clean clothes have been rationed to clients because the organizations have inadequate funds; nevertheless, an important aspect of the professional evaluation of clients in these organizations has been their cleanliness—a condition over which they have little control (Biklen, 1978).

By concentrating on the client as the object of evaluation, the professional record may become a self-serving instrument that can be used to "blame the victim" of organizational neglect and abuse (Ryan, 1971). Put differently, because they represent the assessments of professionals, professional records are political tools which reflect the relations of power between clients and professionals. It is therefore important to pay attention to what the records do not mention as well as the assessments made within them. Another indication of the political nature of professional records is their use in evaluating the effectiveness of different approaches to a problem. If a professional has an interest in one approach over another, then he or she may gather information that is biased. That is not to say that professionals engage in a conscious conspiracy to create inaccurate findings, although they may; rather, the collecting of information about the effectiveness of professional services involves decisions about events that are not always easily classifiable. If the professional has an interest in the outcome of evaluation, then he or she may influence the outcome of the research in a variety of subtle, nonconspiratorial, and often unconscious ways. An example is the way in which the children at Cedarview (see chapter four) were evaluated by staff based on their everyday experiences with the children and their interest in generating findings that could be used to secure new funding of the program (Buckholdt and Gubrium, 1979a).

The empowerment movement, then, is concerned with the ways in which professionals keep and use records. Generally, the solution to this problem involves bringing the client directly into the recordkeeping and evaluation process. More specifically, Douglas Biklen (1978) notes four concrete ways in which the empowerment solution can be applied in this area. First, all records should be open to those who are being served, treated, and/or evaluated. Such a practice both reduces the power of the professional to be arbitrary in creating records and provides a means for the client to challenge immediately any errors in the record. The challenge may be due to a total fabrication or to the professional's tendency to dwell on treatments that overemphasize the client's problems and may cloud future decisions by others using the record.

A second means of empowering clients in the area of recordkeeping is to actively evaluate organizational services in the record. If the client is not being provided services which are rightfully his or hers, then the professional should make note of that in the record, as well as any problematic aspects of the client's behavior that may be caused by inadequate treatment organizations. Such recordkeeping may be used to evaluate the effectiveness of treatment organizations, but just as important, it may help the client to change his or her behavior by providing a more accurate description of the client's environment.

A third, and related, means of empowering clients is to open the professional record to them and other (family members, etc.) so that they can add to it. Not only would such a practice add new information to the record—information that the professional may have ignored or could not get—but it would provide an avenue for clients to disagree with professional evaluations. Although such a practice may increase the conflict between professionals and clients, it is necessary to provide a way for professional-client disagreements to surface so that the record expresses a more balanced picture. Unlike the traditional image of the professional, the empowerment movement assumes that the professional does not always know best and certainly may be wrong. It is, therefore, necessary to plan for such developments by allowing the client and others the right of rebuttal.

The fourth and final way to protect the client from professional errors is for professional and service organizations to institute programs of *client advocacy*. In the area of mental retardation, for example, Biklen supports programs in which "individuals with some knowledge of mental retardation and human rights . . . would serve as ombudsmen and advocates by independently observing and evaluating service programs and conditions" (Biklen, 1978: 36). In this way the interests of clients could be represented within the administrative and decision-making centers of human service organizations.

According to advocates of empowerment, then, changes in recordkeeping will result in both greater accountability of professionals to clients and a higher quality of professional service because of the additional information and insight the client provides (Rosenthal, 1974). In addition, empowerment is seen as an effective way of dealing with a major contradiction in contemporary professional practice: although the professions presumably exist to "enable" clients to better deal with their problems and thereby take control of their lives, they frequently "disable" clients by making them dependent on professionals and human service organizations (Illich, 1977). In other words, the rise of professional medicine, law, education, social work, and other professions has solved some important problems, but it has also discouraged people and communities from developing their own solutions to problems of health, conflict, ignorance, and poverty. The proponents of empowerment hope to reverse the disabling trend by creating a new professional-client relationship in which the professional acts as a partner, not a superior, in helping the client to solve his or her problems.

The empowerment movement hopes to affect more than just the professional-client relationship, however. Supporters also want to redefine the professional's responsibilities to the employing organization and the profession as a whole. The professional's first obligation, according to empowerment advocates, is to his or her client, and all other considerations are of secondary importance. If this assumption were widely accepted, professional education would change drastically. For example, instead of criticizing graduate students in social work programs for unprofessional conduct in becoming overly involved in clients' problems, teachers might caution students on too great an identification with an employer (Cloward and Piven, 1976). The empowerment movement, then, could involve more than empowering the client in his or her relationship with the professional; it might also involve a redefinition of professional work and the reform of organizations that are related to it, such as training schools and employing organizations.

An Overview of Empowerment Solutions

In this section we have considered three areas in which the principles of empowerment have been applied. Each of the applications is somewhat unique, because the circumstances surrounding factory, office, and professional work are different. But all share some assumptions. Thus, all would agree with McGregor's Theory Y in holding that human beings can be vitally interested in their lives as workers and clients if they are given the chance and are rewarded for their efforts. Further, all would agree that when people are encouraged to take control of their lives, they will seek cooperation with others, rather than conflict, and they will seek conventional goals. The problem with modern life and work is not with people, but with the work environments which surround and dehumanize them. The sullen, apathetic, passive, petty, and bitchy side of many workers and clients shows the extent to which we have created a world where authoritarianism and inequality prevail.

Central to the empowerment movement, then, is a new social reality—one based on a different vision of human nature than has prevailed in the past. As with other social realities, empowerment has important consequences for the way in which work is organized and given meaning. In particular, work is defined as a potentially meaningful aspect of each person's life and for this reason workers must take control of their work lives. Advocates of empowerment often depict the worker who prefers to remain apathetic toward his or her job and places greater emphasis on leisure and consumption as a problem, because this attitude leads to authoritarian relations in work and an unfulfilled life for the worker. Indeed, one advocate of empowerment has gone so far as to state that a necessary condition for full democracy in the work place is the creation of a new worker consciousness which stresses the personal traits of flexibility, self-reliance, sensitivity to others, openness to new ideas, and the ability to criticize oneself and to analyze situations and options unemotionally (Bernstein, 1976). Consistent with their other assumptions, empowerment advocates also state that the new consciousness will develop as work places are democratized, although special efforts may be needed to encourage a democratic consciousness in the early stages of empowerment.

Empowerment, in other words, is one form of modern liberation. Like other forms it involves a rejection of old beliefs and practices, but it also introduces new constraints into the lives of workers. It is these consequences of empowerment that are the subject of the next section.

THE IMPACT OF EMPOWERMENT

As with countercultural movements, the proponents of empowerment use an organizing myth as a framework for criticizing past practices and for outlining a better future. A basic feature of the organizing myth of empowerment is the claim that egalitarian work places are more humane, and for this reason workers are more productive. Indeed, much of the literature concerning empowerment details the greater productivity and profitability of egalitarian work places (Bernstein, 1976; Blumberg, 1968; HEW, 1973; Rosenthal, 1974). With few exceptions, however, little attention has been paid to the everyday circumstances of life for workers and clients. It is only when such circumstances are considered that a full assessment of this movement can be made. Because of the limited material on the everyday realities of people affected by empowerment, we will present here only a general sketch of some of the problems which the proponents may encounter in the future. Our purpose is to raise issues for consideration, rather then describe research findings.

Perhaps the most general problem with the empowerment movement is the tendency of its proponents to assume that official charts or statements about power relations in work places are an accurate reflection of what goes on within them. In practice, few clients and low-level workers are totally powerless, and many use their knowledge about the routines of work places to carve out niches of influence for themselves. Workers and clients may not be accorded the public esteem of those who hold official positions of power, but they may still be important in affecting the day-to-day operations of the organization. For example, the secretary who handles the appointments of the president of a company may have great influence on company policy if she chooses to allow some executives easy access to the president and makes access difficult for those committed to a different policy. The point is that power is a relative condition, and few workers can be described as powerful or powerless all of the time; rather, they are powerful and powerless within situations, and when those situations change, so does their level of influence. The empowerment movement may alter the balance of power within work situations, but it will not so alter them that the powerless become powerful all of the time: empowerment only introduces new elements into the bargaining processes of modern work places. How the new rules and positions are interpreted will vary from enterprise to enterprise and even from situation to situation.

Looked at in this way, those proponents of empowerment who feel that the movement will revolutionize modern work are doomed to disenchantment, because the impact of empowerment will not be so revolutionary. Even more than countercultural movements, the empowerment movement will be redefined and changed as workers, clients, and others deal with the problems of everyday life. The responses to these problems may encourage even more drastic programs of empowerment, but they may also encourage a retrenchment from this goal. In this section we will briefly look at the ways in which empowerment may be important to work places, the larger society, and individuals, and some possible limits on its full implementation.

Empowerment and the Work Place

Advocates of empowerment have devoted most of their attention to its impact on the work place. They point to the greater profitability of democratic work places as compared to more authoritarian work settings, where they claim alienation prevails. In addition, the proponents of empowerment point to the human advantages of giving workers and clients a voice in managing their lives. They spend less time, however, discussing the ways in which the practical circumstances of work may in the long run undermine the achievement of the empowerment goal. An important reason for their lack of interest is that the empowerment movement is a limited reform effort that will not directly affect conditions in the general environment in which work occurs. Because these environmental conditions remain unchanged, they may give rise to worker and client problems that may affect implementation of empowerment.

Perhaps the most important environmental condition affecting empowered work places is the general economy, which largely determines an enterprise's profitability. Making a profit is important in most empowered work settings—whether they are socialist factories in Yugoslavia or factories, offices, and professional practices in capitalist nations. Although the literature on empowerment indicates that many enterprises can simultaneously achieve profits and egalitarian relationships, in the long run that may not be possible. The empowerment of clients, for example, is likely to result in professionals having to spend greater time with each client, and unless clients are willing to pay for the additional time, the professional is unlikely to find empowerment to be financially advantageous. It is, in other words, easier to process cases than it is to explain carefully to each client all of the nuances of his or her problem and the options.

In a similar way the empowerment goal may be undermined in factories, where managers tend to be responsible for gathering information about market demands, competitors' plans, and options available to the firm's policy makers. The information is an important source of knowledge which managers may monopolize in order to increase their bargaining power with workers. Even if managers are fully committed to empowerment, however, their specialized knowledge is a problem, because the information they receive may be highly technical and of little interest to workers. One solution to this problem is to elect a special council of workers to deal with the technical and day-to-day issues of management. This solution has been adopted in Yugoslavian factories and a number of other empowered enterprises, such as the worker-owned Sunset Scavenger Company (a garbage collection company) in San Francisco (Perry, 1978). An important consequence of this redefinition of empowerment is that the general membership of the enterprise is often transformed into a body similar to stockholders, who are dependent on managers and their representatives to present the company's situation fairly and conscientiously to them so that they can make informed choices. The job of seeing that workers have necessary information becomes increasingly difficult as workers decrease their involvement in the day-to-day management of the enterprise and as the enterprise becomes more complicated.

In the early years of the Sunset Scavenger Company, for example, worker control was easily achieved, because workers and managers shared a similar level of knowledge about how to run the business. Indeed, each of the men who collected garbage was also responsible for collecting payment for the company's services. In recent years, however, the knowledge gap between workers and managers has widened as the company has expanded to become a conglomerate with investments in several garbage collection companies, two equipment leasing companies, a property development company, a computer service firm, a demolition company, two debris box companies, and other business ventures (Perry, 1978). In addition, the process of collecting garbage has become more complicated as environmental concerns have risen in importance, new trucks and other equipment have been purchased, attempts to recycle some refuse have been undertaken, and a computerized billing procedure has been developed to replace worker responsibility for bill collection. Each of these changes has increased the dependence of workers on management to collect and disseminate accurate and complete information about the company's operations and the options that they have in making general policy.

One outcome of the growth of the Sunset Scavenger Company, then, is that workers, despite their continued ownership of the company, have lost much of their control over it. Similar problems are apparent in the Yugoslavian factory, where the director, who is supposed to be subordinate to the workers, is emerging as the dominant figure because of his access to information about the factory's environment (Adizes, 1971; Kolaja, 1965; Wachtel, 1973). As with the Sunset Scavenger Company, a major reason for the rise of the director has been the emphasis on profits over full worker equality and control. Whatever the reason, an important problem facing the founders of many empowerment programs is their tendency to become elitist oligarchies, which undermines the goal of empowerment even when they have the blessing of the membership (Michels, 1915; Piven and Cloward, 1977). One response to this tendency may be the development of special interest groups—such as the work branches in some contemporary kibbutzim (see chapter seven)—which emphasize the problems and desires of a few workers, not those of the entire enterprise.

Empowerment is also unlikely to eliminate all of the sources of uncertainty found in modern offices and factories. The fact that the economic position of an enterprise may change drastically during any year based on consumer demand or the decisions of government officials about tax, energy, or environmental policies indicates the extent to which much of the uncertainty found in modern factories and offices is related to conditions in the general society. Simply because a company has initiated a policy of promoting secretaries does not mean that these external sources of uncertainty will disappear. Even within the work place empowerment is not likely to eliminate all sources of uncertainty. No matter how well-intentioned the rule makers may be, it is not possible to write evaluation and promotion rules that are so specific that they are totally objective. Even within empowered work places, evaluation and promotion involve decisions made by individuals and committees—decisions based on value judgments and information that workers do not know or cannot control. Thus, although the uncertainties and political relations of empowered work places may be different from those in other settings, they are still present. For this reason, those who wish to be promoted and even those who simply want to protect themselves from attack are likely to develop strategies and practices that reduce uncertainty. Some of those strategies may work to the advantage of one member or a few members at the expense of the advancement of others.

In sum, the practical circumstances of work are more complicated than many proponents of empowerment allow. Because work is a means of making a living, workers must balance this desire against other desires, such as power and equality. Although it is true that some workers are willing to accept a smaller income in exchange for more power and greater equality, social and economic uncertainty makes it difficult to implement that ideal. Workers often feel that their best protection against economic uncertainty is growth and diversification of the enterprise—a policy likely to threaten their desires for power and equality.

Besides workers, the government, competitors, and others may also encourage growth. The Sunset Scavenger Company, for example, has grown in part because of government policies encouraging the development of new methods of dealing with garbage and because of legal and social pressures created by environmentalist and community groups in the San Francisco area. In dealing with these pressures, the managers of the Sunset Scavenger Company have had to hire experts and other specialists who have little in common with the workers who own the company. Similar pressures exist in the empowered factories of Yugoslavia, where the factory's profits are the major source of income for workers and where factory managers are accountable to community leaders; in empowered offices, where promotion remains the most important goal; and in empowered professional practices, where professional income is largely based on service to clients. Because the empowerment movement is based on reform and not revolution, then, its impact will be limited by the practical circumstances of modern work and life that have been left untouched by the movement.

Empowerment and Society

Although proponents of the movement have paid more attention to the consequences of empowerment for the work place than for the larger society, the latter are also important. A significant and desirable consequence is that the empowerment of workers is a major step in the achievement of greater equality and democracy in modern societies. Indeed, it is difficult to imagine a truly democratic way of life in which workers must spend eight or more hours per day in monotonous work under authoritarian supervisors. There are, however, other consequences of empowerment that also deserve mention. One of the most important is the impact of the movement on labor unions.

In Yugoslavia the labor unions have become insignificant institutions. Although they represent worker interests in dealing with management, management is also employed by the workers, and the workers make the final decisions about their pay; consequently, the relationship between management and the unions is not taken very seriously. A similarly difficult situation faces union officials in other countries and industries where empowerment is occurring. There is clearly a place for union bargaining within some forms of empowerment, such as West German codetermination plan and programs of empowerment based on autonomous work groups, but conventional unions are clearly irrelevant in worker-owned and operated enterprises. Even in programs that have a place for unions, the relationship between union and management may be changed. In particular, workers who have control over their work are likely to bring a wider range of concerns to the bargaining table, because they now have an interest in many areas that were previously considered the exclusive province of management. Thus, an important consequence of the empowerment movement is the expansion of union-management negotiations beyond the limited area of wages and fringe benefits.

The empowerment movement may also affect the relationship between government and workers and/or clients. In the past, for example, the U.S. government has been concerned primarily with protecting workers from management abuses, such as attempts to tamper with union elections, to pay less than the minimum wage, or to force people to work in unsafe surroundings. With the exception of a few programs to help people start small businesses, the government has devoted little attention to helping workers buy and operate their own enterprises. This situation is changing as more and more advocates of empowerment are lobbying and cooperating with state and national politicians to write new legislation that makes it easier for workers to buy out their employers. Advocates of empowerment are also attempting to change government policies involving the rights of clients in dealing with professionals and human service institutions and the rights of low-level workers in dealing with their bosses. Although less dramatic than programs facilitating worker ownership and control, laws and regulations have been passed that require professionals and bosses to justify actions which restrict the freedom of clients and keep low-level employees from advancement. Put differently, the person who can legally demand a hearing before being committed to a mental hospital and the secretary who has legal recourse in dealing with the sexual advances and threats of her boss or the overt sexism in a company's hiring and promotion policies are also empowered through government action.

At the same time that some segments of government support empowerment, others oppose some parts of it. Indeed, one of the ironies of empowerment is that much of the conflict over the rights of workers and clients is centered in disputes between government agencies representing differing interest groups. For example, an attorney in the public defender's office may go to court to stop the county welfare department from committing a welfare recipient to a state hospital. Out of these conflicts will emerge new legal definitions of the rights of workers, clients, bosses, and professionals, and for this reason government officials will be key actors in defining the meaning of empowerment in the future.

While it is true that empowerment has many important implications for modern society, it should also be noted that the movement is not a panacea for all social ills. Empowered enterprises are as likely to abuse the public interest as are conventional enterprises. Worker owned factories, for example, can pollute the environment as effectively as other factories, and as long as it is in their best interests, they are likely to do so. There is also little reason to believe that women and other minorities who rise to high-level positions in corporations, universities, and similar institutions will be any more public spirited than their white, male predecessors, other conditions remaining the same. Finally, there is little reason to believe that empowered clients seeking solutions to their problems will put the general public good above their short-run self-interests; indeed, if the past is an indication of future developments, it is likely that many empowered clients will encourage professionals to use ethically dubious, if not illegal, means to solve their problems.

The point is that empowerment is not likely to result in a world where self-interests are suddenly subordinated to the greater public good. Rather, programs of empowerment are important because they offer new settings within which workers, bosses, clients, and professionals can achieve their varying goals. The future of the movement and the meaning of empowerment ultimately will be shaped by compromises as people deal with each other. For this reason, the full implications of the empowerment movement for the general society cannot be fully anticipated.

Empowerment and the Individual

The empowerment movement will also have direct consequences for the individual. Ideally, empowerment makes it possible for workers and clients to have a greater voice in determining their fates. Whether or not this outcome is achieved, it is apparent that empowerment involves a number of other consequences. Most obviously, empowerment requires that workers and clients give more freely of their time and attention than they have in the past. No longer is it possible for a client to turn his or her case over to an attorney or another professional and pursue other activities while awaiting the outcome; rather, the empowered client must be involved in all of the major events affecting his or her case. Similarly, empowered workers are likely to find that much of their time is taken up with meetings and other events which have little to do with their actual work; indeed, they may not even be paid for these responsibilities. Put differently, empowerment involves costs and benefits, and an important problem facing empowered clients and workers is finding a balance of costs and benefits that is personally acceptable.

Juggling the responsibilities of work and family may become particularly problematic. Although tedious work in authoritarian settings takes its toll on workers and their families, it is still possible for many workers to separate much of their work from their family lives (Gans, 1962; Wrobel, 1979). The result is a worker who lives in two worlds in which work is something one does to make a living in order to pay for the more meaningful activities and relationships found outside work. Advocates of empowerment challenge this division by attempting to make work so meaningful that people need not try to separate it from other aspects of their lives. If programs of empowerment are successful, then work will absorb more time and energy—time and energy that may have been devoted to the family in the past. For some workers, the result may be similar to the situations of some highly ambitious managers and professionals who so emphasize their careers that family members must compete for their attention (Kanter, 1977b). A more likely outcome is that old family expectations and obligations will have to be redefined, because work activities and relationships can no longer be left at the office or factory at the end of the day. In this less dramatic way, work will intrude upon the family; the worker's time and attention will have to be rationed to some degree.

One reason that the balance between family and work may change with empowerment is that the movement attempts to extend the notion of having a career to low-level workers. By creating autonomous work teams, short-term work groups, workers' councils, and career reviews, empowerment programs are designed to make it possible for workers to achieve more responsible and challenging work. Looked at this way, empowerment is partly an attempt to introduce many of the concerns of professionalism into the work lives of nonprofessionals. As with professionals, the careers of empowered workers may become institutionalized channels for achieving personal distinctions not possible in the past. But these new career opportunities also may encourage the development of an elite segment of workers aligned with management in the pursuit of policies which may or may not be in the best interests of other workers. In this way, old work-related communities may be broken up and new ones built. Just as in the work-related communities of professionals, it is likely that upwardly mobile factory workers, secretaries, and sanitation workers will justify their personal gains by pointing to the benefits they have created for others. Research in the Yugoslavian factory and the Sunset Scavenger Company indicates that the contributions of empowered workers there have mixed benefits: although they have often helped to improve the incomes and prestige of other workers, they also have pursued policies which have made the workers increasingly dependent on others in making decisions and exercising power. They have, in other words, reduced the level of democracy in the work place.

The Limits of Empowerment

Although the approach to empowerment taken in this section is skeptical about many of the claims made by its advocates, the purpose behind it has not been to reject the movement out of hand. To do so would be to ignore the humanistic concerns and contributions of the sponsors of many empowerment programs. At the same time, it is important to recognize the practical limits of any attempt to reform work. Those limits are too often glossed over by reformers who are caught up in their enthusiasm for the movement's promise of change. The most general and important limit that the movement fails to see is that human beings are not predictable, controllable, or simple; rather, they are pragmatic and opportunistic creatures who assess situations based on both self-interest and altruistic considerations which cannot be fully anticipated by planners. For this reason, some workers will use empowerment programs to improve their positions in the work place, others will unenthusiastically go along with them, and still others will resist them because they perceive the costs as too great. Although the proponents of empowerment are likely to condemn the last group and may even attempt to change that group's direction, a better approach is to recognize that empowerment is an emerging reality that reflects the preferences and interpretations of some workers and clients and violates those of others.

It is unlikely, however, that this more tolerant and pluralistic view will be taken seriously until empowerment advocates begin to look systematically at the varying consequences that empowerment programs have for the lives of workers, clients, managers, professionals and other groups. Only from such studies can we begin to develop an understanding of what can be expected realistically from such reform efforts. Too often persons seeking to reform work begin with unrealistic hopes and, when they are not fully achieved, overreact by ignoring the more limited but important contributions of the reform movement. We have tried to point to some areas in which systematic investigation of empowerment programs might develop a better, more realistic understanding of the movement's potential.

CONCLUSION

Empowerment is a social movement that is having a far-reaching impact on modern work. Its importance is reflected in both the number and types of work affected by it and the variety of countries in which it is found. Empowerment is also important for the lives of workers and clients, because the successful implementation of empowerment programs will undermine many present-day work-related communities formed on the basis of divisions of knowledge and interest separating workers, managers, clients, and professionals. In its ideal form, the empowerment movement promises to replace these old work-related communities with new ones in which equality and cooperation prevail. In practice, the work-related communities that emerge will still be divided and may even breed hostility and suspicion. One reason is that people are affected by and interpret empowerment in different ways, and the differences are used to create differing work-related communities in empowered work settings. Equally important is the fact that human beings seldom stress only general values and goals in their everyday lives; rather, they encounter their work and the other features of their everyday lives as practical problems which require immediate solutions. The solutions often encourage the development of diverse work-related communities which the formulators of the empowerment program did not anticipate or intend. Whatever the consequences of empowerment for specific work places, however, the movement undoubtedly will be important in organizing and giving work meaning in the future.

Chapter Nine

THE SOCIAL ORGANIZATION OF MODERN WORK

Work is a fact of life because most people must devote a significant part of their lives to making their livings. However, not everyone experiences work in the same way, since it can be organized and interpreted differently. The many settings within which work occurs account for the diverse meanings associated with it. The Mundurucú man who works sporadically by hunting and helping his wife clear the land for gardens may share a similar cultural heritage with the man who spends every day collecting rubber from his trees, but how each uses that cultural heritage to make sense out of his work varies with the practical circumstances of the work. A Mundurucú man would find it difficult to sustain an image of himself as a fearless headhunter, for example, when hunting of any kind no longer matters.

More generally, time and space are basic features of work situations, because the flow of human activity and the communities within which it occurs form the framework for building social reality. When major changes occur in either, the meaning of work will be reexamined and probably changed. Consider again the Mundurucú, whose old way of life based on hunting and gardening is being replaced by a new way of life in which rubber collecting is central. Time has changed for the men, since work is more continuous, and space has changed as well now that they work with their wives and other members of the nuclear family rather than alone. New social realities are emerging based on these changing circumstances—circumstances which discourage maintenance of the old ideas and relationships which prevailed in a world of sporadic labor, extreme sexual segregation, and group work.

The social realities associated with modern work are even more varied than they are among the Mundurucú, because the timing of life and the communities within which people give meaning to their lives are more diverse in modern societies. The forms of work considered in this book attest to this fact; indeed, diversity is sometimes poignantly reflected in the landscapes of everyday life, as when a factory dwarfs a peasant village or when a solitary novelty hunter sells his or her wares in front of a large bank. But large differences are found not only among diverse categories of work but within the same category. In the category of countercultural work, for example, great differences exist between the world views of such groups as the Hutterites, the hippies, and the Symbionese Liberation Army. Just as important are the less dramatic differences among workers of the same category. Thus, the factory worker who ends a shift by driving to a distant suburb made up of persons with little in common other than their residences and general income levels, experiences work quite differently from the factory worker who goes home to a peasant village or to an urban neighborhood filled with friends and relatives who share an ethnic and a neighborhood identity. Similarly, the unmarried professional who actively pursues a career experiences his or her work differently from someone who works to supplement the family income or who is the sole support of the family. Finally, the young housewife who must care for several small children within the limited income of her husband experiences her work differently from the middle-aged housewife who has no children at home and whose husband is in his peak earning years.

In each of these examples the actual work of the individuals may be the same, but the meaning of the work varies because of the ways in which it is interpreted. These interpretations are based partly on the relationships that develop at work, and partly on relationships found in the family, neighborhood, or other settings outside the work place. Indeed, an important problem for many workers is balancing the varying and sometimes contradictory demands of persons inside and outside the work place. For this reason, the meaning of work for the individual may change over time as new relationships and expectations are created at work and outside it. Such a change is most apparent at eventful times in people's lives, such as marriage or the birth of a child. It is then that individuals often reassess desires and expectations about work. Thus, old work goals may be redefined as unrealistic dreams which must be abandoned, or a past casual attitude toward work may be replaced by a serious concern for advancement. In less conscious and more subtle ways, individuals continually redefine the meaning of work during less dramatic times in their lives. The worker who has in the past attempted to separate work and family may find, for example, that this distinction is increasingly difficult to maintain as he or she achieves success and gains new work responsibilities. Indeed, this change may occur so gradually that it goes unrecognized by the worker and his or her family until it reaches dramatic proportions.

In sum, work is a human activity that is inseparable from all the other activities and relationships that make up a way of life. It cannot be neatly separated from family, neighborhood, religion, recreation, education, and the many other aspects of modern life. Indeed, a major problem with many of the myths associated with modern work is their tendency to treat work as a distinct area of human activity. When this is done, it becomes easy to describe in a simplistic way all peasants as slaves to tradition, all factory workers as alienated, or all housewives as unfulfilled. Such explanations ignore the symbolic meanings workers can give to even the simplest and most routine tasks. An adequate explanation of modern work, then, must be based on the study of how work is given meaning in the diverse settings of everyday life. One purpose of this book has been to point to some of these settings and the forms of work associated with them.

A second purpose of the book has been to point to some of the ways in which work is given institutional meaning in modern society. Institutional definitions are general public statements about the nature of work and workers. Because they are general statements, institutional definitions are oversimplifications of the multifaceted and contradictory experiences of everyday life, and for this reason earlier chapters treated them as myths. But institutional definitions are also public statements which may be used to make moral evaluations of work and workers; indeed, implicit in each of the myths considered here is a set of value judgments about work and workers. Looked at this way, both the scientific manager who defines workers exclusively in terms of rational criteria, such as money and fatigue, and the proponent of empowerment who claims that all workers really wish to have power over their lives are making value judgments about the "essence" of work and workers. Similar value judgments are apparent in popular statements about housewives and housework, the poor and hustling work, and professional careers and self-actualization. The organizing myths of countercultural groups also contains definitions of the essence of proper work.

The value judgments which underlie institutional definitions are important because they may be used to justify work-related policies that become self-fulfilling prophecies. The scientific managers' practice of breaking down each job into a series of simple, routine tasks, for example, is based on their assumption that workers view their jobs as nothing more than ways of making a living. Consequently, the assignment of tedious work and payment by the piece-rate method are thought of as justified. This assumption may become a self-fulfilling prophecy when the advocates of scientific management so transform the work place that other, nonmonetary rewards are made scarce. Such work situations encourage the worker to adopt a calculating attitude toward work and to treat it primarily as a means to a living. Although based on different assumptions, other institutional definitions—of housework, low-level office work, and the role of the poor—also give rise to self-fulfilling prophecies. In each case, the institutional definitions justify policies which encourage housewives to seek nonmonetary rewards in their work, discourage low-level workers from aggressively seeking advancement, and encourage "work inhibition" among the poor.

Institutional definitions, then, are important in explaining and justifying features of modern work and workers and in creating the conditions which encourage workers to act in predictable ways. But human behavior is not a simple consequence of institutional definitions or the social conditions related to them; it is also motivated by the interpretations of individuals—interpretations which may be contrary to institutional definitions. Well before the empowerment movement, for example, there were low-level office workers who aggressively sought advancement and industrial workers who retarded the implementation of scientific management programs by their resistance. For this reason, the relationship between institutional definitions of work and workers and the conditions of everyday life is always problematic to some degree. Indeed, academic researchers, managers, and others who create institutional definitions spend a great deal of their time and energy attempting to reconcile the differences between their statements and the observable events of everyday life. Sometimes the reconciliation results in a modification of the institutional definitions; for example, the academic advocates of empowerment have concluded that widely accepted scientific management principles actually reduce productivity and must be replaced.

The tension between institutional definitions and the circumstances of everyday life is never fully resolvable. The reason is that institutional definitions are general statements which contain a set of value judgments that oversimplify the complex and contradictory nature of modern work and workers. Everyday life, on the other hand, occurs within concrete situations that are unique; that uniqueness springs from the diverse interpretations and interests that the participants bring to each situation. A third purpose of this book, then, has been to point to the uneasy coexistence of institutional definitions and the social realities of everyday life. On the one hand, institutional definitions give rise to policies which affect the everyday lives of workers, and they may even act as self-fulfilling prophecies by encouraging workers to respond in predictable ways. On the other hand, workers may create new institutional definitions by reinterpreting their work in light of the ways they experience it.

The vitality—indeed the very "essence"—of modern work is found in the continuing efforts of workers to deal with the practical circumstances of their everyday lives and the attempts of others to explain and give direction to the interpretations and actions of workers. It is for this reason that a historical approach is important: it provides a broad framework for seeing the diverse and often contradictory ways in which work is given meaning in modern society and the way those meanings change over time. Only by taking such an approach can researchers see that work is not just a way of making a living but a means by which human beings give personal and symbolic meaning to their lives.

This chapter continues the discussion of these two features of modern work but the issues considered here are broader. Our purpose here is to go beyond the specific forms of work considered in each of the chapters and to come to some general conclusions about modern work and workers. We will begin by considering how work opportunities are distributed in modern society and the consequences for workers' attempts to make a living. The discussion that follows will concentrate on the modern need to work—a need that is only partly related to physical survival. Central to this discussion is the belief that work is complex and cannot be fully understood without considering the many dilemmas workers face.

THE NATURE OF MODERN LABOR MARKETS

When the problem of work opportunities is raised, it is usually discussed within the context of the labor market, because government officials, business leaders, academics, and others concerned with the problem typically treat workers as commodities like automobiles, meat, and houses that are bought and sold in the marketplace. That does not mean that labor specialists are uncaring people who ignore the human problems of work and unemployment; rather, they simply accept the prevailing assumption that the marketplace for human workers operates on the same principles as other markets. Thus, the solution to the current employment problem requires that such basic issues as the supply and demand of different types of workers be considered apart from the personal feelings and problems of workers. Using this assumption, modern governments generate an immense amount of data on work and workers, ranging from monthly unemployment figures to sophisticated projections of future work opportunities and needs.

Clearly some evaluation of the concept of "labor market" and its usefulness in understanding and dealing with modern workers is needed. We will begin that evaluation here by considering the assumptions and policy implications of orthodox economic theory as summarized in the work of David Gordon (1972) and Duane Leigh (1978). The more radical approach known as "segmented labor market theory" is also considered. Because of the problems associated with these approaches, we will conclude by discussing an alternative way of looking at work opportunities.

Orthodox Economic Theory

Basic to orthodox economic theory is the assumption that only one labor market exists in each modern society and everyone competes within that market. As a corollary, the same factors which account for the success of some also account for the failure of others. If, for example, affluent and prestigious workers are better educated than others, then one solution to the problems of the unemployed and *underemployed*—those who cannot support themselves with the jobs they have—is to give them education. Orthodox economic theorists also assume that the modern labor market operates in a perfectly competitive way so that the best qualified receive the best jobs, and they treat the issue of discrimination as largely irrelevant. Finally, they assume that workers are always rationally motivated and will therefore take advantage of opportunities to improve their work skills or to find better-paying jobs.

Based on these assumptions, orthodox economic theorists describe a world in which the opportunity for work, and the pay associated with it, is primarily determined by supply and demand. Workers who have skills that are in short supply and for which there is great demand, for example, have the best jobs, and those who have less competitive skills have poorer jobs. At the bottom of the labor market are all those who have skills that are in abundant supply and for which there is little demand. According to this explanation, the maid who works in a hotel and the person who works in a car wash are both paid low wages because their work skills are so simple that almost everyone in the society can do them and employers therefore do not have to pay higher wages to find workers. The ultimate outcome of this way of distributing workers, pay, and work opportunities is a state of equilibrium, or balance, in which the best interests of both individuals and the general public are achieved. The modern labor market is thus seen as an equitable way of arriving at a harmonious solution to the problem of work. In Gordon's words, "Everyone has a stake in maintaining the present arrangements . . . because everyone is ultimately better off" (Gordon, 1972: 33).

Changes in equilibrium resulting from competitive pressures in the labor market must be approached with great care, because they may be disruptive and hurt the poor and affluent alike. Despite these risks, it is possible to introduce change by making low-ranking workers more competitive. This can be done, for example, by supporting programs which provide public transportation from poor areas to areas where jobs are available, such as locales where a large number of factories or offices are concentrated. Most of the reforms associated with orthodox economic theory, however, deal more directly with the personal attributes of workers, because it is assumed that they will be able to find better jobs if only they can acquire the skills and values that are in demand in the marketplace. Thus, orthodox economic theory has been used to justify the creation of job training and rehabilitation programs, which presumably give workers useful skills and "good" attitudes toward work. Put differently, workers are treated as "human capital," and the job training and rehabilitation programs are forms of investment, similar to investments made in buildings and equipment. In both cases, the investment is intended to pay dividends in the future.

Unfortunately, the human capital investments of the orthodox economists have not always paid dividends. Income figures, for example, show that although the incomes of the poor have increased since World War II, the income gap between the poor and others has remained unchanged since 1940 (Gordon, 1972). Despite the well-intentioned suggestions of the orthodox economists, investment in human capital has thus not always been effective. One explanation often offered is that programs intended to help have been operated by unscrupulous people who have used the poor to make money while giving them little in return. Such programs are the contemporary counterparts of the workhouses of an earlier time, when the poor were also "rehabilitated" through idleness. But the programs of orthodox economists are plagued by more problems than the self-interested actions of a few people; indeed, the very assumptions they make about the modern world of work may impede the effectiveness of their programs. Three of the most important assumptions concern the nature of the poor, the availability of jobs, and the responses of institutional leaders to change (Gordon, 1972).

According to orthodox economists, the modern labor market is made up of three categories of persons—the employed, unemployed, and those not looking for jobs at all. They further assume that the employed are not a problem because their jobs provide an adequate income. The real problem lies with those people who are unemployed, and the solution is training for a job. A major limitation of this way of looking at the poor is that most poor people have jobs during at least some part of the year. Their poverty is based on underemployment, which results from the seasonal nature of much of their work or the inadequate wages they receive from full-time work. In other words, the problem stems less from permanent unemployment than from the cycle of work and being laid off prevalent in some industries and from the low wages paid waitresses, dishwashers, janitors, domestics, and others who work forty or more hours per week. Indeed, one of the ironies of job training programs is that they often train people for low-ranking jobs which offer them a future of continuing underemployment.

Even when training programs concentrate on giving workers skills that will lead to more secure and better-paying jobs, they are not able to change the distribution of good jobs in modern society. Contrary to the assumptions of orthodox economists, the problem of getting a good job is not solved by having the skills to do it or many years of experience. The applicant must also find a job that is open, which often poses a more difficult problem than acquiring the skills in the first place. In addition, employers, union officials, government officials, and other institutional leaders respond to the changing supply of workers rather than sitting passively by and maintaining their old policies, as the orthodox economists assume. One way of dealing with an increased supply of workers is to increase the educational or experience requirements associated with a job. Whether such a policy means that the employer now gets a more capable employee for the same money is uncertain, but it does reduce the number of people who can qualify for the job. In some industries the unions may also respond by voluntarily restricting their membership in order to control the supply of people who can be employed, even though the number of people with the relevant job skills may be quite large. Whatever the responses by institutional leaders, however, a critical weakness in the orthodox approach is the inability of theorists and policy makers to anticipate the results of their programs.

Segmented Labor Market Theory

Because the simplifying assumptions of orthodox economic theory lead to public policies that are often contradictory and ineffective, some economists, sociologists, and others interested in the nature of modern labor markets are advocating a new approach. The new theory, known as *segmented labor market theory*, rejects the orthodox economists' assumptions that there is only one labor market and that it operates based on pure competition (Edwards, Reich, and Gordon, 1975; Gordon, 1972; Kalleberg and Sørensen, 1979; Leigh, 1978; Montagna, 1977, 1979; O'Connor, 1973). Some of the advocates of this approach argue, for example, that the modern economy is made up of two major labor markets which operate on different principles (Bonacich, 1972, 1976; Doeringer and Piore, 1971; Harrison, 1972; Kerr, 1954; Piore, 1975). On the one hand, there is the *primary*, or *institutionalized, labor market*, which is made up of good-paying and secure jobs in which opportunities for advancement are available and workers are rewarded on the basis of relatively clear-cut evaluation criteria. The *secondary*, or *noninstitutionalized, labor market*, on the other hand, is made up of various low-paying and insecure jobs—jobs in which few avenues for advancement exist, the criteria for advancement are vague, if they are stated at all, and interruptions in the work schedule, such as layoffs, are common. Indeed, theorists argue that these two labor markets are so distinct that economic conditions encouraging great prosperity or depression in one labor market frequently have little impact on the other (Friedlander, 1972). It is possible, for example, for workers in the primary labor market to experience nearly unlimited opportunities for employment and advancement while workers in the secondary labor market are experiencing a depression in work opportunities. The reason is that few workers are able to move from one labor market to another to take advantage of the opportunities found there.

Other segmented labor market theorists describe an even more complex economic arrangement. Some claim that the modern economy is made up of three parts: a core, peripheral, and irregular sector (Bluestone, Murphy, and Stevenson, 1973; Ferman and Ferman, 1973). The *core* and *peripheral sectors* correspond with the primary and secondary labor markets identified by others, but in addition there is an *irregular sector* made up of the poor who work in marginal or sometimes deviant occupations. The local handyman who does general home and appliance repairs, the novelty hustler, and many drug pushers who work intermittently and run small-scale operations are all included in this sector. Each possesses work skills for which there is little demand outside the poor community, and for this reason each has limited access to the better-paying and more secure jobs in the peripheral and core sectors of the modern economy. If this division of the labor market is accepted, it is possible to describe different workers as experiencing different sets of work opportunities simultaneously. For example, workers in the core sector may be experiencing a great expansion in work opportunities while workers in the peripheral sector are experiencing no significant change and workers in the irregular sector are experiencing a depression.

There are still other segmented labor market theorists who argue that modern economies are made up of as many as sixteen different markets that are all somewhat distinct (Freedman with Maclachlan, 1976). Regardless of the number of markets identified, however, the theorists agree that each market operates on unique principles that make it difficult for low-ranking workers to move up. The reason is that modern labor markets are not based on pure competition; rather, they operate to discriminate against women, some ethnic and racial minorities, the young, the old, and others who have not received equal treatment historically or have been made superfluous by recent changes in technology. Labor market segmentation, then, stems partly from the past efforts of employers to encourage ethnic, sexual, and other forms of competition and antagonism among workers in order to better control them and to keep wages low, but the persistence of this arrangement goes deeper. It involves the ways in which some jobs have become monopolized by relatively small segments of the population, the relationship between the expectations associated with different jobs and the personal traits developed by persons holding those jobs, and the ways in which government policies are used to limit the work opportunities of some people.

The monopolization of good jobs arises because of the development of *job shelters*, which are institutionalized ways of protecting workers from full competition with others (Freedman with Maclachlan, 1976). Major examples of job shelters are licensing requirements, which limit the number of jobholders to those who can get licenses; civil service regulations, which protect the jobs of employees who have passed the probationary period; professional and other training schools, which may restrict enrollments in order to control the number of workers in a field; and labor union regulations, which may be used to restrict membership and access to unionized jobs. In each of these cases entry into a line of work depends on more than competition: it is also affected by the decisions of other persons who are seeking to control the number of eligible applicants in order to keep wages and job security high. In addition, job advancement is often made into a routine, bureaucratic process; for example, rules about seniority limit the degree to which promotion decisions may be based purely on the job performance of candidates.

Each of these features of sheltered work is absent from unsheltered jobs, where workers have little control over their work fates. There are few, if any, restrictions on who is eligible to apply for a job, and there are few rules protecting the jobholder from continuing competition from outsiders. There are also few rules protecting the worker during depressed periods, when he or she may be laid off for a time; rather, the worker is largely dependent on the good intentions of the employer, and since the small-scale enterprises in this sector of the economy are easily threatened by changing economic conditions, even the well-intentioned employer is limited in the job security that he or she can offer employees. Finally, workers in unsheltered jobs have few guarantees of promotion or other forms of job advancement. These are decisions made by employers and supervisors, who may utilize a variety of criteria in evaluating and promoting workers. Often getting along with the employer or supervisor is as important as job performance in making promotion decisions. Moreover, employers and supervisors are often limited in the opportunities for advancement they can offer employees. Thus, a clerk in a small, corner drugstore may be very dependable and competent but it is difficult to promote that person when the entire work force consists of the employer and the clerk.

The problems of unsheltered workers, then, are not simply the result of the greedy actions of owners and supervisors, for they are related to the way in which the modern economy is organized in segments that operate on different principles. Those persons who have sheltered jobs in the primary sector of the economy work in the best world, since they have greater control over their fates and the enterprises that they work in tend to be larger and offer greater opportunities for advancement. An obvious conclusion is that all workers should seek sheltered jobs in the primary sector of the economy. Workers' ability to do that, however, is limited by the institutional restrictions surrounding sheltered jobs, the discriminatory practices of some schools, unions, and employers, and the number of jobs available in the primary sector. In addition, the ability of workers to move from unsheltered to sheltered jobs is limited by the ways in which work expectations and experiences affect the job histories and personal traits of workers (Gordon, 1972). Put differently, persons who have held unsheltered jobs for several years are unlikely to be seen as desirable candidates for even those sheltered jobs that are open.

Employers in the primary sector want dependable workers who will keep their jobs for many years. Consequently, they look for a stable work history in evaluating job candidates. It is difficult for many workers in the secondary labor market to have stable work histories because their jobs are often short term or cyclical. Thus, they may work at several different jobs during the course of a year and then repeat the cycle the next year. Equally important is the fact that there are few rewards associated with steady employment in the secondary labor market. Not many employers can offer advancement, for example, and so the worker who wants to increase his or her salary or level of responsibility must seek a different job continually. Unlike the ambitious executive who seeks advancement by becoming adept at the politics of a single corporation, the ambitious worker in the secondary labor market must adopt a strategy which gives the impression of an unstable work history, because the operating principles of this sector of the economy are different from those in the primary sector.

In addition, moving from unsheltered to sheltered jobs is complicated by the personal traits workers develop because of their work (Gordon, 1972). The most important traits for workers in the primary market are dependability, an ability to work without supervision, an aggressive or self-assertive style, and an ability to deal with abstract issues. The jobs which make up the secondary labor market offer few opportunities for developing these traits. Dependability is desirable, but many employers recognize that they cannot offer their workers sufficient pay and job security to demand dependability. Thus, the undependable worker is as likely to be rewarded in the secondary labor market as the dependable one. Similarly, independence, assertiveness, and abstraction are traits that are discouraged in jobs where workers are often closely supervised, must be subservient to the employer or supervisor, and spend their time doing simple, routine tasks. Thus, the worker's problem of moving from the secondary to the primary labor market is not a simple matter of having a stable job history: the problem is complex, subtle, and filled with irony.

One of the most notable ironies is the way in which government policies, which are often intended to improve the economic circumstances of poor workers, help maintain segmented labor markets. An obvious example is the creation of public schools, which presumably exist to improve the opportunities of all children but which often operate to give the poor inadequate instruction and channel them into programs that lead to jobs in the secondary labor market. The government also contributes to the problem by establishing programs designed to train workers while ignoring the lack of good jobs in the economy, the ways in which civil service, licensing, unionization, and professional training exclude persons from good jobs, and the many problems of enterprises in the secondary sector of the economy where poor workers are concentrated. So long as these conditions persist, worker training will be meaningless. Finally, government welfare policies requiring welfare recipients to take low-paying and short-term jobs help to maintain segmented labor markets by making it unnecessary for employers to reorganize their work so that greater pay and job security are offered.

The world of work described by segmented labor market theorists is thus much different from the world described by orthodox economists. It is a world in which few good jobs exist, competition for those jobs is limited to a few workers, persons must develop strategies of survival that undermine their efforts to move up, and government policies designed to improve the situation often perpetuate old problems. Each of these facts of modern life must be addressed if the problem of underemployment and inadequate job opportunities is to be solved. For some segmented labor market theorists, the solution is the total destruction of the existing economic organization and the construction of a new one based on principles of equality. Others are less radical in their prescriptions, but they too point to the need for fundamental reforms in the economy so that all workers, not just a privileged elite, can enjoy interesting, well-paying, and secure jobs. Whatever the specific program, however, segmented labor market theorists reject the orthodox view that the modern economy is the most equitable and effective way of distributing work opportunities.

An Alternative Theory

Of the two theories of modern labor markets considered here, the most comprehensive is clearly segmented labor market theory. Advocates of this theory take greater account of the diverse social realities found in the everyday lives of modern workers. They recognize, for example, that there are a variety of ways in which modern work is organized and that the situations of different types of workers are not comparable. Contrary to the claims of the orthodox economists, the work situations of the aged street hustler and the president of a major bank cannot be fully understood through a supply-and-demand analysis. The segmented labor market theorists also recognize that what government, business, professional, and union leaders say about the world and the ways in which they act are often quite different. Indeed, while they use the rhetoric of competition, these people often advocate policies that encourage monopolization. They create opportunities for some and limit them for others, and the outcome of this process cannot be explained away as a harmonious equilibrium in which the best interests of each person and of society as a whole are taken into account. Finally, segmented labor market theorists recognize that work has an influence on the characteristics of individuals and that those characteristics may be important in shaping the individuals' future opportunities. We cannot, in other words, understand the problem of inadequate job opportunites by looking only at supply-and-demand curves.

At the same time that segmented labor market theorists take us beyond the ivory tower world of orthodox economics, they stop short of fully considering the diverse nature of modern work. If they had begun by looking at the everyday lives of modern workers, they would have seen that the experiences of modern workers cannot be adequately captured in two or three categories. It may be true that the Irish Tinkers and persons working in small businesses may do low-paying and insecure work, for example, but the circumstances surrounding those forms of work and the meanings the workers give to their low pay and insecurity are quite different. For the employee in a small business those factors may be sources of shame, whereas the Irish Tinker sees them as signs of independence and therefore feels proud. Thus, the segmented labor market theorists also oversimplify the diverse social realities of modern work by reducing all work experiences to a few variables, such as level of income and job security.

A more comprehensive approach to understanding how work opportunities are distributed in modern society is to begin by looking at concrete work situations and worker interpretations of them. When that is done, it becomes apparent that the characteristics associated with different labor markets and workers are not so easily classified as economic theorists indicate. Segmented labor market theorists argue, for example, that workers in the primary labor market are rewarded for being independent, assertive, dependable, and able to deal with abstract ideas. But a look at work settings in that market shows that many jobs there do not reward those traits; rather, much of the work there involves quite routine tasks and gives workers little chance to display independence, assertiveness, or abstraction. Indeed, in some work places a key to success is creating the appearance of independence and assertiveness while not really taking any chances (Kanter, 1977a). In a similar way, many of the dependable, independent, assertive, and abstract qualities of workers in the secondary labor market are overlooked, because workers there are assumed to be involved in undemanding jobs. In failing to take account of such contradictions the segmented labor market theorists have committed the error of accepting common-sense claims at face value rather than attempting to understand them and their consequences.

An alternative to orthodox economic and segmented labor market theory, then, must begin with detailed descriptions of the ways in which different workers encounter opportunities for work. When this approach is taken, it becomes apparent that the amount and type of knowledge an individual possesses about work opportunities are limited by the mundane circumstances of everyday life. Thus, the fact that a large number of confidence operators come from the state of Indiana can be explained in part by the work circumstances of that state. Historically circuses have wintered there, and since confidence operators have often traveled with circuses, persons living in Indiana have been more likely to learn the trade and be given a chance to practice it than persons in other states (Maurer, 1974). In a similar way, other people in modern society encounter some work opportunities and find that they have little access to others. Some of the work opportunities may be classified roughly as jobs in the primary sector and others in the secondary sector, but however broadly classified by academics and government officials, they are interpreted by individuals within the contexts of their everyday lives. For this reason, the work histories of individuals cannot be understood as the consequence of government policies, job shelters, and labor market processes alone.

Many women who become strippers, for example, have previously worked as actresses, cocktail waitresses, go-go dancers, hatcheck girls, or in similar entertainment-related jobs. They generally take up stripping when they face a major financial crisis in their lives, such as a divorce, which makes them the sole provider for the family, or a show closing, which leaves them with no money to get home (Miller, 1978). Looked at one way, the decision to become a stripper is a simple consequence of a woman's need for money, because stripping is a better paying job than the others which are available. The problem with this conclusion is that it ignores all of those women who face similar problems but deal with them differently. Some women who need money choose to deal with it by accepting an offer of marriage and becoming a housewife, while others seek better-paying (nonstripping) jobs or part-time work to supplement their main source of income. Whatever decision a woman makes, it cannot be understood as the sole result of an "objective" calculation of the costs and benefits of each option. The decision will be made based on those considerations, the influence of friends and family, the value judgments the woman makes, and the consequences of each option for her life style.

In a similar way, others make work decisions based on a variety of considerations. Some young men and women turn down better-paying work opportunities outside their neighborhoods because they want to be near their families and friends, while others choose to leave a good-paying and secure job with the family business and take work that is less prestigious, secure, and financially rewarding because it is more interesting or satisfying. In addition, decisions are made about college majors and careers based on a few courses or instructors that the individual finds interesting or exciting, even though the content of the courses may have little to do with the type of work that a graduate in that field is likely to do.

The point is that although academic researchers, government officials, and others may find it helpful to reduce the world of work to a labor market approach in which human beings are assumed to be calculating actors seeking to improve their work situations, a closer look at everyday life indicates that their focus is only part of the story. Work is a way of making a living, but it may be interpreted as more than this. It may be seen as a means of transcending this world and entering a better, more spiritual one, as a source of creativity and individual expression, as a way of providing service to others, or as a mode of creating meaningful relations with others. Public policies which are directed only at the "labor market" aspect of the work world and ignore the full relationship between the work opportunities of workers and the way in which workers and others interpret them are likely to fail, because they oversimplify human motives. Put differently, we may recognize that our labor is bought and sold in the labor market, much as other commodities are bought and sold, but human beings cannot be equated with washing machines. At the same time that we recognize that we sell our labor and that some workers have more job security and greater incomes than others, we also frequently ask for more than job security and an income in return; indeed, we are sometimes willing to trade a certain degree of job security and income for other work-related goals.

A full understanding of modern work, then, must include a consideration of both the distribution of work opportunities in modern society and the experience of those opportunities in everyday life. How people experience work depends on how they define their needs and wants, because work is an important way in which wants are satisfied.

WORK AND THE SATISFACTION OF HUMAN NEEDS AND WANTS

Although in theory it is possible to distinguish between human needs (or those materials and experiences that are necessary for a way of life) and human wants (or those materials and experiences that are deemed desirable but not absolutely necessary), in practice they are difficult to separate, because our conceptions of what is necessary or just desirable change over time and even from situation to situation. An example of the meshing of needs and wants is found in the description by William H. Whyte, Jr. (1956) of inconspicuous consumption in a Chicago suburb, where the value of economic equality was stressed. That value was not always easy to achieve in practice, however, because clear differences in income developed as some residents advanced in the corporate hierarchy faster than others and could therefore afford to buy more household items. The solution which emerged was a general emphasis on *inconspicuous consumption*; that is, those families that could afford more household items were discouraged from "showing off" their wealth. Some items were treated as luxuries which were desirable but not a necessary part of a proper household. As the incomes of other families rose, however, a curious change in interpretation took place, because many of the old luxuries suddenly became affordable to all. The result was that the old luxuries were slowly and subtly transformed into necessary parts of a fully equipped and proper household, and those families which could not afford or refused to buy the necessary items were subjected to the same gossip and bewildered looks by neighbors as those who were too "showy" with their luxuries.

In much the same way the distinction between human needs and wants is continually defined and redefined in other groups and situations. In hunting and gathering societies, for example, human needs are usually few in number; sufficient food, adequate clothing and shelter, sex, and perhaps access to some type of alcohol or other drug are considered sufficient. The practical limitations of hunting and gathering life encourage this definition of human need, for it is impossible for people to store large amounts of food and other perishable materials and sell it in order to become wealthy. The nomadic life style of many hunting and gathering societies also encourages it, for the hoarder and the wealthy are punished when they must move more goods than others. Finally, the limited definition of need found in such societies is related to the small size of groups and the close ties among members, because those who hoard must do so at the expense of friends and relatives.

Each of these practical circumstances of everyday life encourages the sharing of food and the other resources needed for life, and for this reason the amount of wealth enjoyed by members of hunting and gathering societies is relatively equal. It is this feature of hunting and gathering societies that has led one noted anthropologist to conclude the following:

> The world's most primitive people have few possessions, *but they are not poor*. Poverty is not a certain small amount of goods, nor is it just a relation between means and ends; above all it is a relation between people. Poverty is a social status. As such it is the invention of civilization (Sahlins, 1972: 37–38).

In part, poverty is a unique condition of civilization or modern society, because the conditions of modern life make it feasible for persons to hoard and obtain great wealth without placing themselves or their friends and relatives at a disadvantage. Poverty exists in modern society, then, because of the great inequalities of wealth that characterize it. But that is only part of the story. In addition to being characterized by great discrepancies in wealth, modern societies are also notable for a variety of definitions of human need—definitions that go well beyond acquiring minimally adequate levels of food, clothing, shelter, sex, and recreation. Indeed, Marshall Sahlins argues that one of the great ironies of human history and cultural development is that as the means for meeting the basic needs of human beings have become more sophisticated and the direct threat of starvation due to natural circumstances has decreased, we have "erected a shrine to the Unattainable: *Infinite Needs*" (Sahlins, 1972: 39).

Considered as a general summary of modern life, that conclusion is clearly an overstatement because it ignores the variety of goals toward which people strive. Such goals may include both a desire for a high standard of living and a desire for a more equitable distribution of wealth in the society. At the same time, Sahlin's conclusion points to a number of features of modern life that are important in understanding our motivation to continue to work even after we have provided for our basic survival needs. Indeed, the evolution of human needs and motivations to work is similar to the evolution of wants into needs in the suburb Whyte studied. As human beings have gained greater control over nature and become wealthier, they have transformed many of their wants into needs which must be satisfied if a proper life is to be achieved.

This pattern of development is evident in the history of the Mundurucú, where movement to settlements along the Cururú River has been accompanied by contact with traders, who are bringing the outside world of mass-produced goods into this way of life. One consequence is that the wants and needs of the Mundurucú are now more extensive than in the past. Thus, as the Mundurucú increase their wealth and as the requirement to work in order to meet their traditional needs decreases, they must work longer hours and more continuously in order to satisfy newly developed wants and needs that may not be satisfied through traditional work routines and practices. In a similar way, the wants and needs of others in modern society have developed through contact with persons who interpret the meaning of work and its relationship to the "good life" differently. The modernization of peasant life, for example, has developed out of the complex actions and interactions of the wives and children of traditional peasant men with priests, teachers, government officials, and others who are intentionally and unintentionally undermining the traditional peasant way of life and work. The histories of industrial work, professional work, hustling, and housework also point to changing definitions of human wants and needs—definitions that justify some life and work styles and reject others.

The ongoing task of defining human needs and wants, then, is also a process by which the need for work, its proper organization, and its primary rewards are defined. For this reason, it is important to consider some of the major institutional sources that define modern wants and needs and their implications for workers. We turn to this issue next and conclude by considering briefly how both the modern counterculture and everyday life transform institutional definitions of modern wants and needs.

Major Institutional Sources for Defining Modern Wants and Needs

Perhaps the most obvious institutional sources for defining contemporary wants and needs are the various mass media, which simultaneously convey entertainment or information and a vision of a proper way of life. For example, in radio and television shows devoted to exploring the major issues of the day, such as crime, feminism, family problems, health, and work, what frequently emerges is a vision or perhaps several visions of human needs and wants and the best way of living to fulfill them. Thus, a great deal of recent mass media attention has been devoted to the various needs and wants of housewives in relation to those of their husbands and children. Depending upon the situation and the wants and needs that are emphasized within it, housewives are advised to care enough about themselves and their families to keep their homes spotless and well organized, to care enough to ignore the house and devote themselves to talking and listening to their families, to care enough to keep themselves slender, physically fit, and sexually attractive, or to care enough to become actively involved outside the home in order to make themselves more interesting to others.

In the process of defining the basic needs and wants of women, husbands, and children, then, shows also define the work role of the housewife and the legitimate expectations that women may have about that role. Although their formats are different, movies, books, television, radio, newspapers, and magazines may all be used to create a vision of basic human wants and needs—visions which may affect the lives of workers.

In some ways the most important and certainly the most pervasive use to which the mass media are put is advertising. Much of contemporary advertising involves selling both a product or service and a life style which makes it necessary (Ewen, 1976; Henry, 1963). In selling the life style, the advertisers are also defining the needs and wants of their customers. Within the world of advertising, for example, human beings *need* mouthwashes, deodorants, scented soaps, shampoos and similar items in order to be acceptable to others and thereby live a proper life style. In similar ways, advertisers tell us that we need to dine out occasionally, to engage a professional in arranging the burial of a family member, and to buy a large and expensive recreational vehicle in order to get away from it all and to enjoy nature.

Taken together, these attempts to define human needs in terms of products and services that must be purchased are part of the general orientation toward consumption pervasive in modern societies, particularly the United States (Leiss, 1976). This general orientation is important because it helps justify the continuing need for work in modern society. No longer is it sufficient to work until adequate food and shelter have been acquired; rather, the need to make a living is tied directly to the need to consume more products and services. Karl Marx (1867/1967) has described this tendency as the "fetishism of commodities," because the individual is so oriented toward consumption that it becomes an end in itself; from his or her constantly increasing levels of consumption, the individual seeks respectability, self-esteem, and the meaning of life.

In its simplest and most obvious form the tendency to consume can be observed among those people who seemingly devote their entire lives to finding and buying the "latest" and most prestigious commodities available. But to look only at such people is to miss the subtlety and pervasiveness of consumption in modern society; indeed, a high level of consumption is a basic feature of many of our most important roles and relationships. Certainly one part of the modern definition of being a good parent involves devoting time and attention to one's children, but just as important is providing them with a minimal number of material goods. Indeed, there is no clear distinction between meeting the material and nonmaterial needs of children in modern society, because we frequently define our intellectual, physical, emotional, and social needs in such a way that consumption is basic to their satisfaction. Looking after the health needs of one's children, for example, may involve the purchase and use of vitamins to see to it that their nutritional needs are met, regular visits to the pediatrician, and encouragement in getting adequate exercise, such as joining a Little League baseball team, which may require an investment in baseball shoes, a uniform, and a glove. The cultivation of an appreciation for refined music among one's children may require the purchase of an expensive stereo and numerous records, a piano or other musical instrument and the requisite number of lessons, and tickets to hear the local symphony occasionally.

The point is that consumption is so basic to modern life that it is inseparable from most aspects of it. Even when we pursue goals involving generosity and self-sacrifice, as in raising our children, consumption is an integral part of achieving those goals, and parents who cannot consume at the same levels as others often feel shame or at least wish that they could provide the same opportunities for their children as other parents. Much more important than the blatant forms of consumption found around us, then, are these subtler forms, because it is within these forms that we can see more fully the transformation of human wants into needs. In the course of this transformation, we also create a need for work to earn the required income for meeting our human needs.

When the subtler tendencies toward consumption are considered, it becomes apparent that human needs are defined in a number of institutional contexts, not just in response to the self-interested claims of advertisers. When government officials attempt to define "the poverty line" or to define a minimal standard of living, they are also establishing an official cutoff point for the level of income that must be achieved in order to meet the basic human needs for persons living in modern society. The fact that the official income level may have emerged as a compromise from political negotiations among a number of competing interest groups is irrelevant. The income figure, once announced and given official sanction, becomes a standard for use by legislators, social workers, and others who must assess the needs of individuals and the society.

In similar ways, academic researchers, representatives of labor unions, the professions, and other worker associations, and members of social movements attempt to define basic human needs. Sometimes they concentrate on broad issues, such as the determination of an adequate income, but at other times they define needs more specifically. For example, the members of the early Charity Organization Societies, who devoted much time and energy to the "treatment" of the poor, were frequently concerned about the possibility of political radicalism among urban immigrants. One solution was to encourage the poor to save their money so that they could move out of their tenements, where the Charity Organization supporters felt radicalism could easily grow, to single-family dwellings, where the political radicals would be separated from the rest of the immigrant poor. They did not present the argument in this way, however; rather, they encouraged the poor to see the purchase of a single-family dwelling as a necessary part of a proper and truly American way of life. Owning a home, in other words, was defined as an American need—one that required a higher income than was necessary to maintain an apartment. Those among the immigrant poor who accepted this definition of their needs, then, also found that the need for stable and well-paying employment took on new importance in their lives.

The relationship between human needs and consumption is also apparent in the area of human services; indeed, much of the activity of professionals and their associations involves defining human needs. We are told, for example, that we all need to draw up a will in order to simplify the transfer of property upon our deaths, and basic to drawing up a will is the employment of an attorney. Put differently, professionals forge a link between the public interest and their own self-interest by creating a *need* for their services—one which justifies both their work and their claim that they understand clients' problems better than anyone else. It is important to recognize, however, that such claims and the definitions of human needs associated with them are subject to change because the circumstances of everyday life change. New circumstances may encourage the professional to call into question old definitions of need.

A common medical claim in the past, for example, was that each person should have an annual physical checkup by a physician trained to recognize symptoms of disorder before the problem becomes serious. In some prepaid health-care programs, which are presumably based on preventive medicine, physicians discourage their patients from getting an annual checkup, claiming that it reveals little useful information. In part, this response reflects the economic interests of the physicians in those programs, who get paid at a prescribed rate regardless of the number of patients they treat. Consequently, they are not encouraged to overtreat as some fee-for-service physicians are. Their response also indicates the way in which a change in the circumstances of everyday life may encourage a questioning of traditional practices. The emphasis on efficiency of operation in prepaid health-care programs introduces a new concern into the lives of physicians, who previously were often more concerned with treating their patients than with efficiency reports. In reviewing standard medical practices from the administrator's point of view, many physicians have discovered that the annual checkup is a waste of time and money for many people, and they therefore reject it as a basic medical need for their patients who are in good health.

The problem of making a living, then, cannot simply be dismissed as one of providing for basic wants and needs. How human wants and needs are defined by the individual and, more generally, within the social institutions of a society is basic to understanding how human beings experience the need for work. Indeed, the relationship between the need for work and other needs and wants is often less clear in modern societies than in other societies, where success and failure at hunting and gathering have immediate and easily observable consequences for the well-being of individuals. In modern societies, on the contrary, work affects how often and well a person eats, but it also affects a number of other needs and wants that are not so obviously linked to survival. Many men and women work, in part, to buy the braces that their children need to be attractive and popular, to buy a dress or sports coat that their spouse wants and perhaps needs, and to pay for a vacation trip that the whole family needs to get away from the pressures of their usual routines of life and work. As these wants and needs escalate to include more and more goods and services, the family's level of consumption will increase and the need for work will be affected and perhaps dramatically redefined.

To this point we have discussed the relationship between work and the satisfaction of wants and needs by concentrating on the goods and services that can be obtained from modern work. There is another side to this relationship which involves how work itself is defined as a need. Although it is true that some people experience the need for work primarily as a problem of securing an income, others see it as a more complex human need. For the latter, work should offer the individual both an income and other rewards. Many craftspeople and other workers, for example, seek to derive direct satisfaction from their work. In pursuing that goal, they define the need to work in terms of both an income and self-expression. Similarly, factory workers who choose to live and work in the old ethnic neighborhoods of their childhood often implicitly define the need for work as more than a source of income: it is also a part of a more general way of life. Even corporate executives who actively seek well-paying jobs do not define the need for work in purely monetary terms. One corporate executive states, for example, that "money is not a motivator. . . . It's just a way for the company to cut its losses by ensuring that people do their job at all. The reward we really control is the ability to promote" (Kanter, 1977a: 129).

This vision of the need for work is best developed among persons committed to a goal of self-actualization, because work is often treated as an important means of achieving new levels of personal growth and satisfaction. Their vision is given institutional sanction by management theorists who emphasize the effectiveness of nonauthoritarian approaches, government sources that report on the debilitating impact of uninspiring work on individuals, academic theorists who dwell on the relationship of human nature and modern work, proponents of work-related social movements (such as empowerment), representatives of workers' associations (such as labor unions and professional associations) seeking to articulate the interests of their memberships, and some representatives of the mass media, such as journalists who recount the problems of modern workers (Terkel, 1972; Garson, 1972). Central to the vision of all such individuals is a definition of work as a humanly essential activity which should provide people with an opportunity to achieve their potential and to express themselves. We need to work, in other words, even if we have an adequate income, because work is one of the most important avenues for achieving self-actualization.

This definition of human nature and human needs is evident in a number of work-related areas of modern life. It is a frequent assumption underlying treatment programs for the poor and handicapped, who are seen as suffering from their dependence on others. By giving such people work training and jobs, professionals claim that they will achieve both independence and personal dignity. The definition is also implicit in the early domestic science movement, which defined full-time housework as a socially important activity and a major source of satisfaction and growth for women. Historically the professions also have accepted this definition of work and human nature; indeed, the professions are a preeminent example, because even as the advocates of professionalization have proclaimed the higher quality of their services and their primary commitment to public service, they also have stressed the self-actualizing consequences of success in the world of work. The greatest joys and the true meaning of professional work, then, come less from the income, prestige, and power that may accrue to the individual than from the satisfactions and growth that accompany service to others. Recently, the empowerment movement has extended this vision of human nature and work to workers who have been ignored in the past. Thus, advocates argue that secretaries, factory workers, and other low-ranking workers in modern society possess the same human need as others to exercise control over their work and to develop their unique individual potentials.

This vision of human nature is important in understanding the way in which many modern workers experience the need for work. They see satisfying and challenging work as a fundamental human need and not as something that many of us would prefer but can live without. Thus, the relationship between work and the process of defining human wants and needs involves more than the ways in which we transform desired goods and services into necessities; it also involves the ways in which we transform the process of making a living (work itself) into a basic human need. In so transforming work, we give it a meaning that transcends the mundane problem of making a living: we recognize that as we work we are also creating ourselves and giving meaning to our lives. As with the mindless pursuit of goods and services, the goal of self-actualization can also become an "infinite need," because there is no limit to the number of challenges and experiences that may be sought in the name of personal growth and satisfaction. The modern "shrine to the Unattainable," then, includes both the potentially infinite number of goods and services that we seek from others and the potentially infinite feelings of growth and satisfaction that we expect to derive from ourselves. Both sources of need also make work a continuing fact of everyday life in modern society.

The Implications of Institutional Definitions of Needs for Workers

The way in which human wants and needs are defined within a society or group, then, has important implications for how individuals define and experience work. Besides affecting the way in which the need for work is experienced, the definition of wants and needs also influences the organization and rewards of work. Within those institutions where work is primarily defined as a source of income, for example, there is little need to consider how the organization of work affects the lives of workers; rather, a primary concern for productivity can easily prevail in these work settings. Scientific management theory assumes this definition when it proclaims that workers are best understood as simple, calculating creatures who are primarily motivated by money. Thus, productivity is enhanced when work is broken down into many simple routines and workers are paid piece rates on the basis of their productivity. In defining human nature and needs in this way, scientific managers have justified work organization that depends on a complex division of labor, highly specialized work tasks, and authoritarian relations with supervisors. They have also defined the primary reward of work as income and nothing more.

Within other modern institutional settings, however, human wants and needs are defined differently and so are the need for work, its proper organization, and its primary rewards. Social definitions historically associated with housework take this perspective, because it is difficult to define workers as motivated primarily by income when they are unpaid. One vision of human nature, or more precisely feminine nature, and its relationship to work is found in the domestic science movement, which at one time argued that although women cannot and should not compete with men in the work world outside the home, they need to work and to make a contribution to their families and the society. It argued further that such a need could be met by building "rational households," in which work was organized according to the general principles of scientific management, and the primary rewards of work stemmed from family relationships and the satisfactions deriving from "right living."

The institutional settings associated with the peasantry, professional workers, the poor, and empowerment are also organized around a variety of definitions of human nature, the need for work, its proper organization, and its primary rewards. Indeed, much of the vitality of modern social institutions as well as a great deal of conflict found within them stem from competing definitions given human nature and human wants and needs. Ongoing conflicts over the proper definition of human nature and work are important because they influence the way work is experienced by workers and how it is justified to them.

To this point the discussion has centered on "mainstream" institutional definitions linking work with human wants and needs. But human beings are not mere captives of institutional definitions, for they are quite capable of rejecting conventional definitions and creating new ones. They are also capable of modifying and even ignoring institutional definitions that get in the way of their goals and activities in everyday life. Thus, it is important to recognize that human wants and needs are defined in a variety of ways in modern society, and for this reason the need for work, its proper organization, and its primary rewards frequently are experienced and justified in everyday life in ways which differ from publicly stated institutional definitions. Two sources of variation which we have dealt with previously—countercultural movements and communities and the practical circumstances of everyday life—deserve further attention here.

Work and Needs in the Counterculture

Central to countercultural criticisms of modernity is a rejection of consumption as a value in itself and a redefinition of human nature and needs in more general and abstract ways (John Hall, 1978). In Hutterite colonies, for example, human nature and needs are defined in relation to the divine order, and although it may be human nature to sometimes stray from sacred traditions or at least occasionally look longingly at the many possessions of outsiders, each person is obliged to suppress this tendency. Among the Hutterites, then, human needs are defined within the context of community needs and the requirements of tradition and the divine order. Thus, each proposal for change in Hutterite colonies is interpreted in light of traditional religious beliefs and practices and the immediate needs of the community as they are defined by community leaders. This approach is obvious in decisions made about tractors and other farm implements that may be used to increase the productivity of the entire community, but it is also evident in the process of *controlled acculturation*, through which luxuries taken from the outside world are incorporated slowly into Hutterite life (Eaton, 1952). The basic question underlying decisions such as these is not whether community members need or merely want these items; rather, it is whether or not current use is extensive and how adoption can be justified within religious tradition. In this way, Hutterite wants become needs. Anyone who uses an alternative argument based on the unique needs of each individual, as opposed to the general needs of the entire community, will surely fail.

In other countercultural groups, the process of defining human wants and needs is different. In synchronic movements and communities the present is the most important consideration in defining human needs and wants, and it is therefore possible for needs and wants to be in a continual state of flux as situations change. Indeed, the definition of needs and wants in synchronic countercultural groups may be highly inconsistent as the individual moves from situation to situation and as the same object or experience is transformed from a need to a want and back again. In apocalyptic groups, on the other hand, there is greater emphasis on consistency, because human needs and wants are defined in relation to revolutionary or transcendental goals. In the ISKCON temple, for example, the needs of each member are assumed to be only partly understandable, because true insight into human nature and needs only comes with full Krishna consciousness. For this reason, temple members are dependent on those who have achieved higher levels of consciousness to direct their lives and define their needs. In a similar way, revolutionary groups like the SLA define human needs and wants in terms of the goals and needs of the group, and a general evaluation of the group's ultimate mission typically precedes the process of transforming human wants into needs.

Each of these general approaches to defining human needs and wants has implications for the work of countercultural members. In the Hutterite colony, for example, work is a necessary fact of life, because it is needed to make a living and it is an important aspect of the religious traditions of the group. Work is not a special value in itself, however, and those who too actively and openly seek public acclaim or self-actualization in their work are likely to be treated as a problem and not as persons to be admired and emulated. The need for work is also subordinated to other, more general needs in apocalyptic movements and communities, where the immediate problem of making a living is treated, at worst, as an unfortunate fact of life and, at best, as something that may further the cause of revolution or transcendence. In synchronic groups the need for work, its proper organization, and its primary rewards are always being redefined, because the meaning of life and work are always found within the present.

In developing alternative definitions of work and human wants and needs, the groups making up the modern counterculture give new direction and meaning to patterns of consumption in the larger society. For example, though the Hutterites reject adoption of material comforts simply for the sake of having them, they are regular consumers of the latest farm equipment and they frequently borrow ideas about farming techniques from agricultural magazines and reports which are primarily intended for conventional farmers. Hippies may also reject much of the consumption orientation of conventional people, but they frequently make exceptions for musical equipment, certain items of clothing, some drugs, and the other items of the hippie life style. Thus, members of the counterculture criticize many of the most important features of modernity, but they seldom reject it totally. They accept those goods and services which are useful in sustaining their alternative way of life, and in the process they give new symbolic importance to those goods and services.

In similar ways, countercultural groups redirect conventional conceptions of work as a value in itself or, more precisely, work as a special human need. In the kibbutz, for example, work is treated as an important and meaningful activity for both the individual and the community. For this reason, an individual's willingness to do hard work is a major criterion in evaluating a candidate for membership in the kibbutz. The "religion of labor" of the kibbutz is different from the conventional goal of self-actualization through work, however, because the object of work in the kibbutz is to achieve personal growth and fulfillment by subordinating one's individual interests to those of the community. That vision of the human need for work is quite different from one which stresses the necessity for reorganizing work so that each person can achieve his or her idiosyncratic potential. Perhaps the countercultural group that comes closest to the conventional emphasis on work as an avenue to individual liberation is the hippie community, which defines legitimate work as any way of making a living that each person finds immediately satisfying; that is, legitimate work is "doing your own thing." A fundamental difference between this vision of work and the more conventional emphasis on work as a value in itself is the absence of a notion of careerism in the hippie vision. For hippies, legitimate work is something that is satisfying in the present, and its value is unrelated to future rewards or opportunities; in contrast, most conventional definitions of work as a value link present work activities and requirements to future rewards and opportunities.

In sum, countercultural groups are an important source of criticism of mainstream institutional definitions concerning human nature, needs, wants, and work. To the extent that they implement their critiques, they also represent alternative institutions within which the need for work, its proper organization, and its primary rewards are defined. An important reason for studying the ways of life and work of countercultural groups, then, is to contrast their definitions with those that prevail in mainstream institutions. For this reason, countercultural groups provide us with insight into conventional assumptions about work and human nature, and they are an example of how human beings may reject conventionality and act to create alternative realities.

For most people, however, modifying and changing the assumptions underlying mainstream institutional definitions require not so much a systematic evaluation and rejection of the basic features of modernity as an almost unconscious adaptation of everyday behavior and beliefs. It is therefore important to consider some of the ways in which work, human nature, and wants and needs are shaped by the practical experiences of everyday life.

Work and Needs in Everyday Life

Central to an adequate understanding of the relationship between work and the definition of human wants and needs in everyday life is the way in which the individual combines basic, pragmatic concerns, such as making enough money to pay the rent, with longer-term and perhaps idealistic goals. Among the latter goals are a desire to be of service to others, to achieve great fame, power, or self-actualization, or simply to be a respected member of the neighborhood or society. Whatever the specific concerns of each individual, the continual combination and recombination of practical and idealistic goals help define the need for work and what a person considers basic wants and needs. For some, the process of balancing long-term and short-term goals is highly conscious and rational, because they regularly evaluate their present circumstances in light of where and what they want to be in the future. Indeed, some work places encourage this type of evaluation by institutionalizing periodic career reviews. In universities, corporations, police departments, and other large bureaucratic work settings, for example, it is common for supervisors and other superiors to evaluate the performances of their subordinates annually, and in the process the individual may be encouraged to review his or her long-term work goals and expectations.

The conscious evaluation of the need for work and its relationship to basic wants and needs involves more than career reviews, however, because individual reflection and evaluation may also be involved. Losing a job, being offered a promotion or new job that requires relocation, or just becoming bored with one's way of life may all be occasions for reassessment of what one wants out of life, and since work is a major source for achieving most wants and needs, these evaluations also involve a reassessment of what one wants and needs from work. The conscious reassessment of basic wants and needs and work may also be occasioned by the changing circumstances associated with different phases of the life cycle. There are profound differences, for example, in the interpretations, expectations, and experiences of young men and women who are beginning careers as factory workers, professionals, or peasants and those of older men and women who are near retirement. Such differences exist even though the practical circumstances of the work of each group may appear on the surface to be the same. Indeed, to look only at surface reflections easily leads to the superficial and self-serving conclusions drawn by many young workers, who claim that those near retirement have lost their commitment to their jobs and are only putting in time, and by older workers, who consider the young to be greedy, lazy, undependable, or in some other way unreasonable.

Housewives provide one of the best and most important examples of how short-term and long-term goals and expectations are reassessed based on the changing circumstances of everyday life. Although marriage entails a number of constraints on housewives because they must take account of the demands and desires of their husbands, a full-time housewife without children enjoys a great deal of autonomy. She may, for example, choose to do all of the wash and ironing on Monday so that she can devote most of Tuesday to recreation with her friends. Much of this freedom vanishes with the birth of children, because accompanying their arrival are a variety of anticipated and unanticipated limitations. Infants and small children almost continuously demand both attention and food, clothing, and similar items of subsistence. Such demands dramatically increase the workload of the housewife, and they reduce her freedom to leave the home to be with other adults and to set her own work schedule. Thus, the birth of children changes the practical circumstances of the everyday lives of these workers. This event is also frequently accompanied by a conscious reassessment of the short-term and long-term wants and needs of the housewife. Many women, for example, find themselves taking a new look at their former life styles and concluding that they were based on an "immature" orientation in which self-centeredness, irresponsibility, and the desire for pleasure prevailed (Lopata, 1971). The birth of children, then, becomes an occasion for developing a new vision of oneself as a "mature" person who has reasonable expectations about work and life. When her children leave home, her husband retires, or she is widowed, the same woman may once again reassess her past, present, and future and conclude that she has acted in an immature way by being too self-sacrificing while raising her children. That reassessment may become a rationale for redefining herself as a mature, liberated woman who is not ashamed to be somewhat self-centered, irresponsible, and pleasure seeking.

In everyday life, then, the process of defining basic human wants and needs is continuous and characterized by frequent change. For this reason, the need for work and the rewards that people seek in their work are also subject to great change. Such changes are not always based on conscious and rational calculation, however; indeed, many of the most important changes affecting our lives are given little importance until a later time, when we discover that decisions and choices made about issues that on the surface appeared to be unrelated to work were critical in affecting our future options. One explanation that takes account of this aspect of everyday life is *side-bet theory*, which was developed to explain the process by which individuals choose to leave or remain in their jobs (Becker, 1960; Ritzer and Trice, 1969, 1970). Essentially, the theory argues that workers who have made a large number of side bets, or investments in a way of life, that will be disrupted or destroyed by a job change are less likely to take advantage of new job opportunities than are others with fewer side bets. Some side bets are directly work related, and they may have been consciously sought. As a side bet, an individual may strive for an office with a nice view or a division of a factory that is quiet and clean; the greater pay or authority another job may offer may not be sufficient to offset such a side bet. Equally important are other side bets that may have seemed totally unconnected to one's work at the time they were made but which eventually constrict the freedom of workers. Indeed, a major reason why side bets are often treated as irrelevant to one's work is that they involve nonwork aspects of the individual's life.

The decision to have children is an obvious and important side bet, because a household with several children has many more needs, wants, and expenses than a childless household, where an individual is freer to leave a well-paying job for one that is more interesting or to move to take advantage of new opportunities without being concerned about the educational, social, and emotional consequences of the move for the children. There are other important side bets frequently made without conscious reflection on their full implications. Among them are decisions about housing, because an expensive home limits the freedom of the worker to seek other work that pays less; location decisions, because the work opportunities found in different cities and rural areas vary; and recreation choices, because many hobbies require great amounts of time and/or money and cannot always be pursued in any location. Sailing, for example, is an expensive and time-consuming pastime which requires that the sailor live near a large body of water. The decision to invest in a sailboat and to become an avid sailor, then, may in the long run be a source of constraint in the world of work, because other job opportunities require a move to an area without a large body of water, pay too little to support the worker's hobby, or require so much time that too little is left for sailing.

Human beings create wants and needs in their everyday lives, then, through a subtle process. The importance of many choices goes unrecognized, but the consequences are often very important in understanding how people interpret the need for work, its proper organization, and its primary rewards. When workers report that they feel alienated from their work or that they are stuck in their jobs, they are describing the facts of life as they see and experience them. Workers often interpret these facts of life as conditions beyond their control, but a more careful analysis often shows that they have intentionally and unintentionally contributed to the conditions. Workers who wish to assess their work situations rationally, then, must consider the context of their entire way of life and the wants and needs that make it up. When that is done, it becomes apparent that those persons who choose to treat satisfying and stimulating work as a basic human need must pay a price in time and energy that cannot be directed toward other sources of satisfaction and meaning, such as family and recreation. Indeed, the problem is one faced by both individual workers as they go about their everyday lives and many institutional leaders, particularly advocates of empowerment, who have yet to fully confront it. As those leaders succeed in giving low-ranking workers more opportunities for advancement, influence, and self-actualization, they will also be asking workers to create new definitions of and expectations about work, family, and recreation.

CONCLUSION

The major purpose of this chapter has been to bring together the specific types of modern work discussed previously by placing them in a more general framework. Two of the most important problems facing modern workers are access to work and the need for work. Although unquestionably the institutions of modern life give rise to both, people also experience them as personal problems which can be solved only within the unique everyday life circumstances of each individual. For this reason, highly generalized theories about abstract labor market processes must be viewed skeptically and used carefully. The traditional French peasants may be analyzed from a labor market point of view, for example, but that type of analysis is quite foreign to traditional peasant life and the social realities of those men and women. From the point of view of the traditional peasant, becoming a worker has little to do with the abstract relationships between supply and demand or between different sectors of the economy; rather, each person works because it is necessary and the right thing to do, and the kind of work that each does is related to traditional sex and age divisions, the amount and quality of land inherited from one's ancestors, the weather, and, more generally, the unpredictable actions of the World Bitch (Hélias, 1978). In similar ways, the peasants' wants and needs are primarily defined within the localized worlds of their everyday lives.

Although many features of peasant life and work are unique, other workers in modern society also live in segmented worlds in which each individual encounters only a portion of the diverse experiences, relationships, and realities that surround them. Theorists often see this claim as obvious when they consider the lives of industrial workers living in traditional ethnic neighborhoods, housewives and some hustlers, because those workers are frequently described as simple, provincial folk who lack the sophisticated and wider-ranging experiences and perspectives of professionals, managers, and other "respectable" workers. Aside from the self-serving nature of such a claim, it also glosses over the segmented experiences of the latter types of workers. Factory managers may possess a sophisticated understanding of the latest accounting techniques and management theories or they may have international contacts with a variety of business, governmental, and educational leaders, but it is also likely that they possess little or no knowledge about day-to-day work in the factory. How, for example, do workers on the shop floor actually go about their jobs, or how do company's salespeople actually market their products? They are likely to glean knowledge about the everyday activities of workers from official organization charts, other descriptions of how the work is supposed to be done, and sales and efficiency reports, which are supposed to indicate how well it is being done. In this way, the several worlds of work present in the modern factory are kept separate.

One general conclusion to be drawn from the analysis of modern work, then, is that although the scope and nature of modern workers' worlds vary, the decision to take up a particular line of work carries with it a set of practical limitations affecting the types of economic opportunities available to the worker and the types of social experiences and realities that he or she may encounter. Indeed, because modern work is made up of so many different worlds, Peter Berger (1964) argues that it is best understood as a Mad Hatter's Party; that is, work settings are carnivallike arenas wherein assorted clowns, jesters, villains, and innocent bystanders intently pursue their diverse and absurd goals. The peasant who takes out a large government loan with no intention of repaying it and knowing that government officials are powerless to insist upon its repayment, the factory worker who deals with an authoritarian supervisor by sabotaging the assembly line, the secretary who deals with an unsupportive boss by neglecting to correct grammatical errors in the executive's letters and reports, the hustler who grudgingly cooperates with the rehabilitation efforts of a social worker in order to get the welfare funds that he or she feels are deserved without such treatment, and the housewife who insists that she is a "domestic engineer" are all examples of how modern work settings can be approached from this point of view.

Although it is useful in characterizing some of the most important aspects of modern work, the analogy of the Mad Hatter's Party can easily be interpreted so that modern work and the lives of workers are depicted as meaningless and inconsequential. Anyone who has developed a stomach ulcer or black lung disease or has lost an arm or leg due to the conditions of his or her work knows that such a conclusion is too simple. In less spectacular ways, those persons who feel humiliated, exploited, or alienated in their work also know that the games played in modern work settings have serious consequences for workers. To concentrate only on the carnivallike features of modern work, then, is to ignore the ways in which making a living are combined with other concerns to make work an important and meaningful aspect of modern life. Indeed, when we move beyond surface appearances, it becomes apparent that one of the most important features of modern work is that workers confront many dilemmas.

Perhaps the most important of those dilemmas is the proper definition of work. Is it only a way of making a living or does it involve more? The dilemma can be seen in the discussions of the several types of work considered in this book, and as those discussions make clear, no consensus about the proper solution to the dilemma exists in modern society. The lack of consensus is obvious in the assumptions made about work and workers by advocates of scientific management and empowerment, but it is also frequently observable in the divisions between traditional peasants and the carriers of modernity, clients and professionals, hustlers and welfare bureaucrats, housewives and their families, and between those committed to a countercultural life and those committed to conventionality. Indeed, a full understanding of modern discord about the true meaning of work must go beyond the simple issue of whether it is only a way of making a living or something more. We must also ask what more work should entail. Included in the response to this question are such divergent visions as self-actualization, living in concert with the universe, revolution, and belonging to a meaningful work group which is making an important contribution to the good of others.

The dilemma of modern work is more than a matter of philosophical interest, because the solutions chosen have important implications for the way in which work is organized and experienced. Two recent proposals for dealing with the problem of modern work illustrate this point. The first is offered by Peter Berger and Richard Neuhaus (1977), who argue that modern life is divided into a public and a private sphere, each of which individuals experience quite differently. The public sphere is made up of large, impersonal, and alienating institutions, which include most governmental bodies as well as large conglomerates, big labor, and growing bureaucracies in such fields as education and the professions. In contrast, the private sphere is made up of small, localized, and personalized institutions, such as the churches, small businesses, voluntary associations, and families in the setting of the local neighborhood and town. According to Berger and Neuhaus, this institutional division is important in developing public policies to empower people. Institutions found in the public sphere are so large, complex, and bureaucratized that they offer few opportunities for giving people significant control over their lives. Consequently, advocates of empowerment should be realistic and recognize that alienation in the public sphere is going to be a fact of life in the future, and they should concentrate on developing public policies which increase the influence of institutions in the private sphere, where people can assert a greater level of control over their lives.

In effect, Berger and Neuhaus are recommending that since there is little we can realistically hope to do about the large, bureaucratized settings where many of us work, we should direct our attention to those features of our nonwork lives that have greater potential for achieving the goal of empowerment. In pursuing this approach we would also create a definition of work which emphasizes its importance as a way of making a living and deemphasize its potential as a source for self-actualization, religious expression, or meaningful relations with others. Their interpretation assumes that the dominant wants and needs of persons living in modern society are economic and that there is little interest in giving priority to other wants and needs involving the quality of work lives. Lawrence Haworth (1977) challenges this assumption in his recent proposal for dealing with the modern problem of work.

Basic to Haworth's proposal is his belief that modern life has become decadent because individuals focus almost exclusively on events and relationships in their personal lives. They thus ignore the general issues affecting humanity and do not cultivate a "vision of an ideal state of affairs" toward which we should all strive (Haworth, 1977: 3). The great stress placed on consumption in modern society and the related tendency to treat work as little more than a way of making a living give evidence of this modern-day preoccupation. Other indications are a general lack of respect for the ecological balance of the natural environment and a willingness to live with alienating institutions in order to enjoy high levels of consumption.

Unlike Berger and Neuhaus, who argue that those features of modern life must be accepted as limitations on public policy, Haworth states that a major goal of public officials and other leaders must be to counter this tendency by encouraging a commitment to meaningful work which produces goods and services that are of high quality and are important in maintaining a high quality of life. It is important, in other words, to challenge prevailing assumptions that encourage people to equate their basic needs with the number of goods and services they consume and to redefine work as both a way of making a living and a way of contributing to the well-being of others. Both can be done by applying the general principles of professionalism to all forms of modern work; that is, work should be evaluated based on the degree to which it contributes to the well-being of others and is rewarding to the worker. Those forms of work that do not measure up must be professionalized, and those that cannot be so transformed should be eliminated. After all, when looked at from a point of view that rejects decadence and consumption, there are few types of modern work that are truly essential to meeting our most important human needs. The elimination of those forms of work that cannot be professionalized, then, will have little effect on the quality of modern life, only the quantity of trivial goods and services available to us.

Although the proposals of both Berger and Neuhaus and Haworth can be criticized because of the simplifying assumptions about modern work and life that underlie them, they are useful examples of how the problem of defining the purpose of modern work may be resolved in contradictory ways. Indeed, both visions of work are evident in the inconsistent and sometimes contradictory policies of government, employers, and labor unions, which at times treat work as only a way of making a living and therefore stress income and related issues and at other times reflect a broader concern for the ways that work can be organized to improve the quality of life. These inconsistencies and contradictions show up constantly in the never-ending process of creating, evaluating, and changing the policies of public and private organizations.

But defining the purpose of work is not simply a matter of organizational policy; it is also a dilemma many workers face. The problem is encountered and resolved differently as the circumstances of everyday life change in response to changing economic cycles, the different phases of the life cycle, and a multitude of other factors. Under some conditions and at some times, workers stress the importance of work as a way of making a living, and at other times they want more than this from their work. However each person resolves this dilemma, it is important to recognize that the value a worker associates with a type of work is only partly related to the standard of living that accompanies it. Its value also depends on the ways members of different segments of modern society define the need for work, its proper organization, and its primary rewards.

For this reason, a full understanding of the meaning of modern work must include a concern for how individuals combine rational calculations about the advantages and disadvantages of different types of work with value judgments and emotional states—such as feelings of shame, fear, pride, and vanity—in their everyday lives (Douglas, 1977; MacIver, 1964). When work is approached in this light, it becomes a diverse, changing, and contradictory part of human life. Thus, some women see themselves as "just housewives," while others take great pride in their work; the Irish Tinkers put up with the poverty of their traditional life because of the feelings of pride and independence their nomadic life style allows them; and some work for money, but feel they are stuck in jobs too small for their spirit (Terkel, 1972). It is from these diverse definitions and concerns that the modern drama of work is created and played out—a drama which has important consequences for the lives of both the players and the audience (Berger, 1964; Hughes, 1951). The general purpose of this book has been to point to some of the settings within which the modern drama of work is acted out, the actors involved, and the plots in which they are embroiled.

References

Abrahamsson, Bengt
1972 *Military Professionalization and Political Power*. Beverly Hills, Cal.: Sage Publications.
1977 *Bureaucracy or Participation*. Beverly Hills, Cal.: Sage Publications.

Adizes, Ichak
1971 *Industrial Democracy: Yugoslav Style*. New York: The Free Press.

Altheide, David L.
1976 *Creating Reality*. Beverly Hills, Cal.: Sage Publications.

Altheide, David L., and Johnson, John M.
1980 *Bureaucratic Propaganda*. Boston: Allyn and Bacon, Inc.

Ariès, Philippe
1960 *Centuries of Childhood*. New York: Random House.

Aronowitz, Stanley
1973a *False Promises*. New York: McGraw-Hill Book Company.
1973b "Trade Unionism and Workers' Control." In *Workers' Control*, eds. Gerry Hunnius, G. David Garson, and John Case, pp. 62–116. New York: Random House.

Ash, Roberta
1972 *Social Movements in America*. Chicago: Markham Publishing Company.

Axinn, June, and Levin, Herman
1975 *Social Welfare*. New York: Harper & Row, Publishers, Inc.

Banfield, Edward C.
1958 *The Moral Basis of a Backward Society*. New York: The Free Press.
1968 *The Unheavenly City Revisited*. Boston: Little, Brown and Company.

Baritz, Loren
1960 *The Servants of Power*. Middletown, Conn.: Wesleyan University Press.

Barker, Elizabeth Faulkner
1964 *Technology and Woman's Work*. New York: Columbia University Press.

Barthes, Roland
1972 *Mythologies*. Translated by Annette Lavers. New York: Hill and Wang.

Becker, Howard S.
1960 "Notes on the Concept of Commitment." *American Journal of Sociology* 66: 32–42.

Becker, Howard S., Geer, Blanche, Hughes, Everett C., and Strauss, Anselm L.
1961 *Boys in White*. Chicago: University of Chicago Press.

Benet, Mary Kathleen
1972 *The Secretarial Ghetto*. New York: McGraw-Hill Book Company.

Bennett, John W.
1966 "Communal Brethren of the Great Plains." *Trans-Action* 4 (December): 42–47.
1967 *Hutterian Brethren*. Stanford, Cal.: Stanford University Press.

Bennis, Warren G., and Slater, Philip E.
1968 *The Temporary Society*. New York: Harper & Row, Publishers, Inc.

Bensman, Joseph, and Lilienfeld, Robert
1973 *Craft and Consciousness*. New York: John Wiley & Sons, Inc.

Benston, Margaret
1969 "The Political Economy of Women's Liberation." *Monthly Review*, 21 (September): 13–27.

Berg, Ivar
1979 *Industrial Sociology*. Englewood Cliffs, N.J.: Prentice-Hall, Inc.

Berger, Peter L.
1964 "Some General Observations on the Problem of Work." In *The Human Shape of Work*, ed. Peter L. Berger, pp. 211–241. Chicago: Henry Regnery Company.
1977 "Toward a Critique of Modernity." In *Facing up to Modernity*, ed. Peter L. Berger, pp. 70–80. New York: Basic Books, Inc., Publishers.

Berger, Peter L., and Luckmann, Thomas
1966 *The Social Construction of Reality*. Garden City, N.Y.: Doubleday & Company, Inc.

Berger, Peter L., and Neuhaus, Richard John
1977 *To Empower People*. Washington, D.C.: American Enterprise Institute for Public Policy Research.

Berheide, Catherine White, Berk, Sarah Fenstermaker, and Berk, Richard A.
1976 "Household Work in the Suburbs." *Pacific Sociological Review* 19 (October): 491–517.

Berk, Richard A., and Berk, Sarah Fenstermaker
1979 *Labor and Leisure at Home*. Beverly Hills, Cal.: Sage Publications.

Berkanovic, Emil, Reeder, Leo G., Marcus, Alfred C., and Schwartz, Susan
1974 *Perceptions of Medical Care*. Lexington, Mass.: Lexington Books.

Bernard, Jessie
1974 "The Housewife: Between Two Worlds." In *Varieties of Work Experience*, eds. Phyllis L. Stewart and Muriel G. Cantor, pp. 49–66. New York: John Wiley & Sons, Inc.

Bernstein, Paul
1976 *Workplace Democratization*. Kent, Ohio: Kent State University Press.

Beynon, H., and Blackburn, R. M.
1972 *Perceptions of Work*. Cambridge: Cambridge University Press.

Bhaktivedanta, A. C.
1969 *Śri Isophanishad*. New York: The Bhaktivedanta Book Trust.

Biklen, Douglas
1978 "Mental Retardation and the Power of Records." In *Client Participation in Human Services*, eds. Constance T. Fischer and Stanley L. Brodsky. New Brunswick, N.J.: Transaction Books.

Bledstein, Burton
1976 *The Culture of Professionalism*. New York: W. W. Norton & Company, Inc.

Bluestone, Barry, Murphy, William M., and Stevenson, Mary
1973 *Low Wages and the Working Poor*. Ann Arbor, Mich.: The Institute of Labor and Industrial Relations, The University of Michigan–Wayne State University.

Blumberg, Paul
1968 *Industrial Democracy*. New York: Schocken Books.

Bogdanich, George
1974 "Steel: No-Strike and Other Deals." *The Nation* 219 (September 7): 171–174.

Bonacich, Edna
1972 "A Theory of Ethnic Antagonism: The Split Labor Market." *American Sociological Review* 37 (October): 547–559.
1976 "Advanced Capitalism and Black/White Relations in the United States: A Split Labor Market Interpretation." *American Sociological Review* 41 (February): 34–51.

Boraston, Ian, Clegg, Hugh, and Rimmer, Malcolm
1975 *Workplace and Union*. London: Heinemann Educational Books.

Bose, Christine
1979 "Technology and Changes in the Division of Labor in the American Home." *Women's Studies International Quarterly* 2: 295–304.

Bott, Elizabeth
1957 *Family and Social Network*. New York: The Free Press.

Braude, Lee
1975 *Work and Workers*. New York: Praeger.

Braverman, Harry
1974 *Labor and Monopoly Capital*. New York: Monthly Review Press.

Brecher, Jeremy
1972 *Strike!* Boston: South End Press.

Bromley, David G., and Shupe, Anson D., Jr.
1979 *"Moonies" in America*. Beverly Hills, Cal.: Sage Publications.

Brooks, Thomas R.
1964 *Toil and Trouble*. New York: Dell Publishing Co., Inc.

Bucher, Rue
1962 "Pathology: A Study of Social Movements Within a Profession." *Social Problems* 10: 40–51.

Bucher, Rue, and Stelling, Joan G.
1977 *Becoming Professional*. Beverly Hills, Cal.: Sage Publications.

Bucher, Rue, and Strauss, Anselm
1961 "Professions in Process." *American Journal of Sociology* 66 (January): 325–334.

Buckholdt, David R., and Gubrium, Jaber F.
1979a *Caretakers*. Beverly Hills, Cal.: Sage Publications.
1979b "Doing Staffings." *Human Organization* 38: 255–264.
1980 "The Underlife of Behavior Modification." *American Journal of Orthopsychiatry* 50 (April): 279–290.

Bullock, Paul
1973 *Aspiration Vs. Opportunity*. Ann Arbor: Institute of Labor and Industrial Relations, The University of Michigan–Wayne State.

Burns, Scott
1975 *Home, Inc*. Garden City, N.Y.: Doubleday & Company, Inc.

Cabet, Etienne
1848 *Voyage en Icarie*. Paris: Bureau du Populaire.

Caplovitz, David
1970 "Economic Aspects of Poverty." In *Psychological Factors in Poverty*, ed. Vernon L. Allen, pp. 229–241. Chicago: Markham.

Carden, Maren Lockwood
1971 *Oneida*. New York: Harper & Row, Publishers, Inc.

Cavan, Sherri
1972a "The Class Structure of Hippie Society." *Urban Life and Culture* 1 (October): 211–237.
1972b *The Hippies of the Haight*. St. Louis: New Critics Press, Inc.

Champion, Dean J.
1967 "Some Impacts of Office Automation Upon Status, Role Change, and Depersonalization." *The Sociological Quarterly* 8 (Winter): 71–84.

Cloward, Richard A., and Piven, Frances Fox
1976 "Notes Toward a Radical Social Work." In *Radical Social Work*, eds. Roy Bailey and Mike Brake, pp. vii–xlviii. New York: Pantheon Books.

Cohen, Rueven
1972 *The Kibbutz Settlement*. Translated by Harry Statman. Israel: Hakibbutz Hameuchad Publishing House Ltd.

Cowan, Ruth Schwartz
1974 "A Case Study of Technological and Social Change." In *Clio's Consciousness Raised*, eds. Mary Hartman and Lois Banner, pp. 245–253. New York: Harper & Row, Publishers, Inc.
1976 "Two Washes in the Morning and a Bridge Party at Night: The American Housewife Between the Wars." *Women's Studies* 3: 147–172.

Criden, Yosef, and Gelb, Saadia
1974 *The Kibbutz Experience*. New York: Schocken Books.

Cunnison, Sheila
1966 *Wages and Work Allocation*. London: Tavistock Publications.

Curley, Anne
1980 "Take a Letter." *Milwaukee Journal*, Part II (April 22): 9–10.

Dalla Costa, Mariarosa
1972 "Women and the Subversion of Community." *Radical America* 6 (January–February): 67–102.

Damrell, Joseph
1978 *Search for Identity*. Beverly Hills, Cal.: Sage Publications.

Daner, Francine Jeanne
1976 *The American Children of Krsna*. New York: Holt, Rinehart and Winston.

Daniels, Arlene Kaplan
1969 "The Captive Professional: Bureaucratic Limitations in the Practice of Military Psychiatry." *Journal of Health and Social Behavior* 10 (December): 255–265.

1973 "How Free Should Professions Be?" In *Professions and Their Prospects*, ed. Eliot Freidson, pp. 39–57. Beverly Hills, Cal.: Sage Publications.

Davidoff, Leonore
1976 "The Rationalization of Housework." In *Dependence and Exploitation in Work and Marriage*, eds. Diana Leonard Barker and Sheila Allen, pp. 121–151. London: Longman.

Davies, Margery
1974 "Woman's Place is at the Typewriter." *Radical America* 8 (July–August): 1–28.

Dawley, Alan
1976 *Class and Community*. Cambridge, Mass.: Harvard University Press.

Doeringer, Peter B., and Piore, Michael J.
1971 *Internal Labor Markets and Manpower Analysis*. Lexington, Mass.: D. C. Heath and Company.

Douglas, Jack D.
1970 "Understanding Everyday Life." In *Understanding Everyday Life*, ed. Jack D. Douglas, pp. 3–44. Chicago: Aldine Publishing Company.

1977 "Existential Sociology." In *Existential Sociology*, eds. Jack D. Douglas and John M. Johnson, pp. 3–73. Cambridge: Cambridge University Press.

Dow, Leslie M., Jr.
1977 "High Weeds in Detroit." *Urban Anthropologist* 6 (Spring): 111–128.

Drucker, Peter F.
1949 *The New Society*. New York: Harper & Row, Publishers, Inc.

1973 *Management*. New York: Harper & Row, Publishers, Inc.

Dublin, Thomas
1979 *Women at Work*. New York: Columbia University Press.

Duncan, Hugh Dalziel
1962 *Communication and Social Order*. New York: Bedminster Press.

1968 *Symbols in Society*. New York: Oxford University Press.

Easton, Barbara
1976 "Industrialization and Femininity: A Case Study of Nineteenth Century New England." *Social Problems* 23 (April): 389–401.

Eaton, Joseph W.
1952 "Controlled Acculturation: A Survival Technique of the Hutterites." *American Sociological Review* 17: 331–340.

Edelman, Murray J.
1974 *The Political Language of the Helping Professions*. Madison, Wis.: Institute for Research on Poverty, University of Wisconsin, Madison.

Edwards, Richard C., Reich, Michael, and Gordon, David M., eds.
1975 *Labor Market Segmentation*. Lexington, Mass.: D. C. Heath and Company.
1979 *Contested Terrain*. New York: Basic Books, Inc., Publishers.

Ehrenreich, Barbara, and English, Deirdre
1975 "The Manufacture of Housework." *Socialist Revolution* 26 (October–December): 5–40.

Elman, Richard M.
1966 *The Poorhouse State*. New York: Pantheon Books.

English, Clifford, and Stephens, Joyce
1975 "On Being Excluded." *Urban Life* 4 (July): 201–212.

Epstein, Cynthia Fuchs
1970 *Woman's Place*. Berkeley, Cal.: University of California Press.

Erasmus, Charles J.
1968 "Community Development and the Encogido Syndrome." *Human Organization* 27 (Spring): 65–74.

Erlich, John L.
1974 "The Domestic Workers Rebel." *The Nation* (September 28): 273—275.

Ewen, Stuart
1976 *Captains of Consciousness*. New York: McGraw-Hill Book Company.

Faunce, William A.
1968 *Problems of An Industrial Society*. New York: McGraw-Hill Book Company.

Ferman, Patricia R., and Ferman, Louis A.
1973 "The Structural Underpinnings of the Irregular Economy." *Poverty and Human Resources Abstracts* 8 (March): 3–17.

Ferree, Myra Marx
1976 "Working-Class Jobs: Housework and Paid Work as Sources of Satisfaction." *Social Problems* 23 (April): 431–441.

Fine, Kertha Sapin
1973 "Worker Participation in Israel." In *Workers' Control*, eds. Gerry Hunnius, G. David Garson, and John Case, pp. 226–264. New York: Random House.

Fischer, Constance T., and Brodsky, Stanley L., eds.
1976 *Client Participation in Human Services*. New Brunswick, N.J.: Transaction Books.

Foner, Philip S.
1977 *Factory Girls*. Urbana, Ill.: University of Illinois Press.

Form, William H.
1976 *Blue-Collar Stratification*. Princeton, N.J.: Princeton University Press.

Foster, George M.
1965 "Peasant Society and the Image of Limited Good." *American Anthropologist* 67 (April): 293–315.

Franklin, S. H.
1969 *The European Peasantry*. London: Methuen & Co., Ltd.

Freedman, Marcia K., with the assistance of Maclachlan, Gretchen
1976 *Labor Markets: Segments and Shelters*. Montclair, N.J.: Allanheld, Osmun and Co. Publishers, Inc.

Freidland, William H., and Nelkin, Dorothy
1971 *Migrant*. New York: Holt, Rinehart and Winston.

Freidson, Eliot
1970 *Profession of Medicine*. New York: Dodd, Mead & Company.
1973 "Professions and the Occupational Principle." In *Professions and Their Prospects*, ed. Eliot Freidson, pp. 19–38. Beverly Hills, Cal.: Sage Publications.
1978 "The Official Construction of Occupations: An Essay on the Practical Epistemology of Work." Paper presented at the Ninth World Congress of Sociology, August, at Uppsala, Sweden.

Freilich, Morris
1963 "Toward an Operational Definition of Community." *Rural Sociology* 28 (June): 117–127.

French, David, and French, Elena
1975 *Working Communally*. New York: Russell Sage Foundation.

Fried, Marc, with Fitzgerald, Ellen, Gleicher, Peggy, Hartman, Chester, Blose, James, Ippolito, Charles, and Benz, Edwina Nary
1973 *The World of the Urban Working Class*. Cambridge, Mass.: Harvard University Press.

Friedan, Betty
1963 *The Feminine Mystique*. New York: W. W. Norton & Company, Inc.

Friedlander, Stanley L.
1972 *Unemployment in the Urban Core*. New York: Praeger Publishers.

Galper, Jeffrey H.
1975 *The Politics of Social Services*. Englewood Cliffs, N.J.: Prentice-Hall, Inc.

Gamst, Frederick C.
1974 *Peasants in Complex Society*. New York: Holt, Rinehart and Winston.

Gans, Herbert J.
1962 *The Urban Villagers*. New York: The Free Press

Garraty, John A.
1978 *Unemployment in History*. New York: Harper & Row, Publishers, Inc.

Garson, Barbara
1972 *All the Livelong Day*. New York: Penguin Books.

Gaskin, Ina May
1978 *Spiritual Midwifery*. Summertown, Tenn.: The Book Publishing Company.

Gaskin, Stephen
n.d. *This Season's People*. Summertown, Tenn.: The Book Publishing Company.
1977 *Volume One: Sunday Morning Services on the Farm*. Summertown, Tenn.: The Book Publishing Company.

Glazer-Malbin, Nona
1976 "Housework." *Signs* 1 (Summer): 905–922.

Glenn, Evelyn Nakano, and Feldberg, Roslyn L.
1977 "Degraded and Deskilled." *Social Problems* 25 (October): 52–64.

Gmelch, George
1977 *The Irish Tinkers*. Menlo Park, Cal.: Cummings Publishing Company.

Gmelch, George, and Gmelch, Sharon Bohn
1978 "Begging in Dublin." *Urban Life* 6 (January): 439–454.

Gmelch, Sharon Bohn
1975 *Tinkers and Travellers*. Dublin: The O'Brien Press.
1976 "The Emergence of an Ethnic Group." *Anthropological Quarterly* 49 (October): 225–238.

Goldberg, Lawrence G., and Greenberg, Warren
1977 *The Health Maintenance Organization and Its Effects on Competition*. Washington, D.C.: Federal Trade Commission.

Goldner, Fred H., and Ritti, R. R.
1967 "Professionalization as Career Immobility." *American Journal of Sociology* 72: 489–502.

Goode, William J.
1957 "Community Within a Community: The Professions." *American Sociological Review* 22: 194–200.

Gordon, David M.
1972 *Theories of Poverty and Underemployment*. Lexington, Mass.: Lexington Books.

Greenlick, Merwyn R.
1975 "The Impact of Prepaid Group Practice on American Medical Care: A Critical Evaluation." *The Annals of the American Academy of Political and Social Science* 399 (January): 100–113.

Greenwood, Ernest
1957 "Attributes of a Profession." *Social Work* 2: 45–55.

Grob, Gerald N.
1961 *Workers and Utopia*. Chicago: Quadrangle Books.

Gubrium, Jaber F., and Buckholdt, David R.
1979 "The Production of Hard Data in Human Service Institutions." *Pacific Sociological Review* 22 (January): 115–136.

Gusfield, Joseph R.

1967 "Tradition and Modernity." *American Journal of Sociology* 72 (January): 351–362.

1970 "Introduction: A Definition of the Subject." In *Protest, Reform and Revolt*, ed. Joseph R. Gusfield, pp. 1–18. New York: John Wiley & Sons, Inc.

1973a "The Social Construction of Tradition." In *Traditional Attitudes and Modern Styles in Political Leadership*, ed. J. D. Legge, pp. 83–104. London: Angus and Robertson.

1973b *Utopian Myths and Movements in Modern Societies*. Morristown, N.J.: General Learning Press.

1975 *Community*. New York: Harper & Row, Publishers.

Hall, Catherine

1974 "The History of the Housewife." *Spare Rib* 26: 9–13.

Hall, John

1978 *The Ways Out*. London: Routledge and Kegan Paul.

Halperin, Rhoda, and Dow, James, eds.

1977 *Peasant Livelihood*. New York: St. Martin's Press.

Harris, Richard N.

1973 *The Police Academy*. New York: John Wiley & Sons, Inc.

Harrison, Bennett

1972 "Employment, Unemployment and Structure of the Urban Labor Market." *Wharton Quarterly* 6 (Spring): 4–7, 26–31.

Haug, Marie R.

1973 "Deprofessionalization: An Alternate Hypothesis for the Future." In *Professionalization and Social Change*, ed. Paul Halmos, pp. 195–211. Keele: The University of Keele.

Haug, Marie R., and Sussman, Marvin

1969a "Professional Autonomy and the Revolt of the Client." *Social Problems* 17: 153–161.

1969b "Professionalism and the Public." *Sociological Inquiry* 39 (Winter): 57–67.

Haworth, Lawrence

1977 *Decadence and Objectivity*. Toronto: University of Toronto Press.

Hays, Samuel P.

1957 *The Response of Industrialism 1885–1914*. Chicago: University of Chicago Press.

Hélias, Pierre-Jakez

1978 *The Horse of Pride*. Translated by June Guicharnaud. New Haven, Conn.: Yale University Press.

Henry, Jules

1963 *Culture Against Man*. New York: Random House.

HEW (United States Department of Health, Education, and Welfare)

1971 *Toward a Comprehensive Health Policy for the 1970's*. Washington, D.C.: Government Printing Office.

1973 *Work in America*. Cambridge, Mass.: M.I.T. Press.

Holmstrom, Lynda Lytle
1973 *The Two-Career Family*. Cambridge, Mass.: Schenkman Publishing Company, Inc.

Holzner, Burkart
1972 *Reality Construction in Society*. Rev. ed. Cambridge, Mass.: Schenkman Publishing Company, Inc.

Homans, George
1950 *The Human Group*. New York: Harcourt Brace and Jovanovich.

Hostettler, John A.
1968 *Amish Society*. Rev. ed. Baltimore: The Johns Hopkins University Press.
1974 *Hutterite Society*. Baltimore: The Johns Hopkins University Press.

Hostettler, John A., and Huntington, Gertrude Enders
1967 *The Hutterites of North America*. New York: Holt, Rinehart and Winston.

Hughes, Everett C.
1951 "Work and Self." In *Social Psychology at the Crossroads*, eds. John Rohrer and Muzafer Sherif, pp. 313–323. New York: Harper & Row, Publishers.
1963 "Professions." *Daedalus* 92: 655–668.
1970 "The Humble and the Proud." *The Sociological Quarterly* 11 (Spring): 147–156.

Huizer, Gerrit
1970 "'Resistance to Change' and Radical Peasant Mobilization." *Human Organization* 29 (Winter): 303–313.

Hunnius, Gerry
1973 "Workers' Self-Management in Yugoslavia." In *Workers' Control*, eds. Gerry Hunnius, G. David Garson, and John Case, pp. 268–321. New York: Random House.

Hunnius, Gerry, Garson, G. David, and Case, John, eds.
1973 *Workers' Control*. New York: Random House.

Illich, Ivan
1977 "Disabling Professions." In *Disabling Professions*, eds. Ivan Illich, Irving Kenneth Zola, John McKnight, Jonathan Caplan, and Harley Shaiken, pp. 11–39. London: Marion Boyars.

International Labour Office
1960 "Effects of Mechanisation and Automation in Offices," Parts I, II, and III. *International Labour Review* 81 (February): 154–173; 81 (March): 254–273; 81 (April): 350–369.

Jamous, H., and Peloille, B.
1970 "Changes in the French University-Hospital System." In *Professions and Professionalization*, ed. J. A. Jackson, pp. 111–152. Cambridge: Cambridge University Press.

Jenkins, David
1973 *Job Power*. New York: Penguin Books, Inc.

Johnson, Terence J.
1972 *Professions and Power*. London: The Macmillan Press Ltd.

Johnson, William R.
1974 "Education and Professional Life Styles: Law and Medicine in the Nineteenth Century." *History of Education Quarterly* 14 (Summer): 185–207.

Jolas, Tina, and Zonabend, Françoise
1977 "Tillers of the Fields and Woodspeople." In *Rural Society in France*, eds. Robert Forster and Orest Ranum, trans. Elborg Forster and Patricia M. Ranum, pp. 126–151. Baltimore: Johns Hopkins University Press.

Judah, J. Stillson
1974a *Hare Krishna and the Counterculture*. New York: John Wiley.

1974b "The Hare Krishna Movement." In *Religious Movements in Contemporary America*, eds. Irving I. Zaretsky and Mark P. Leone, pp. 463–478. Princeton, N.J.: Princeton University Press.

Kalleberg, Arne L., and Sørensen, Aage B.
1979 "The Sociology of Labor Markets." *Annual Review of Sociology* 5: 351–379.

Kanter, Rosabeth Moss
1972 *Commitment and Community*. Cambridge, Mass.: Harvard University Press.

1977a *Men and Women of the Corporation*. New York: Basic Books, Inc.

1977b *Work and Family in the United States*. New York: Russell Sage Foundation.

Kerr, Clark
1954 "The Balkanization of Labor Markets." In *Labor Mobility and Economic Opportunity*, eds. E. Wight Bakke, Philip M Hauser, Gladys L. Palmer, Charles A. Myers, Dale Yoder, and Clark Kerr, pp. 92–110. New York: The Technology Press of the Massachusetts Institute of Technology and John Wiley & Sons, Inc.

Kett, Joseph F.
1977 *Rites of Passage*. New York: Basic Books, Inc., Publishers.

Kincaide, Kathleen
1973 *A Walden Two Experiment*. New York: William Morrow.

Kolaja, Jiri
1965 *Workers' Council*. New York: Frederick A. Praeger, Publishers.

Komarovsky, Mirra
1962 *Blue-Collar Marriage*. New York: Random House.

Kornblum, William
1974 *Blue Collar Community*. Chicago: University of Chicago Press.

Kornblum, William, and Lichter, Paul
1972 "Urban Gypsies and the Culture of Poverty." *Urban Life and Culture* 1 (October): 239–253.

Kotelchuck, David, ed.
1976 *Prognosis Negative*. New York: Random House.

Langer, Elinor
1970a "Inside the New York Telephone Company." *New York Review of Books* 14 (March 12): 16, 18, 20–24.

1970b "The Women of the Telephone Company." *New York Review of Books* 14 (March 26): 14, 15–21.

Lantz, Herman R.
1958 *People of Coal Town*. Carbondale, Ill.: Southern Illinois University Press.

Larson, Magali Sarfatti
1977 *The Rise of Professionalism*. Berkeley, Cal.: University of California Press.

Lasch, Christopher
1977 *Haven in a Heartless World*. New York: Basic Books, Inc.

Latour, Bruno, and Woolgar, Steve
1979 *Laboratory Life*. Beverly Hills, Cal.: Sage Publications.

Leach, Edmund R.
1954 *Political Systems of Highland Burma*. London: G. Bell.

Leiberman, Jethro K.
1970 *The Tyranny of the Experts*. New York: Walker and Company.

Leigh, Duane E.
1978 *An Analysis of the Determinants of Occupational Upgrading*. New York: Academic Press.

Leiss, William
1976 *The Limits to Satisfaction*. Toronto: University of Toronto Press.

Leon, Dan
1969 *The Kibbutz*. Oxford: Pergamon Press.

Lewis, Oscar
1966a "The Culture of Poverty." *Scientific American* 215 (October): 19–25.
1966b *La Vida*. New York: Random House.

Lockwood, David
1958 *The Blackcoated Worker*. London: George Allen & Unwin Ltd.

Lofland, John
1966 *Doomsday Cult*. Englewood Cliffs, N.J.: Prentice-Hall, Inc.

Lopata, Helena Z.
1971 *Occupation: Housewife*. London: Oxford University Press.

Lubove, Roy
1973 *The Professional Altruist*. New York: Atheneum.

Luft, Harold S.
1978 *Poverty and Health*. Cambridge, Mass.: Ballinger Publishing Company.

Lupton, T.
1963 *On the Shop Floor*. Oxford: Pergamon Press.

Macarov, David
1980 *Work and Welfare*. Beverly Hills, Cal.: Sage Publications.

MacIver, R. M.
1964 *Social Causation*. New York: Harper & Row, Publishers, Inc.

Manning, Peter K.
1977 *Police Work*. Cambridge, Mass.: The MIT Press.

Marglin, Stephen A.
1974–1975 "What Do Bosses Do?" Parts I and II. *The Review of Radical Political Economics* 6 (Summer): 60–112.

Marx, Karl
1964 *The Eighteenth Brumaire of Louis Bonaparte*, 1832. New York: International Publishers.
1967 *Capital* 1867. Vol. 1. Edited by Frederick Engels. New York: International Publishers.

Marx, Karl, and Engels, Friedrich
1969 *The German Ideology*, 1845–1846. London: Lawrence and Wishart.

Maslow, Abraham H.
1954 *Motivation and Personality*. New York: Harper & Row, Publishers, Inc.
1965 *Eupsychian Management*. Homewood, Ill.: Irwin and Dorsey.

Maurer, David W.
1974 *The American Confidence Man*. Springfield, Ill.: Charles C Thomas.

May, Joel
1971 "Introduction—Restructuring the Health Delivery System—Will the Health Maintenance Strategy Work?" In *Health Maintenance Organizations*, pp. 12–23. Chicago: University of Chicago Press.

Mayo, Elton
1945 *The Social Problems of an Industrial Civilization*. Cambridge, Mass.: Harvard University Graduate School of Business Administration.
1946 *The Human Problem of Industrial Civilization*. Cambridge, Mass.: Harvard University Graduate School of Business Administration.
1947 *The Political Problem of Industrial Civilization*. Cambridge, Mass.: Harvard University Graduate School of Business Administration.

McBride, Theresa
1976 *The Domestic Revolution*. London: Croom Helm.

McGregor, Douglas
1960 *The Human Side of the Enterprise*. New York: McGraw-Hill Book Company.

Mendras, Henri
1970 *The Vanishing Peasant*. Translated by Jean Lerner. Cambridge, Mass.: M.I.T. Press.

Michels, Robert
1915 *Political Parties*. New York: Hearst's International Library Co.

Miller, Gale
1976 "Organizational and Professional Responses to Change." Unpublished Ph.D. dissertation, University of Kansas, Lawrence, Kansas.
1978 *Odd Jobs*. Englewood Cliffs, N.J.: Prentice-Hall, Inc.
1980 "The Interpretation of Nonoccupational Work in Modern Society: A Preliminary Discussion and Typology." *Social Problems* 27 (April): 381–391.

Miller, Gale, and Warriner, Charles K.
1980a "Professional Power and Social Change at the Community Level." *The Social Science Journal* 17 (October): 1–19.
1980b "Purposive Social Change and Interorganizational Networks." *Journal of Sociology and Social Welfare* in press.

Mills, C. Wright
1951 *White Collar*. New York: Oxford University Press.

Mills, C. Wright, with Schneider, Helen
1948 *The New Men of Power*. New York: Harcourt Brace Jovanovich.

Mills, Herb
1976 "The San Francisco Waterfront," Part I. *Urban Life* 5 (July): 221–251.
1977 "The San Francisco Waterfront," Part II. *Urban Life* 6 (April): 3–32.

Mills, Richard
1973 *Young Outsiders*. New York: Random House.

Mitchell, Juliet
1966 "Women: The Longest Revolution." *New Left Review* 40 (December): 11–37.

Mithun, Jacqueline S.
1973 "Cooperation and Solidarity as Survival Necessities in a Black Urban Community." *Urban Anthropology* 2 (Spring): 25–34.

Modell, John
1979 "Changing Risks, Changing Adaptations: American Families in the Nineteenth and Twentieth Centuries." In *Kin and Communities*, eds. Allan J. Lichtman and Joan R. Challinor, pp. 119–144. Washington, D.C.: Smithsonian Institute Press.

Montagna, Paul D.
1977 *Occupations and Society*. New York: John Wiley & Sons, Inc.
1979 "Labor Market Segmentation." Unpublished paper presented as a didactic seminar at the Annual Meeting of the American Sociological Association, August, in Boston.

Morel, Alain
1977 "Power and Ideology in the Village Community of Picardy." In *Rural Society in France*, eds. Robert Forster and Orest Ranum, trans. Elborg Forster and Patricia M. Ranum, pp. 107–125. Baltimore: Johns Hopkins University Press.

Morin, Edgar
1970 *The Red and the White*. Translated by A. M. Sheridan-Smith. New York: Random House.

Murphy, Richard F.
1960 *Headhunter's Heritage*. Berkeley, Cal.: University of California Press.
1971 *The Dialectics of Social Life*. New York: Basic Books, Inc., Publishers.

Murphy, Yolanda, and Murphy, Richard F.
1974 *Women of the Forest*. New York: Columbia University Press.

Nelson, Daniel
1975 *Managers and Workers*. Madison, Wis.: University of Wisconsin Press.

Nichols, Theo, and Armstrong, Peter
1976 *Workers Divided*. Glasgow: Fontana/Collins.

Nichols, Theo, and Beynon, Huw
1977 *Living with Capitalism*. London: Routledge and Kegan Paul.

Niederhoffer, Arthur
1969 *Behind the Shield*. Garden City, N.Y.: Anchor Books.

Niehoff, Arthur H., and Anderson, J. Charnel
1966 "Peasant Fatalism and Socio-Economic Innovation." *Human Organization* 25 (Winter): 273–283.

Noble, David F.
1977 *America by Design*. New York: Oxford University Press.

Nofziger, Margaret
1978 *A Cooperative Method of Birth Control*. 2nd ed. Summertown, Tenn.: The Book Publishing Company.

Oakley, Ann
1974a *The Sociology of Housework*. New York: Random House.
1974b *Woman's Work*. New York: Random House.

O'Connor, James
1973 *The Fiscal Crisis of the State*. New York: St. Martin's Press.

Orbach, Eliezer
1968 *Cooperative Organization in Israel*. Madison, Wis.: Center for the Study of Productivity Motivation, Graduate School of Business, The University of Wisconsin.

Parsons, Talcott
1949 "The Social Structure of the Family." In *The Family*, ed. Ruth Nanda Anshen, pp. 241–274. New York: Harper & Row.
1951 *The Social System*. New York: The Free Press.

Parsons, Talcott, and Bales, Robert F.
1955 *Family, Socialization and Interaction Process*. New York: The Free Press.

Partridge, William L.
1973 *The Hippie Ghetto*. New York: Holt, Rinehart and Winston.

Pelling, Henry
1960 *American Labor*. Chicago: University of Chicago Press.

Percivall, Julia, and Burger, Pixie
1971 *Household Ecology*. Englewood Cliffs, N.J.: Prentice-Hall, Inc.

Perrucci, Robert
1973 "In the Service of Man: Radical Movements in the Professions." In *Professionalisation and Social Change*, ed. Paul Halmos, pp. 179–194. Keele: University of Keele.

Perry, Stewart E.
1978 *San Francisco Scavengers*. Berkeley, Cal.: University of California.

Peters, Victor
1965 *All Things Common*. New York: Harper & Row, Publishers, Inc.

Pilcher, William M.
1972 *The Portland Longshoremen*. New York: Holt, Rinehart and Winston.

Piore, Michael J.
1975 "Notes for a Theory of Labor Market Stratification." In *Labor*

Market Segmentation, eds. Richard C. Edwards, Michael Reich, and David M. Gordon, pp. 125–150. Lexington, Mass.: D. C. Heath and Company.

Piotrkowski, Chaya S.
1978 *Work and the Family System*. New York: The Free Press.

Piven, Frances Fox, and Cloward, Richard A.
1971 *Regulating the Poor*. New York: Random House.
1977 *Poor People's Movements*. New York: Random House

Pleck, Elizabeth H.
1976 "Two Worlds in One: Work and Family." *Journal of Social History* 10 (Winter): 178–195.

Polanyi, Karl
1957 "The Economy as Instituted Process." In *Trade and Market in Early Empires*, eds. Karl Polanyi, Conrad M. Arensberg and Harry W. Pearson, pp. 243–270. Glencoe, Ill.: The Free Press and The Falcon's Wing Press.

Poll, Solomon
1962 *The Hasidic Community of Williamsburg*. New York: Schocken Books.

Popkin, Samuel L.
1979 *The Rational Peasant*. Berkeley, Cal.: University of California Press.

Rapoport, Rhona and Rapoport, Robert N.
1976 *Dual-Career Families Re-examined*. New York: Harper & Row, Publishers, Inc.

Rayack, Elton
1967 *Professional Power and American Medicine*. Cleveland: The World Publishing Company.

Reader, W. J.
1966 *Professional Men*. New York: Basic Books, Inc., Publishers.

Redekop, Calvin Wall
1969 *The Old Colony Mennonites*. Baltimore: The Johns Hopkins University Press.

Reiter, Rayna R.
1975 "Men and Women in the South of France: Public and Private Domains." In *Toward an Anthropology of Women*, ed. Rayna R. Reiter, pp. 251–282. New York: Monthly Review Press.

Resnick, James L.
1976 "The Emerging Physician." In *Professions for the People*, eds. Joel Gerstl and Glenn Jacobs, pp. 175–214. New York: John Wiley & Sons, Inc.

Richardson, Dorothy
1972 "The Long Day." In *Women at Work*, ed. William L. O'Neill, pp. 3–303. Chicago: Quadrangle Books.

Richmond, Mary
1917 *Social Diagnosis*. New York: Russell Sage Foundation.

Riemer, Jeffrey W.
1979 *Hard Hats*. Beverly Hills, Cal.: Sage Publications.

Ritzer, George
1975 "The Emerging Power Approach to the Study of the Professions." Unpublished paper presented at the Annual Meeting of the American Sociological Association, August, San Francisco.

Ritzer, George and Trice, Harrison
1969 "An Empirical Study of Howard Becker's Side-Bet Theory." *Social Forces* 47: 475–478.
1970 "On the Problem of Clarifying Commitment Theory." *Social Forces* 48: 530–533.

Robinson, H. A., and Finesinger, Jacob E.
1957 "The Significance of Work Inhibition for Rehabilitation." *Social Work* 2 (October): 22–31.

Roebuck, Julian B., and Frese, Wolfgang
1976 *The Rendezvous*. New York: The Free Press.

Roethlisberger, F. J., and Dickson, William J.
1939 *Management and the Worker*. Cambridge, Mass.: Harvard University Press.

Rosenthal, Douglas E.
1974 *Lawyer and Client*. New York: Russell Sage Foundation.

Ross, H. Laurence
1970 *Settled Out of Court*. Chicago: Aldine Publishing Company.

Rosser, James M., and Mossberg, Howard E.
1974 *An Analysis of Health Care Delivery*. New York: John Wiley & Sons, Inc.

Roth, Julius A.
1963 *Timetables*. Indianapolis, Ind.: The Bobbs-Merrill Company, Inc.
1972 "Staff and Client Control Strategies in Urban Hospital Emergency Services." *Urban Life and Culture* 1 (April): 39–60.
1974 "Professionalism: The Sociologist's Decoy." *Sociology of Work and Occupations* 1 (February): 6–23.

Rothman, David J.
1971 *The Discovery of the Asylum*. Boston: Little, Brown and Company.

Rothman, David, and Rothman, Sheila M.
1972 "Introduction: The Experience of Poverty in America." In *On Their Own*, eds. David J. Rothman and Sheila M. Rothman, pp. v–xxv. Reading, Mass.: Addison-Wesley Publishing Company.

Rothstein, William G.
1973 "Professionalization and Employer Demands: The Cases of Homeopathy and Psychoanalysis in the United States." In *Professionalisation and Social Change*, ed. Paul Halmos, pp. 159–178. Keele: The University of Keele.

Roubin, Lucienne
1977 "Male Space and Female Space Within the Provençal Community." In *Rural Society in France*, eds. Robert Forster and Orest Ranum, trans. Elborg Forster and Patricia M. Ranum, pp. 152–180. Baltimore: Johns Hopkins University Press.

Roy, Donald
1952 "Quota Restriction and Goldbricking in a Machine Shop." *American Journal of Sociology*, 57: 427–442.

1959–1960 "'Banana Time' Job Satisfaction and Informal Interaction." *Human Organization* 18: 158–168.

Rubin, Lillian Breslow
1976 *Worlds of Pain*. New York: Basic Books, Inc., Publishers.

Ryan, William
1971 *Blaming the Victim*. New York: Random House.

Sahlins, Marshall
1972 *Stone Age Economics*. New York: Aldine-Atherton, Inc.

Saward, Edward, Blank, Janet, and Lamb, Henry
1973 *Some Information Descriptive of a Successfully Operating HMO*. Washington, D.C.: Department of Health, Education, and Welfare.

Saward, Ernest, and Greenlick, Merwyn R.
1972 "Health Policy and the HMO." *The Milbank Memorial Fund Quarterly* 50 (April): 147–176.

Schlesinger, Philip
1979 *Putting 'Reality' Together*. Beverly Hills, Cal.: Sage Publications.

Schutz, Alfred
1967 *Collected Papers*. Vols. 1 and 2. The Hague: Martinus Nijhoff.

Schutz, Alfred, and Luckmann, Thomas
1973 *The Structure of the Life-World*. Translated by Richard M. Zaner and H. Tristram Engelhardt, Jr. Evanston, Ill.: Northwestern University Press.

Scott, James C.
1976 *The Moral Economy of the Peasant*. New Haven, Conn.: Yale University Press.

Scott, Robert A.
1970 "The Construction of Conceptions of Stigma by Professional Experts." In *Deviance and Respectability*, ed. Jack D. Douglas, pp. 255–290. New York: Basic Books, Inc., Publishers.

Scull, Andrew T.
1977 *Decarceration*. Englewood Cliffs, N.J.: Prentice-Hall, Inc.

Sennett, Richard, and Cobb, Jonathan
1972 *The Hidden Injuries of Class*. New York: Random House.

Serrin, William
1973 *The Company and the Union*. New York: Alfred A. Knopf.

Shepard, Jon M.
1971 *Automation and Alienation*. Cambridge, Mass.: M.I.T. Press.

Shostak, Arthur B.
1969 *Blue-Collar Life*. New York: Random House.

Siegal, Harvey A.
1978 *Outposts of the Forgotten*. New Brunswick, N.J.: Transaction Books.

Smelser, Neil J.
1959 *Social Change in the Industrial Revolution*. Chicago: University of Chicago Press.

Smith, C. Henry
1957 *The Story of the Mennonites*. 4th ed. Newton, Kans.: Mennonite Publication Office.

Smith, Elmer L.
1958 *The Amish People*. New York: Exposition Press.

Spencer, Charles
1977 *Blue Collar*. Chicago: Lakeside Charter Books.

Spiro, Melford E.
1970 *Kibbutz*. New York: Schocken Books.

Stack, Carol B.
1974 *All Our Kin*. New York: Harper & Row, Publishers, Inc.

Steidl, Rose E., and Bratton, Esther Crew
1968 *Work in the Home*. New York: John Wiley & Sons, Inc.

Stephens, Joyce
1976 *Loners, Losers, and Lovers*. Seattle: University of Washington.

Stevens, Rosemary
1971 *American Medicine and the Public Interest*. New Haven, Conn.: Yale University Press.

Stone, Katherine
1974 "The Origins of Job Structures in the Steel Industry." *Journal of Radical Political Economics* 6 (Summer): 113–173.

Strasser, Susan M.
1978 "The Business of Housekeeping: The Ideology of the Household at the Turn of the Twentieth Century." *Insurgent Sociologist* 8 (Fall): 147–163.

Street, David, Martin, George T., Jr., and Gordon, Laura Kramer
1979 *The Welfare Industry*. Beverly Hills, Cal.: Sage Publications.

Sutherland, Edwin H.
1937 *The Professional Thief by a Professional Thief*. Chicago: University of Chicago Press.

Tabachnik, Leonard
1976 "Licensing in the Legal and Medical Professions, 1820–1860: A Historical Case Study." In *Professions for the People*, eds. Joel Gerstl and Glenn Jacobs, pp. 25–42. New York: Schenkman.

Terkel, Studs
1972 *Working*. New York: Random House.

Tessler, Richard, and Mechanic, David
1975 "Consumer Satisfaction with Prepaid Group Practice." *Journal of Health and Social Behavior* 16 (March): 95–113.

Thomas, W. I.
1923 *The Unadjusted Girl*. Boston: Little, Brown and Company.

Thompson, James D.
1967 *Organizations in Action*. New York: McGraw-Hill Book Company.

Tiffany, Donald W., Cowan, James R., and Tiffany, Phyllis M.
1970 *The Unemployed*. Englewood Cliffs, N.J.: Prentice-Hall, Inc.

Tilgher, Adriano
1958 *Homo Faber*. Translated by Dorothy Canfield Fisher. Chicago: Henry Regnery Company.

Trattner, Walter I.
1979 *From Poor Law to Welfare State*. 2nd ed. N.Y.: Free Press.

U.S. Congress
1973–1974 "Health Maintenance Organization Act of 1973." In *United States Code*, 0.1, pp. 1015–1042. St. Paul, Minn.: West Publishing Co.

Valentine, Bettylou
1978 *Hustling and Other Hard Work*. New York: The Free Press.

Valentine, Charles A.
1968 *Culture and Poverty*. Chicago: The University of Chicago Press.
1971 "The 'Culture of Poverty.'" In *The Culture of Poverty*, ed. Eleanor Burke Leacock, pp. 193–225. New York: Simon and Schuster.

Vallier, Ivan
1962 "Structural Differentiation, Production Imperatives, and Communal Norms: The Kibbutz in Crisis." *Social Forces* 40: 233–241.

Vanek, Joann
1974 "Time Spent in Housework." *Scientific American* 231 (November): 116–120.

Van Til, Sally Bould
1976 *Work and the Culture of Poverty*. San Francisco: R and E Research Associates.

Veblen, Thorstein
1953 *The Theory of the Leisure Class*, 1899. New York: Mentor.

Veysey, Laurence
1973 *The Communal Experience*. Chicago: University of Chicago Press.

Wachtel, Howard M.
1973 *Workers' Management and Workers' Wages in Yugoslavia*. Ithaca, N.Y.: Cornell University Press.

Wallace, Anthony F.C.
1978 *Rockdale*. New York: Alfred A. Knopf.

Walshock, Mary Lindenstein
1979 "Occupational Values and Family Roles: Women in Blue-Collar and Service Occupations." In *Working Women and Families*, ed. Karen Wolk Feinstein, pp. 63–83. Beverly Hills, Cal.: Sage Publications.

Warner, W. Lloyd, and Low, J. O.
1947 *The Social System of the Modern Factory*. New Haven, Conn.: Yale University Press.

Wax, Murray L., and Wax, Rosalie H.
1971 "Cultural Deprivation as an Educational Ideology." In *The Culture of Poverty*, ed. Eleanor Burke Leacock, pp. 127–139. New York: Simon and Schuster.

Wax, Murray L., Wax, Rosalie H., and Dumont, Robert V.
1964 *Formal Education in an American Indian Community*. Monograph No. 1. Society for the Study of Social Problems.

Weber, Eugen
1976 *Peasants into Frenchmen*. Stanford: Stanford University Press.

Wheeler, Stanton, ed.
1969 *On Record*. New York: Russell Sage Foundation.

Wheeler, Wayne, Hernon, Peter, and Sweetland, James H.
1975 "Icarian Communism: A Preliminary Exploration in Historiography, Bibliography, and Social Theory." Unpublished paper, Department of Sociology, University of Nebraska at Omaha, Omaha, Nebraska.

Whyte, William H., Jr.
1956 *The Organization Man*. Garden City, N.Y.: Simon and Schuster.

Wiebe, Robert H.
1967 *The Search for Order, 1877–1920*. New York: Hill and Wang.

Wilensky, Harold L., and Lebeaux, Charles N.
1958 *Industrial Society and Social Welfare*. New York: The Free Press.

Wolf, Eric R.
1957 "Closed Corporate Peasant Communities in Mesoamerica and Central Java." *Southwestern Journal of Anthropology* 13 (Spring): 1–18.

1966 *Peasants*. Englewood Cliffs, N.J.: Prentice-Hall, Inc.

Women's Work Study Group
1976 "Loom, Broom and Womb: Producers, Maintainers and Reproducers." *Radical America* 10 (March-April): 29–46.

Woodroofe, Kathleen
1962 *From Charity to Social Work in England and the United States*. Toronto: University of Toronto Press.

Wright, Gordon
1964 *Rural Revolution in France*. Stanford, Cal.: Stanford University Press.

Wrobel, Paul
1979 *Our Way*. Notre Dame, Ind.: University of Notre Dame Press.

Wylie, Laurence
1964 *Village in the Vacluse*. Rev. ed. New York: Harper & Row, Publishers, Inc.

1966 *Chanzeaux*. Cambridge, Mass.: Harvard University Press.

Young, Michael, and Willmott, Peter
1973 *The Symmetrical Family*. New York: Random House.

Zablocki, Benjamin
1971 *The Joyful Community*. Baltimore: Penguin Books, Inc.

Zaretsky, Eli
1976 *Capitalism, the Family and Personal Life*. New York: Harper & Row, Publishers, Inc.

Zeldin, Theodore
1973 *France 1848–1945*. Vol. 1. Oxford: Oxford University Press.

Zwerdling, Daniel
1978 *Workplace Democracy*. New York: Harper & Row, Publishers, Inc.

INDEX